LAW, DEATH, AND ROBOTS

Can the law keep up with AI? This book examines liability and regulation for artificial intelligence causing serious physical harm, both now and in the future.

While AI moves quickly, regulation follows more slowly – an increasing problem for an evolutionary, fast-paced emerging technology. AI has the potential to save lives, but in doing so will have the potential to take them as well. How do we future-proof law and regulation to incentivise life-saving innovation as safely as possible?

This book details how to regulate AI in high-risk civil applications (for example, automated vehicles and medicine), addressing both liability and regulatory structure. It highlights crucial liability themes for technology governance; provides tools to bridge the gap between regulators and technologists; examines jurisdictional approaches to AI regulation in the EU, UK, USA, and Singapore; and ultimately suggests a jurisdiction-agnostic blueprint for regulation.

Law, Death, and Robots

The Regulation of Artificial Intelligence in High-Risk Civil Applications

Keri Grieman

•HART•
OXFORD • LONDON • NEW YORK • NEW DELHI • SYDNEY

HART PUBLISHING

Bloomsbury Publishing Plc

Kemp House, Chawley Park, Cumnor Hill, Oxford, OX2 9PH, UK

1385 Broadway, New York, NY 10018, USA

29 Earlsfort Terrace, Dublin 2, Ireland

HART PUBLISHING, the Hart/Stag logo, BLOOMSBURY and the Diana logo are trademarks of Bloomsbury Publishing Plc

First published in Great Britain 2024

First published in hardback, 2024

Paperback edition, 2026

A catalogue record for this book is available from the British Library.

A catalogue record for this book is available from the Library of Congress.

Library of Congress Control Number: 2024940132

ISBN: PB: 978-1-50997-740-6
ePDF: 978-1-50997-741-3
ePub: 978-1-50997-743-7

Typeset by Compuscript Ltd, Shannon

Dedicated to Rick, Mary, and Jon

FOREWORD

According to the Bletchley Declaration (signed by the countries represented at the AI Safety Summit in November 2023), 'AI should be designed, developed, deployed, and used, in a manner that is safe, in such a way as to be human-centric, trustworthy and responsible'. Echoing recent concerns about the safety of foundation models, the Declaration emphasises that there is an urgent need to address the 'potential for serious, even catastrophic, harm, either deliberate or unintentional, stemming from the most significant capabilities of these AI models'. Given that China, the European Union, the United States, India, Australia and more than 20 other countries – as well as the United Kingdom who hosted the Summit – were represented at Bletchley, we can take it that there is a significant global consensus that, while we want beneficial AI innovation, above all we want AI that is safe.

When we say that we want AI that is 'safe', this covers a broad spectrum of risks. We certainly do not want AI that presents an 'existential threat' to humanity. Humans have no desire to be enslaved by super-intelligent AI or to go the same way as the dinosaurs. Governance, both international and national, needs to ensure that we do not sleepwalk into a catastrophe. Making the perhaps optimistic assumption that we can control for and contain existential threats, we still have to reckon with ubiquitous AI. Functioning as a utility in much the same way as electricity, AI might still be dangerous. In an AI-enabled world, accidents might still happen as a result of which human lives might be lost and serious personal injury occasioned. For the individuals who are impacted in this way, it is no consolation that such risks are quotidian. Zero risk might not be achievable, but the accidental death of humans is a matter for regret. Governance that is both effective and socially acceptable is required, but what steps should be taken for the sake of AI safety? How are accidents of this kind to be prevented and, in the event of the use of AI leading to the death of humans, who is to be liable and on what basis? These latter questions are the focus for Keri Grieman's timely book.

While autonomous transport systems that take humans out of the driving seat, or AI that replaces humans in dangerous workplaces, or AI that makes surgical procedures more precise and effective might reduce the number of humans who are in accident zones or who might otherwise be killed or injured, this is not an unqualified good. For one thing, taking humans out of these loops might mean that jobs are lost. For present purposes, though, the point is that there will still be plenty of humans who are at risk of being killed or injured while using transport that is AI-enabled, or who are recipients of AI-enabled goods and services, and so on. Questions of ex ante prevention and ex post liability and compensation will still arise. As Grieman rightly observes: 'Ultimately, AI needs a regulatory system that combines both ex ante and ex post approaches: what safeguards AI should have to go through to reach the market, and what will be done when an accident occurs' (193). With this in mind, where should our governance of AI start?

If we adopt a traditional starting point for our ex post governance of accidents, and if we assume that the victim was not at fault, then our opening question is to ask: who was 'at fault'? Unpacking this compressed question, we ask whose acts caused the accident, whether the relevant actor failed to take reasonable care, and whether the resulting death or injury was reasonably foreseeable. There is much devil in the doctrinal detail and the general principle that those parties who are judged to be 'at fault' should be liable to compensate the victims of their careless acts leaves plenty of scope for contextual application. Even with such flexibility, where the parties who are potentially to be held liable are the producers of AI or the providers of AI-enabled goods and services, it might be felt that there needs to be some regulatory adjustment of the general principle. This adjustment might be designed to make it easier for victims to make out the case for liability (as with product liability regimes or by reversing the burden of proof) or simply to ensure that victims are compensated (as with no fault compensatory schemes). Conversely, the purpose of the regulatory adjustment might be to shield producers or providers with a degree of immunity against liabilities that might hinder the development and availability of AI applications that are expected to be collectively beneficial.

We can argue endlessly about the extent to which these various kinds of ex post compensatory schemes might have a collateral deterrent or preventive effect. To the extent that provision for compensation does have some preventive effect, all well and good; nevertheless, where, as in the European Union, the culture is precautionary, there will be ex ante regulatory safety checks and, typically, the higher the perceived risk (as with the risk of death or serious personal injury) the more intensive the assessment will be. In regimes of this kind, regulatory compliance will be a foreground consideration for developers and providers of AI-enabled goods and services and ex post liability regimes will need to take a position on the significance of regulatory compliance or non-compliance.

Against this relatively familiar background, Grieman offers readers an informative and accessible introduction to the technology of AI; a wide-ranging commentary on liability for AI accidents (particularly arising from the use of autonomous vehicles and in relation to AI-enabled medical practice); an insightful review of such matters as explainable AI; some reflections on the different regulatory approaches being articulated in Singapore, the European Union, the United States and the United Kingdom; and, last but not least, a proposed blueprint for liability which is then applied to a test case of harm caused by an AI-enabled product (a chainsaw) and which is designed to show 'how to structure regulation to incentivise safe, explainable AI, and provide a way to deal with [harmful] incidents when they occur, without formalising standards that fossilise the state of the art too early' (249).

Although the book is not directly concerned with questions about the compatibility of AI laws with the fundamental values of a particular community, for example whether regulation is compatible with human rights and human dignity, picking up on the Bletchley Declaration, we might ask to what extent the approach taken, including the proposed regulatory blueprint, is orientated towards 'human-centric, trustworthy and responsible' design, development, deployment and use of AI.

As a first step, it is proposed that 'a new general regulator for AI liability' should be created, the regulator's responsibilities particularly being focused on 'AI with high or unknown levels of harm' (195). The key roles of the regulator would include 'identifying and banning unacceptable AI', laying out the regulatory requirements for 'pre-approval of the riskiest AI applications', receiving 'the results of quasi-independent investigations where an AI causes serious harm', imposing sanctions for failure to comply with regulatory obligations, and issuing guidelines as well as communicating with 'industry, government and the public' (222). In this respect, Grieman joins others in proposing a bespoke regulator for AI and, while there might be several reasons for so proposing, a properly resourced and dedicated AI regulator would seem to be a sound basis for building public confidence in the use and application of AI.

If the general regulator decides that a particular AI application is too risky, a ban should be imposed. However, where AI applications pass this initial filter, a distinctly human-centric approach to any questions of liability is to be taken. Crucially, two standards will be applied to determine the liability of producers: one standard is that of 'a reasonable human performing the same task'; and the other is that of 'a reasonable producer of [the]sub-speciality' (196). In both cases, the burden of proof is on the producer. Elaborating on the first standard, Grieman emphasises that AI is not required to be perfect (humans, after all, are far from perfect) but, even if AI statistically out-performs humans, it will not pass the human test if it 'malfunctions in a way that a human would not' (200). As to the second standard, the question of whether a particular producer has acted with the care of a reasonable producer will depend on best practice (including the use of explainable AI tools during production) and on the state of the art. Presumably, if AI tools are commonly used to acquire knowledge of the state of the art, and even if knowledge so acquired would go beyond the capacity of humans unaided by such tools, producers will be held to the higher standard. In this way, the blueprint remains anchored to reasonable human performance as the minimum standard while requiring due diligence by producers and entertaining the hope that a culture of responsible production will grow and will serve to drive up standards.

Finally, we should welcome Keri Grieman's book, not only as a valuable addition to the burgeoning literature on the governance of AI, but as a fine example of the way in which lawyers can make a contribution to debates about governance that span historic legal principles, regulatory policy and breakthrough technologies. Governance matters, good governance is to be preferred to poor governance, and in all phases of lawyering we should follow Grieman's lead in aspiring to find ways of making governance better.

Roger Brownsword
June 2024

PREFACE

> We can only see a short distance ahead, but we can see plenty there that needs to be done.[1]
>
> Alan Turing

This book examines the question of how autonomous artificial intelligence (AI) agents in high-risk civil applications should be regulated and liability allocated. Regulation in this regard includes examining the AI throughout its lifecycle: both in production and after an accident has occurred. This examination needs to begin by analysing how liability is treated in non-AI cases; then investigating the practical tools used for AI development – examining how they might interact with traditional liability.

This book is a technology-led enquiry into the law. The examination begins with research into AI and how it works – its various forms and approaches, followed by a specific focus on how to explain the workings of AI. After an analysis of the issues raised by AI, I then explore the existing regulatory efforts, and ultimately potential opportunities and parallels in ideally regulating AI as an ever-expanding field. This desk-based methodology involves reviewing literature in the fields of law and computer science, as well as substantive case law and legislation for legal and regulatory analysis. Research was also supplemented by conversations with colleagues in the technical field of AI – thanks in large part to the Alan Turing Institute.

In terms of jurisdictional scope, the book takes UK law as a starting point, but looks to the endeavours of other jurisdictions to expand and contrast the UK approach. While the United Kingdom, the United States and Singapore are all common law systems, the European Union is a mix of common law and civil law systems. The difference between common and civil law systems is not necessarily as great as it may initially appear, as will discussed in chapter eight, but may have some impact on liability depending on how liability is dealt with in each Member State. The comparison of the four jurisdictional approaches provides a basis for grounding the blueprint: what approaches taken thus far have been optimal, and how they have been shaped by their constituents. The blueprint takes the lessons learned from classical approaches to

[1] A Turing, 'Computing Machinery and Intelligence' (1950) 59 *Mind* (New Series) 433.

liability and regulation, as well as AI-specific endeavours and sectoral regulation to craft an approach that is jurisdictionally agnostic. The blueprint is then applied to each of the four jurisdictions, illustrating how it could be applied. While the book specifically addresses AI causing accidental death, the lessons learned and approaches recommended have broader applicability and value for AI regulation.

ACKNOWLEDGEMENTS

Deepest thanks to Chris Reed, without whom this book would never have happened. Thank you for your support, your time, and perhaps above all, your sense of humour.

Thank you to the Alan Turing Institute for its support via the doctoral studentship, but also for its dedicated and welcoming community.

Thank you to the Centre for Commercial Law Studies, and to the many wonderful people I met in my time there. Particular thanks to the Cloud Legal Research team whose support and expertise were always appreciated, and to Laura Edgar for her helpful supervision comments.

Thank you to the Responsible Technology Institute for their continual encouragement and enthusiasm.

Last but never least, thank you to my family, friends and those who wander that line.

TABLE OF CONTENTS

A NOTE ON THE FUNDING

This work was supported by the Economic and Social Research Council (ESRC) through the Alan Turing Institute Doctoral Studentship Programme, with support during the final stages of preparation for publication from the Microsoft Cloud Legal Project.

ABBREVIATIONS

AI	artificial intelligence
AV	automated vehicle
AV START	American Vision for Safer Transportation Through Advancement of Revolutionary Technologies Act
CheXNeXt	deep learning application for chest radiograph diagnosis
EU	European Union
FAVP	American Federal Automated Vehicles Comprehensive Plan
GDPR	European Union's General Data Protection Regulation
GPS	global positioning system
ICO	Information Commissioner's Office
IEC	International Electrotechnical Commission
ISO	International Organisation for Standardization
LiDAR	light detection and ranging
RADAR	radio detection and ranging
SELF DRIVE	American Safely Ensuring Lives Future Deployment and Research in Vehicle Evolution Act
TR	Singapore Technical Reference
UK	United Kingdom
US	United States
XAI	explainable artificial intelligence

LIST OF FIGURES

TABLE OF CASES

United Kingdom

Canada

Ireland

Singapore

United States

TABLE OF LEGISLATION

European Union:

Singapore:

United States:

Federal:

California:

Other:

1

State of AI and its Regulation

This book investigates how to regulate artificial intelligence (AI) which risks causing accidental death or serious injury, taking into account the technical realities and legal requirements of a regulatory system. It reconciles the societal desirability of high-benefit AI with the inherent risks thereof, balancing potential benefit with the critical need for safe development and use.

1.1. Introduction

Few concepts have captured the human imagination like artificial intelligence (AI). Whether we dream of a being to take on our workloads or with which to share the loneliness of existence, non-human intelligences have long had a place in human stories. Man-made automata have had a place in Greek mythology,[1] Jewish legend[2] and Ancient China, circa 400 BCE.[3] While the pop-culture wheel inexorably turns – zombies lasting several years, vampires perhaps fewer but returning more frequently – artificial intelligences are a consistent thread in the background. It is perhaps one of the most enticing possibilities for humanity; the peak of creativity – to build something capable of thinking and creating. It is also one of the most terrifying: while humanity does not trust or understand itself, it trusts even less an existence that lacks the frailties and context of the human condition. Thus, we have our villains, our wonderful cultural mainstays of an existence clever enough to rival or better our own, but alien and different to confound and defy us. Robotic villains, sentient programme bad guys, and lunatic artificial lifeforms[4] give us Ultron, The Cybermen, The Borg, The Matrix (machines), False Maria, The Terminator, Roy Batty, and HAL 9000 – we have so many AI villains that we rank them.[5] Isaac Asimov in particular deserves a large share of

[1] 'Robotics and Artificial Intelligence in the Homeric Epics' (*Novo Scriptorium*, 22 April 2019): novoscriptorium.com/2019/04/23/robotics-and-artificial-integillence-in-the-homeric-epics/.

[2] R Jones, 'Archaic Man Meets a Marvellous Automaton: Posthumanism, Social Robots, Archetypes' (2017) 62 *Journal of Analytical Psychology* 338: onlinelibrary.wiley.com/doi/abs/10.1111/1468-5922.12316.

[3] J Needham, *Science and Civilisation in China: Physics and Physical Technology – Mechanical Engineering*, vol 4, 2nd edn (Cambridge University Press 1965).

[4] 'Artificial Intelligence' (*Villains Wiki*): villains.fandom.com/wiki/Category:Artificial_Intelligence.

[5] 'It's Here: The Top 10 Greatest Cyborg and AI Villains' (*Horror Made*, 21 August 2015): horror-made.com/2015/08/20/its-here-the-top-10-greatest-cyborg-and-ai-villians/.

credit for the modern conceptions of AI, laying out a perfectly credible set of rules to balance humanity and AI, and then proceeding to demonstrate the ambiguities and difficulties of those rules, to the detriment of his human protagonists.[6] Yet this brings us to problem one with our fascinating cabal of villainy: AI does not think like humans. At the very least, it does not do so yet.[7]

Our second problem arises with the very existence of AI: why, exactly, do we want it? For all that an automated workforce has its benefits, this can be accomplished without a human level of intelligence, as seen by the level of non-AI automation already employed. While AI might perhaps share the deep philosophical questions of humanity, there is no guarantee it will do so. Why, then, should humanity persist in the development of AI? Many technologically adept commentators have pointed out the very pertinent dangers that AI may pose to humanity.[8] Yet we persist. We persist because there are benefits to AI that can not only better current practices but help to undo the damage that humanity has wrought. The potential benefits of AI are boundless, hampered only by humanity's collective creativity, drive and resources. Given the leaps in AI development so far, it is difficult to imagine a field in which AI could not be beneficially employed: AI is being used in ecology, epidemiology, earth-science, economy, education, energy and e-commerce – and that is not even all the 'e's, much less the entire list of AI applications. It would be negligent to ignore life-saving and earth-saving potential developments out of fear wrought of fiction. This is not to say that fears are unfounded, but that potential benefits must enter the discussion of risk.

One application with clear potential benefits is self-driving vehicles.[9] Self-driving vehicles offer benefits in traffic congestion, fuel costs, human hours, accessibility and green transport.[10] However, there is the obvious concern that not only do such vehicles have the potential to kill or harm humans, but that they have already done so.[11] Social acceptance is a key factor for self-driving vehicles to become widely used, and surveys have indicated that this trust is lacking: one survey in the United States had 82 per cent ranking safety as the most important factor of self-driving adoption, with 74 per cent not trusting the vehicle to drive

[6] Such as his 1950 'positronic robot' short story collection of 1950, 'I, Robot'. I Asimov, *I, Robot* (Gnome Press 1950).

[7] R Abbott and A Sarch, 'Punishing Artificial Intelligence: Legal Fiction or Science Fiction' (2019) 53 *University of California Davis Law Review* 323.

[8] B Marr, '28 Best Quotes About Artificial Intelligence' (*Forbes*, 25 July 2017): www.forbes.com/sites/bernardmarr/2017/07/25/28-best-quotes-about-artificial-intelligence/.

[9] There are also potential negative impacts, such as lack of availability of organs for transplant, job losses in the transportation industry, and increased competition against air travel. K Grieman, 'Hard Drive Crash' (2019) 9 *Journal of Intellectual Property, Information Technology and Electronic Commerce Law* 294: jipitec.eu/issues/jipitec-9-3-2018/at_download/CompleteIssue.

[10] ibid.

[11] K Richmond, '15 Unbelievable Self-Driving Car Statistics & Facts' (*Future Insights*, 2019): future-insights.com/15-unbelievable-self-driving-car-statistics-facts-2019/.

better than a human, and 74 per cent believing the vehicles would be prone to malfunction.[12]

Additionally, this tying of mistrust to potential harms frequently invokes the parallel of 'The Trolley Problem'; a classic philosophical problem wherein there is a trolley speeding along a track towards three individuals, and the person to whom the question is put has the opportunity to throw the switch, putting the trolley onto a different track, on which it will kill only one person. The problem is classically framed to examine the moral implications of acting in order to mitigate but directly cause harm, versus passively allowing greater harm to happen. The scenario has evolved to include personas or backstories for the potential victims. Overall, it has become the byword of moral panic around AI and transportation, and attempts to find some sort of morally cohesive answer have cropped up in various ways: experiments such as the 'Moral Machine', which is a 'platform for gathering a human perspective on moral decisions made by machine intelligence, such as self-driving cars'.[13] Participants are asked to choose 'the lesser of two evils, such as killing two passengers or five pedestrians. As an outside overseer, [one judges] which outcome … is more acceptable'.[14]

This is a fundamental mis-framing of the question. It is not the car choosing to kill one person or three. It is humanity. We look at a system we do not understand, and either assume it functions as we do, or that it is making deep philosophical decisions, rather than understanding that it is a composition of probabilities and sensors. We propose questions such as the moral machine to determine whether humanity really has an underlying approach as to who should live and who should die based on the attributes of each (the moral machine). Yet at the base of the trolley problem in its original form is the question: is it better to take action and directly cause the death of one, or to take no action and allow the death of many? That is the question that we as a society are answering when deciding whether or not to turn to self-driving vehicles. Human drivers are objectively bad at what they do.[15] But we are used to them being bad, so we let this continue. Yet the move to self-driving vehicles has the potential to not only harm fewer humans, but to harm progressively fewer humans as it continues to improve. It is the job of regulation to ensure that as few humans as possible will be harmed in the transition to self-driving vehicles. But make no mistake, it is not a case of the AI 'deciding' which human to kill. It is a question of devising and enforcing a system that is best equipped to stop the trolley.

This book investigates how we could build such a system, one that best enforces our safe-braking 'trolley', or more generally entices innovation without sacrificing safety and reliability. Specifically, it examines AI applications resulting

[12] K Othman, 'Public Acceptance and Perception of Autonomous Vehicles: A Comprehensive Review' (2021) 1 *AI and Ethics* 355: doi.org/10.1007/s43681-021-00041-8.

[13] 'Moral Machine' (*Moral Machine*): moralmachine.mit.edu.

[14] ibid.

[15] A Davies, 'Oh Look, More Evidence Humans Shouldn't Be Driving' (*Wired*, 21 May 2015): wired.com/2015/05/oh-look-evidence-humans-shouldnt-driving/.

in death or serious injury: those applications for which death or injury is never an intended consequence, unlike in military applications where death may be intended, but mistakes may still occur. These applications will be referred to in this book as high risk – a definition that does not specifically align with the EU's definition of high risk; a definition discussed in depth in section 5.3.2. Two areas in particular illustrate how negligence liability will work in their own and other domains. Medical liability is an important example given its additional intricacies in liability, while driving liability serves as an example of how generic liability may be applied. Automated driving liability has also attracted a great deal of judicial analysis, making it an ideal candidate for analysing how other risks may be treated, and whether it has the potential to ultimately be treated under strict liability (given the extensive backdrop of insurance within the sector). There will also be additional examples added into chapter four ('Law Using XAI'), demonstrating that these two areas examined in depth are illuminating for other areas.

Medicine and transportation illustrate distinct areas of AI application. Self-driving vehicles operate on a fixed-state model, or at very least a series of fixed-state models: a journey from point A to point B will be completed using the same, fixed-state AI model. While this model may be changed or updated between journeys, it will be fundamentally the same model during the journey. Medical applications, however, address a human at different stages of their medical journey: at diagnosis, during surgery, while in aftercare, etc, and may either be an updated model throughout that journey, or a series of different models entirely, for example a diagnostic tool followed by an infection treatment. Also, while medical liability has particular intricacies beyond general fault-based liability, driving is an example of more broadly applicable fault-based liability, accompanied by a large body of case law for non-AI driving. Lastly, both have the potential for regulators to introduce strict liability alongside pre-existing insurance schemes – a set-up already employed in some jurisdictions for human physicians, and to varying extents in driving.

Before diving in, we must address what is captured by the term AI generally. Then we must recognise that some AI systems represent a conceptual break from preceding technologies, as they can act as an intermediary decision-maker, and factor in this recognition into regulation rather than relying solely on traditional conceptions of regulation which account only for humans and human decision-making.

The definition of AI is oft debated. A 2018 survey on the definition of artificial intelligence found the most agreed-upon definition to be Pei Wang's:[16]

> The essence of intelligence is the principle of adapting to the environment while working with insufficient knowledge and resources. Accordingly, an intelligent system

[16] D Monett, CWP Lewis and KR Thórisson, Introduction to the JAGI Special Issue 'On Defining Artificial Intelligence' Commentaries and Author's Response (2020) 11 *Journal of Artificial General Intelligence* 1, 2.

> should rely on finite processing capacity, work in real time, open to unexpected tasks, and learn from experience. This working definition interprets 'intelligence' as a form of 'relative rationality'.[17]

This definition had a positive response ('strongly agree' or 'agree') of 58.6 per cent of 567 respondents.[18] Needless to say, debate continues. However, it is reasonable for the purposes of this book to note that definitions tend to centre around the AI in question's ability to perform a task which requires a level of cognition. This is still very broad – it includes both an autonomous vacuum cleaner and a self-driving vehicle – but nonetheless is central to understanding AI, and serves to underline why, exactly, there is a conceptual difference between AI and that technology which came before it. While AI does not make a decision in the way that humans make a decision, decisions are nonetheless being made. From the legal perspective, this is a fundamental break: no matter how 'smart' the smart car, if it was driven into another car there was no break in the chain of causation between a human decision-maker and a consequence. Questions such as fault and foreseeability rely on a human decision-maker undertaking an action, and the consequences of that action. The introduction of AI means that a human decision, for example to deploy a self-driving car, may not as a matter of law have caused the consequence, the accident, because of the introduction of a non-human decision-maker between the human and the consequence.

This chain of causality underpins much of law conceptually. Without delving into arguments of natural law or fundamental elements, concepts such as culpability and, more importantly, responsibility, rely on there being a direct connection between a human decision-maker and a consequence. This is not to say that exceptions do not exist – animals make decisions, as do humans who are exempted from consequence by virtue of mental condition – but that fundamentally the law hangs its hat for concepts such as liability on an action, and the foreseeable consequences of that action.

When there is an AI decision-making entity between a human and a consequence, what becomes of foreseeability? How can someone be held liable when they cannot be said to have made the decision that caused a consequence? How can regulation reconcile the potential positives of AI with the desperate need to ensure they are as safe as possible? Where is regulation left with liability? These bring our questions of regulation for AI causing accidental death to a series of sub-questions, the first asking what laws currently exist that address AI? What effects might these laws have? The second set of sub-questions addresses how regulation should best be structured: what technical aspects of AI itself lend themselves to understanding the technology? What concepts form parallels with existing

[17] ibid, citing P Wang, 'What Do You Mean by "AI"?' in P Wang, B Goertzel and S Franklin (eds), *Artificial General Intelligence: Proceedings of the First AGI Conference, Frontiers in Artificial Intelligence and Applications* vol 17 (IOS Press 2008).

[18] Monett, Lewis and Thórisson (n 16).

legal concepts? Ultimately, what must regulation address to induce societally beneficial AI?

The first step in answering all of these questions is to look at the technology itself. This is not a simple thing, as AI advancements are as quick as they are plentiful, yet it is exceptionally important. If regulation is based on misconceptions surrounding AI the regulation will be ineffective at best, and at worst stifle innovation. There is a distinct tightrope to walk: over-regulation has the potential to quash potential avenues of development and innovation, while under-regulation has the potential to allow for greater damage and casualties.[19] So where, then, is AI currently?

1.2. Technological Introduction to AI

The first step in dispelling myths around AI is to specify what it is not. Specifically, that AI is not yet at a state of advancement that would allow a single AI to learn multiple, different tasks by itself. AI development is currently at what we would term narrow or specific AI, which performs a single task, rather than general AI. On the whole, the concept of general AI is what fuels our pop-culture phenomena: artificial minds that learn as quickly and variably as humans, with the ability to pick up on context and nuance as a human would. Happily, or unhappily, we are simply not here yet.

AI today is at the stage of narrow AI. This does not mean that it is not useful or effective, but rather that it tends to be useful and effective for a specific task. Some AI applications even learn as they go and can become more accurate or more efficient through their lifetime as the algorithm refines itself.[20] Yet there are basic similarities to AI development, whether or not they learn as they go.

The first step in creating an AI is to determine what the AI is intended to do: whether it is to devise a game strategy, identify potholes, or any number of applications, the starting point is to determine the problem. Second, appropriate data is gathered in order to build the AI. Third, to examine the process by which a human would accomplish this task: identify end goals of the game; look for irregularities in the road surface, etc. This also requires recognising that there are some things which humans do which are difficult to explain – why certain musical notes sound 'better' in a particular order, or how we evaluate multiple inputs while driving.

[19] Under-regulation means that companies or individuals can enter the field with no regulation whatsoever. Consider here the internet: there are clear harms that states are now trying to address, but internet regulation came much, much later than the internet itself. Because of the lack of regulation, harms that occurred could not be pursued, or pursued only with the added difficulty of trying to create ad hoc parallels to other legislation, such as taxation, defamation, etc.

[20] There is, conversely, a concern of 'over-fitting' an AI, wherein it learns lessons (re: patterns) too specifically fitted to a particular set of parameters. For example, if a model were over-fitted to its training data, it may not be as effective on data that is not its training data.

A model is then built that tries to approximate, to an extent, the way that a human might accomplish that task: telling the AI what aspects of a game give certain amounts of points; providing the AI with inputs about potholes – for humans this would be what they look like, but for an AI might include a map where potholes have been previously identified. Third, the AI model will be trained so that it meets or exceeds human performance and is tested against appropriate benchmarks.

Machine learning is a form of AI that uses data and algorithms to incrementally improve its own function. This means that the machine learning algorithm is not specifically written or created, but rather improves from a baseline as it is used. While data and training will be discussed in greater detail, the pertinent point at this stage is that a machine learning AI can 'learn' from data, using various mechanisms to both improve its function and to perform tasks on data it was not trained on.

There are two points of interest here. First is whether the data used to train the AI model is structured, or unstructured. Structured data has a distinct consistency of formatting, whereas unstructured data does not. In other words, structured data might be tabular data on aspects of a house for sale: how many rooms it has, how many bathrooms, its price, its postcode, etc. The structuring of the data is deliberate, and correlates to known or expected categories. Whereas unstructured data is not necessarily numerically driven, and can include images, audio, words and any other information not strictly confined to formal parameters. The second note is that the AI's training on the data can take on a variety of forms. These include supervised, unsupervised, reinforcement, self-supervised and semi-supervised.

Supervised learning is an approach wherein the AI is shown a series of examples of what it is intended to do in order to emulate them. For example, an AI that is intended to identify pictures of moose might be shown pictures of moose, labelled 'moose', and pictures that do not include moose, labelled 'lacking moose'. Essentially, labelled training data provides the AI with information to make the connections that its creators want. This is useful for tasks such as classification, which would include identifying objects in images, recognising gestures, detecting voices and transcribing conversations.[21] Such decisions can also critically affect outcomes, for example if a developer were to create a self-driving vehicle that did not include classification for wet or icy roads, so that the vehicle did not alter its behaviour to deal with them.

Unsupervised learning is when the AI is provided with a lot of data which is unlabelled. The AI then makes connections of its own accord, grouping data by analysing it and finding patterns and features that may or may not have been evident to its human creators. Such an approach works well for applications such as clustering and anomaly detection:[22] clustering, for example, might be grouping a

[21] A Bonner, 'The Complete Beginners Guide to Deep Learning' (*Medium*, 13 January 2019): towardsdatascience.com/intro-to-deep-learning-c025efd92535.

[22] ibid.

photoset into animals with four legs and animals with two legs. Anomaly detection includes functions such as fraud detection: finding data that has unusual features and flagging it. Unsupervised AI might skip the broad steps identified before that relate to how a human would complete a task: the creators are not informing the AI of a particular kind of data to look for, such as potholes, but seeing what the AI groups together without human input.

Semi-supervised learning combines supervised and unsupervised approaches in providing the AI labelled and unlabelled data. It can be 'referred to as transductive (inferring correct labels for the given data) or inductive (inferring the correct mapping from X to Y)'.[23] Self-supervised learning, conversely, involves providing part of a data example and having the AI predict out the remaining part.[24] The aim of semi-supervised learning 'is to understand how combining labeled and unlabeled data may change the learning behaviour, and design algorithms that take advantage of such a combination'.[25]

Reinforcement learning involves providing no direction to the AI between the data and desired results, but provides either rewards or penalties for the AI's predictions. The AI is designed to maximise the reward function. Essentially, reinforcement learning does not 'teach' the AI, which means that behaviours are modified incrementally through the AI's trial and error.[26]

At the moment, these are three of the most common approaches to training. One can note that there is a basic progression of:

input → AI → output

While this is of course an over-simplification, it is a useful one because law relies on causal chains: that an action was reasonably seen to cause an outcome. It also brings us to another potential division of AI: how the AI achieves its goals. AI can be enabled entirely digitally – such as an AI that sorts images – or act upon the physical world, such as a self-driving vehicle. Essentially, some AI is embedded in a physical system, and some is not. AI that is not embedded in a physical system are much more likely to have a human intermediary between their actions or decisions and the world – we call this a 'human in the loop' system. AI systems that are embedded can also be 'human in the loop systems', wherein a human must approve the AI's actions or has some control over them, but 'human out of the loop' systems are most likely to be embedded: there is not necessarily a human intervention between the AI's action and the consequences thereof. For example, this could be anything from an autonomous weapon to an autonomous tea robot. While these will be discussed in greater detail further on, we will call these 'human out of the loop' AI systems autonomous agents 'embedded'.

[23] ibid (emphasis removed from original).

[24] N Sinha, 'Self-Supervised Learning' (*Medium*, 3 October 2019): towardsdatascience.com/self-supervised-learning-78bdd989c88b.

[25] X Zhu and A Goldberg, 'Introduction to Semi-Supervised Learning' (2009) 3 *Synthesis Lectures on Artificial Intelligence and Machine Learning* 1.

[26] ibid.

Expanding upon the input → AI → output progression, the output will sometimes have an effect on the system in which the AI functions. In the same way that human actions have consequences, so too does the AI's. Consequences can occur in two ways: directly, or systemically. This provides us with:

input → AI → output → consequence

Let us examine these components individually. The input that the AI receives is all of the data put to it after it is created and tested. There are no limits on the types of data this could be: visual, auditory, tabular, etc. It must simply be the – or a – type of data that the AI is equipped to use. Some AI combines inputs from multiple types of sources: for example the AI behind a fully autonomous self-driving vehicle might be interpreting input from cameras, sensors, RADAR,[27] LiDAR,[28] GPS[29] and other connected vehicles. Input is not necessarily always so complex, however, and could be coming from a single source such as the tabular aspects of a house to be priced. Types of input are always known, as the AI is created in a way that can receive them, but the input that an AI is making use of in a particular moment might not be known. In the self-driving vehicle for, example, it may not be easily evident which source of information the car is acting on at any given moment: sensor, LiDAR, etc.

The AI itself has been created, tested and trained. The process by which it reaches decisions may be more or less well inherently understood depending on its design, which will be discussed later in greater detail,[30] but what is knowable is the type of output it is intended to produce. While humans must find their purpose, AI is created to address a problem.[31] This output may be more or less accurate, or more or less functional for what it is intended to do, but the intended output is inherently knowable.

The consequence of the AI is the impact that the AI has on the system in which it functions. This depends on several factors. First, whether the AI is an autonomous agent or not. If an AI is not an autonomous agent, there may be a human between the AI and any intended consequences. This means that the AI could be used more classically as a tool, rather than a free-'thinking' agent.[32] Alternatively, the non-autonomous AI might be put purely to digital tasks, such

[27] Radio detection and ranging.

[28] Light detection and ranging.

[29] Global positioning system.

[30] See ch 3, 'Explainable AI (XAI)'.

[31] This might not be the case for general AI, but it is for narrow AI – this is necessary for the training, testing and refining of the AI.

[32] There are of course caveats to this statement. For example, if a radiology AI that interprets X-rays creates interpretations that are passed to an untrained human simply for the purposes of feeding the interpretation to a surgical AI, there has not been nor is there intended to be a meaningful interjection in the decision-making process by the/a human. The human intermediary is only a 'human in the loop' if they have any say or meaningful review of the AI's decision-making process. Where things become more complicated, however, are if a human intermediary is required by the AI producer but is clearly only required in an attempt to escape liability when the AI is clearly intended, marketed and agreed to function autonomously.

as an AI application that plays video games. Either way, harms are still possible. Essentially, there are three types of consequences: insignificant, direct or systemic. An insignificant consequence might be an AI sugar scooper that spills a few grains of sugar. If the AI cannot otherwise move or interfere with other operations,[33] its consequences are insignificant. Direct or systemic consequences are where our more classical legal conceptions of harm enter the discussion. A direct harm is physical harm that the AI causes to a human or property. These can be simple: the AI tea robot bumps into the feet of the human in the kitchen. Or they can be severe: the AI zeppelin flies into a building, causing millions in damage. Systemic harms, conversely, are more insidious: the use of the AI may be obvious, but the way in which it shapes the system in which it functions might not be: one might never know that decisions for interviewing job candidates depended on biased data. This is a deep underlying concern for the use of AI as a whole.

In looking at the knowability of consequences for direct damage specifically, the question becomes, 'what happens if the AI functions perfectly? And 'what happens if it does not? If the answer to either of these questions is unknown, then the consequences may not be known. Conversely, even if the potential consequences are serious, they may still be knowable, for example the potentially harmful effects of chemotherapy, such as cell damage, are serious but knowable, direct effects.

Where types of consequences are known, we encounter the same sorts of questions that we ask of human counterparts. For example, in a medical context, one might use a diagnostic AI to examine x-rays. If the AI works perfectly, there are two possible outcomes: the AI correctly diagnoses the patient's issue and flags it for treatment, or the AI correctly diagnoses that the patient does not have an issue and does not recommend them for further treatment. If the AI does not work perfectly, there are two possible outcomes: the AI incorrectly diagnoses an issue with the patient and flags it for treatment, or the AI incorrectly diagnoses the patient as having no issues and fails to flag them for treatment. It should be noted here that there is already an AI – called CheXNeXT – which can detect 14 different pathologies 'including pneumonia, pleural effusion, pulmonary masses, and nodules in frontal-view chest radiographs, with internal performance similar to practising radiologists',[34] with similar accuracy but a time of 1.5 minutes against the radiologists' 240 minutes on a 420 image dataset.[35] So the risks of misdiagnosis are similar to the AI's human counterparts, and the AI has the benefit of speed. The consequences, while potentially serious, are known.

In summary, of input, output and consequences, output is always known but may be functional within a relative measure – how accurately it can sort images, how well it drives, etc. Both input and consequences may be known or unknown

[33] Such as heating the sugar sufficiently to explode.

[34] S Saria, A Butte and A Sheikh, 'Better Medicine through Machine Learning: What's Real, and What's Artificial?' (2018) *15 Public Library of Science Medicine* 12: dx.plos.org/10.1371/journal.pmed.1002721.

[35] ibid.

in relative measure. This provides four potential outcomes: both input and consequences are known; input is known and consequences are not; input is unknown and consequences are known; neither input nor consequences are known. Visually speaking, this can be represented as:

Figure 1 Input and consequences of AI

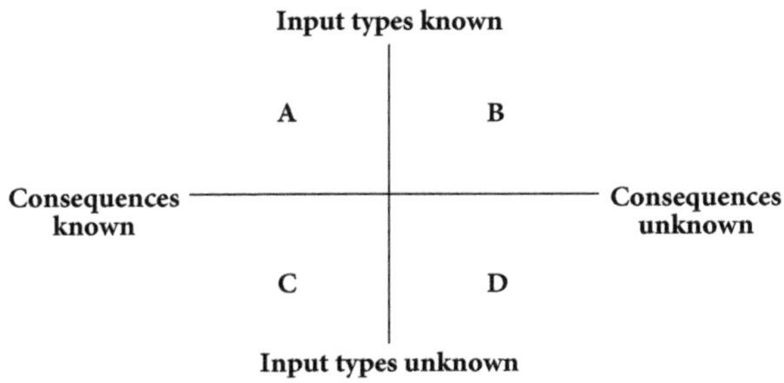

There are several inherent assumptions to this division. First is that AI will only have the tools to achieve its purpose – that one does not outfit the toaster with a rocket launcher. Second is that AI has the potential to move categories depending on its purported use. For example, a facial recognition AI that is used to determine age for the purposes of purchasing a video game, and wherein the data is immediately deleted,[36] has a very different impact from that same facial recognition programme used in law enforcement. The input types are the same, the output may be identical, but the potential impacts are radically different. This category hopping can also occur when more than one AI interacts with another towards a common purpose: an AI-enabled sonar detector has predictable data input, and a definable output. However, if it is then used in a self-driving vehicle, its output is combined with other AI applications to the AI 'driving' the vehicle – the output taken as a whole is thus less knowable. Third, certain elements are important for all types: scoping, which approach to use, training, and testing. These will be discussed later.[37] Fourth, the more complicated the world with which the AI interacts, the less foreseeable the impact it will have. Using again the self-driving vehicle example, the car must contend with other vehicles, pedestrians, cyclists, dogs, traffic lights and weather, to name a few. The chess AI, conversely, needs only to contend with the inherent rules of the game.

This depiction does not include an examination of systemic harms and whether they can be known or unknown, which are outside the scope of this book.[38]

[36] This is of course simplified, and not considering whether such data can be perfectly anonymised at the source.

[37] See ch 3, 'Explainable AI (XAI)'.

[38] Bias or biased AI can also cause damage and liability. AI has the capacity to be unbiased, but the issue is that the data on which they are trained comes from the data which humans have so far, which can be incredibly biased. Many have written in the vein of the use of artificial intelligence in

The quadrants are also a relative binary: certain tools can help make inputs more obvious, and the area of consequences might be known but with exact details lacking. A more realistic depiction would show that how 'known' the consequences are is relative, and that the knowability of input types may depend on the tools being used to assess them.

In any case, the importance is – without losing sight of the granularity of AI types themselves – to highlight the knowability and lack thereof of AI applications.

1.3. Scope of the Book

As discussed with respect to the societal approach to the trolley problem, we are at a crossroads in deciding how and whether or not to employ AI. There may be applications for which the risks of AI outweigh their potential benefits: either in terms of human rights, such as sentencing applications; or physical risk, such as freestyle hairdressing.[39] Yet some of the most exciting applications are those where risk is not only involved, but inevitable: the applications which can save the most lives will also have the by-product of taking lives as well. Applications that cause physical harm that does not ultimately result in death are included in this analysis.

The AI focused on in this book are applications that are designed to carry out activities that carry inherent risks to physical safety. There are many more types of AI which are potentially dangerous, but whose activities are nonetheless not inherently focused on inherently physically dangerous activity. Other types of AI include generative AI, such as large language models. Large language models, such as those popularised by Chat-GPT and LLaMA 2, are certainly capable of causing physical harm, such as by instructing someone to do something dangerous like drinking a cleaning product, but their intended activity is, in the case of large language models, to create a language-based response, not a physical outcome or an outcome that produces a physical effect. While the use of large language

public and private decision-making in the public and private sectors posing a significant human rights threat. See, eg, MK Land and JD Aronson, 'Human Rights and Technology: New Challenges for Justice and Accountability' (2020) 16 *Annual Review of Law and Social Science* 223: doi.org/10.1146/annurev-lawsocsci-060220-081955; J-W Hong and D Williams, 'Racism, Responsibility and Autonomy in HCI: Testing Perceptions of an AI Agent' (2019) 100 *Computers in Human Behavior* 79: www.sciencedirect.com/science/article/abs/pii/S0747563219302389; J Angwin, J Larson, L Kirchner and S Mattu, 'Machine bias' (2016) ProPublica in J-W Hong and D Williams, 'Racism, Responsibility and Autonomy in HCI: Testing Perceptions of an AI Agent' (2019) 100 *Computers in Human Behaviour* 79.

[39] eg, an AI that custom-cuts long hair. While shorter, buzz-cut hair could be safely accomplished with a covered razor, custom cuts of longer hair involve wielding sharp instruments around the face of the human. There are certainly workarounds to this, such as feeding hair into a safety envelope within which sharp instruments are contained, but the general concept puts risk over benefit.

and other generative models produce liability,[40] they are out of the main scope of this book focused on inherently physically dangerous activity.

While the entire purpose of using AI is to solve a problem better than could be done with a human,[41] AI applications will, at the very least initially, be imperfect. The potential benefits of such applications are sufficient that advancements should be pursued, hopefully to the eventual point of perfection. The largest two cross-sections of such applications – those that have the greatest potential for life-saving, but also direct and serious consequences – are transport and medical AI, as previously discussed. These two fields share a variety of challenges: deeply impactful damage; potentially unknowable consequence prior to deployment; and a distinct desire for embedded use. This book will focus on the regulation of those transport and medical applications that are autonomous AI agents: those which do not have a human in the loop and have the potential to take human lives. There are of course applications of AI that would take human lives directly as an intended consequence such as military applications; these will not be addressed herein.[42]

The examination of AI causing accidental death or injury in the following chapters will proceed first by examining traditional liability in areas causing accidental death: driving, the medical system and product liability. This will include a discussion of strict liability, a possible regulatory path which does not necessarily preclude the kinds of questions that would be asked for traditional fault-based liability. Second, there will be a discussion of the tools for AI development, training and analysis, and how these tools interact with legal concepts. Third, an examination of the regulatory playing field of four distinct approaches: Singapore, the European Union, the United States and the United Kingdom. These examples will be used to analyse the essence of regulatory approaches in the area broadly, and explain how states are beginning to assess AI, followed by a look at how these states are beginning to regulate AI applications sectorally in areas causing accidental death. These jurisdictions were chosen by virtue of their heavy investment into AI, differing approaches to AI regulation, and availability of both legislation and commentary in English. Each jurisdiction has striven to be world leading in a particular way, whether in providing a regulatory system for others to adopt; growing human expertise in AI; growing a market in AI; or in providing favourable government/industry relationships to foster AI. While there is a broader focus on common law systems in terms of discussing fault-based liability, there is nonetheless discussion of civil law approaches, such as in Germany and France, and the provision of case study examples on all four jurisdictions, including EU civil law systems.

[40] See, eg, M Garcia, 'What Air Canada Lost in "Remarkable" Lying AI Chatbot Case' (*Forbes*, 19 February 2024): www.forbes.com/sites/marisagarcia/2024/02/19/what-air-canada-lost-in-remarkable-lying-ai-chatbot-case/.

[41] Faster, more efficiently, more safely, or any combination of these.

[42] An obvious example being autonomous weapons. See, eg, N Bhuta et al (eds), *Autonomous Weapons Systems: Law, Ethics, Policy* (Cambridge University Press 2016).

This book brings the analytical discussion together by proposing a regulatory blueprint for autonomous AI causing accidental death, informed by current regulation, the tools available for the production and examination of AI, practical existing legal parallels, and regulatory theory. The penultimate chapter provides a case study analysis of how the blueprint would function in practice in the four chosen jurisdictions. The conclusion will touch on the blueprint's importability to other types and areas of AI.

For simplicity's sake, this book will refer to the entity creating, training and testing the AI as the producer. This may in practice be multiple parties, or indeed require a differentiation between producers and those making the AI available on a particular market,[43] but while these discussions are valuable, they are outside the scope of this particular endeavour.

[43] The EU AI Act makes this distinction.

2

Drivers, Doctors, Devices

Liability is a core concept of every legal system: how, when and why a party is at fault. There are two primary reasons why the law imposes liability: to deter deleterious action or inaction; and to compensate victims when harm occurs. In UK law/common law systems, liability can be found through the tort of negligence, contractual liability and statutory liability. Within these, fault is assessed subjectively in negligence cases, where there is a broad obligation of care on the party in question – a duty to others operating in the same sphere. For example, this could be a duty to a patient; to one's neighbour by proximity; to other drivers. Fault is often assessed objectively in cases such as contractual obligation and statutory liability (such as product liability): where there is a more closely defined obligation of provision – a specific service in a particular style; a particular object of a particular quality.

Across both common and civil law systems, particular sectors or sub-sectors may specifically be deemed to have 'strict liability'. In strict liability areas, the nature of the event means that if it occurs, the party is automatically in the wrong – there is no question of fault or negligence. In the United Kingdom, for example, there is strict liability for contempt of court.[1] The United Kingdom and Singapore[2] do not employ strict liability for driving, and neither do any US states, but some Member States of the European Union, including France and the Netherlands, have strict and 'semi-strict' approaches respectively to liability for driving.[3] In healthcare, the United Kingdom,[4] Singapore[5] and the United States[6] all use a medical negligence approach; in the European Union, while Member States' approaches do vary, '[l]iability for fault remains the predominant basis of liability' in medicine. 'However, strict liability has an important role in Spain, and in the Czech Republic contractual liability is equated to a form of strict liability'.[7] While strict liability for offences will

[1] Contempt of Court Act 1981, ss 1–2.

[2] N Morgan and S Yeo, 'Defining the Fault Elements of Driving Offences' (2007) 19 *Singapore Academy of Law Journal* 205.

[3] 'Report on Strict Liability' (*Cycle Law Scotland*, 2012): parliament.act.gov.au/__data/assets/pdf_file/0006/534678/05_Research-Report-on-Strict-Liability.pdf.

[4] R Goldberg, 'Medical Malpractice and Compensation in the UK' (2012) 87 Chicago-Kent Law Review: heinonline.org/HOL/LandingPage?handle=hein.journals/chknt87&div=9&id=&page=.

[5] DQ Anderson, 'Medical Negligence Proceedings in Singapore: Instilling a Gentler Touch' [2021] *Global Studies in Comparative Law* 53: doi.org/10.1007/978-3-030-67000-9_14.

[6] BS Bal, 'An Introduction to Medical Malpractice in the United States' (2009) 467(2) *Clinical Orthopaedics and Related Research* 339: www.ncbi.nlm.nih.gov/pmc/articles/PMC2628513/.

[7] S Taylor, 'Introduction' (2019) 2 Journal Du Droit de la Santé et de l'Assurance – Maladie 9: cairn.info/revue-journal-du-droit-de-la-sante-et-de-l-assurance-maladie-2019-2-page-9.htm; www.cairn.info/revue-journal-du-droit-de-la-sante-et-de-l-assurance-maladie-2019-2-page-9.htm.

be discussed further in chapter three, it is sufficient temporarily to note that (a) strict liability is not, or at least not yet, a widespread approach, and (b) AI will cause accidental death beyond those in driving and medicine specifically, and fault elements are unlikely to be abandoned wholesale across all sectors in which AI will be employed.

To understand how liability for AI might be imposed, we need to start by outlining the liability rules for human defendants and then assessing how liability for AI might be decided using the current regime. Drivers, doctors and devices have been selected for analysis for two reasons: first, they are obvious areas for harm to be caused; and second, they already carry a heavy level of regulation – liability and regulation frequently go hand-in-hand and are likely to continue to do so in these cases. As will be demonstrated in this chapter, the current scheme of liability for humans is based on the foreseeability of harm and precautions taken to prevent that harm. Section 2.6 will examine whether AI is a product or a service, and if the distinction is in fact meaningful in the case of AI, and section 2.7 provides a summary analysis: how traditional conceptions of human-centred liability should be reconsidered for AI.

2.1. Subjective Liability

Subjective liability is based on a failure of care on the part of the defendant, usually described as negligence. At its core, negligence is based on the foreseeability of harm by action or inaction. *Blyth v Birmingham Waterworks Co* provides the essential definition: 'negligence is the omission to do something which a reasonable man, guided upon those considerations which ordinarily regulate the conduct of human affairs, would do, or doing something which a prudent and reasonable man would not do'.[8] This was expanded upon in *Lochgelly Iron & Coal Co Ltd v McMullan* in the statement that 'negligence means more than heedless or careless conduct, whether in commission or omission: it properly connotes the complex concept of duty, breach, and damage thereby suffered by the person to whom the duty is owing'.[9] This brings us to three essential points: the existence of a duty of care, the breach of that duty of care, and loss caused by that duty of care.

2.1.1. Duty of Care and Breach thereof

The most well-known statement of the general duty of care for negligence, also known as the neighbour principle, comes from the case of *Donoghue v Stevenson*:

> You must take reasonable care to avoid acts or omissions which you can reasonably foresee would be likely to injure your neighbour. Who, then, in law is my neighbour?

[8] *Blyth v Birmingham Waterworks Co* (1856) 11 Exch 781; 156 ER 1047, 1049.

[9] *Lochgelly Iron & Coal Co Ltd v McMullan* [1934] AC 1, 25 (HL).

> The answer seems to be persons who are so closely and directly affected by my act that I ought reasonably to have them in contemplation as being so affected when I am directing my mind to the acts or omissions which are called in question.[10]

While interpretations of this statement have been argued, the principle has been distilled to a few essential elements: the foreseeability of harm, the proximity or degree of connection between the action and the harm, and whether imposing liability would be fair, just and reasonable.

The essential element is whether it was reasonably foreseeable whether the act in question would cause the harm in question. The two classic examples are cases involving cricket: in *Bolton v Stone*, the claimant was struck and injured by a cricket ball while standing outside her home, and brought a case against the cricket club for negligence.[11] To quote, '[m]embers of the club of twenty years' standing or more agreed, in evidence, that the hit was altogether exceptional in comparison with anything previously seen on that ground'.[12] While hitting the cricket ball out of the cricket ground to this location was clearly possible, it was also historically unusual. While harm clearly could not be ruled out, the very low 'quantum of danger' meant that a reasonable person would not anticipate it and recognise a need to guard against it.[13] Conversely, in a case where 'quite a number of balls came over the boundary of the fence', a cricket club was indeed found liable.[14] Essentially, it must be reasonably foreseeable, and above a certain quantum of possibility, that harm will occur. This quantum is judged against both past occurrences and common sense.

Proximity between parties is broadly concerned with the degree of connection between the party causing the harm and the party suffering. In *Bourhill v Young*, a pregnant woman witnessed a fatal collision between a motorcycle and a car and subsequently sued the motorcyclist's estate on the basis that she had suffered shock that caused a miscarriage.[15] It is also noted that there was no 'element of reasonable fear of immediate bodily injury to [the pregnant woman]'.[16] The court discussed the consideration of whether a duty of care was owed both in terms of remoteness of damage, but also in relevance to the existence of a duty, ie, proximity. The court found that 'such a duty only arises towards those individuals of whom it may be reasonably anticipated that they will be affected by the act which constitutes the alleged breach', and that '[one] is not liable for negligence in the air'.[17] In other words, the potential victim must fall within a range of those reasonably contemplated to be affected within the context of the situation at hand.

[10] *Donoghue v Stevenson* [1932] AC 562, 580.
[11] *Bolton v Stone* [1951] AC 850.
[12] ibid, 852.
[13] ibid.
[14] *Miller v Jackson* [1977] 3 WLR 20 (CA).
[15] *Bourhill v Young* [1943] AC 92.
[16] ibid, 94.
[17] ibid, 101–02.

Whether imposing liability would be fair, just and reasonable is particularly slippery to nail down. Cases such as *Rich & Co v Bishop Rock Marine*[18] note that the requirement 'is a policy control mechanism' which takes into account the effects that decisions would have on other realities – a subjective assessment of the elements of the case at hand. In *Rich & Co v Bishop Rock Marine*, this included the decision of whether or not to hold a classification society liable for having approved a ship to sail after only temporary repairs, given that the ship then sank. It was decided on the basis that it would be unfair, unjust and unreasonable for a duty of care to exist on the classification society when '[t]he insurance system is structured on the basis that the potential liability of shipowners … is limited under the Hague Rules', and if a duty of care were to be recognised, 'it must have a substantial impact on international trade'.[19] Essentially, for practical, policy, and social reasons a duty of care was found not to exist. One additional element of the 'fair, just, and reasonable' portion is whether finding a duty of care to exist would leave defendants liable for an 'indeterminate amount for an indeterminate time to an indeterminate class',[20] something courts have chosen to avoid and may continue to avoid by not imposing liability on some AI producers.

2.1.2. Causation

In terms of causation, the court will assess whether the conduct in question was sufficiently connected to the damage to justify liability. In other words, whether the conduct in question was sufficiently causative of the harm in question. This is often posed through the 'but for' test: but for the actions of the party in question, would the harm have occurred? For example, but for the pub leaving its trapdoor on the pavement open, the patron would not have fallen in and sustained injury. The 'but for' test takes into account the context of the case in question, such as in *Calvert v William Hill Credit Ltd* wherein the bookmaker's failure to close the compulsive gambler's account was not found to be cause for liability, as the gambler would have continued his behaviour with other bookmakers.[21] Beyond sole and direct causation, there can also be contributory negligence, wherein the victim's actions contributed to the harm in question. In such cases, the monetary compensation is generally split along the proportionality of action as determined by the court.

In summary, liability for negligence can be broken down to duty of care, breach of duty of care, and sufficient connection between that breach and the harm being considered. Even cursory examination suggests that this will not be straightforward to apply to AI: when examining duty of care, should this be applied to the AI itself, its developers, its users, or some combination thereof? What is the level of

[18] *Marc Rich & Co AG v Bishop Rock Marine Co Ltd (The Nicholas H)* [1996] AC 211.
[19] ibid, 239.
[20] *Ultramares Corp v Touche* (1932) 174 NE 441, para 180.
[21] *Calvert v William Hill Credit Ltd* [2008] EWCA Civ 1427.

care to be provided, and should the standard against which to measure the duty of care be what a human would do? How can fault be shown where the vast majority if not all the information about the AI's workings is held solely by the developer? These questions will be examined throughout this chapter.

While this is the briefest of overviews, it serves to provide the general principles to which the law looks: relationships between the parties, foreseeability of consequence, acknowledgement of context, and the imposition of obligations, considered subjectively as a whole. There are of course more specific areas of subjective liability, particularly in areas entailing accidental death. For subjective liability, this includes doctors and drivers.

2.2. Doctors

Medical or clinical negligence is one area where subjective liability is particularly specialised. This is for several reasons: the greater ability expected of professionals; the dangers and complexity of the field; and the necessity of the service. The element of professionalism means an expectation of a level of knowledge beyond a layman: a person off the street knows why not to stab someone with a pen; a doctor knows when and why that might be a good idea.[22] The dangers and complexities of the field are commingled: while not all areas of medical fields have immediate and deadly effects on individual health, they are intertwined with those that are. A minor indicator such as loss of taste can be a symptom of a deadly virus (Covid-19), or simply of new medication.[23] The human body is a complex instrument, and doctors must have a sufficient level of knowledge not only of their area of expertise, but of the human body as a whole, in order to practise effectively and circumspectly. Lastly, the societal importance of the medical system and medical advancement cannot be understated, and both policies and insurance systems have arisen to protect both victims and the functioning of the system as a whole.

Clinical negligence has the same initial starting point as general negligence: a party has a duty of care; the standard of care was insufficient; and another party suffered harm. Generally speaking, a duty of care within the medical system is not difficult to prove: it exists where a medical practitioner 'has assumed some sort of responsibility for the patient's care [including] basic personal care or a complex procedure'.[24] While a medical professional does not have a legal duty to help in an emergency situation, there is often a professional duty to aid in emergency

[22] Such as an emergency tracheotomy. See 'Tracheotomy: Does TV Get it Right?' (American Lung Association, 2016): lung.org/blog/tracheotomy-does-tv-get-right.

[23] '4 Reasons For Loss of Taste' (Atlanta ENT Institute/Ear, Nose and Throat Specialists in Georgia, 19 September 2019): entinstitute.com/4-reasons-for-loss-of-taste/.

[24] 'Duty of Care | Advice Guides | Royal College of Nursing' (The Royal College of Nursing, 4 December 2015): rcn.org.uk/get-help/rcn-advice/duty-of-care.

situations to the limit of their competency.[25] For brevity of narrative, the medical professional will be referred to here as a medical doctor – not to state that theirs is the only role that matters, but merely to focus on the role that is potentially most inclusive of procedures undertaken.

How or against whom clinical or medical negligence claims are brought can be specific to a jurisdiction. This is true even between EU Member States, an issue provided for in EU Regulation 1215/2012.[26] While the aforementioned fault-based system is the most common, some jurisdictions have moved to a 'no-fault' system wherein the need to prove 'that the cause of harm was unconscionable, or beyond normal or reasonable practice, is removed'.[27] Such approaches are underwritten by insurance regimes, and pursue only questions of what happened, rather than applications of fault. Sweden and New Zealand, for instance, have no-fault systems: the victim must still prove that the doctor in question caused the harm in question, but not whether there is an element of fault.[28] The additional difference between systems includes whether there are duties and requirements on participants in the process to assist the complainant, ranging from providing funds for legal advice, to providing information on complaint procedures.

2.2.1. Standards

While the United Kingdom remains on a negligence-based liability system, as many jurisdictions do, there is a question of the standard of care present within the duty of care between the doctor and patient. For a doctor to have been negligent, they must be shown to have fallen below the standard of reasonable care. In non-medical settings, this is the standard of a reasonable person: what would a reasonable person, given the settings and context, have done? The standard is of course more specific for medical professionals and is found in *Bolam v Friern*: a doctor 'is not guilty of negligence if he has acted in accordance with a practice accepted as proper by a responsible body of medical men skilled in that particular art'.[29] In other words, so long as the doctor acts as a reasonable professional of that particular specialty, they do not act negligently. While the word 'reasonable' does not appear in the original, that the act be 'accepted as proper' provides a fundamentally similar grounding for broad acceptability: put in the negative, if something

[25] ibid.

[26] 'In Which State Can You Sue and Which Law Applies?' (National Contact Point for cross-border healthcare): eu-patienten.de/en/behandlung_deutschland/behandlungsfehler/klageort_und_anwendbares_recht/klageort_und_anwendbares_recht.jsp.

[27] European Commission. Directorate General for Health and Food Safety, and others, *Patients' Rights in the European Union: Mapping Exercise: Final Report* (Publications Office 2016): data.europa.eu/doi/10.2875/751285.

[28] P Fenn, A Gray and N Rickman, 'The Economics of Clinical Negligence Reform in England' (2004) 114 *Economic Journal* F272: academic.oup.com/ej/article/114/496/F272-F292/5089438.

[29] *Bolam v Friern Hospital Management Committee* [1957] 1 WLR 582, 587.

were not 'accepted as proper', it would not, as a medical act, be considered to have been reasonable. The assessment remains subjective, as there is no explicit definition of the exact steps of care that may apply – medicine being a holistic practice – and that there is often no defined correct action in providing care.

Bolam v Friern provides additional clarity as well on what a 'body' of medical persons might entail: 'a man is not negligent, if he is acting in accordance with such a practice, merely because there is a body of opinion who would take a contrary view'.[30] This is a particularly crucial point, as it acknowledges that medicine is not a binary practice of right and wrong; not only is there a potential range of acceptable care and treatment, but also that disagreements on what is appropriate does not inherently constitute negligence. Such disagreements occur even within sub-specialties, or patients would never seek a second opinion. It further underscores the lack of defined boundaries on what constitutes 'a responsible body': there is neither number nor designation to provide any sort of specificity. The body of medical experts must be 'skilled in that particular art' – an anesthesiologist's actions would be judged by an anesthesiologist, and not, say, a general practitioner or an endocrinologist.

The dicta of *Bolam v Friern* has of course been refined by further cases. These include the statement of the court in *Bolitho v City and Hackney Health Authority* that

> there are cases where, despite a body of professional opinion sanctioning the defendant's conduct, the defendant can properly be held liable for [medical] negligence … if, in a rare case, it can be demonstrated that the professional opinion is not capable of withstanding logical analysis, the judge is entitled to hold that the body of opinion is not reasonable or responsible.[31]

While 'it will very seldom be right for a judge to reach the conclusion that views genuinely held by a competent medical expert are unreasonable',[32] *Bolitho* nonetheless provides a theoretical limit on the decisions of the medical profession, but not an objective assessment of the duty of care.

Muller v King's College Hospital[33] introduces a distinction between cases concerning treatment as a whole and cases concerning solely a diagnosis. Treatment decisions can include whether or not to treat a condition, such as if the patient's quality of life must be weighed against the potential effectiveness and outcome of a treatment. If the case involves advice, treatment, or the practice of medicine more generally, the *Bolam* and *Bolitho* standards apply: there may be opposite opinions held (and possibly disagreed with by a judge as to their reasonableness). However, if the case is purely diagnostic, and 'there is no weighing of risks and benefits, only misreporting which may or may not be negligent', there is a fixed standard

[30] ibid.
[31] *Bolitho v City & Hackney Health Authority* [1997] 3 WLR 1151, 243 (HL).
[32] ibid.
[33] *Muller v King's College Hospital NHS Foundation Trust* [2017] EWHC 128.

'of reasonable skill and care, fixed by law' and the court may weigh contradictory expert evidence in determining negligence.[34] This is particularly interesting given the impact of an earlier case, *Gregg v Scott*, which addressed liability for diagnostic cases: negligence for a missed diagnosis can only be shown where the chance of survival would have otherwise been available on the balance of probabilities.[35] The facts in *Gregg v Scott* involved a missed diagnosis; a delay which lowered the patient's chances of surviving more than a decade from 42 per cent to 25 per cent.[36] In other words, even had the (inarguably negligent) missed diagnosis been correct, the patient's chances of long-term survival would still have been less than 50 per cent. The patient was unable to prove on the balance of probabilities that the negligence removed the chance of recovery.[37] It is important to note that while the determination of the process for survival is arguably more objective, the assessment of negligence specifically is still a subjective assessment based on the context of action and inaction.

Lastly but notably, the court acknowledges and supports the medical system's pursuit of advancement in practice through its approval of what Farrell and Dove call 'super-specialist[s,] who may undertake procedures which others might regard as being inappropriate or even too risky'.[38] This both underscores the idea that treatment comes from a range of acceptable alternatives, and takes this concept a step further by acknowledging that new treatments are an inherent part of modern medicine. This idea is supported by the Access to Medical Treatments (Innovation) Act 2016, legislation 'aimed at improving patient access to innovative treatments'.[39] While there have been debates as to whether the Act was necessary or in fact introduced real change, it is clear that both medicine and law are intended to allow medical professionals to make use of innovative procedures and treatments at their disposal.[40] While this embrace of metamorphosis will be further discussed, it is important to note that it is an existing portion of both medical case law and practice.

2.2.2. Doctors: Analysis

The assessment of negligence for doctors reflects the complexities of practice: that there is no one correct path to 'correctly' practise medicine, and the field is in a

[34] ibid.

[35] *Gregg v Scott* [2005] UKHL 2.

[36] ibid.

[37] Also referred to as 'loss of chance'. In other words, loss of chance was not applicable as the odds of recovery when properly diagnosed were less than 50%.

[38] A-M Farrell and ES Dove, 'Clinical Negligence' in Mason and McCall Smith (eds), *Law and Medical Ethics*, 12th edn (Oxford University Press 2023) 367, citing *De Freitas v O'Brien* [1995] PIQR P281.

[39] 'Access to Medical Treatments (Innovation) Act' (MRC Medical Research Council, 11 September 2018): mrc.ukri.org/about/policy/mrc-position-statements/access-to-medical-treatments-innovation-act/.

[40] 'Access to Medical Treatments (Innovation) Bill Will Not Serve Healthcare Professionals' (*Pharmaceutical Journal*): pharmaceutical-journal.com/article/opinion/access-to-medical-treatments-innovation-bill-will-not-serve-healthcare-professionals.

constant state of advancement. Assessments must allow for the fact that evidence towards conflicting treatment does not necessarily mean that there has been inappropriate conduct, nor does the fact that the practice in question does not yet have an established history of use. Treatment decisions differ from diagnostic decisions, and focus on how, in that particular case, a missed treatment would have affected the outcome for the individual. Clinical negligence broadly examines whether the practitioner acted as a reasonable member of their profession. This is more specific than general negligence, in which the standard is a reasonable person, and perhaps deepens the question of foreseeability: would a reasonable practitioner, weighing the multiple inputs towards foreseeable impacts of a course of action or treatment, have considered the course of action (or lack thereof) reasonable?

There are several potential points of difficulty in applying the liability of doctors to the use of AI in healthcare. First, causation: whether the harm suffered is sufficiently connected to the fault – but for the actions of the decision-maker, would the harm have occurred? This question transposes neatly from a human decision-maker to an AI decision-maker, and the 'but for' test can be applied similarly. As with cases of multiple human actors, there may be cases of responsibility allocation between multiple entities, including scenarios with an AI/human combination: liability would be allocated similarly to a human/human scenario.

Second, duty of care: if medical care is being provided, there is an assumption of responsibility. While there may be questions at the fringes of medical care, such as whether medical recommendations by an AI-powered app constitute medical care, for medical AI providing care directly there is an exact parallel with the AI's human counterpart.

Third, standard of care: whether the medical personnel in question have provided reasonable care. As discussed, there are particular considerations for medical standards of care such as whether a sub-specialist would consider the course of action reasonable, and whether the case is a diagnostic one, but it is sufficient for the moment to note that the current standard is reasonable care, as defined in the context of the treatment.

2.3. Drivers

As in other jurisdictions, drivers in the United Kingdom need to follow a list of requirements in order to be allowed to drive. These include practical measures such as vision tests, driving tests and acquiring insurance.[41] Autonomous vehicles will need similar authorisation, at the very least for driving tests, but the essential demands are the same – whether or not the entity driving has the capacity to do so safely. More specific requirements for autonomous vehicles are discussed in section 6.1.5.

[41] 'Legal Obligations of Drivers and Riders' (GOV.UK): gov.uk/legal-obligations-drivers-riders.

While liability for the medical system necessarily reflects the complexities of the practice of medicine, liability for drivers is based broadly on following the rules of the road. Because the act of driving a motor vehicle on land occurs on a fixed plane, in a relatively constrained number of types of scenarios,[42] there are a fixed set of rules to follow, with the necessary vagaries filled in by the general principles of liability – to act as a reasonable person.

Case law: Standard of Care

Drivers owe a duty of care to those on or surrounding the road. While there are limits to this duty for more remote parties – discussed below – anyone who would foreseeably suffer harm by the driver's actions is included in this remit. The duty (or duties) of care for an AI driver will be owed to the same persons.

The level of care is to drive to the same standard as other, reasonable drivers, and the case law explains this in more detail. *Nettleship v Weston* provides that the standard of care of a driver is no different for learner drivers than for experienced drivers, and is that of the 'reasonable care and skill' of other drivers.[43] This was in due course expanded by *Mansfield v Weetabix Ltd*, wherein the court found that where the driver is unaware of their own disability, and the condition impairs driving ability, the standard of care is 'that which is to be expected of a reasonably competent driver unaware that he is or may be suffering from a condition that impairs his ability to drive'.[44] In *Mansfield v Weetabix*, the defendant (Tarleton) drove into a shop due to overly high blood glucose levels that resulted in a brain malfunction. While the initial trial found him liable on the grounds that he had, in fact, driven into a shop,[45] this was overturned given that Tarleton was unaware of the malignant tumour that caused the glucose level issue, or indeed the issue itself.[46] The court held that an objective standard that did not take into account the driver's unknown condition would effectively have inappropriately inserted strict *or objective* liability. Essentially, *Mansfield v Weetabix* emphasised the court's acceptance of context in assessing driving behaviour, as long as the cause of unacceptable behaviour is unknown by the driver in question.[47]

Stewart v Glaze and *Ahanonu v South East London and Kent Bus Co Ltd* further address the standard to which the duty of care is held. In *Stewart v Glaze*, Stewart was drunk, inexplicably ran into the road, and was struck by Glaze's car causing a brain injury. Expert evidence included the speed of the moving vehicle, point of impact, Stewart's path, and Stewart's alleged rate of movement. The question for the court was whether Glaze was driving reasonably in having failed to apply the

[42] As decipherable by humans, eg, types of traffic interchanges, some(one/thing) in the road.
[43] *Nettleship v Weston* [1971] 2 QB 691.
[44] *Mansfield v Weetabix Ltd* [1998] 1 WLR 1263, 1268.
[45] Evidence suggests it was not, until that point, a drive-through.
[46] *Mansfield* (n 44).
[47] Context is a particularly difficult issue for AI, and one that is not generally solved yet. Further discussion in section 4.2.

brakes. The court emphasised that 'it is important to ensure that the Court does not unwittingly replace the test with the standard of the ideal driver[; and] that the Court is not guided by what is sometimes referred to as "20–20" hindsight'.[48] Glaze was not found negligent in failing to stop, and the judge did not rebuke Glaze for failing to see Stewart before Stewart stepped into the road given the situational context: Stewart was waiting at a bus stop, a common area for pedestrians to loiter without intent to enter the road.

Ahanonu involved a pedestrian (Ahanonu) who was 'squashed between the defendant's bus, a double decker and a bollard'.[49] The driving area in question involved a particularly tight corner, and a sign to pedestrians stating 'Warning. Buses Turning. Pedestrians must keep to footways'. Ahanonu was not on the footpath at the time she was squashed by the bus. The argument made for negligence was that the corner was known to be hazardous, 'as shown by the marks on the bollard of repeated collision by buses against it, and the accident was foreseeable because many pedestrians jaywalked across the carriageway'.[50] On appeal, the court ruled no negligence given the circumstances: namely the 'extraordinarily dangerous action of the claimant' in entering the road; and the need for the bus driver to be actively looking at the other bus in front of him as the turn was made. Had he made the turn without this attention, the lack thereof would have been negligent.[51] The court noted that the lower court had 'in effect sought to impose a counsel of perfection on the bus driver', and that 'there is sometimes a danger in negligence cases that the court may evaluate the standard of care owed by the defendant by references to fine considerations elicited in the leisure of the court room, perhaps with the liberal use of hindsight'.[52]

While the Highway Code sets out how drivers should ideally behave, case law provides that the Code is not in fact an instruction on negligence – although it will influence the courts' interpretation of the reasonable driver standard. Cases such as *Goad v Butcher* give guidance in interpreting the Highway Code with regard to negligence. In summary, Butcher was making a turn towing a tractor-trailer; Goad as a motorcyclist saw the turn being made, braked hard and lost control. Details include Butcher slowing down to make the turn, cutting the corner and therefore entering the exit lane rather than the entry lane, and having started the turn before Goad was in sight. Goad had been travelling above the posted speed limit. Goad alleged Butcher had been negligent in making the turn. The ultimate judgment stated that 'failure to observe [The Highway] Code may be evidence of negligence, but whether it is will depend very much on the circumstances in which the act in question was committed and who is the claimant'.[53] In the circumstances of the case,

[48] *Stewart v Glaze* [2009] EWHC 704, para 5 (QB).
[49] *Ahanonu v South East London and Kent Bus Co Ltd* [2008] EWCA Civ 274, para 1.
[50] ibid, para 7.
[51] ibid.
[52] ibid, para 23.
[53] *Goad v Butcher* [2011] EWCA Civ 158, para 9.

> Butcher had a duty to take reasonable care to avoid causing injury to other road users whom he should reasonably have foreseen might be affected by his actions. That means he had a duty to act as a reasonably prudent and careful driver of a slow-moving and lengthy vehicle.[54]

The court further cites *Clayton v Lambert* in stating that 'judges must take care not to hold a motorist liable in negligence just because the accident might have been avoided if a different decision had been taken'.[55] Both of these statements are upheld by the Road Traffic Act section 38.7:

> A failure on the part of a person to observe a provision of the Highway Code shall not of itself render that person liable to criminal proceedings of any kind but any such failure may in any proceedings (whether civil or criminal, and including proceedings for an offence under the Traffic Acts), be relied upon by any party to the proceedings as tending to establish or negative any liability which is in question in those proceedings.[56]

The Road Traffic Act 1991 also substitutes where relevant into the 1988 act a definition of

> Careless, and inconsiderate, driving [:] If a person drives a mechanically propelled vehicle on a road or other public place without due care and attention or without reasonable consideration for other persons using the road or place, he is guilty of an offence.[57]

In summary, the need to take reasonable care to avoid injury involves acting in a 'reasonably prudent' manner but is not precluded by the fact that other decisions could have been made. Much like the aforementioned standard for doctors, drivers will not be held to the fiction of a perfect course of action and thus liable, as long as the driver was driving with reasonable care and consideration for other road users.

2.3.1. Drivers: Analysis

In terms of applicability to AI, the areas of interest are duty of care and standard of care. The case law provides an informative boundary for duty of care: while a driver has a duty of care to those around them – those to whom their actions would reasonably cause harm – the duty of care does not extend to bystanders who witness an accident, as per *Bourhill v Young*. Standard of care, however, raises a particularly interesting point: it is not possible to exhaustively describe what driving should look like, or how one should drive to avoid liability. The law is forced to rely on the standard of reasonable care, with the Highway Code providing non-binding guidance as to what this might look like. Additionally, reasonable care as a concept clearly depends on context: what should be done given the circumstances in which a choice is being made; a concept that will be discussed in detail in chapter four.

[54] ibid, para 10.
[55] ibid citing *Clayton v Lambert* [2009] EWCA Civ 237, [2010] RTR 3.
[56] Road Traffic Act 1988.
[57] Road Traffic Act 1991 s 2, substituting s 3 of the Road Traffic Act 1988.

The technical requirements of driving listed above are, though not exhaustive,[58] a demonstration of the decades if not centuries-long incredibly effortful attempt to quantify as many potential aspects of the driving experience as possible. There is of course far more detail provided than given here – the rules for pedestrians alone are 35 sections long, with 10 devoted to crossing the road.[59] The Highway Code itself mentions the word 'reasonable' in just three sections, two of which relate to providing paperwork.[60] Rules for drivers include the statement in section 97 that '[b]efore setting off, you should ensure that you have planned your route and allowed sufficient time'.[61] Yet the case law clearly demonstrates, and outright states, that the Traffic code, and other legislation, are 'more what you'd call "guidelines" than actual rules'.[62] It is in fact difficult to settle on any particular part of the code from which the court would under no circumstances be swayed: while eyesight has a quantifiable metric required to be tested in advance, one can lose eyesight suddenly and for unpredictable reasons. While motorcyclists and passengers are required to wear helmets, the Highway Code itself deliberately provides for those who are religiously compelled to wear a turban.[63] Some rules provide something that a driver 'MUST NOT' do, then immediately caveat this with an exception for emergencies.[64] Both the Highway Code and the Road Traffic Act (1991) rely on the concept of reasonableness for the act of driving itself:

> The Highway Code Rule 144:
>
> 'You MUST NOT … drive without reasonable consideration for other road users'.[65]

The Road Traffic Act defines careless and inconsiderate driving as driving 'without due care and attention or without reasonable consideration for other persons'.[66]

While the relevant regulatory and legislative efforts make a valiant effort to define the often incontrovertible mundanity of driving, there is a clear reliance on the concept of reasonableness for standards of care. This is for several reasons. First, the sheer variety of human experience. It is impossible to define each and every situation that one might face in driving, similarly to in life. The hazards of the road differ by a variety of factors: weather, time of year, population density, country, and cow infestation, to name a few.[67] Drivers in Canada are instructed

[58] eg, the Road Traffic Act of 1991 further details driving offences, cycling offences, construction and use, licensing of drivers (eg, physical fitness and effects of disqualification), insurance, information (as to driver identity), trial, penalties, miscellaneous and 32 sections on traffic in London.

[59] Chickens have presumably mastered this section, although not the philosophical implications.

[60] Highway Code 2015, Rules 268 and 287.

[61] ibid.

[62] *Pirates of the Caribbean: Curse of the Black Pearl*, directed by Gore Verbinski, performance by Geoffrey Rush, (Walt Disney 2003).

[63] Highway Code 2015, Rule 83.

[64] eg, ibid Rule 271: 'You MUST NOT pick up or set down anyone, or walk on a motorway, except in an emergency'.

[65] ibid.

[66] Road Traffic Act 1988 (as amended).

[67] Claire Harrison, 'Holy Cow! Cops Step in as Herd of Cattle Blocks Road in Warwickshire' (*CoventryLive*, 28 July 2021): coventrytelegraph.net/news/local-news/holy-cow-police-step-herd-21166875.

to aim at deer, but swerve at moose, with the idea that deer will dodge, but moose are sturdier than cars. English drivers are unlikely to be taught the same, given the dearth of moose on English roads. No ruleset, published or otherwise, can possibly cover all possible worlds that a driver may face – no llamas in London, no peacocks in Philadelphia. Even where events are covered in codes or regulations, there is a clear statement by the courts that such proscriptions and prescriptions may not in fact be the foundations of negligence, as each case depends on the facts.

The facts of each case are the second point of sensibility for grounding negligence and liability in reasonableness. The facts of each case are the context – not the physics of the crash, but the pachyderm in the room. The *Ahanonu* case provides the unfortunate image of a young woman squashed between a bus and a bollard. This is instinctively a scenario that driving regulations seem proposed to avoid. Yet an examination of the context – a pedestrian with every warning not to run into an extremely busy and complex roadway, and a driver focused on the demanding task of balancing a turn with traffic front and rear – provides a scenario that no human who has ever driven would want to find themselves in, but where they would not feel responsible for the injury. *Ahanonu* provides a further point of examination: the inherent frailties of human drivers.

The court in *Ahanonu* noted that while the pedestrian victim was not in fact in the bus driver's blind spot when squashed, the driver was required to keep eyes and attention on the bus in front of him in order to drive forwards, and that he would in fact have been driving negligently had his attention been elsewhere. This highlights a necessary reality of human drivers: they are, axiomatically, human, and thus human-shaped. While some individuals may be able to separate the directions of both eyes,[68] a human's visual attention is assumed to be limited to a singular focal point. In other words: humans can only look one way at once, and in driving there is often one direction the driver is required to look. The court does not and will not demand that drivers be perfect, but rather that they be reasonably skilled and attentive. The court does not demand that human drivers have Cerberian heads, although they may require that AI demonstrate greater capabilities – see section 4.2.

Fourth, the reliance on the flexibility of reasonableness is not, ironically, unreasonable. Life changes quickly, and regulations do not. Car company Daimler points to the first stationary gasoline engine as being the first form of the modern car as we know it, with its patent filed in 1886.[69] The first case of a pedestrian struck and killed by a car in the United Kingdom occurred in 1896, with the car alleged to be driving five miles an hour.[70] Neither the patent filer nor the pedestrian would have

[68] See, apparently, Bill Skarsgård: Rebecca Alter, 'Bill Skarsgård's Eyes Really Did Spook Sweet Angel Bill Hader on the Set of *It*' (*Vulture*, 9 September 2019): vulture.com/2019/09/bill-hader-bill-skarsgard-eyes-memes.html.

[69] 'Benz Patent Motor Car: The First Automobile (1885–1886)' (Daimler): group.mercedes-benz.com/company/tradition/company-history/1885-1886.html.

[70] A McFarlane, 'How the UK's First Fatal Car Accident Unfolded' *BBC News* (17 August 2010): bbc.com/news/magazine-10987606.

imagined a distracted driving charge based on texting while driving. Regulations do evolve with time – there are now many prohibitions on distracted driving based on texting – but there is a clear gap between the introduction of something that may affect driving or a driver, and regulation to manage it. This balance and dichotomy will be explored in further depth,[71] but suffice to say that there will always be a gap. For example, Elon Musk, head of car company Tesla, stated in 2016 that fully autonomous driving was 'basically a solved problem'.[72] This is not a problem accepted by others as solved, but the fact of such driving is known, and yet many governments around the world have not yet introduced legislation to address the partial autonomy clearly present in the driving world. Those that have begun to address partial or full autonomy in driving have often held long consultation periods, such as the UK Law Commission's consultation and report on Automated Vehicles.[73]

In essence, detailed rules do not work for human driving, and cannot work for AI driving. The standard is that of a reasonable driver: a driver who, with the benefit of context, decides on a reasonable course of action with the information available to them at the time and subject to any and all practical limitations such as only being able to see in one direction. Trying to define an acceptable way to drive prior to a specific situation is impracticable: the most one can do is compare, after the fact, whether the actions taken by the AI driver were comparable to those we would expect of a human driver. One potential way to resolve this is to implement no-fault liability, leaving arguments of appropriateness to insurers.

The United Kingdom mandates very clearly that one 'must have motor insurance to drive [a] vehicle on UK roads', with '[t]hird party insurance [a]s the legal minimum'.[74] The Automated and Electric Vehicles Act 2018 for automated vehicles further states that[75]

Where

(a) an accident is caused by an automated vehicle when driving itself on a road or other public place in Great Britain,
(b) the vehicle is insured at the time of the accident, and
(c) an insured person or any other person suffers damage as a result of the accident,
the insurer is liable for that damage.[76]

[71] The importance of neither over nor under-regulating, nor regulating without an accurate picture of what impact the introduced aspect may have.

[72] Timothy B Lee, 'Tesla Autopilot Director Contradicts Musk's Self-Driving Timeline' (*Ars Technica*, 5 July 2021): arstechnica.com/cars/2021/05/tesla-autopilot-director-contradicts-musks-self-driving-timeline/. He did, however, admit in August 2021 that the Tesla's fully autonomous driving system was 'not great'. Rebecca Bellan, 'Musk Admits Full Self-Driving System "Not Great", Blames a Single Stack for Highway and City Streets' (*TechCrunch*): social.techcrunch.com/2021/08/24/musk-admits-full-self-driving-system-not-great-blames-a-single-stack-for-highway-and-city-streets/.

[73] Law Commission, *Automated Vehicles: joint report*: www.lawcom.gov.uk/project/automated-vehicles/.

[74] 'Vehicle Insurance' (GOV.UK) gov.uk/vehicle-insurance.

[75] Automated and Electric Vehicles Act 2018, s 2(1).

[76] Although it does account for incidents where a vehicle might be driving itself and not insured, such instances are covered in more detail by the Law Commission reports in section 6.1.5.

Essentially, no-fault liability is a pragmatic fix where identifying fault is difficult, and/or adds greatly to the cost and expense of the process: the insurer covers the costs associated with the incident. The insurer can then seek to claim against a party at fault, which would ultimately re-raise the question of what negligence looks in the case of an automated vehicle – the comparison would be reasonable care on the part of a human driver. Where automated vehicles will likely if not inevitably increase the complexity of accident investigation, reducing the burden on individuals involved is a benefit – where AI producers and insurers have both the financial and functional expertise to investigate an incident, an individual owner may not. However, the fundamental question of the standard of a reasonable driver remains.

2.4. Summary of Liability for Drivers and Doctors

In summary, liability of both drivers and doctors is fundamentally assessed on the circumstances and subjective context of the action in question.[77] The broad framework of duty of care, breach of the standard of care, proximity, and causation are the tiles of the mosaic, but the subjective assessment of liability is of the larger picture. The standards are specific to context: the reasonable practitioner acting with the knowledge available to them; the driver with reasonable care under the circumstances. There are stopgaps for common sense: if the court determines that a course of treatment could not 'withstand logical analysis', or if a turn could only realistically be made while a driver looked in the other direction, the court will provide a conclusion that more closely responds to the foreseeable consequences than the potentially prescribed action.

This will be difficult to overlay onto AI sans any adjustments. While the elements discussed above such as the existence of a duty of care do not present inherent issues, standard of care does: it relies on the foreseeability of harm, which itself is an assessment of the driver or doctor's situation at the time they make the decision – all knowns and unknowns at that point in time. While AI can progressively improve, it is nonetheless reliant on a decision-making process that does not have the benefit of a *human* decision-making process: a benefit, in this case, because the standard of reasonableness is set to what is reasonable for a human in a particular circumstance at a particular time. Just because the AI is making a decision 'in the moment' does not mean that it benefits that the context that an analogous human would have in that same moment.

[77] Although some jurisdictions apply strict liability for driving offences, which means that if the damage in question occurred, then liability is applied automatically and irrefutably.

2.5. Devices: No-Fault Liability?

As regards drivers and doctors, the previous discussion makes clear that liability is based on fault, as determined by a lack of reasonable care. Reasonable care includes considerations such as foreseeability of risk, likeliness of harm, etc. Yet this approach does not necessarily port over to devices or products: when a physical device causes loss and damage, the liability is typically based not on the idea of fault, but on the binary question of whether the device meets an expected level of quality – if it does not, there is strict or 'no-fault' liability, which does not attempt to address questions such as reasonableness of a person's actions. The question for AI, then, becomes how this no-fault liability might be affected in cases where a device causes injury due to the direction of the AI controlling it.

This also raises questions of how and which AI might be characterised as a device. An AI that has no physical presence is arguably not a device, for example a purely software AI that examines x-rays. Additionally, there are AI which are software inextricably linked with hardware to achieve their purpose, such that considering one without the other would be to consider another aspect altogether: the self-driving vehicle, for example, is piloted by an AI, and to consider the vehicle without the AI means assessing the car as simply a car-shaped mechanism, and not a self-driving car.[78] This brings us to the unresolved question of whether law will conceptualise an AI application as specifically the AI, such as the algorithm that creates a response to inputs, or the entire operation controlled by the AI, such as the AI and the rest of the vehicle.

There are two general types of objective liability: statutory liability and contractual liability. While cases involving harm can also include subjective liability due to negligence, the categories are distinct and negligence liability will be assessed on the aforementioned criteria. Objective liability is, as per the name, intended to be objective: the criteria for the device to achieve are set out in legislation or contractual agreement, and failure is to be judged on an objective standard – not taking into account its surrounding context. In practice, however, this too incorporates varying degrees of subjectivity – an objective liability test may be slightly subjective, or particularly subjective.

Consumer protection law deals with what consumers can expect and demand from suppliers in products purchased. Contractual liability functions similarly, though based on contractual terms as well as statutory ones, and often includes relationships dealing with goods or services between businesses, and between consumers and businesses. Notably, contractual relations cannot serve as a bar to subjective liability. The Consumer Rights Act 2015 provides that

[78] While this may raise questions in the case of aspects such as driver-assist technologies, the line is blurred: having additional sensors is a requirement of a self-driving vehicle but may still be beneficial to a human driver.

65(1) A trader cannot by a term of consumer contract or by a consumer notice exclude or restrict liability for death or personal injury resulting from negligence.

(2) Where a term of a consumer contract, or a consumer notice, purports to restrict a trader's liability for negligence, a person is not to be taken to have voluntarily accepted any risk merely because the person agreed to or knew about the term or notice.

...

65(4) In this section 'negligence' means the breach of –

(a) any obligation to take reasonable care or exercise reasonable skill in the performance of a contract where the obligation arises from an express or implied term in the contract,

(b) a common law duty to take reasonable care or exercise reasonable skill

...

65(5) It is immaterial for the purposes of subsection (4)

(a) whether a breach of duty or obligation was inadvertent or intentional, or

(b) whether liability for it arises directly or vicariously.[79]

This does not mean, however, that there are no elements of subjective liability found in contractual and statutory liability.

2.5.1. Statutory and Contractual Liability

The Consumer Protection Act 1987 deals with product liability and safety in England and Wales. The Act implements the EU Product Liability Directive,[80] which as of 31 December 2020 is part of UK domestic legislation as well.[81] The second source is the Consumer Rights Act 2015. Consumers may have additional applicable rights under contract, although these rights would of course depend on the contract itself, and general contract law by extension. Product liability claims can and are frequently framed as common law actions of negligence, as breach of contract, or as a Consumer Protection Act claim.[82] Establishing negligence by a manufacturer is much the same as establishing negligence generally: establishing a duty of care between the manufacturer and the harmed party; establishing a breach of the standard of care by the manufacturer; establishing that the breach caused the harm in question, etc. The Consumer Protection Act provides an even more straightforward approach for consumers, and provides for strict, no-fault liability: if a product is defective, the manufacturer ('producer') has responsibility. Defect is defined thus:

[79] Consumer Rights Act 2015, s 65(1–2), 65(4–5).

[80] Council Directive 85/374/EEC on the approximation of the laws, regulations and administrative provisions of the Member States concerning liability for defective products [1985] OJ L210/29 (Product Liability Directive).

[81] 'EU Legislation and UK Law': legislation.gov.uk/eu-legislation-and-uk-law.

[82] 'Product Liability and Safety in the UK (England and Wales): Overview' (*Practical Law*): uk.practicallaw.thomsonreuters.com/w-013-0564?transitionType=Default&contextData=(sc.Default).

(1) Subject to the following provisions of this section, there is a defect in a product for the purposes of this Part if the safety of the product is not such as persons generally are entitled to expect; and for those purposes 'safety', in relation to a product, shall include safety with respect to products comprised in that product and safety in the context of risks of damage to property, as well as in the context of risks of death or personal injury.

(2) In determining for the purposes of subsection (1) above what persons generally are entitled to expect in relation to a product all the circumstances shall be taken into account, including –

   (a) the manner in which, and purposes for which, the product has been marketed, its get-up, the use of any mark in relation to the product and any instructions for, or warnings with respect to, doing or refraining from doing anything with or in relation to the product;
   (b) what might reasonably be expected to be done with or in relation to the product; and
   (c) the time when the product was supplied by its producer to another; and nothing in this section shall require a defect to be inferred from the fact alone that the safety of a product which is supplied after that time is greater than the safety of the product in question.[83]

There are several points to note in this definition. First, that the safety of the product is what 'persons are generally entitled to expect' – expectations being further refined to include marks or marketing. Second, that defect includes thought towards 'what might reasonably be done with or in relation to the product'. In other words, how one might reasonably expect it to be used, or the impacts it may be reasonably assumed to affect. Lastly, the test is applied at the time when the product was supplied, and a product is not inherently defective if it was succeeded by a safer product. This strikes a very similar note to the standards of medical professionals: that the product was produced to the known standard of the time. Leaded gasoline was not considered defective when it was originally provided to consumers, although it certainly would be now in terms of its unsafe health effects.

The Sale of Goods Act 1979 provides further guidance as to what attributes a product should have, and how such expectations interact with contractual obligations:

14(2): Where the seller sells goods in the course of a business, there is an implied term that the goods supplied under the contract are of satisfactory quality.

(2A) For the purposes of this Act, goods are of satisfactory quality if they meet the standard that a reasonable person would regard as satisfactory, taking account of any description of the goods, the price (if relevant) and all the other relevant circumstances.

(2B) For the purposes of this Act, the quality of goods includes their state and condition and the following (among others) are in appropriate cases aspects of the quality of goods –

[83] Consumer Protection Act 1987, s 3(1–2).

(a) fitness for all the purposes for which goods of the kind in question are commonly supplied;
(b) appearance and finish,
(c) freedom from minor defects,
(d) safety, and
(e) durability

(2C) The term implied by subsection (2) above does not extend to any matter making the quality of goods unsatisfactory –

(a) which is specifically drawn to the buyer's attention before the contract is made,
(b) where the buyer examines the goods before the contract is made, which that examination ought to reveal, or
(c) in the case of a contract for sale by sample, which would have been apparent on a reasonable examination of the sample.

14(3) Where the seller sells goods in the course of a business and the buyer, expressly or by implication, makes known –

(a) to the seller … any particular purpose for which the goods are being bought, there is an implied term that the goods supplied under the contract are reasonably fit for that purpose, whether or not that is a purpose for which such goods are commonly supplied, except where the circumstances show that the buyer does not rely, or that it is unreasonably for him to rely, on the skill or judgment of the seller[.][84]

Contractual liability provides for compensation for damage caused by a defective product, but claims can generally only be made against the seller of the product – not directly by a consumer against a manufacturer.[85]

For business to business contracts, the Unfair Contract Terms Act 1977 also provides that liability for breach of the obligations arising from the 1979 Sale of Goods Act relating to conformity, quality, or fitness for a particular purpose, 'cannot be excluded or restricted by reference to a contract term except in so far as the term satisfies the requirement of reasonableness'.[86] The Consumer Rights Act provides – for consumers – that '[a] term of a contract to supply goods is not binding on the consumer to the extent that it would exclude or restrict the [supplier's] liability' arising from, among others, that the goods be 'of satisfactory quality' and 'fit for particular purpose'.[87]

The Consumer Protection Act, the Sale of Goods Act, and the Unfair Contract Terms Act raise questions surrounding reasonableness and context: that satisfactory quality is achieved 'if they meet the standard that a reasonable person

[84] Sale of Goods Act 1979 c 54, s 14(2–3).

[85] This general restriction is called privity of contract, and there are exceptions, such as where a third party was intended to benefit from the contract.

[86] Unfair Contract Terms Act 1977, s 6(1a).

[87] Consumer Rights Act 2015, s 31(1)(a) and (b). The Consumer Rights Act also provides further limitations to exclusions of liability: equivalent terms in a digital content supply contract (s 41); liability for service to be performed with reasonable care and skill (s 57); the general unenforceability of unfair terms (s 63); and exclusion of death or personal injury caused by negligence (s 65).

[would expect]'; the context of the purpose for which the product is sold; the 'fitness for purpose' of the product. The 'objective standard' is an assessment of how well the product will fit its contextually appropriate use: a subjective assessment of the foreseeable context of the product; its uses and harms. In other words, this is an objective test that nonetheless incorporates a degree of subjectivity.

These interpretations are borne out in the case law. Whether or not a contract limits liability between parties, a product will be considered defective if it does not provide the safety the purchasing party is reasonably entitled to expect or is not reasonably fit for the purpose for which it was intended. *Wilkes v DePuy* marked a departure from earlier case law and concerns an allegedly defective artificial hip implant. While the claimant alleged negligence, a claim was also brought under the Consumer Protection Act 1987 – that 'when the [implant] component was put into circulation by the Defendant, there was a "defect" in it, as defined by the Act, because its safety was not such as persons were generally entitled to expect'.[88] The defendants argued that the issue with the implant was a rare but recognised issue, with warnings being provided in the instructions for use. The court ultimately held that the product was not defective, and that the risk–benefit balance of a product should be considered, including, potentially, cost: 'the ease and extent to which a risk can be eliminated or mitigated may be a circumstance that bears upon the issue of the level of safety that the public is generally entitled to expect'.[89] A purely strict-liability approach, or an objective application of an objective test – such as interpreting that the product broke, and was thus defective – would not have been upheld. The court upheld a subjective application of an objective test. While warnings provided with the product will also be considered, and the product in question must still align with the appropriate sectoral standards, the reasonableness of the standard of production will be examined by the court.

The development risks defence was introduced as part of the European Directive on Product Liability and provides the defence to liability that 'the defect could not have been discovered in the current state of scientific and technical knowledge'.[90] The development risks defence has been rarely successful, and has been interpreted narrowly by the European Court of Justice, such as in *[European] Commission v United Kingdom*, stating that the article in question

> refers solely to the 'scientific and technical knowledge' at the time the product was marketed … it has no bearing on the exclusion of the manufacturer from liability that no one in that particular class of manufacturer takes the measures necessary to eliminate the defect or prevent it from arising, if such measures are capable of being adopted on the basis of the available knowledge.[91]

[88] *Wilkes v DePuy International Limited* [2016] EWHC 3096 (QB).

[89] ibid.

[90] C Newdick, 'The Development Risk Defence of the Consumer Protection Act 1987' 47 *Cambridge Law Journal*: 455: cambridge.org/core/product/identifier/S0008197300120458/type/journal_article.

[91] Case C-484/04 *Commission v United Kingdom* (2006).

This interpretation was followed in the UK case *A v National Blood Authority*, which found that the defence 'ceases to be a development risk and becomes a known risk not if and when the producer in question … had the requisite knowledge, but if and when such knowledge were accessible anywhere in the world'.[92] The intention of the defence is to protect those parties taking on development risks by investing in the creation of new technologies and products, yet the case law restricts the defence to the narrow interpretation of availability of knowledge of risk: that it be knowable to any party, inside the field or out of it.

2.5.2. Assessment of Objective Liability

Objective liability is realised by its delineation in statute and prior agreement. Legislation aimed at consumer protection is laid down to ensure that providers cannot avoid responsibility by merely contracting out of providing what they have agreed to provide. While contractual agreement can bar certain types of liability, this is not so generous a loophole as it may seem: traders cannot contract out of liability of personal injury resulting from negligence; negligence being the obligation to take reasonable care.[93] The Consumer Protection Act provides that a product is defective if its safety is not what persons are generally entitled to expect: taking into account its marketing, what might reasonably be done with the product, and the time at which it was provided for sale.[94] The Sale of Goods Act adds that there is an implied term of satisfactory quality to goods: what a reasonable person would regard as satisfactory, including fitness for purpose and safety.[95] The Unfair Contract Terms Act tops off this trifecta of legislation by stating that, for business to business contracts, obligations of conformity, quality, or fitness for particular purpose cannot be excluded 'except in so far as the term satisfies the requirement of reasonableness'.[96] Leading cases such as *Wilkes v DePuy* assess the reasonableness of the standard of the product in context of the risk–benefit analysis of the product that was being provided. *A v National Blood Authority* underlines the idea that while difficult to prove, the court does intend to protect development, but does so by examining the contextual knowledge of the field at the time the product is provided.

In other words, objective liability is not applied objectively after all: objective liability still has a degree of subjective liability. Products must be what consumers are reasonably entitled to expect, based on the context of its marketing and reasonable understandings of the product's use – the foreseeability of its use and, much like liability for doctors, the state of knowledge of the field at the time. The

[92] *A v National Blood Authority* (2001) EWHC QB 446.
[93] Unfair Contract Terms Act 1977, ss 1(1) and 2(1).
[94] Consumer Goods Act 1987, s 3(2).
[95] Sale of Goods Act 1979, s 14(2).
[96] Unfair Contract Terms Act 1977, s 6(1A)(b).

Sale of Goods Act provides that 'goods are of that satisfactory quality if they meet the standard that a reasonable person would regard as satisfactory, taking account of any description of the goods, the price (if relevant) and all the other relevant circumstances'.[97] A risk–benefit analysis of the intended use and cost of the product clearly reflects an interpretation of the intended context of use. An examination of the knowledge of the field at the time may provide a narrow loophole for developers, but as the exception that proves the rule: the court will examine the knowledge of the field, and just how foreseeable risk might have been with a dedicated due-diligence effort.

While the timing of questions of foreseeability and context may be slightly different between subjective and objective liability, there is less functional difference in the questions ultimately asked.

2.6. AI: Product or Service?

Liability is not affected by the philosophical implications of this designation, instead posing a relatively mundane conundrum: is AI a product, or a service? Liability standards are, in theory at least, different for each: liability is absolute for products, and fault-based for services. This question may have less import than initially proposed, given that the questions asked of subjective and objective liability are ultimately not dissimilar, but it is informative to consider nonetheless.

AI, or at least narrow AI, occupies a conceptually unusual space in liability. First and foremost, it is not human, and it does not operate as humans do. It is a misstatement to say that AI 'thinks' – it does not recreate the human or animal neurological processes that we call thinking. Typically, the legal decision maker is the 'reasonable person': the idea of the 'reasonable person' depends on an ability to foresee probable futures from context, evaluate the likely risks from that context, and act to mitigate those risks. AI lacks the capacity to evaluate context in the way that we expect human decision-makers to do, and it must rely on internal rules, whether or not it 'learns' as it goes. These rules are, broadly speaking, what the AI is created to achieve; something that is a specific course of action, whether to drive (safely) from A to B, to make a cup of tea, or to play with a child. Even the most complex AI processes such as neural networks are layering probabilities and weights of information in a deeply detailed fashion to simulate human thinking as closely as possible, but do not and cannot yet imitate the incredibly complex processing of a biological mind. This is clearly demonstrated in the inability of AI to grasp the nuance of context, something that humans inherently understand very early on. As will be discussed in section 3.2, AI is the combination of advanced mathematics, statistics, and probabilities. AI interacting physically, such as robots

[97] Sale of Goods Act 1979, s 14(2)(a).

and self-driving vehicles, 'consist of nothing other than probabilities about states and events arising in the environment'.[98] An AI is simply a stat in a hat.

Yet for all that AI does not 'think', it has the ability to create and/or implement 'decisions' – the application of internal rules to an external system. While one could certainly debate the appropriateness of the term 'decisions', it is sufficient as a stop-gap to have a term that includes taking action, either physically or digitally, in a similar fashion to a human.

2.6.1. AI as a Service

Consider AI as a service. For this purpose, there are two types of AI: embedded, and non-embedded. Non-embedded AI is purely digital, for example, a content recommendation service; a bank-loan analyser. Embedded AI is AI that is enabled by a physical presence – what we would generally call a robot, though not necessarily as humanoid as they are typically portrayed. In either case, one can frame the work done by the AI similarly to its human counterparts – booking a flight, moving a box.

In a liability question regarding service, the question becomes whether the person providing the service provided the service with reasonable skill and care. These questions do not have sufficiently analogous actors in scenarios involving AI. Treating the AI as if it were the human providing the service requires attributing some level of legal personhood to the AI. While this argument has been much discussed,[99] it is unsuitable in this particular arena for several reasons. First, it treats AI as an entity as static as a human – where humans can change their minds, they cannot change their abilities or their fundamental thought processes. One of the most desirable benefits of AI is that it can, for example when an AI-driven vehicle is in an accident, the AI can be amended to never have that same accident for the same reason. Humans, conversely, have the same accidents all the time, as will be discussed at length below. Second, providing AI with a level of personhood would require the AI to be able to own assets in order to recompense claimants. Third, treating the AI as a legal person provides a level of insulation between the producer and AI liability claims, when the producer is realistically the only party that can functionally set the parameters and therefore actions of the AI: what is used to train, test and validate the AI, and eventually putting it on the market. Ultimately, asking whether the AI as an entity took reasonable care is not a sensible question. Finally, as Abbott points out, while corporations are permitted to be parties to a contract and own property, '[t]heir legal rights exist only to improve

[98] F Sprenger, 'Microdecisions and Autonomy in Self-Driving Cars: Virtual Probabilities' (2020) *AI & SOCIETY*: doi.org/10.1007/s00146-020-01115-7.

[99] LB Solum, 'Legal Personhood for Artificial Intelligences' in W Wendell and P Asaro (eds), *Machine Ethics and Robot Ethics* (Routledge 2017).

the efficiency of human activities such as commerce and entrepreneurship … They are a member of our legal community but not our moral community'.[100]

When deciding who bears responsibility for the consequences of the AI's actions, one could conceptualise the service as being provided by the AI user, with the AI analogous to a human agent. In the case of a human agent, the question to be asked is whether the agent was negligent. This not only requires some level of personhood, as per the issues discussed immediately prior, but also requires that the AI be examined as if it thinks like a human, with human levels of context, reasonableness and appropriateness, none of which it has.

Alternatively, one could place the AI user as the service supplier, with the AI itself as the service. This provides the question of whether the user was negligent in deciding to use the AI, or the way in which the user deployed the AI.[101] This does not require attributing any human levels of context or agency to the AI, nor allow human parties to use the AI as a shield to liability.

If the user was not negligent – they used the AI in an appropriate manner and for the purpose for which it was intended – then we are left with the AI developer as the only reasonable party to address questions of whether the AI was negligently created. This includes questions such as whether the producer considered reasonably foreseeable risks, and whether the steps taken in the AI's creation were negligent.

2.6.2. AI as a Product

If AI is treated as a product, and there is an incident, we are left with the objective liability of contract and statute. In such cases, the questions asked are first whether death or personal injury occurred, and if so, whether such harms resulted from negligence. The second question is whether the AI, as a product, was defective. This hinges on questions such as first, what persons are generally entitled to expect in the product they purchase, which relies on contextual evidence such as the manner in which it was marketed, and what might reasonably be expected to be done with or in relation to the product. Second, whether the product was of a standard that a reasonable person would regard as satisfactory: whether it was fit for its intended purpose, taking into account considerations such as safety and durability. As previously discussed, such questions look very similar to subjective liability: was it reasonably foreseeable that the way the AI was produced would mean it was defective? Was the creation of the AI negligent?

[100] R Abbott, *The Reasonable Robot* (Cambridge University Press 2020).

[101] Such as, eg, using the AI for a purpose it was not designed to suit. HR Sullivan and SJ Schweikart, 'Are Current Tort Liability Doctrines Adequate for Addressing Injury Caused by AI?' (2019) 21 AMA Journal of Ethics 160: journalofethics.ama-assn.org/article/are-current-tort-liability-doctrines-adequate-addressing-injury-caused-ai/2019-02. M Simmler and N Markwalder, 'Guilty Robots? – Rethinking the Nature of Culpability and Legal Personhood in an Age of Artificial Intelligence' (2019) 30 *Criminal Law Forum* 1: doi.org/10.1007/s10609-018-9360-0.

2.6.3. The Product or Service Distinction for AI

Both the product and service address of liability ultimately rely on negligence. The distinction is, in practice, when the liability arose – in creation of the AI, or in its use. If AI is a product and the liability arises in use, the question is whether the user was negligent – if the user is negligent, then there may also be a question of whether the negligence of the developer also played a part, and if so whether the developer should be liable to the victim, the user, or both. If the liability arises in creation, then in theory liability is objective, but in practice, as discussed, whether or not the AI was defective comes down to a question of negligence at the design, training and testing stage. If AI is a service, then the question is simply whether the service was negligent in design and development, or in implementation.

To expand on this: if the use of the AI was negligent, there are two possible scenarios: the user had clear warning of the limitations of the AI and used it contrary to those warnings; or the AI does not fit the definition of defective and the fault lies with the way it was used. This could be a scenario such as a consumer purchasing an AI vacuum cleaner and putting it in a horse paddock, where it is promptly overwhelmed by mud and political promises, causing it to explode. The more concerning scenario, however, is of course where the use of the AI was negligent because there was an issue with the AI – the AI being defective, and not holding up to what one would reasonably expect for its purported use. In such a case questions of responsibility will be mirrored up the supply chain until such a question lands on the creator who originally produced the defective product.[102] In other words, in the case of harm caused by an AI, it is the case that either (a) the AI was not defective and was put to a use beyond what would be considered reasonable, or (b) the AI was defective, and questions of context and foreseeability must be put to the original AI creator.[103] This is particularly important as there is a massive knowledge imbalance between what the purchaser can be aware of in investigating the AI, and what the producer can be aware of having produced the AI.

2.7. Conclusion

What the previous section indicates is that the question of liability, when put to AI, is still fundamentally a question of human liability: both of the user and their actions with regard to the AI, but also the producer: whether in producing the AI they acted to the standard of a reasonable person of that particular field.

[102] There may be questions on other parties in the chain if there was a sufficiently high level of knowledge of the internal workings of the AI, but there will indisputably be questions on the producer in the case of defect.

[103] While there may be cases of contributing negligence, these pose no additional burdens beyond those imposed by investigating AI in questions of sole negligence, and contributory negligence is a long-accepted concept in liability.

All the liabilities discussed in this chapter depend on foreseeability. When looking at foreseeability broadly, three themes emerge. First, that foresight is one of the obligations placed on a party in advance of their actions, such as driving, treating a patient or placing a device on the market. Here we see the manufacturer; the diagnostician; the cricket club. A manufacturer producing a product with a known defect can, should and must reasonably foresee the harm it may cause. While the definition of defect will depend on any specific legislation, the details of the product, the marketing and the foreseeable use of the product, the manufacturer must consider the reasonably foreseeable consequences. The manufacturer's obligations are in advance of the moment the harm occurs: a sharp child's toy does not cause harm in the factory; it will cause harm after it is sold and played with by a child. The diagnostician failing to order the necessary test does not cause the harm, but by inaction fails to stop it. The cricket club ignoring a series of balls hit into a garden has not yet hit someone but is guilty by inaction of allowing the eventual harm. The AI producer who fails to train and test their self-driving vehicle in rainy conditions wilfully ignores a potential danger.

In essence, foreseeability for obligations in advance is a time bomb: decisions are put into place that will cause or contribute to an event down the line. Decisions must be made around reasonably foreseeable issues, and without the benefit of the specific context brought by hindsight. This is particularly crucial in the case of AI, because these decisions are made by humans, but will be enacted by AI.

The distance between obligations in advance and obligations in the moment is decidedly on a continuum: an advance obligation might be breached years before, at the time of designing a product, or minutes before in leaving the lawnmower on the hill. The exact space between the two is unimportant; the essential difference is that for obligations in advance the actor in question does not have the context through which their actions will be judged – for an obligation in the moment, those contextual conditions are already present. For AI, it is even less clear than with other products or actions, because the AI's actions, even with training and testing, may not be inherently predictable to its human audience – this will be expanded on in chapter three.

Incidents themselves are typically a short reel rather than a snapshot: a pedestrian trips on an unduly uneven pavement and falls into the road to be struck by a driver. There is no nanosecond in which liability crystallises – perhaps the pedestrian wobbles before falling; perhaps they dive headlong. Either scenario would find the pavement owner liable for the unduly uneven pavement. There are also 'Schrödinger's Cat' scenarios, wherein the specific context in which an action takes place may not cause an incident in the moment, but may later on: a cleaning staffer mops a floor of a busy event hall but fails to put up 'wet floor' signs; no one falls during the conference, but another staffer falls later on. The act is still negligent in the moment, whether or not it may cause or contribute to a later incident. The essential question of foreseeability is this: what could be reasonably foreseen to cause an issue, and how could that obligation be addressed? The same 'wet floor' example could be used, but with a robot mopper that can, say, plug into a digital sign and have it display a warning message.

The second theme of foreseeability for humans is that it depends on context in two respects – context that includes the humans in the scenario, accounting for, if not outright embracing, human frailties, and context both of the exact moment of current action, and for the future predictable context. While liability for doctors does not at all times focus on physical intricacies, they are there nonetheless: a surgeon must have a steady hand, but it is recognised that human vision and muscle control can only cut so fine an incision. By contrast, a higher level of precision might be expected of an AI surgeon.

Because of its 'slightly larger than infinitesimal' range of dynamics, liability for drivers is a more accessible lens through which to view this issue: the court, and the law more broadly, take into account the imperfection of human drivers. Human driving need not be perfect to be reasonable: a perfect driver may never hit a pedestrian, but a reasonable driver can only look in one direction while someone darts around their vehicle. Decisions must be made around reasonably foreseeable issues, but with the enormous impact of specific context. Actions might be specific reactions, or actions taken in specific response to context. Context confers obligations on the human in the moment. However, while AI might not have the benefit of obligations in the moment, it has the potential to be informed by a greater range of information than a human driver – connected vehicle information, more sensors, and 360 degrees of input.

The third theme of foreseeability is that reasonableness is a convenient fiction: it is 'all but impossible to specify, in advance, what kind of behaviour constitutes adequate caution or due care in given situations'.[104] This is not to say that anything short of perfect is, as already discussed, unreasonable, but that there is the fundamental need for an understanding of 'this' and not 'that' for acceptable actions, albeit an understanding that changes by location, culture and even weather. The background, the facts and the situation in which they occur are crucial. Context is inevitable, but the threads of problems are far simpler to pull out of a tapestry after something has already gone wrong: a driver pulling a tractor-trailer onto a road would, if in possession of a crystal ball, wait until the speeding motorcyclist had passed. Contamination via microcracks in vials is an understandable issue if one knows that glass can have microcracks. The law does not depend on humans to be perfect, but the reason that court cases on negligence still occur is that reasonableness is not an objectively verifiable fact and thus becomes a contested matter, particularly given that just because an alternative act exists does not mean that the original act was unreasonable. Obligations in advance turn into obligations in the moment somewhere between the immediate and the indefinite, and AI is caught in this trap: we should not accept a lower standard of behaviour for AI based on

[104] E Green, 'The Reasonable Man: Legal Fiction or Psychosocial Reality?' (1968) 2 *Law & Society Review* 241: jstor.org/stable/3052783.

the idea that its creators could not be informed by the context of the moment. However, holding out for perfect actions by AI means that humanity would be denied their improvements on human behaviour in the meantime.

Where, then, does this leave us for AI? AI systems do not think, do not feel, and even if they do dream of electric sheep[105] they are unlikely to dream of electric tractor-trailers. What is the meaning of an obligation of foreseeability for AI, and on whom does it fall? In terms of obligations in the moment, AI does not have the benefit of human levels of context: '[c]ontextual AI doesn't exist yet'.[106] AI cannot interpret the context of a situation it is in, in the moment it 'makes' a decision. This does not remove the impact of and need for context, yet it means that manufacturers must deal with all obligations effectively in advance – through training, testing and recursive maintenance obligations – rather than having the benefit of the context of the moment. In other words, they need to predict the context in advance.

An AI's state of existence – its ability to produce an output, either physical or digital – depends on the information it is given, and it cannot be given information about all possible situations. Any foreseeability, any obligations in advance, are on the humans creating the AI: it is they who design the AI for its intended use; they who train and test the AI on what data they deem appropriate; they who have the obligation in advance to foresee what issues the AI will create and encounter. Reasonable foreseeability falls on the creators, because the AI is unlikely to be able to interpret a scenario in the same sense that a human would.

Thus, an important legal question is whether the *actual* context should have been foreseen. This means that for AI, the law will essentially look at obligations in the moment as obligations in advance: obligations on the humans involved. How, then, do creators substitute their own foresight about the actions of an entity that cannot foresee in any human sense of the word? To do this they need to understand what the AI will do, when and why. In order to answer these questions, the human who has an obligation of foreseeability needs to understand how the AI makes its decisions – in other words, an explanation of the AI's 'reasoning' is needed. How far such an explanation can be possible is the subject of the next chapter.

[105] PK Dick, *Do Androids Dream of Electric Sheep?* (Doubleday 1968).

[106] Oliver Brdiczka, 'Contextual AI: The Next Frontier of Artificial Intelligence' (*Digital Transformation*, 8 April 2019): blog.adobe.com/en/publish/2019/04/09/contextual-ai-the-next-frontier-of-artificial-intelligence.html.

3

Explainable AI (XAI)

In the previous chapter we saw that in practical terms, liability is based on fault. Fault is based on the idea of the foreseeability of risk, and the reasonable steps taken to mitigate those risks based on context. AI does not think like humans, and therefore does not have context. Because of this, the only time at which a human-level understanding of context and reasonable action affects the AI fundamentally is during the AI's creation. This means that those who create and ultimately produce the AI – particularly in the case of complex AI – need a deep level of understanding of what the AI will do and why. Explainable AI provides a way to ensure certain levels of reliability and approach in AI, which the law can use in a similar way as it does human explanations.

3.1. Introduction

Explainability is inextricably linked to artificial intelligence as a field. Some AI systems are interpretable, which means that the potential outputs of such an AI can be understood and predicted at its base level without delving into the AI's workings for individual outputs. However, for many AI systems this is not the case, and explainability methods, or explainable AI (XAI), are used to examine why the AI does what it does, when and why. While developers cannot test against each and every circumstance that the AI will encounter, XAI provides the testing ground for what developers know, or ought to know,[1] that the AI will encounter, including scenarios in which it cannot identify all factors.

3.2. How to Divide AI

AI is not inherently opaque, nor understandable. As per the quadrant division in section 1.1.2, some AI actions are more easily understood – whether in terms of what the AI does, or why it does it. But it is important to put these workings into a broader context. AI is not a completely separate entity from data science, computing or computation. As the figure below shows, machine intelligence is part of a broader world of sciences.

[1] Wilful ignorance being no bar to foreseeability.

Figure 2 Interacting disciplines[2]

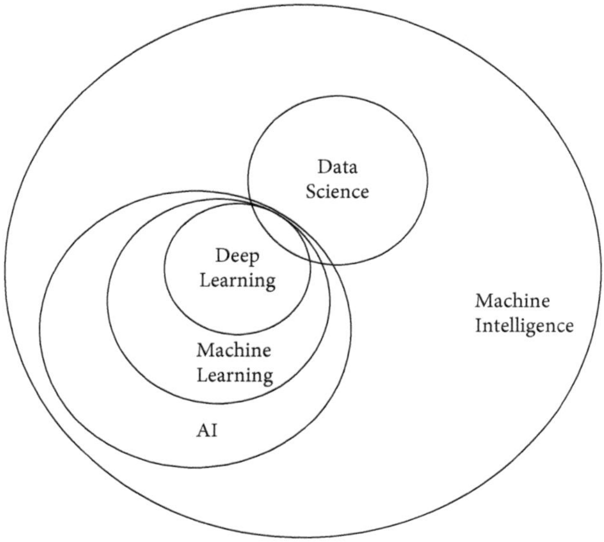

What concerns this book, however, is where AI makes a fundamental leap from direct human input to machine-generated decision-making. To narrow these categories, albeit simplistically, this provides the following:

Figure 3 Artificial intelligence subcategories[3]

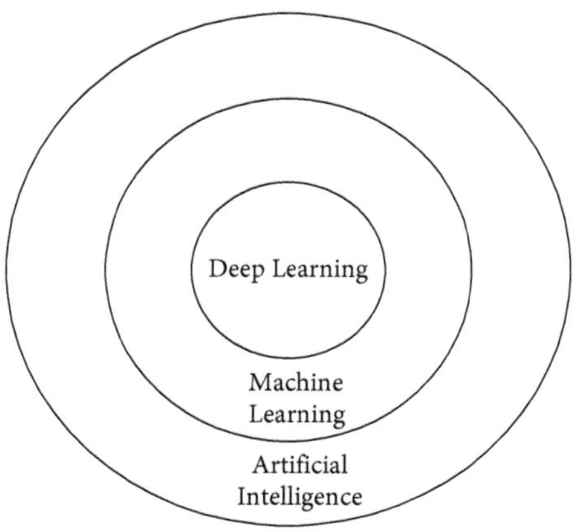

[2] Based on R Pradeep Kumar, 'Are ML, DL, DS the Unique Relations of AI?' (*Medium*, 29 March 2020): medium.com/@4deep.prk/are-ml-dl-ds-the-unique-relations-of-ai-a52d7735c88.

[3] Based on Fahmi Nurfikri, 'Artificial Intelligence, Machine Learning, and Deep Learning – What the Difference?' (*Medium*, 14 June 2020): towardsdatascience.com/artificial-intelligence-machine-learning-and-deep-learning-what-the-difference-8b6367dad790.

Artificial intelligence is an exceptionally broad concept. Within it are sub-categories, which include machine learning, and within machine learning, deep learning. What makes machine learning distinct as an AI category is that it is the depth or complexity at which it 'learns' on its own: the AI can act without being explicitly programmed; without a programmer telling it how to produce certain outputs. This means that the producer of the AI, and the individuals who work on it, will not necessarily understand why the AI makes the decisions that it does: we refer to this as the AI being 'opaque', or a black box.

Generally speaking, the closer to the centre of the AI diagram we go, the more complex the decision-making processes of the AI become. Because the AI is not being told what to do, when to do it, and how to do it, the connections between the information Machine Learning AI receives and what is done with it gets more complex. Deep learning is a more complex form of machine learning and is inspired by the abstraction levels of the human brain: pieces of information are given tiny weightings towards an outcome as they progress through a series of neuron-inspired connections called 'nodes'. Broadly speaking, the more complex the intended function of the AI, the more opaque its decision-making will be: the greater the predictive power, the greater the relative complexity.[4] There is an 'interpretability/performance trade-off' for black box models.[5]

This is why complex models can be desirable: their capacity for nuance and predictive power is increased. This is desirable for AI that engages in complex tasks such as combining multiple sources of data in order to move in the physical world. It does, however, add to the difficulty in interpreting why the AI does what it does. While terminology is not universally agreed,[6] it is helpful to specify terms for the discussion in this book: for these purposes the term 'interpretable' will be used to refer to the ability (likely of an expert) to understand a model without additional tools, whereas 'explainability' refers to the need for tools to be applied to a machine learning model in order to understand it when it is not inherently interpretable. The more opaque an AI is, or the more of a 'black box' it is, the less interpretable it is, and the more helpful explainability techniques become.

3.3. Interpretability of AI

Some types of AI models are inherently interpretable. These kinds of models include linear regression, logistical regression, generalised linear models, decision trees, decision rules, and rule fit models.[7]

[4] This has been debated, such as in C Rudin, 'Stop explaining black box machine learning models for high stakes decisions and use interpretable models instead' (2019) 1 *Nature Machine Intelligence* 206: doi.org/10.1038/s42256-019-0048-x. Yet it is sufficient to at this stage know that more complex AI can, in cases, accomplish a level of granularity that is not necessarily shared by solely interpretable AI.

[5] G Ciatto et al, 'Agent-Based Explanations in AI: Towards an Abstract Framework' in D Calvaresi et al (eds), *Explainable, Transparent Autonomous Agents and Multi-Agent Systems* (Springer International Publishing 2020).

[6] These terms are sometimes used interchangeably, or defined slightly differently.

[7] C Molnar, *Interpretable Machine Learning*: christophm.github.io/interpretable-ml-book/index.html.

An example of a decision tree:

Figure 4 DIY assistance

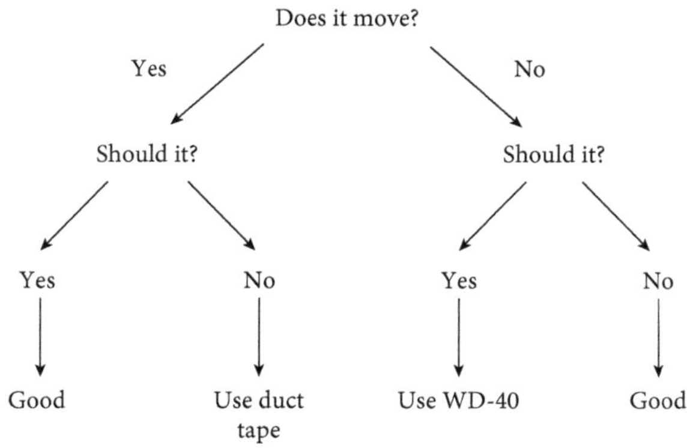

It is not necessary to delve into the function and methods of each of these models but suffice to say that not only can they be understood, but the methods used to create them can be evaluated. For the purposes of regulation, they present no particular obstacle as there is no fundamental disconnect between the human creating the AI and the AI's actions. Because the actions of the AI are predictable for a set of inputs, it is foreseeable how the AI might malfunction and potentially cause harm. The AI is in this way a proxy for the human: when each step of the AI's process or function is wilfully created, there is no question of subsumed responsibility by a non-human entity. This is not to say that care and due diligence is unnecessary, merely that the benchmarks for both are reasonably catered for by existing regulation that deals with machines or programs generally. Knowing that definitions of AI include entities that mimic human action, there are certainly companies that employ AI methods who would not need to define them in such a way: automated factory lines fall under such a definition. If one were to argue that all AI entities must be regulated, this would entail the unnecessary duplication of existing regulation for safety and market purposes in many cases, while not necessarily providing an inherent benefit.

Difficulty arises for AI systems which are not inherently interpretable, but which are best understood by explainability tools. This discipline and these methods are referred to as XAI, or explainable artificial intelligence.

Molnar's hitherto unparalleled *Interpretable Machine Learning* provides the following, using 'interpretability methods' where this paper uses XAI: some portion of the world is described in a collection of data; that data is used to train a black box model; interpretability methods are used to extract an explanation from the black box; then the explanation can be provided to a human.[8]

[8] ibid.

Essentially, data attempts to describe something about the world. The AI model takes that data and makes its approximation, a model, of how the portion of the world at issue functions. The explainability method (here interpretability method) then attempts to inform the human recipient how and why the AI model is making the assumptions and interpretations that it does.[9]

There are many reasons that it is important to understand why an AI does what it does. Several reasons, all of which are relevant to liability, include:

1. Detecting and correcting bias.
2. Highlighting functionality issues.
3. Ensuring the model acts for the right reasons.
4. Ensuring reliability of the model.

Detecting and correcting bias is absolutely crucial. While this is a topic explored at length elsewhere, it is important to highlight that not only can AI create bias where none existed by making connections between hitherto unconnected categories, but it can also go a long way into entrenching existing bias when trained on historical data. Web retail giant Amazon, for example, created a machine learning program to aid in recruitment. The model was 'trained to vet applicants by observing patterns in resumes submitted to the company over a 10-year period. Most applications came from men, a reflection of male dominance across the tech industry'.[10] This led to the program developing an inherent bias against female candidates, including applications with references to connections such as 'women's chess club' and 'all-women's colleges'.[11] Thankfully the program was scrapped after Amazon felt that neutrality could not be guaranteed, but it clearly demonstrates the danger of assuming that just because an AI is inhuman, that it is unbiased. While areas of AI use such as recruitment tools are of course inherently concerning, there are areas that have even more dangerous impact such as sentencing in criminal justice systems.[12]

While death may seem like a human rights issue, and assuredly in most cases it is, the concerns here are different. An AI application that is not completely interpretable and deals fundamentally with human rights will embed systematic human rights abuse in a way that makes it not only difficult to catch, but to question. Physical damage, however, is much easier to catch because it is immediately noticeable. While it may be very difficult to catch a year or two difference in sentencing of an accused due to a biased system, it is conversely very easy to notice that someone has been hit by a car. This is not to say that physical damage,

[9] ibid.

[10] Jeffrey Dastin, 'Amazon Scraps Secret AI Recruiting Tool That Showed Bias against Women' *Reuters* (10 October 2018): www.reuters.com/article/us-amazon-com-jobs-automation-insight-idUSKCN1MK08G.

[11] ibid.

[12] R Simmons, 'Big Data, Machine Judges, and the Legitimacy of the Criminal Justice System' (2018) 52 *University of California Davis Law Review* 1067: lawreview.law.ucdavis.edu/issues/52/2/articles/52-2_Simmons.pdf.

particularly to a human, is not important – it absolutely is – but that the switch to AI in such applications as transport has the capacity to drastically reduce such problems, rather than embed them. For example, the AI in a Tesla is not evaluating the intangible characteristics of the human in their field of scanning, it is evaluating whether the human is an 'object' or an 'in-path' object.[13] It is not assigning a value or impact based on any characteristics of the human and is in fact less likely to do so than a human driver as it is not equipped to determine individual characteristics and therefore form any associations thereof.

What this chapter will address more in depth are the latter reasons that AI explainability are important: highlighting functionality issues, ensuring the model acts for the right reasons, and ensuring reliability of the model. These are the areas necessary for technical robustness and are most important when examining AI applications that cause accidental death – immediate, rather than systemic, harm. In order to examine these and how XAI tools can be used to address them, it is important to first understand what XAI tools are and how they work.

First, recall that while interpretability is a characteristic a model inherently does, or does not, have, explainability is an interaction with an AI (usually machine learning) model. Explanations can take many different forms, such as 'text explanations, visualizations, local explanations, explanations by example, explanations by simplification, and feature relevance'.[14] XAI techniques can also be used at many stages of the AI process: in training the data; training the model; debugging the model and the training data; deploying the model; and after the model is trained.[15] Techniques after the AI is trained are referred to as post-hoc. The same XAI technique or method may also have a different intended audience. This has been split by some practitioners into AI *consumers*, or those receiving an explanation, and their different types as *personas*.[16] What an explanation should provide in and of itself will be discussed later in more depth.

There are many ways that XAI tools can be divided. Some XAI tools work on tabular data, some on images, some on text. Some work before a model is finalised, some after. There is no one metric that makes an XAI tool better than another, because each use depends on the circumstance. Some of the ways to divide explanations are whether they are:[17]

1. **Static or interactive:** static explanations provide a single explanation for what an AI has done at a particular point in time. An interactive explanation allows a consumer or expert to ask clarifying questions of an explanation to refine the answer they receive.

[13] 'Autopilot': www.tesla.com/autopilot.

[14] AB Arrieta et al, 'Explainable Artificial Intelligence (XAI): Concepts, Taxonomies, Opportunities and Challenges toward Responsible AI' (2019): arxiv.org/abs/1910.10045.

[15] V Arya et al, 'One Explanation Does Not Fit All: A Toolkit and Taxonomy of AI Explainability Techniques' (2019): arxiv.org/abs/1909.03012.

[16] ibid.

[17] ibid.

2. **Local or global:** a global explanation looks at the function of a model as a whole – how the grand design of the model leads it to decisions generally. A local explanation examines a single AI decision, prediction or action, and attempts to explain the intricacies of reasoning behind it.
3. **Directly interpretable versus post-hoc explanation:** whether the model is inherently interpretable or uses an auxiliary method to explain the model after it is trained.
4. **Surrogate model:** a second, more clearly interpretable model approximates the more complex model.
5. **Visualisation:** a visualisation technique may focus on parts of a more complex model, rather than attempting to explain the entire model. For example, this could be a heat map of what parts of an image the AI based its categorisation – such as a moose's antlers and hooves in identifying one in a photo.

Figure 5 Taxonomy of explanations[18]

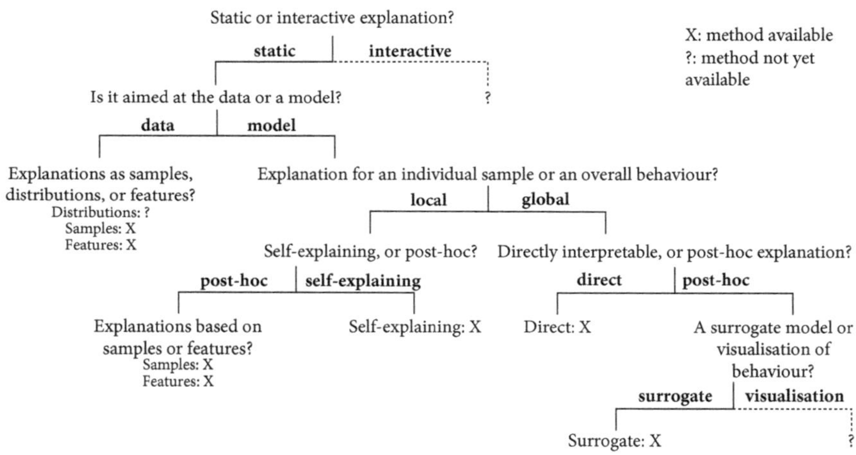

This figure, based on that of Arya et al, proposes a taxonomy based on what is explained, how it is explained, and the level at which it is explained.[19] While there are certainly other viable ways to divide explanations, this method has several advantages:

1. It fills in the gaps even where we cannot yet provide certain measures: 'interactive explanations', 'explanations as samples', and 'visualise behaviour' models. While it does not propose tools that specifically accomplish these approaches, it provides for their existence and where they might fit in the hierarchy of questioning.

[18] Based on ibid.
[19] ibid.

2. It provides a viable hierarchy of questions to ask to triangulate what an explanation produces, and in what manner.
3. It identifies the types of data that an explanation might address.
4. It proposes a '[single] taxonomy that is simple yet comprehensive enough that it is useful for different types of users'.[20]

The authors of this proposed toolkit and taxonomy illustrate its use with a series of examples via the personas of different potential users in a loan application scenario: the loan officer, applicant and bank executive. The loan officer would follow the 'static' branch to 'model', 'local', 'post-hoc' and 'samples' in order to validate whether the AI's recommendations for a loan grant or denial are justified, based on other similar individuals.[21] An applicant seeking to understand why their loan was rejected might want a tool that follows 'static', 'model', 'local' and 'post-hoc' before choosing a method under 'features', providing a method that can show the grounds on which the decision was made.[22] The bank executive, concerned with the overarching decision-making process of the model rather than a specific instance, might want a tool following 'static', 'model', 'global, 'post-hoc' and 'surrogate', wherein the XAI tool would provide a more interpretable, second AI model.[23]

These three theoretical individuals give an example of how stakeholders in a particular circumstance might benefit from the provision of an explanation of the decision-making AI. It should be reiterated here that there are indeed other goals: trustworthiness, causality, transferability, informativeness, confidence, fairness, accessibility, interactivity and privacy awareness, to name a few.[24] Each of these play a part in not only why explanations are desired, but the areas that XAI tools can be best utilised to support.

XAI tools are perhaps easiest visualised for regulators as a tool which can be applied at the end of the AI production pipeline in assessing the above criteria to evaluate an AI. While this is certainly a valuable stage, it is certainly not the only stage of impact. XAI tools can and should be used throughout the AI production pipeline:

Figure 6 Explanations in the AI creation process 1[25]

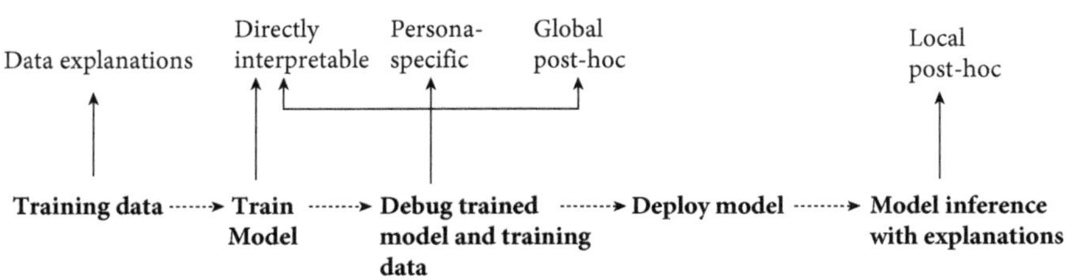

[20] ibid.
[21] ibid.
[22] ibid.
[23] ibid.
[24] Arrieta et al (n 14).
[25] Based on Arya et al (n 15).

In this figure by Arya et al, the lower track sets out the AI production process itself: training data is acquired; an AI model is trained; the training model and training data are debugged; the model is deployed; and the model inference is provided.[26] The top line provides what XAI tools can offer at various stages. Data explainers providing 'abstract methods for explainers that use unsupervised techniques to explain datasets'; directly interpretable explainers which support tools that 'train interpretable models directly from labelled data'.[27] Local post-hoc explainers can be divided into black-box and white-box explainers, with black-box explainers being capable of addressing any type of model with only the requirement of the model's predictive function, whereas white-box models require access to a model's internal functions.[28] Global post-hoc explainers are divided similarly, and address the entire model rather than an individual case.[29]

Explanations: Who needs what?

As briefly discussed in the bank loan examples, different parties surrounding an AI entity may want different things from the AI. Referring again to the AI production pipeline, consider which stakeholders appear where: numbering the lower line from one to five, the AI producers alone occupy parts one to four. The training data, model training, model and data debugging, and deployment are the province of the AI producers, be they a sole producer, a multinational organisation or anywhere in between. This process is the same for each production, unless one fails to debug the model (rendering it untrustworthy at best, and actively bad at worst). Recall again the simplified AI production process of previous chapters: input is provided, output occurs and impact follows. Here, the AI user – the person using the AI for its ultimate intended purpose – steps in between deployment and output. The more in-depth process provides a greater level of detail as to what goes into that input, and what makes the AI itself. The stages of AI explainability can be split into three: pre-modelling explainability (to understand and describe the data used for the model); explainable modelling (where the model itself is explainable); and post-modelling explainability (to provide explanations to describe an already-developed model.[30]

What, then, does this mean for explanations? It means that while the AI consumer would benefit from one style of explanation, the producers and regulator would benefit from others. Indeed, they would benefit from several – in-depth explanations not only on the end product, but also on the product as it is developed. It also means that XAI tools, by necessity, reflect the stage and type of AI they

[26] ibid.
[27] ibid.
[28] ibid.
[29] ibid.
[30] Bahador Khaleghi, 'The How of Explainable AI: Post-Modelling Explainability' (*Medium*, 3 August 2019): towardsdatascience.com/the-how-of-explainable-ai-post-modelling-explainability-8b4cbc7adf5f.

examine. An example-based explanation, for instance, works well 'if the feature value of an instance [carries] more context, meaning the data has a structure, like images or texts do',[31] whereas tabular data will be much more challenging to interpret. Yet things are more complicated than they seem, and for three reasons:

1. There is no closed list of XAI options.
2. Many XAI options may be equally appropriate.
3. The Rashomon effect, also known as the 'multiplicity of good models'.[32]

First, even for a particular stakeholder wanting an explanation on a particular system or even a particular decision of that system, to be produced in a particular type, there is no closed list of XAI tools available. There is no fixed list as to what XAI tools are possible. Consider again the taxonomy chart from above: it does not provide an exhaustive list of tools, but merely types of questions to consider when choosing tools or grouping them. Tools are used at different stages in the process. And while some tools are model-agnostic and can be applied to any AI model, others are developed for and around particular AI architectures.[33] For models as complicated as neural networks, it has been suggested that model-specific interpretation methods are needed,[34] making it impossible to mandate even model-agnostic methods effectively.

Second, there is no given XAI tool for a given type of circumstance. This is not to say that in a particular circumstance there is no one optimal choice. The difference is a fine one, but one faced everywhere in life: consider, for example, telling a child that they should not talk to strangers. This is not a terrible rule inherently, but one that is inapplicable in so many situations as to be problematic if followed: every person is a stranger at first, and the child should inarguably talk to other children, their teacher, their healthcare providers, etc. Similarly, mandating that a particular type of XAI be used in a type of circumstance does not take into account the context of the needs of that choice: while a Local Interpretable Model-Agnostic Explanation (LIME) might be a popular saliency method for highlighting the portion of an image on which a local explanation is based, mandating its use, even for graphic-based instances, fails to account for circumstances surrounding the explanation.

Third, the Rashomon Effect or the 'multiplicity of good models', occurs

> where, for a given set of data, it's possible to construct many equally well-performing models that may differ greatly in their internal structure … their accuracies are so close to one another that we cannot be sure that the differences aren't due to random factors. Each of those models suggests a different explanation, even though they all have similar input-output mappings.[35]

[31] Molnar (n 7).

[32] L Hancox-Li, 'Robustness in Machine Learning Explanations' (Proceedings of the 2020 Conference on Fairness, Accountability, and Transparency, 27 January 2020) 640: doi.org/10.1145/3351095.3372836.

[33] Khaleghi (n 30).

[34] Molnar (n 7).

[35] Hancox-Li (n 32).

At first glance, this seems fantastical: there may not inherently *be* a correct answer, and each is potentially valid; 'each' referring to the explanation proffered by a different explanation method model. Without 'convergence of multiple methods on the same explanation', there is a lack of robustness to an explanation.[36]

All this to say that XAI tools as a class are nearly as large as AI itself,[37] and growing all the time. While XAI tools vary in form, function and timeline of use, so too do the phenomena they attempt to explain. Demanding explanations of producers or products at all times is simply not feasible: there are too many potential types of explanations possible, and demanding an explanation of each echelon of a complex AI is simply too onerous. Additionally, some explanations require access that AI producers would be loath to provide, such as the information about the algorithm that might be considered trade secrets – 'white-box' explainers require access to an AI's internal material. While AI as a field is in the midst of finding a balance between publishing knowledge and reducing misuse,[38] it seems certain that complete openness is not a workable stance to enforce.

So if the vast world of XAI is broad, why not set objective standards? First, as previously noted, setting rules for types of scenarios does not mean that those rules are sufficiently responsive, especially where the standard required is one of reasonable competence. Second, setting a certain type of XAI tool or test to meet means that that benchmark can be gamed for specifically. For example, consider the Volkswagen 'diesel dupe', wherein the Environmental Protection Agency found that many Volkswagen vehicles 'could detect when they were being tested, changing the performance accordingly to improve results'.[39] While a concrete benchmark is not inherently negative, it lends itself to this sort of workaround: rather than building to the *purpose* of the test, the product is built to the test itself. Without an overarching benefit to a particular test, which broadly mandating particular XAI tools would not provide, the potential negatives outweigh the potential benefits. This is not to say that particular industries will not or should not mandate certain types of tests – these will be crucial in industry-specific regulation – but that they are ill-guided as a point of general technical robustness. The best XAI tools are not those that are used most commonly; the best XAI tools are those most suited to the AI at hand. A hammer might be the most recognisable tool for attaching one piece of wood to another with a piece of metal but is a suboptimal choice when using a screw.

What use, then, are XAI tools? As part of the technical creation and testing process, they are useful if not essential in testing the robustness, accuracy and decision-making structure. But for all their difficulty to mandate, they are incredibly useful in regulation as well: not as pillars to build around, but as proof-positive evidence of due diligence.

[36] ibid.

[37] Only nearly as broad because some AI is so simplistic as to not require explanation.

[38] T Shevlane and A Dafoe, 'The Offense–Defense Balance of Scientific Knowledge: Does Publishing AI Research Reduce Misuse?' (Proceedings of the AAAI/ACM Conference on AI, Ethics, and Society, 2020): dl.acm.org/doi/10.1145/3375627.3375815.

[39] Russell Hotten, 'Volkswagen: The Scandal Explained' *BBC News* (10 December 2015): bbc.co.uk/news/business-34324772.

3.4. Explanations in Law

Generally speaking, society does not 'demand an explanation for every suboptimal decision … the utility of explanations must be balanced against the cost of generating them'.[40] Additionally, humans are 'notoriously inaccurate' when providing their rationale for decisions after the fact.[41] Yet there are situations where the need for explanations arises, particularly in law.

Explanations are demanded where decisions have particular impact, such as judges and administrative agencies for their decisions.[42] Outside strict liability offences, much of criminal law relies on the presence of both an *actus reus* and a *mens rea* – the committed act, and the guilty mind: 'the physical element alone is, generally speaking, not enough to constitute criminal liability'.[43] The *mens rea* is an explanation of a choice, and is used to determine whether the individual in question acted 'knowingly, recklessly, negligently, or innocently – all of which can bear legal significance'.[44] AI does not bear these human-centric concerns, because it is not burdened with human context. Even if it were clear that general AI could understand human concepts such as moral right and wrong, society is still at the stage of specific rather than general AI. Furthermore, humans do not always agree on a concrete answer for such questions.[45]

So, while AI may not be capable of questions regarding a 'guilty mind', the need to understand why certain decisions are made remains. This is particularly true because AI can be *changed*. While humans can certainly change and grow as individuals, it is not possible to unilaterally 'upgrade' humanity to fix certain decisions, and it would be unethical to do so if it were possible. Yet this is one of the biggest advantages of AI: the area of AI that *learns*. If a problem has occurred, and it is determinable or explainable *why* that problem occurred, there is a high likelihood that that problem can be fixed. This is especially evident in areas such as transportation: human driver accidents occur over and over for the same reasons. For example, the reported road casualty statistics in Great Britain estimate that in 2018, between 220 and 260 people died in accidents where at least one driver or rider was over the legal blood alcohol limit.[46] Clearly just telling humans that driving over that blood alcohol limit is illegal does not work, nor does the overwhelmingly

[40] F Doshi-Velez et al, 'Accountability of AI Under the Law: The Role of Explanation' (2019): arxiv.org/abs/1711.01134.

[41] T Storey, *Unlocking Criminal Law*, 7th edn (Routledge, 2019), citing RE Nisbett and TD Wilson, 'Telling More than We Can Know: Verbal Reports on Mental Processes' (1977) 84 *Psychological Review* 231; CM Funk and MS Gazzaniga, 'The Functional Brain Architecture of Human Morality' (2009) 19 *Current Opinion in Neurobiology* 678.

[42] ibid.

[43] ibid.

[44] Doshi-Velez et al (n 40).

[45] As evidenced by the moral machine, 'A platform for gathering a human perspective on moral decisions', MIT Media Lab: moralmachine.net.

[46] 'Reported Road Casualties in Great Britain, Final Estimates Involving Illegal Alcohol Levels: 2018' (Department for Transport, 2020).

common knowledge of the dangers thereof. While there is no direct comparison for AI driving – it is very difficult to get an AI drunk – issues that are known have the capacity to be fixed. Consider the Tesla crash wherein a driver was killed while the autopilot mode was engaged: the Tesla failed to differentiate between a bright sky and a white tractor-trailer crossing the highway, and crashed directly into it.[47] This is not the first Tesla crash, nor even the last Tesla crash to occur when a large truck turned across the road in front of the Tesla.[48] While it should be noted that in both these cases the driver was obliged to maintain full control of the vehicle, clearly the autopilot did not engage as intended. Yet these accidents highlight not only the promise of AI that learns, but of the necessity of explanations, both to fix the problem and to examine whether that problem was reasonably preventable.

3.5. Due Diligence and the Burden of Proof

Due diligence is clearly relevant to civil liability because it is used to show that reasonable care has been employed. Although a claimant normally has to prove negligence, in some cases the court might use the doctrine of *res ipsa loquitur* to reverse the burden of proof.[49] Where the burden of proof is reversed, the defendant has to provide a satisfactory explanation to discharge that burden.

A reverse burden of proof, by way of strict liability subject to a defence that reasonable care was taken, is often found in laws which impose criminal or regulatory liability. Where such a defence exists in the legislation – although the England and Wales Draft Criminal Code of 1989 included the potential for due diligence to become a general defence, the Code has not been enacted[50] – again the defendant needs to give a satisfactory explanation.

While new statutory offences tend to provide for due diligence as a specific defence, other jurisdictions, such as Canada, allow due diligence as a general defence.[51] In Canada, there is a distinction between strict liability and absolute liability: the former has defences, the latter does not.[52] The case of *R v Sault Ste Marie* cemented strict liability as a 'halfway house' between fault-based liability, such as criminal offences, and absolute liability, where *mens rea* is irrelevant and

[47] Danny Yadron and Dan Tynan, 'Tesla Driver Dies in First Fatal Crash While Using Autopilot Mode' *Guardian* (30 June 2016): theguardian.com/technology/2016/jun/30/tesla-autopilot-death-self-driving-car-elon-musk.

[48] David Shepardson, 'Tesla Driver in Fatal 'Autopilot' Crash Got Numerous Warnings: US Government' *Reuters* (20 June 2017): reuters.com/article/us-tesla-crash-idUSKBN19A2XC.

[49] See section 5.3.2 for further details.

[50] Storey (n 41).

[51] ibid.

[52] NJ Strantz, 'Beyond R v Sault Ste Marie: The Creation and Expansion of Strict Liability and the Due Diligence Defence' (1992) 30 *Alberta Law Review* 1233: canlii.org/en/commentary/doc/1992CanLIIDocs182#!fragment//BQCwhgziBcwMYgK4DsDWszIQewE4BUBTADwBdoByCgSgBpltTCIBFRQ3AT0otokLC4EbDtyp8BQkAGU8pAELcASgFEAMioBqAQQByAYRW1SYAEbRS2ONWpA.

liability is automatic on proof of the committed act.[53] The defence of due diligence requires that a party has taken 'all reasonable steps to avoid the particular event'.[54] The determination of what constitutes 'reasonable steps' is 'contingent on the nature of the offence, the specific industry involved, and the individual circumstances of each case'.[55] The decision was a unanimous one by the Supreme Court of Canada, and has been described by (former) Chief Justice Dickson as 'a good example of creating doctrine to serve important legal purposes'.[56]

The three categories of liability of offences in Canada have been described thusly:[57]

1. Offences in which *mens rea*, consisting of some positive state of mind such as intent, knowledge, or recklessness must be proved by the prosecution either as an inference from the nature of the act committed or by additional evidence.
2. Offences in which there is no necessity for the prosecution to prove the existence of *mens rea*; the doing of the prohibited act *prima facie* imports the offence, leaving it open to the accused to avoid liability by proving that he took all reasonable care, this involves consideration of what a reasonable man would have done in the circumstances. The defence will be available if the accused reasonabl[y] believed in a mistaken set of facts which, if true, would render the act or omission innocent, or if he took all reasonable steps to avoid the particular event. These offences may properly be called offences of strict liability.
3. Offences of absolute liability where it is not open to the accused to exculpate himself by showing that he was free of fault.

If we examine each of these three approaches to criminal liability for AI, it becomes clear that we have to reject the first and the third.

The first approach asks whether the accused had criminal intent. If a human who was responsible for the AI had such an intent, such as in creating an AI designed to commit fraud, then the human can be prosecuted under existing laws. Here the AI is just the tool used by the accused to commit the offence. Asking whether an AI itself had *mens rea* does not make sense: an AI does not intend to do something with negative consequences, it does what it is trained to do, which may result in negative consequences. Not only does an AI lack human context such as emotions or motivation, but it also lacks the context of how the physical world works. If an AI is trained to make a cup of tea, and only to make a cup of tea, it is not inherently 'aware' that bumping into a human and spilling the tea on them will harm that human. There is no intent or negligence on the part of AI. There may be negligence on the part of the human who created the AI, but such concerns will be addressed under foreseeability in section 4.1.2.

[53] *R v Sault Ste Marie* [1978] 2 SCR 1299, 85 DLR (3d) 161; 40 CCC (2d) 353; 3 CR (3d) 30 (SCC).
[54] ibid.
[55] Strantz (n 52).
[56] P Bowal and L Iss, 'Whatever Happened to R v Sault Ste Marie: The Due Diligence Defence' (2013) 37(3) *Lawnow* 63: hdl.handle.net/1880/49667.
[57] ibid.

In the third approach of imposing absolute liability, the accused has no chance to defend themselves against the charge so long as the negative consequences have occurred and been caused by the AI. This is cause for pause. AI as a field shows the most promise for society in areas that will indeed cause harm, in transportation and medical applications in particular. These applications are imperfect and are unlikely to suddenly become perfect in the near future. Yet their promises of benefits are credible enough that to ignore or quash them would deprive society of a true step forward in healthcare,[58] environmental[59] and individual benefits.[60] As previously discussed, the intent of regulation should be not to quash AI innovation, but to usher in its use as safely as possible. Absolute criminal liability would clearly quash this immediately.

However, it is worth considering the impacts of absolute civil liability using insurance. Lawmakers may choose to pursue this route, albeit with the risk that concentrating liability on one group – the AI producer – may shut down certain sectors if AI is too expensive to insure, even if the net harm of the AI is lower than its human counterparts.

Lawmakers also need to recognise that absolute liability for producers risks disincentivising beneficial AI by making the risks, particularly financial risks, too high to put those AI systems into use. This balance could be redressed if the producer has a way to distribute the risk, such as through insuring the AI. This will, however, increase the cost of the AI's purchase and/or use. Conversely, putting absolute liability on the users of AI would be less logical in that they have less impact in determining how and why the AI accomplishes tasks. However, if portioning absolute liability to the user, the insurance burden could be put on the user rather than the producer, similar to, for example, requiring human drivers to hold car insurance. This works for driving because the insurance system is already set up; it would be a costly and time-consuming system to initiate across the broad field of activity that AI will impact, even specifically high physical risk AI.

The role of regulation is to make technological developments as safe as possible, and to encourage beneficial innovation. Absolute liability on either party is an option but does not reflect the goal of optimal facilitation of high-benefit AI.

Consider this relationship in other areas of science, such as vaccines. While the law is loath to commit to hard and fast numbers, realistically, if an application is of overwhelming benefit to humanity, it will be approved.[61] Vaccines do pose a risk to

[58] 'Automated Deep Learning May Allow Doctors to Develop AI Systems for Healthcare' (Moorfields Eye Hospital NHS Foundation Trust, 2019): moorfields.nhs.uk/news/automated-deep-learning-may-allow-doctors-develop-ai-systems-healthcare.

[59] Julia Pyper, 'Self-Driving Cars Could Cut Greenhouse Gas Pollution' (*Scientific American*, 15 September 2014): scientificamerican.com/article/self-driving-cars-could-cut-greenhouse-gas-pollution/.

[60] DL Silver, 'Machine Lifelong Learning: Challenges and Benefits for Artificial General Intelligence' in J Schmidhuber, KR Thórisson and M Looks (eds), *Artificial General Intelligence* (Springer 2011).

[61] The World Health Organization, for example, produced a target profile for Covid-19 vaccines stating that vaccines should as a measure of efficacy, provide a '[c]lear demonstration of efficacy (on population basis) ideally with ~50% point estimate'. 'WHO Target Product Profiles for COVID-19 Vaccines' (World Health Organization, 9 April 2020): www.who.int/publications/m/item/who-target-product-profiles-for-covid-19-vaccines.

a very, very small percentage of the population. For example, a review of 10 years of the US National Vaccine Injury Compensation Program found five deaths in children and adolescents with the cause of anaphylaxis post-vaccination.[62] Given the known (though very statistically minute) possibility for negative reactions, it seems likely that such extreme reactions occurred even with care. Has damage occurred? Certainly. Are such deaths devastating? Unquestionably. Yet vaccines are still of such overwhelming benefit to humanity that it would be negligent not to pursue them. The pandemic of Covid-19 makes this all the more poignant. The problem with absolute liability is that it not only slows production in trying to achieve perfection but may stop the process entirely. This is not to say that faulty vaccines are not cause for liability: it has been stated that in the United States, '[a] manufacturer who produces and sells a defective vaccine that creates a risk of significant injury to the recipient is liable to any person injured by that defect'.[63] Even with this, it continues to be the case that successful cases against manufacturers are uncommon.[64]

This leaves us with the second approach to criminal liability (and perhaps civil liability as well). A system under which liability is assumed but can be defended against, seems to be the best way to encourage growth without restricting progress in areas of overwhelming societal benefit.[65] This is not to say that liability and accounting for damages are not important, but that direct and overwhelming culpability should not be used as a stick. Instead, the demand and push for improvement should be used as a carrot. Additionally, high-impact potential AI must carry the recursive obligation to examine the AI's function periodically, particularly in cases of AI that learns, or in providing updates to AI systems. Under strict liability with a due diligence defence, this recursive obligation includes a requirement to update the AI for known problems: once an accident or issue occurs that is clearly or substantially caused by the AI in question, the issue forms part of the body of

[62] R Johann-Liang et al, 'Analysis of anaphylaxis cases after vaccination: 10-year review from the National Vaccine Injury Compensation Program' (2011) 106(5) *Ann Allergy Asthma Immunology* 440.

[63] National Research Council (US) Division of Health Promotion and Disease Prevention, 'Liability for the Production and Sale of Vaccines' in *Vaccine Supply and Innovation* (National Academies Press (US) 1985): www.ncbi.nlm.nih.gov/books/NBK216813/.

[64] ibid. What vaccines demonstrate is that there are times when absolute liability can be problematic. There might be areas, however, in which it would sensibly apply. For example, New Zealand's Accidental Compensation Corporation is a crown-corporation accidental insurance injury board. The fund is paid into by New Zealand employees and business owners, as well as levies on vehicle licensing and fuel-filling.* Incentives such as levy discounts for safe workplaces apply, but overall there is a no fault, no examination system towards accident and injury. In such a case, absolute and no-fault liability overlap in the lack of examination of due diligence. Similarly, absolute liability may not be problematic in cases such as road vehicles, as there is already an obligation to insure the vehicle. For a fully automated vehicle, this may mean that there would be no claims which failed for lack of fault, but that costs should ultimately be outweighed by the reduced number of claims and lack of litigation costs. However, assuming this approach for all AI has the potential to disincentive automation even in beneficial ways, such as per the vaccine example. A more granular approach could be beneficial. *'What we do' (Accidental Compensation Corporation, 2018): www.acc.co.nz/about-us/who-we-are/what-we- do/ 8.

[65] 'Societal' being a broad categorisation intended to reflect overarching good that does not unduly disadvantage any particular group.

knowledge surrounding that AI, and other areas of AI. Again, referring to the Tesla autopilot mistaking the tractor-trailer for a cloud; light-painted vehicles on sunny days are a known issue for camera sensors on self-driving vehicles. While it may not have been reasonably known before, it is certainly part of the knowledge of the field now. The due diligence defence does not include the defence against an issue which is known to the field, and therefore should have been tested for. While this will be expanded upon in section 7.2, one can proceed with the knowledge that this potential for growth in the field means that due diligence is not a fixed or permanent state, and like fields such as medicine, expand to include new adaptations and discoveries.

How, then, does this relate to XAI? XAI forms the largest part of the body of evidence that can be produced in defence of due diligence. Recall the XAI use sequence:

Figure 7 Explanations in the AI creation process 2 (see also above, Figure 6)[66]

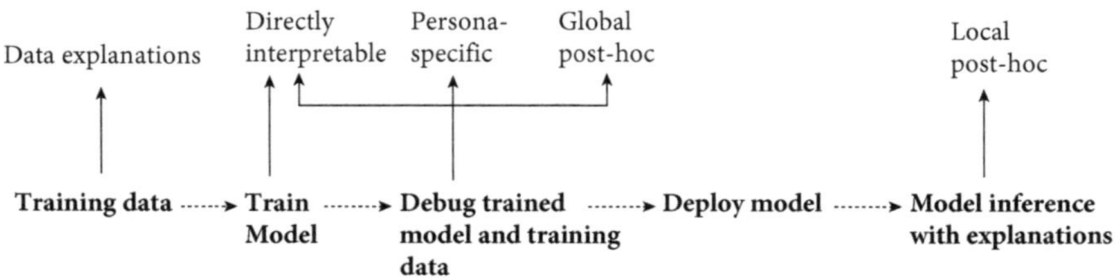

XAI tools are not simply used after an accident has occurred. Their use is an inherent part of the AI production process, or at the very least the AI production process that generates concerns regarding societal or human-focused harm.[67] There are certainly questions that will be asked once the process is complete. These questions include checking the system's response to natural points of interest: for self-driving vehicles various obstacles, vehicles, pedestrians, traffic lights, etc. For medical applications, this should certainly include whether the process is reliant on extraneous factors, or whether the individual's medical factors are taken into account. Yet XAI is applied at multiple points in the process, and, from a regulatory perspective, the more robustly such tools are applied the better.

In drawing on their XAI processes as evidence of due diligence, producers will be forced to account for several factors: the care taken to test the system throughout; the reasonability of their choices; the suitability of their resources to their ultimate product; and the reasons for using black box over interpretable models. While reasonableness and suitability will be addressed in chapters four and seven respectively, testing and the interpretability trade-off are intrinsic parts of the explainability process.

[66] Arya et al (n 15).

[67] This book in no way suggests that less directly harmful processes, such as music creation, share or should share this level of testing.

Interpretability is a key point for AI. The perfect AI application is both perfectly accurate, and interpretable. However, a real-life AI is likely to be neither. Perfect accuracy or function is of course a goal, as AI producers strive to improve the AI in all metrics. Yet if one is to wait for an application to be perfect, that application is likely to remain unfinished. Toleration of a certain level of imperfection is necessary, be it from human professionals or technological functions. This does not mean that perfection should not be striven for, but that one must acknowledge that there is a point at which waiting for perfection deprives one of the benefits of use in the meantime. Interpretability, meanwhile, is also very desirable.

Rudin points out the real-world impacts of a lack of transparency and accountability: those incorrectly denied parole; accidental release of dangerous criminals; inaccurate testing of the safety levels of polluted air; and 'generally poor use of valuable resources in criminal justice, medicine, energy reliability, finance[,] and in other domains'.[68] Rudin (and others, elsewhere) argue(s) that interpretable models can be as accurate and efficient as non-interpretable models; that explainability methods lack fidelity to the original model; that no single XAI explanation is adequate; and that ultimately black-box methods should be rejected in favour of interpretable models.[69] While the human rights implications – as previously discussed – are certainly important, there are other considerations, particularly when the AI application in question interacts with the physical world. First, let us treat interpretability as a binary question rather than a spectrum, and also assume that Rudin is unilaterally correct that interpretable models can always be as accurate and efficient as their non-interpretable counterparts. In such a case, it is clear that their use should be strongly encouraged if not mandated: interpretable models bring benefits in terms of reliability; debugging; informing feature engineering; directing data collection; informing human decision-making; and building trust.[70] There should be a clear and definable exploration into the feasibility of an understandable model rather than an opaque one. Yet interpretability, even on a spectrum, is not the only consideration. The most obvious contender is the aforementioned accuracy – by and large, prediction accuracy decreases as explainability increases.[71]

A plain reading of Rudin's argument would suggest that models such as neural networks should not be used, purely on the basis that they are less explainable. Yet there is clearly a potential trade-off between model performance and explainability.[72] Rudin herself notes that the high-level performance of deep neural networks in computer vision, speech and language cannot yet be matched by interpretable

[68] Rudin (n 4).

[69] ibid.

[70] Parul Pandey, 'Interpretable Machine Learning' (*Medium*, 10 April 2019): towardsdatascience.com/interpretable-machine-learning-1dec0f2f3e6b.

[71] A Richardson and A Rosefeld, 'A Survey of Interpretability and Explainability in Human-Agent Systems' (Proceedings of the 2nd Workshop on Explainable Artificial Intelligence, 2018).

[72] Thomas G Dietterich, 'Exchange between Thomas G Dietterich and Cynthia Rudin on Explainable Machine Learning and Interpretability': twitter.com/tdietterich/status/1053487106193002496.

models.[73] Areas of application with high levels of complexity to consider, such as transport and medical AI, also have multitudinous sources of input. It also raises an issue with the idea of complexity versus interpretability in and of itself: one node of a neural network may be interpretable, but billions altogether certainly are not. There is no hard and fast number that defines when a number of interpretable entries combine to make an uninterpretable entity, and there is a vast range between what a domain expert might understand, what someone else in the field might understand, and what a non-expert might understand.

To Rudin's point that explainability methods lack fidelity to the original model – because if the explanation was completely faithful it would *be* the original model – is only relevant where an exact replication is intended or required. Humans are completely incapable of providing an exact explanation for their actions, and law does not demand such an explanation. While in the case of the technical – such as AI – as close an explanation as possible is desirable, for the purposes of regulation there is no need for an exact, perfect replication if there is indeed a tangible benefit in performance given the model type. For example, humans are typically adept at recognising familiar voices. Barring outliers such as a very unique voice pitch or unfamiliar accent, it would be very difficult for most humans to explain why they knew a voice belonged to a particular person. There is a risk of mis-identification, but the potential damage tends to be low. There would be limited benefit to requiring an AI or indeed a human to accurately explain precisely how a voice was identified, unless the potential risks of mis-identification were unusually high.

Law and regulation typically look for high-level abstraction to equate explanations to performance in the form of motivation and reasonableness. If someone acted in their own self-defence, the court in question will not be looking to the exact height, weight and physical training of the potential opponent, but to the reasonableness of the supposed self-defendant – whether they had reason to fear for their safety or had other reasonable means of recourse in the situation. Further to this point, different audiences need different explanations. An expert AI creator might be capable of understanding each nuance that the AI has to offer, but an explanation to others will need to be phrased in broader terms. It is important that the explainability method be as exact as possible, and proof of this will be part of the due diligence defence, but perfection is the exception, rather than the rule.

Another point is that no single XAI explanation is adequate. This may in fact be the case, but there is no reason that a single tool must be used. Further, even if one is using a single tool[74] this does not mean that no valuable information is produced: as Dietterich points out,

> [a] saliency map may not tell you how the network discrimination discriminates between dogs and cats [for example], but it does tell you whether the network is looking at the dog or the cat rather than the background [which] is important debugging information.[75]

[73] ibid.
[74] Rudin cites a saliency map as an example. Rudin (n 4).
[75] Dietterich (n 72).

A robust examination through XAI techniques may well require examination from different angles, and this is no detriment to the law: the ideal case has multiple witnesses.

Rudin's final point that black-box methods should ultimately be rejected in favour of interpretable models does not bear out from the regulatory perspective. It may eventually do so from the technical side if interpretable methods do indeed conform in metrics to their uninterpretable counterparts, but this again highlights why non-rigid regulation is essential: it allows the field to grow and establish an equilibrium of beneficial norms, rather than trapping such norms and best practices at a place in time.

Ultimately, XAI must be used not only for robust testing but also to explain choices. One aspect of this is explaining choices for the AI to be less interpretable. Where an interpretable model shares an accuracy close to the non-interpretable model, the interpretable model should certainly be used. Yet where there is a definable gap in performance between the two, XAI tools should be used in as many ways as reasonably feasible to make the non-interpretable model more knowable. The exact tools and explanation types will depend on the model itself, but explanations intended to overcome opacity should be aimed at their consumer.

3.6. Facets of Explanations

What should an explanation look like? As previously addressed, there are multiple potential consumers for the same AI application. Miller emphasises explanations in AI as a way to 'increase trust and transparency of intelligent agents', as well as being useful for 'justifying autonomous agent behaviour, debugging … machine learning models, explaining medical decision-making, and explaining predictions of classifiers'.[76] In other words, not only should XAI tools be used throughout the development timeline, but the consequences of those explanations also need to be considered.

In his comprehensive survey of existing social science research, Miller highlights four major findings that are important for explainable AI:

1. Explanations are *contrastive* – they are sought in response to particular *counterfactual cases* … That is, people do not ask why event *P* happened, but rather why event *P* happened instead of some event *Q*. This has important social and computational consequences for explainable AI.

   …

2. Explanations are *selected* (in a biased manner) – people rarely, if ever, expect an explanation that consists of an actual and complete cause of an event.

[76] T Miller, 'Explanation in Artificial Intelligence: Insights from the Social Sciences' (2019) 267 *Artificial Intelligence* 1, 1.

Humans are adept at selecting one or two cases from a sometimes infinite number of causes to be *the* explanation. However, this selection is influenced by certain cognitive biases.

...

3. Probabilities don't matter – while truth and likelihood are important in explanation and probabilities really do matter, *referring* to probabilities or statistical relationships in explanation is not as effective as referring to causes. The most likely explanation is not always the *best* explanation for a person, and importantly, using statistical generalisations to explain why events occur is unsatisfying, unless accompanied by an underlying *causal* explanation for the generalisation itself.
4. Explanations are *social* – they are a transfer of knowledge, presented as part of a conversation or interaction, and thus are presented relative to the explainer's beliefs about the explainee's beliefs.

...

These explanations are not just the presentations of associations and causes (*causal attribution*), they are *contextual*.[77]

3.6.1. Explanations are Contrastive

Let us examine these statements. First, that functional explanations are contrastive. It has been argued that law relies on contrastive explanations implicitly, for example in liability wherein a defendant's breach of care must be shown to have caused the damages in question, it is insufficient to show the results had the cause not occurred – one must look 'to a specific replacement for the cause, which in this case is the hypothetical scenario in which the defendant acted *lawfully*'.[78] Schaffer suggests that law employs a contrastive approach, if not explicitly, and that applying such a lens explicitly aids in understanding causation as a concept.[79] In the law of negligence, the very concept of the 'but for' test provides a contrastive scenario: but for the action of the defendant, the plaintiff's loss would not have occurred. While there can of course be mitigating factors, the law is, to a point, willing to focus on a primary cause to the exclusion of others if there is a sufficiently weighty contrastive point.

At the very least, the law employs such reasoning in several regards. Common law judgments, for example, rely on the principle of '*stare decisis*', which means 'to stand by things decided',[80] ie, to follow the doctrine of precedent. In so doing, judges differentiate outcomes between cases by pointing out contrastive fact patterns: the

[77] ibid, 3 (emphasis in original).

[78] J Schaffer, 'Contrastive Causation in the Law' (2010) 16(1) *Legal Theory* 259: cambridge.org/core/journals/legal-theory/article/contrastive-causation-in-the-law/C649A3D07D99D8FB05FD1EF0042338A3 (emphasis in original).

[79] ibid.

[80] 'Stare Decisis' (Legal Information Institute, 2021): law.cornell.edu/wex/stare_decisis 4.

'material facts' of each case, which influence the decision and establish similarity or dissimilarity.[81] Rarely if ever will a court examine a case and decide that the case bears no similarity to another, or that it is exactly similar but deserves a different result for no reason. A judge will not state that X case does not follow its predecessor case Y even though the fact patterns were similar. The judge would state that case X does not follow its predecessor case Y even though the fact patterns were similar, because Z detail was different: had Z detail been the same, they would have the same judicial outcome.[82]

On a purely common-sense basis, the contrastive explanation is helpful. Even if there are two major explanations rather than one, the ability to provide explicit counter-scenarios makes the information more intuitive to examine. For the Tesla crash involving mis-sensing a tractor-trailer for a cloud, all but the most expert witness would struggle to interpret the data from the many inputs to the car's AI: data from multiple cameras, sensors and radars, that will at best[83] be represented as probabilities. Conversely, a contrastive explanation makes a more intuitively understandable explanation, for example if the car had not interpreted the unusually bright reflection coming off the white tractor-trailer as a cloud, it would have stopped before it made contact; and if the light levels had not been interpreted as 'optimal' given the clear and sunny day, the car would have given less weight to the camera input over other kinds of sensor input.[84]

3.6.2. Explanations are Selected

Miller asserts that

> people rarely, if ever, expect an explanation that consists of an actual and complete cause of an event. Humans are adept at selecting one or two cases from a sometimes infinite number of causes to be *the* explanation. However, this selection is influenced by certain cognitive biases.[85]

This accords broadly with courts' treatment of trial participants. When examining a witness, one asks why something was done, not the probabilities behind various

[81] O Shulayeva, A Siddharthan and A Wyner, 'Recognizing Cited Facts and Principles in Legal Judgements' (2017) 25 *Artificial Intelligence and Law* 107: doi.org/10.1007/s10506-017-9197-6 4.

[82] In greater detail: in case one, the co-defendants shared a house. Co-defendant one had purchased an illicit substance and kept it on the coffee table of the home he shared with co-defendant two. The substance was in a clearly labelled container. The court finds co-defendant two guilty of joint possession, even though he did not purchase the illicit substance. In case two, the co-defendants again shared a house. Co-defendant one had purchased an illicit substance and kept it hidden in his own closet. The container was clearly labelled with the name of the substance. In the second case, the court would constructively distinguish between the two cases by noting that in the second, co-defendant two had no knowledge of the object, had not consented to its possession, and had no degree of control over it, all of which co-defendant two had in case one.

[83] Best here to mean most easily interpretable.

[84] Not necessarily the explanation for this crash, but a plausible explanation for *a* crash.

[85] Miller (n 76) 3.

reasons that something was done. In asking why a driver entered an intersection, they are far more likely to respond that the light was green than the myriad of 'real' reasons: their light was green, the other direction's light was red, they saw no pedestrians, cyclists, or other potential dangers, there were no audio cues to indicate that any danger was present, and their overall understanding of safe driving indicated that entering the intersection was a reasonable course of action.

Additionally, testimony is not necessarily reliable. Various studies have shown that testimony – the human-centric, court equivalent of an explanation – can be influenced. One such way is by a co-witness: 'blame-conformity' involves a co-witness incorrectly blaming an innocent bystander for a crime, influencing the other witness.[86] Researchers and experts on eyewitness psychology also note that

> [a] particular utterance may have more or less probative value, depending on such *contextual issues* as the *personal histories* of the maker of the statement of those who hear it, *what else* was occurring concurrently, *when* the conversation took place, *who else* might have witnessed it, and *which of many* conversations in which a particular exchange took place.[87]

While a witness's testimony would be influenced by these and other factors, the courts are not privy to the context of each and must contend with the explanations proffered them, influenced though they are by their circumstance. This conflict extends further when considering those giving explanations for their own actions: '[n]avigating a conflict of interest is not only a problem for the intentionally corrupt, but also for well-meaning individuals who unintentionally succumb to conflicts but then post hoc rationalise their actions so as to appear (to themselves and others) to be objective'.[88] Further, and more bluntly, '[e]veryone is prone to rationalizing their actions and beliefs'.[89] This is no less true in formal court explanations than in everyday life, because the rationalisation is not conscious.

3.6.3. Probabilities do not Matter

As previously mentioned, explanations to courts are unlikely to depend on the percentage contribution of various facts to an action – green light, no cars, etc. There may be variance in this, such as a case in which an expert witness can give a statistical measure of an outcome, or a concrete measurement: the percentage likelihood of a car's brakes to fail, or the negative temperature at which a fire hydrant might fail.[90] Yet these numbers and probabilities are not the entirety of

[86] C Thorley and D Kumar, 'Eyewitness Susceptibility to Co-Witness Misinformation Is Influenced by Co-Witness Confidence and Own Self-Confidence' (2017) 23 *Psychology, Crime & Law* 342.

[87] MP Toglia et al, *The Handbook of Eyewitness Psychology: Volume I: Memory for Events* (Psychology Press 2017) 1934 (emphasis in original).

[88] DM Cain and AS Detsky, 'Everyone's a Little Bit Biased (Even Physicians)' (25 June 2008) 299(24) *Journal of the American Medical Association* 2893: doi.10.1001/jama.299.24.2893.

[89] ibid.

[90] *Blyth v Birmingham Waterworks Company* (1856) 11 Ex Ch 781.

the questions asked: the court might enquire as to whether the brake failure risk was known by all parties, or perhaps solely the supplier (rather than the manufacturer). The temperature at which a hydrant might fail is relevant, but unfortunately for Mr Blyth, it is relevant in that the Birmingham Waterworks Company were not determined to be negligent because that temperature was much colder than could reasonably be expected by the company in Birmingham.[91]

Miller points to the ideas of truth and probability, with the example of a sack full of red balls. The answer to 'why is the ball red?' could be answered statistically with the response that all balls in the bag are red, but a better explanation is that someone painted it red.[92] Yet for the question, 'why did we observe a red ball coming out of the bag', the fact that all balls in the bag are red is a good explanation 'because having only red balls in the bag does cause us to select a red one'.[93] The work cited by Miller – Josephson and Josephson – provides that the difference between the two statements are that one is explaining the observed fact and the other the event explaining the fact: to explain via statistics, the cause of the generalisation is needed as well.[94]

In explanations to courts, it seems that probabilities are only important in a general sense: criminal cases ask questions such as whether someone was guilty beyond a reasonable doubt; civil cases might ask on the balance of probabilities which party was responsible. Each is looking for an ultimate explanation, but there is no percentage certainty requirement. It would be rare indeed for a jury to be asked whether a defendant was, in a murder trial, at least 95 per cent guilty.

3.6.4. Explanations are Social

This is an important point. Human explanations are invariably contextual, and tie directly into the legal concepts of reasonableness. Many if not all defences depend on their context, social and otherwise: self-defence is acceptable, but only under certain circumstances. A driver's surprise at seeing an elephant in the road and subsequent acceleration into a telephone pole is much more reasonable in central London than it is in a safari park in Tanzania.

Explanations are a framing of knowledge, of circumstance and of context. Nowhere is this more evident than the narrative of law: 'the recounting of events … with interpretation of those events … is central to all legal processes and the many different kinds of legal story interwoven with each other to form the grand fabric of law'.[95] Explanations are required for accountability from judges and

[91] ibid.

[92] Miller (n 76).

[93] ibid.

[94] ibid, citing JR Josephson and SG Josephson, *Abductive Inference: Computation, Philosophy, Technology* (Cambridge University Press 1996).

[95] M Hanne and R Weisberg, *Narrative and Metaphor in the Law* (Cambridge University Press 2018) 2.

administrative agencies, and 'an explanation for a particular choice can provide evidence as to whether the defendant acted knowingly, recklessly, negligently, or innocently – all of which can bear legal significance'.[96] Doshi-Velez et al further state that '[w]here the focus is on individual responsibility and restitution, such as with criminal law and personal injury liability, individual explanations are often central to legal outcomes'.[97]

In the legal context, explanations are not just a pure data reading of an outcome. They provide the actor's relationship to other actors, to the situation and to legal concepts: the reasonableness of the action, the foreseeability of the consequence, and the implications of other actors involved. An explanation without context is one dot in a pointillist piece – accurate, and a part of the greater whole, but not inherently indicative of the entire picture.

3.7. How XAI Meet these Criteria (for Courts)

Given the importance of these four criteria for explanations to courts, how might XAI help AI meet them? The points should not be taken as gospel – probabilities can be demonstrably helpful – but can be a guide as to presenting XAI data to courts. Explainable AI tools providing data may not be inherently contrastive, but an expert witness explaining the data in such a way would be of benefit to the courts. This is easier in certain circumstances than in others; showing that a loan-providing AI was not discriminating on protective grounds can be shown with contrastive explanations, whereas showing that a prescription of medication based on AI recommendations was reasonable may be difficult to portray in contrastive terms. This brings us to the second point: that explanations are selected.

That explanations are selected by humans in an inherently biased manner is clearly not a positive for courts dealing with humans. Rationalising after the fact is not a beneficial aspect, yet an inherently unavoidable one for humans.[98] It is true too that the XAI tools used to examine an AI will be selected by humans, and in the case of an ex-post examination, may be chosen to best portray the decisions made in the AI production process. However, providing a log of the production process and the choices made therein – time stamped before an incident – means that such evidence cannot be altered through retrospective rationalisation. While a court will certainly face rationalisation of choices made in the decision-making process, XAI provides a measure that can be reviewed on a purely factual basis: the probabilities assigned to obstacles perceived on the road, or the highlighted portions of a radiology scan interpreted to be meaningful, for example.

[96] Doshi-Velez et al (n 40).

[97] ibid.

[98] F Cushman, 'Rationalization Is Rational' (2020) 43 *Behavioral and Brain Sciences* 28: cambridge.org/core/journals/behavioral-and-brain-sciences/article/abs/rationalization-is-rational/2A13B99ED09BD802C0924D3681FEC55B.

Probabilities lie at the heart of XAI explanations. Explanations via XAI are very likely to be probabilistic in nature, particularly for complex AI dealing with numerical or tabular data. Producers will have an important line to walk in representing probable likelihoods as causes without overstating their impact on an event. In such a case, expert witnesses will be needed to examine the motivations behind which probabilities are provided and the likely causes thereof, particularly where the most likely and the 'best' explanations are not identical (a distinction posed by Miller).[99]

The social nature of explanations is particularly interesting when examining courts and AI producers. Concepts such as reasonableness hinge on the social nature of a situation, and the human desire for narrative cannot be denied.[100] The concept of the reasonable person – once called the man on the Clapham omnibus – is a legal fiction. Courts have built up through case law and social context an understanding of what actions might be reasonable or not. At this point in time, at the very least, AI lacks this human context. It has no social understanding of interactions, and it would be near impossible to build such context into narrow AI. This lack of context is the basis for small adjustments to automated procedures: at a stand-off, how can a self-driving vehicle and a pedestrian indicate to one another who is to proceed, when there is no cultural backdrop of gestures or eye contact? Why and how should an AI concierge respond to 'thank you', when they do not have a concept for 'you', or 'thank'? To the courts, reasonableness is expectations built over the course of time. We have not yet reached the period of time to determine what a reasonable AI build looks like, even in domain-specific applications. Because AI does not have this context, the human participants in the process must provide it: not in post-hoc fiction, but in the narrative describing the XAI use and decision-making throughout the process. What was reasonable for the human producers to provide in terms of context is a much more reasonable question to ask than 'why didn't the AI pull off the road to let an ambulance through?' AI systems are a product of their design, not of unique, individual, human-like motivations.

This then leads us to the next question: given the limitations of XAI explained above, how can its outputs be used to answer the law's questions about foreseeability and reasonableness?

[99] Miller (n 76).

[100] Sometimes to the point of anthropomorphism and personification.

4

Law Using XAI

What the previous two chapters tell us is that both tort and XAI for law depend fundamentally on foreseeability. Foreseeability is a mixture of what one might expect to happen, and what can be seen to have happened. In order for an assessor to decide whether or not a foreseeability standard has been met, that assessor will need explanations about the various aspects of the AI in question: what information has been received; what it had to work on; and what the AI's 'thought processes' look like. There are elements that need explaining in order for the assessor to determine whether or not the producer is liable. This cannot be done simply by looking at a black-box AI. The tools that the assessor, and indeed other parties, use are XAI. This chapter asks what the law needs in order to understand the answer to the question of foreseeability, and how XAI can provide those answers.

4.1. Where We Are So Far

4.1.1. Technologically

The state of knowledge in AI can change incredibly quickly. Broadly speaking, there are many types, kinds and applications of AI, all of which are progressing in their own and overlapping directions. A single purpose – say, to vacuum a floor – can be accomplished by a relatively complex AI that maps the layout of its surroundings, probable obstacles, optimal timing, etc, or by an incredibly simple AI – a vacuum that redirects when its sensor bumps into something. However, the more complex the task at hand, the more complex the AI designed to complete the task needs to be. An AI log cutter that simply chops in a singular downward motion at regular intervals can be designed in a way that its actions and internal logic are easily explainable. An AI surgeon requires more nuance – not only what, when and whom to cut, but how, with what pressure, when to cease cutting, what tissue to remove, etc. A decision tree is a useful example of a simple algorithm but is unlikely to allow for sufficient nuance to perform complex tasks – unless, of course, it is a decision tree with thousands of weighted inputs, and as such is not inherently interpretable. Even relatively simple relationships such as decision trees (if X, then Y) can become difficult to understand if there are a thousand or more inputs, each with different weights. Essentially, complex and nuance-intensive tasks are the domain of the AI areas of machine learning and deep learning – those areas of AI which are not inherently interpretable. The nuance and specificity of input is a barrier to understanding, but they provide the necessary levels of complexity to achieve the level of performance desired. AI causing accidental death is most likely in domains where they are employed because of their capacity to proportionately improve or even save lives, such as transportation and medical domains: applications where the benefit to risk-balancing is high. If such applications were simple and straightforward, more progress would have been made in their automation before complex AI existed.

While the AI used in critical domains may not be inherently interpretable, this does not mean that there are no clues to interpretation. As previously discussed, XAI provides tools with which to examine AI. There are a variety of angles that XAI explanations can take: they can be static or interactive; local or global; inherent to the model or done after it is trained; there can be a second more interpretable model; and pertinent data can be visualised.[1] Data is collected from the system with which the AI will interact, the data is modelled into an AI, and the AI is interpreted via XAI. XAI techniques are used along the lifecycle of AI: to examine the data; to train the model; to debug the model; and to explain after the model has done something. Explanations reflect the AI design and development stage that they examine, and should be chosen with a variety of factors in mind: what is being examined for; what the model is likely to face when deployed; whether the data is sufficiently robust and reflective, etc. XAI tools are not perfect, but neither do they lie: they do not turn a light on over the black box in a dark room, but they can be used as a torch to examine the box from one angle at a time.[2]

The inherent usefulness of the AI is that it can take over a portion of human labour in a given circumstance. This can be additional to the human, such as with surgical-assistive tools, or in place of the human, such as a fully automated vehicle. As discussed, however, this has implications for foreseeability when harm occurs; it is not an active human mind making a decision with the benefit of context in the moment. There is a disconnect between the human decision-maker and the result. However, '[i]nterpretability and explainability can resolve the foreseeability challenge in some cases … while the foreseeability challenge AI poses for negligence is not absolute, it is still a difficulty'.[3]

[1] V Arya et al, 'One Explanation Does Not Fit All: A Toolkit and Taxonomy of AI Explainability Techniques' (2019): arxiv.org/abs/1909.03012.

[2] It helps, of course, to have multiple torches.

[3] AD Selbst, 'Negligence and AI's Human Users' (2020) 100 *Boston University Law Review* 1315, 1341.

4.1.2. Foreseeability

There are some limited scenarios in which foreseeability does not apply. For example, the Court of Appeal has held that damages flowing from fraudulent inducement are not limited to what could be reasonably foreseen: normally,

> [i]n contract, the damages are limited to what may reasonably be supposed to have been in the contemplation of the parties. In fraud, they are not so limited. The defendant is bound to make reparation for all the actual damages directly flowing from the fraudulent inducement.[4]

Furthermore, there are cases in which parties could, at least in theory, accept absolute obligations via contract or prior agreement. For example, 'Volvo, Google, and Mercedes-Benz have already pledged to accept liability if their [self-driving] vehicles cause an accident'.[5] Companies making such commitments benefit from a potential increase and goodwill and trust in their products, although cases have not yet arisen to test the specificities of how such a commitment would turn out in practice.

Beyond these exceptions and caveats, foreseeability is the main basis by which the law imposes obligations on a party in advance. This raises questions about how to foresee the risks which using AI introduces 'the very essence of liability considerations is potentially affected by the involvement of AI'.[6] More practically,

> [i]f artificial intelligence companies are sued for the negligent development of their software, courts will be faced with a difficult question of foreseeability. When proving a case of negligence, plaintiffs are required to show that the harm occurred was a foreseeable consequence of the defendant's negligent conduct.[7]

The AI provides a level of decision-making that 'disrupts our typical understanding of responsibility for choices gone wrong'[8] – AI provides an intermediary decision-making entity that may not match its human counterparts. For example, the DeepMind AI 'Alpha Go' beat world-leading Go champion in 2016, by employing the now dubbed 'move 37', which human experts initially thought to be made in error, but which ultimately won Alpha Go the match.[9] A human employing an AI hedge-trimmer might have no idea it would take off a layer of the neighbour's

[4] *Doyle v Olby (Ironmongers) Ltd* [1969] 2 QB 158, 167.

[5] O Ben-Shahar, 'Should Carmakers Be Liable When a Self-Driving Car Crashes?' (*Forbes*, 22 September 2016): perma.cc/U22K-B4H4.

[6] B Schütte, L Majewski and K Havu, 'Damages Liability for Harm Caused by Artificial Intelligence – EU Law in Flux' (Social Science Research Network 2021): papers.ssrn.com/abstract=3897839.

[7] W Kowert, 'The Foreseeability of Human–Artificial Intelligence Interactions' (2017) 96 *Texas Law Review* 181: semanticscholar.org/paper/The-Foreseeability-of-Human%E2%80%93Artificial-Intelligence-Kowert/f512cdf9a190b32af0e730a404944c677f8278d0 4.

[8] ibid.

[9] J Vincent, 'Former Go Champion Beaten by DeepMind Retires after Declaring AI Invincible' (*The Verge*, 27 November 2019): theverge.com/2019/11/27/20985260/ai-go-alphago-lee-se-dol-retired-deepmind-defeat.

car as well. Yet it is difficult to justify an argument that would remove the foreseeable categories of harm for the sole reason that AI is used,[10] particularly given that the AI's human counterparts' liability would not change in their activities: whether an AI or human driver causes harm by striking another road user, that same human is harmed and the principles for determining liability are unchanged.

There are some levels of sliding scale appropriate here, for example, for cases in which a human is in full control of the AI, such as where the AI is providing additional information to assist the human in making a decision, rather than a direct action (such as non-embedded versus embedded AI). While this can be defined in terms of 'human in the loop', 'human out of the loop', or 'human over the loop',[11] and while there are likely to be gradations of responsibility, the starting question is the case where a human is the final decision-maker in the process:

> If a doctor relies on a tool to help her decide to inject a drug or release a patient, we still analyze the case in malpractice despite a tool being involved; we expect the doctor to understand her tools well enough to satisfy her duty of care while using them.[12]

For example, if a surgeon is sent a radiological exam on which the AI has highlighted an area of concern, one would expect the human doctor to treat the scan and recommendations with at least as much care and examination as they would treat the scan and recommendations of a colleague. The foreseeability issues caused by AI are thus less relevant, given that a human holds ultimate decision-making power.[13]

It has also been argued that humans act as 'liability sponges' in situations where machines are seen as infallible: '[e]ven though the human operators may not be able to avert the danger, failure to do so manifests as a decision they can be blamed for – such as not taking the wheel back in time or not paying enough attention to alerts'.[14] Such arguments are not unimportant, and should be given particular examination from sectoral legislation: while driving, for instance, what the human response time actually is, versus how quickly they are assumed to be able to regain control, should both be carefully examined and explicitly defined where the car is designed to hand back control. This will be discussed in further detail in section 6.1.5.

There comes a point, however, where we reach those AI applications which are most problematic: those which are embedded, autonomous, opaque and

[10] Kowert (n 7).

[11] T Grønsund and M Aanestad, 'Augmenting the Algorithm: Emerging Human-in-the-Loop Work Configurations' (2020) 29 *Journal of Strategic Information Systems* 101614: sciencedirect.com/science/article/pii/S0963868720300226.

[12] Selbst (n 3) 1319.

[13] Although they should perhaps be examined through other lenses, such as overreliance on the AI's recommendations – '[p]eople may trust computers more than humans'. University of Georgia, 'People may trust computers more than humans: New research shows that people are more likely to rely on algorithms (*ScienceDaily*): sciencedaily.com/releases/2021/04/210413114040.htm.

[14] Selbst (n 3) 1350.

undertaking societally desirable activities with the potential for significant positive impact – AI whose 'dangerous behaviour and harmful effects stem from their unpredictable self-learning algorithms', or simply their sheer opacity, and 'not from specific risky acts of programming or [human operation]'.[15] In these cases there is no human operator, and it is the most advantageous case not to have one.[16] How will the courts address foreseeability and liability in such cases? The answer is that they will look to the humans involved.

4.1.3. The Humans Involved

First, a brief note on the humans involved: human decision-makers are inherently imperfect, and '[p]eople often lack the information necessary to determine the safest possible course of action, and even if they had it, they could not process all of the information to incorporate it into the decision'.[17] This is known as bounded rationality, and 'foreseeability is how negligence law compensates for bounded rationality'.[18] In other words, the obligations in the moment are not necessarily so different from the obligations in advance – risks must to a certain extent be foreseeable, but humans are not capable of nor expected to read potential harms perfectly.

From a human perspective, obligations in the moment are determined in advance for AI because the decision-making relative to consequences – inputs, types of decision-making, etc – are determined prior to an incident. What the AI is intended to do determines the appropriateness and reasonableness of risks considered and mitigatory actions taken by the producer given the circumstances in which the AI is intended or likely to function. This is a broad look at the circumstances, and includes the ways in which the AI will foreseeably fail to do what is intended: an AI that is intended to make tea will foreseeably be at risk of spilling the tea, causing harm by spilling it directly on the human, causing a slipping hazard, or by combining it with another hazard such as an electrical junction, to name a few. An AI that is intended to aid in human movement by providing additional lifting power will foreseeably malfunction by providing too much or too little lifting power or by applying it unequally.[19]

[15] P Huberman, 'Tort Law, Corrective Justice and the Problem of Autonomous-Machine-Caused Harm' (2021) 34 Canadian Journal of Law & Jurisprudence 105: cambridge.org/core/journals/canadian-journal-of-law-and-jurisprudence/article/abs/tort-law-corrective-justice-and-the-problem-of-autonomousmachinecaused-harm/723467C9EF5CF11C29E1AB2E1BCA2D73.

[16] Autonomous vehicles, for example, have automation levels from zero to five, but significant benefits are reached at level five where there is no possible human involvement, ie, no steering wheel. Such a case realises benefits such as cars for those who cannot drive, those who are impaired, and the lack of need for a driver generally (eg, shipping).

[17] Selbst (n 3) 1360.

[18] ibid.

[19] O Franklin-Wallis, 'Inside X, Google's Top-Secret Moonshot Factory' (*Wired UK*, 2020): wired.co.uk/article/ten-years-of-google-x.

What, then, is the 'reasonableness' in reasonable foreseeability for our opaque, autonomous, oh-so-promising AI? Reasonableness is the build-up of expectations over time. Without that backlog of interpretation to hand, reasonableness is the developers' and designers' evidence of due diligence in design, in training and in testing; the defence of their choices, optimisations and expertise – the reasonable programmer; and the reasonable expertise of the domain in which the AI will function: the reasonable address of issues internal to the AI, and those it will encounter.

4.2. Steps of an AI Harm Incident

As explained in section 2.1.1 the steps to establish negligence are to establish a duty of care, the standard of care, the breach of that standard of care, and whether imposition of liability would be fair, just and reasonable. This will be examined in three parts: the duty of care; the standard of care and its breach; and whether imposition is fair, just and reasonable.

4.2.1. Duty of Care

The duty of care is likely to be relatively straightforward to establish, and addresses who it can be reasonably anticipated that the AI will affect. There may be cases where the AI is being used explicitly outside its intended purpose by using it around people where such interaction is explicitly disavowed, and so no risk to that group can be foreseen, but most specific AI, either embedded or not, will have a foreseeable group of people who might suffer from its actions and thus a duty of care will be owed to that group. In the case of embedded AI,[20] the AI will be expected to either (a) interact with humans, or (b) not interact with humans. If the AI is reasonably expected to interact with humans, there will be a duty of care owed by the producers (through the AI) to the humans with which the AI will interact. Where the AI is reasonably expected not to interact with humans, this has, potentially, several layers: whether the AI is reasonably expected not to interact with humans who are not experts, such as technicians or domain experts, or not to interact with humans at all, either directly or indirectly, such as a robot shot into space.[21] In cases where the AI is reasonably expected to interact only with expert humans, there is still a duty of care both to the expert humans, *and* to those with which the AI does not have direct physical contact, but on whom the AI may foreseeably have effects. This is the same duty of care for non-embedded AI, as AI may have significant effects on humans without physical interaction,

[20] Arguably mostly robots, but the distinction is of minimal importance for this purpose.
[21] Just for Curiosity.

such as those individuals about whom decisions are made by automated systems.[22] This broad level of potential impact may in fact be one of the unique aspects of AI. Essentially, a duty of care owed by the producers to a potential future party is likely to be easy to establish for all but the most obscure cases, particularly for AI causing accidental death.

4.2.2. Standard of Care

For there to be a breach of a duty of care, there first needs to have been a standard to have been breached. Rachum-Twaig suggests that

> [t]he most accepted formulation for a breach of the duty of care is the Hand formula, determining that the injurer breaches the duty of care when (1) the costs of the prevention of harm were lower than the harm expectancy (the cost of the harm multiplied by the probability of its occurrence), and (2) such preventative measures were not taken.[23]

While the Hand formula is unique to the United States, it is nonetheless a reasonable position from which to start: the idea that there is a relationship between the level of harm and the care that should be taken to prevent it. However,

> [i]f the behaviour of AI-based robots is unpredictable or unexplainable to humans, how can the probability that they will eventually inflict harm on others be assessed? Moreover, the harm itself is not only unforeseeable or difficult to assess, but also the types of harm themselves are sometimes unpredictable.[24]

Kingston suggests that '[the] various limitations that AI systems are subject to can be divided into two categories: [1] Limitations that human experts with the same knowledge are also subject to; [and 2] Limitations of artificial intelligence technology compared with humans'.[25]

There are several steps for consideration in assessing the standard of care. While many types of harm are possible – physical, social, psychological, etc – let us concentrate on physical harm. This can be direct, such as by hitting someone with a car, or indirect, such as by giving a false negative diagnosis. In using AI, there are two applicable standards of care. Let us consider them in the order they will be discovered post-hoc: initially, the obligations in the moment. What obligations were on a decision-maker (in such a case, the AI) at the time of the incident? Herein we find our standard of the reasonable professional: the AI must 'act' to the standard of a reasonable professional. This is for multiple reasons. First, this is the bare minimum standard that is acceptable, both to the law and to society

[22] Such as loans, but also health-specific areas such as hospital admission and treatment priority.

[23] O Rachum-Twaig, 'Whose Robot is it Anyway? Liability for Artificial-Intelligence-Based Robots' (Social Science Research Network 2019) papers.ssrn.com/abstract=3339230 4.

[24] ibid.

[25] J Kingston, 'Artificial Intelligence and Legal Liability' (2018): arxiv.org/abs/1802.07782, 4.

for reasons of establishing trust. Particularly in the case of AI causing accidental death, it is unquestionable that the AI must be at least as good as its human counterpart.[26] Second, this is a minimum target which developers must reach – an AI that is not at least as good as its human counterpart is unquestionably below the necessary standard of care. This, however, brings us to two further points: first, that human professionals are imperfect in practice. Second, that there are certain dimensions which are difficult to capture in the metric 'as good as'.

Consider a case in which a pedestrian steps out of the darkness onto the road. The autonomous vehicle may in fact hit the pedestrian. A human driver may also have hit the pedestrian, if in both cases the sensors and human driver could not detect the pedestrian – this is an example of the '[l]imitations that human experts with the same knowledge are also subject to'.[27] But this comparison might not be enough to avoid liability for the autonomous vehicle's accident; we expect that technology will improve on human performance. Consider then a case where without warning an unattended bus barrels width-wise across a road, and then off the road and, as a consequence, another vehicle crashes while avoiding it and damages a parked car.[28] It is hard to state, in such a case, how a human driver of that other vehicle ought to respond to the bus causing unpredictable havoc, and it would be difficult to assign a metric to such a response. Nonetheless, if the other vehicle were an autonomous vehicle, then society might expect, and the law may want to impose, liability even if the automated vehicle had performed to a standard similar to a human driver. In cases where the human standard is unaddressable, either by inherent human imperfection or by difficulty of comparison, and physical harm has occurred, we turn to the second point for standard of care: the standard of a reasonable developer.

4.2.3. Standard of a Reasonable Developer

Recall the three broad themes of foreseeability discussed in chapter two: foreseeability is the culmination of obligations on a party in advance; foreseeability depends on context, and reasonableness is a convenient fiction, albeit a necessary one; obligations in advance turn into obligations in the moment. Examination is left to a crucial piece of legal lore, with one significant addition: what did the producer[29] know, ought to have known, *or should have tested for*?

[26] Furthermore, although not part of the standard of care, the AI should be '(as good as a human) + X' wherein X is something societally desirable: that the AI is more efficient, cheaper, greener, cleaner, capable of functioning continually, etc, to offset the cost both societally and ecologically (energy entailed in creation) of creating and maintaining the AI.

[27] Kingston (n 25).

[28] 'Oxford Bus Company Crash: Second House Evacuated' *BBC News* (8 October 2021): bbc.com/news/uk-england-oxfordshire-58846457.

[29] The producer will in all likelihood be made up of a variety of parties in practice.

Consider here the fatal crash in Tempe Arizona, whereby a woman walking her bicycle across a dark highway in the night was struck and killed by a 'self-driving' Uber vehicle.[30] There are several layers to this crash: first, that there was a safety driver in the Uber vehicle, who was at the time of the crash streaming a video. Investigations reported that the driver 'was in the driver's seat, and had the ability to take over control of the vehicle in an emergency. Dash-cam footage released by police shows [the backup driver] looking down, away from the road, for several seconds immediately before the crash'.[31] The backup driver was indeed charged. However, footage is also publicly available of the crash, and while it is clear that the driver was in fact supposed to be paying attention and have both hands on the wheel, it is unclear whether a fully attentive driver could have stopped in time: the victim is unlit, with no reflectors, and to the viewer appears out of nowhere at a likely insufficient distance to stop.[32] It is entirely possible that, had the backup driver been paying attention, they still may not have been able to react in time. At the very least, there could be an almost identical case where the vehicle was a bit closer, or travelling a bit faster, wherein a human driver could not stop. This is where applying the standard of a reasonable professional – here, the holder of the driver's licence – would not necessarily indicate a breach of the standard of care to drive reasonably.

However, if a human driver had had the information that the driving system did, the human driver would have been negligent. The system detected the existence of some risk in sufficient time to react to the potential incident, but because of development choices did not do so: a breach of the standard that should be expected of a reasonable producer. First, the vehicle detected the bike-walker six seconds before the crash, but only braked 1.3 seconds before the crash[33] – it varied between identifying the pedestrian 'as an unknown object, then as a vehicle, and then as a bicycle, each time adjusting its expectations for her path of travel'.[34] Second, this identification issue was known, and had in fact been reported within the company prior to the crash.[35] Former employees stated that the decision to switch from a lower-seated vehicle to a higher one exacerbated the blind-spot issue.[36] Uber ought to have known, did actually know, and should have tested for this issue – a pedestrian walking their bicycle is unlikely to be considered an unforeseeable or improbable edge case.

[30] Rory Cellan-Jones, 'Uber's Self-Driving Operator Charged over Fatal Crash' *BBC News* (16 September 2020): bbc.com/news/technology-54175359.

[31] ibid.

[32] 'Uber Self-Driving Car Crash in Tempe, Arizona' (Directed by *VentureBeat*, 2018): youtube.com/watch?v=XtTB8hTgHbM.

[33] 'Uber Driver in Fatal Tempe Crash May Have Been Watching The Voice Behind the Wheel' (*Gizmodo*, 22 June 2018): gizmodo.com/uber-driver-in-fatal-tempe-crash-may-have-been-watching-1827039127.

[34] A Marshall, 'Uber's Self-Driving Car Saw the Woman It Killed, Report Says' (*Wired*, 24 May 2018) wired.com/story/uber-self-driving-crash-arizona-ntsb-report/.

[35] Cellan-Jones (n 30).

[36] A Kasap, *Tracing the Locus of Regulation and Liability* (Edward Elgar Publishing 2022) 131.

Is Imposing Liability Fair, Just and Reasonable?

The question of whether the imposition of liability would be fair, just and reasonable is a policy question. Essentially, it is intended to take into account the domino effects of the decision: on future human decisions; on insurance burdens; on the market more broadly; on trade relations, etc. This has the potential for considerable implications for AI: AI is likely to be used across many aspects of life, and it would be impossible to determine the exact sectors or applications without either narrowing the scope for AI or guessing with wild abandon. It seems clear that in the applications where AI is designed to save lives, then the application is broadly desirable. It seems similarly clear that where AI has the capacity to save lives, it is also likely – though hopefully, through testing, planning and regulation less likely than humans – to take lives, at bare minimum in the short term. AI in such areas is therefore something society should encourage, but also carefully regulate: to make such dangerous applications as safe as practically possible, while also acknowledging that in waiting for an application to be perfect, society might miss out on the potentially considerable benefits. While the specificities of this regulation more broadly will be discussed in depth in chapter seven, let us note for now that the law imposing liability should attempt this balance of care and innovation.

Is imposing liability for breaching the standard of care for AI causing accidental death fair, just and reasonable? These are broad terms, and AI defies many of the conventional ways in which the law addresses humans. AI can only capture that which is, to an extent, quantifiable. Natural language processing does not process intent, merely use. AI systems that paint are not themselves reacting to the emotions that paintings inspire, they are combining and reconfiguring data of previous painters. The law recognises the existence of concepts such as fairness, justice and reasonableness because they are human concepts, not because they are inherent quantifiable truths of the universe such as gravity:

> Take the universe and grind it down to the finest powder and sieve it through the finest sieve and then *show* me one atom of justice, one molecule of mercy. And yet … [one acts] as if there is some ideal order in the world, as if there is some … some *rightness* in the universe by which it may be judged.[37]

We cannot put a reasonable course of action to an AI, because we have no grains of reasonableness to give it – no mathematically definable crumb to which such a description would apply. AI does not have the context inherent to humans that is necessary for reasonableness, and so far we cannot provide it. We can at best create AI that acts in the footsteps of reasonable humans, but we cannot make it do so for anything like the same motivations. If AI is allowed, victims will be harmed; even killed. Harm in and of itself is not fair, is not just. But it is, arguably, reasonable, if the quantum of harm that occurs is demonstrably less than the harm that would have occurred without the use of AI, or in aid of a specific further

[37] T Pratchett, *Hogfather* (Corgi Books 1997) 423. Death emphasis (all caps) removed.

purpose: amputating a limb is a harm, but certainly reasonable if it will save a life. In striking a balance in the regulation of AI, we must not override the desirability of life-saving capacity, nor underweight the harm that will be caused, while still acknowledging that human actions in the moment, with all the informed contexts that a human can muster, is absent.

Death is perhaps the most serious of consequences, and its avoidance the most desirable of aims. Encouraging developers, or more realistically AI-producing companies, not to consider such harm would clearly be unjust. Yet so too would be foregoing the life-saving capacity or other benefits. At a practical level, the only party that has a fundamental level of control of an AI – albeit in advance – is the producer.[38] At that same practical level, the AI cannot be expected to exercise control; there is no liability which could coerce, convince, or even particularly be 'noticed' by an AI – an AI does not have assets to withdraw, a desire to live, or shame to be bestowed. The hammer does not care if it is returned to the box, nor if it is melted down. The owner of the hammer cares about the loss of the hammer, and society needs hammers. For practical, policy and social reasons, liability is necessary: to compensate victims, and deter harms. For functional reasons, the subject of potential liability is the developer in cases of accidental death.[39]

There is also the question of how the liability should be established. The law provides different standards across liability, such as strict liability compared with negligence liability. In the case of AI, there is a massive imbalance between the information held by the AI developer, and that held by the victim. Furthermore, the fact that an AI has caused harm engages concepts such as '*res ipsa loquitur*', or 'the thing speaks for itself' – the inference of negligence from the nature of the accident. In the case of harm occurring, *ex post*, the developer must rebut the assumption of negligence. This can be done through proof of due diligence, as evidenced by the provision of results from training, testing and XAI. This means, of course, that records should be kept. It also means that there is a level of pressure for such records to be reasonably communicable to relevant legal parties.

4.3. Sample Application

4.3.1. Duty of Care

Given the broad nature of development of AI, and the likelihood of a multitude of individuals working on a singular AI, the parties involved in development will be referred to here as the AI producer. The producer will, in most cases, be a company – not individual employees, or not inasmuch as public-facing liability is concerned. To whom, when and in what capacity do producers owe a duty of care?

[38] Or developers as a singular entity.

[39] There are, of course, cases where liability will be split with users, co-causers of an accident, etc. But in cases of pure AI mishap, the developing party has liability.

As previously discussed, proving duty of care is unlikely to be a hurdle. For AI applications that are expected to interact with humans, or have direct effects on humans, a duty of care is clear. There will certainly be exceptions:

> [t]he liability of professional operators can be justified by the argument that professionals should only use tools they can consider themselves responsible for ... it could be submitted that the correct bearer of the risk of AI causing an accident is the professional operator who decided to utilise AI.[40]

In terms of duty of care, this could be reflected in a scenario where an AI is only intended to be used by those with appropriate training on the tool, as with other medical tools. In such a case, the AI producer is unlikely to find itself with a duty of care to, say, a patient who was operated on by medical personnel untrained on the AI. Along these lines, there are arguments to be made for lack of duty of care for use extremely outside the AI's intended use, judged on not only a practical application level, but by considerations such as marketing and foreseeable misuse.

In the case of a self-driving vehicle – which for simplicity's sake will be fully automated – there is a clear duty of care towards the occupants of the car, other road users and those nearby. The duty of care of a human driver is fully subsumed by the AI driver, and through the AI to the producers. In the case of an autonomous surgical AI, the duty of care is of the surgeon to their patient, and fellow medical personnel while performing.

Determining duty of care is not inherently technical; however, in the case of AI it is likely that there will be a question of divided liability with multiple providers.[41] Given the complexity of such a situation and the division of precise proportions of contribution, this particular aspect will remain outside the scope of this book.

4.3.2. Standard of Care

The standard of care will depend on the type of application, the reasonable human doing the same thing, and the 'reasonable producer'. In a situation where there is no available comparison for the level of expertise of the comparable human, or where the producer has met the standard of a reasonable human doing the same thing but a higher standard might be expected from an AI, it must be examined whether the producer has acted to the level of a reasonable producer: what the producer knew, ought to have known, or ought to have tested. An examination of the AI and its decision-making will be needed to decide whether the producer met the standard of what they ought to have known or tested for. In the case where a reasonable

[40] Schütte, Majewski and Havu (n 6).

[41] There are further questions here, such as if publicly accessible tools were used. While such questions should certainly be considered on a case-by-case basis, it is reasonable to assume as a baseline that a company would not be considered liable if there were no compensation provided to the party providing open-access code, so long as the code did not purport to have 'abilities' beyond reality – eg, purporting a higher level of accuracy in reporting on radiological scans.

professional standard is available, an examination of the available standards will be needed. For example, there are margins available for certain medical procedures: *Muller v King's College Hospital NHS Foundation Trust* decided that even though an 'excision was later described as "incomplete" because it did not include a margin of 2cm around the wound which would have been standard practice if it were known that the affected area was cancerous',[42] the surgeon had not been negligent because there was a body of surgical opinion which would not remove the margin if the area was not known to be cancerous. In a case purely on the question of whether an excisement of this type was properly undergone, the standard would be 2cm. Where such specific standards are available, AI measurements should conform to this knowledge. However, as explored in section 2.2.1 this is only the case so long as there was not a competing but accepted view among professionals of that sub-specialty of field.

The technical examination of the AI is where standard of care becomes more complex. While many cases involving AI liability are likely to settle before court, let us assume a scenario where an AI has caused an accidental death, and there is an examination of the AI by a panel of expert witnesses.

4.3.3. Breach of Duty: Drivers

Consider a scenario where there has been a festival on a number of closed streets in the centre of a large city. The streets of the festival itself have been blocked off, but as participants disperse, they join road traffic in other areas. Festival participants are unusually dressed. One such participant is a street performer in seven-foot stilts. The performer trips, stumbles into the street still on the stilts, and ultimately falls on the street, where they are struck by an autonomous vehicle. Let us assume that it is unclear whether a reasonable human driver could have avoided the stilt-walker, and an AI examination is to be conducted.

The examination would first examine the basic track record of the vehicle. This is likely to have been required in order for the company to market the vehicle or, as required, get it insured. This is likely to have included a baseline of distance driven, capabilities of handling driving across a variety of scenarios, and demonstration of capability of handling a variety of edge cases. Let us assume that the provider's record for the autonomous vehicle of this type was acceptable, and that the car was on the road legally.

Second, the examination would then proceed to the records of the vehicle. In the case of the Tempe Arizona crash, this included what the car actually detected, whether or not it could be classified, as well as systems' inputs such as how fast the person/object was approaching/being approached by the vehicle, and different likelihoods of identification, for example 10 per cent likelihood of being a human. Such investigation would include whether the vehicle was reporting to be

[42] *Muller v King's College Hospital NHS Foundation Trust* [2017] EWHC 128.

functioning at full capacity; that all sensors and cameras were working and accurate; and that no updates or errors were reported to the car's owner or occupier.

Third, the examination would look at the explanations of the vehicle's actions. This will proceed best if records have been kept at a high standard throughout the development process (which will be expounded upon later). The court will look at two types of explanations: those produced in the moment of error; and those produced throughout the development process.

In many ways, the explanation of the error in the moments of the accident – 'post-modelling explainability' – will be far more straightforward. Because the error has actually occurred, it is far easier to track down: an explanation can be specific, because it is not attempting to cover all possible errors that could occur. It is attempting to find the reason that a particular action occurred, not the fundamental basis for all possible actions. Restricting this investigation to what is currently possible (ie, not theorising how interactive explanations might function), the explanation requirements could be framed as a one-shot static explanation, of the model, on a local, post-hoc level. To unpack this: the model is looking at a single instance that has occurred. The XAI techniques are not attempting to examine the data that was used to train the model as a whole, but the model itself. The XAI is not aiming to explain the entire model, but to look at a single individual action. The XAI is intended to explain a single action after the fact. As 'simple' as this sounds, it must still take into account a variety of factors: the input of a variety of sensors and cameras; and the weights given to each of them. This can be an incredibly extensive process. It will also involve a variety of XAI tools: the car will be examining visual data; classification data; data from communicating with other cars and or navigation tools; and any number of other inputs. There is no closed list as to what such an exploration might look like, but it could include 'backward propagation, proxy models, and activation optimization'.[43]

Without delving into what tools might be most appropriate, the investigators will be entitled to assume that the tools best suited to the task should be used. This will depend on the type of explanation taking place. In examining the results turned up by the XAI examinations, the courts will be looking at three factors:

1. What did the producer know?
2. What ought the producer have known or anticipated?
3. What ought the producer have tested for?

In the case of our stilt-walker, the producer may well not have known that the car would not recognise stilts as part of a human person. This could be for a variety of reasons, but would ultimately come down to the most likely two: first, that the sensors and video of the car would only capture up to seven feet. Second, that the body of the human was located above the seven feet, with up to seven feet

[43] Bahador Khaleghi, 'The How of Explainable AI: Post-Modelling Explainability' (*Medium*, 3 August 2019): towardsdatascience.com/the-how-of-explainable-ai-post-modelling-explainability-8b4cbc7adf5f.

being taken up by the stilts themselves. The producer was presumably unaware that the car would specifically fail to recognise stilt-walkers, or more particularly, stilt-walkers above a particular height (the height above the sensors). There are also case-specific questions about how far away the car was from the stilt-walker when the stilt-walker fell; how fast the car was travelling.

What ought the producer have known? This is a trickier question, and where more familiar foreseeability questions creep in. Ought the producer have known that humans of unusual shapes and sizes could enter the roadway? Yes. But is our stilt-walker within the assumable boundaries of what would enter a recognisable part of the roadway, rather than a particular length above it? There are likely to be questions of whether a human driver would have been able to notice and react to the stilt-walker in time, given that the stilt-walker would be out of the driver's normal range of vision. Human drivers are not required to be perfect, and neither should their automated counterparts.

What ought the producer have tested for? This question is not dissimilar from what they ought to have known, but brings us to the second part of the examination: what factors were the development of AI training and testing based on? In this portion, examiners look at non-singular XAI techniques, aimed at earlier portions of the development process: what did the developer define as relevant with regard to the training data' training the model; debugging the training model and data, etc?[44] Are those tests defensible as appropriate and non-negligent? AI is a selection of stacked probabilities, and both the selected probabilities and the judgement of the stacking matter. Put simply, potential percentage likelihood of one assessment impacts the next. A self-driving vehicle might determine with x per cent certainty that a colour is white. Then it might assign it a 'y' per cent likelihood of being a line on the road. Then a 'z' per cent likelihood of being an indicator of a 'acceptable to cross' line on the road. The vehicle may then assign a 'q' per cent likelihood of a safe merge over that line, taking into account 'a' per cent of the object ahead of it being a vehicle, 'b' per cent likelihood of the movement detected in the other direction being a plastic bag and not a pedestrian, etc. Both what are assessed to be actionable probabilities, and which have precedent over one another, matter a great deal.

This is where the provider's records come into play, and where the rebuttal defence of due diligence becomes relevant. The provider can mount a defence of due diligence over what training and testing was done. They must defend, to expert witnesses, the choices that were made throughout the process: that the training data was robust and representative; that the XAI tools that were chosen were chosen appropriately and represented what the AI was optimised for, not just the tests that showed the best possible results; that the testing data was not only sufficiently removed from the training data but was itself sufficiently robust; and that the AI was trained to respond to edge cases. Our stilt-walker is likely to be just such an edge-case but may fall to its human-driver comparison because of the

[44] Arya et al (n 1).

unusual roadway entry. Yet the examination of the development process is nonetheless important, and provides the point at which negligence can be considered – the decisions made in advance by the provider in order to realise the 'decisions' of the moment by the AI. The provider will be examined as a reasonable provider – whether the decisions made reflected the knowledge of the field at the time and were defensible to a group of professionals in the same sub-field. As with medicine, differing opinions are not a torpedo to a reasonable decision, so long as the decision-maker is supported by evidence and professional opinion. Unlike medicine, however, there must be a recursive responsibility: as knowledge of the field changes, and given AI's capacity to learn, there will be an obligation to respond and adapt to known changes and issues in the field.

4.3.4. Breach of Duty: Doctors

While there are substantial overlaps in assessing standard of care and breach for non-diagnostic medical applications and driving, how courts will treat transport and medical applications, there are some unique properties regarding medical negligence for diagnostics that are worth examining specifically. Duty of care proceeds exactly the same way: whether there is a duty of care by the provider, through the AI, to the individual in question. The proximate connection between the AI providing care and the individual receiving it will be straightforward, whether or not the application is diagnostic.

Let us assume that the AI application in question is a radiological AI, intended to detect and diagnose lung cancer.[45] However, for purposes of our analysis, let us assume that this AI is capable of both detecting and carrying out treatment, as inserting a human in the loop in such a case would be likely to act as a 'liability sponge' by having a responsibility to re-examine and confirm the scan themselves.[46] Let us assume that the AI diagnoses a false negative, ie, clears the patient as not having points of concern in their radiological scans, and recommends against any treatment.

First, we examine the standard of care of a reasonable radiologist, which brings us back to *Gregg v Scott*: missing a diagnosis will only be deemed negligent if the patient's chances of long-term survival are substantially affected.[47] Negligence must be proven on the balance of probabilities that the missed diagnosis would have altered the changes of long-term survival. Additionally, *Muller v King's College Hospital* contributes that while generally speaking opposite opinions may be held by medical professionals and neither opinion be negligently held, purely

[45] Denise Grady, 'A.I. Took a Test to Detect Lung Cancer. It Got an A' *New York Times* (20 May 2019): nytimes.com/2019/05/20/health/cancer-artificial-intelligence-ct-scans.html.

[46] Future regulation may resolve this, and arguably should, but given the accompanying paperwork of complex though not-entirely autonomous AI applications such as semi-autonomous vehicles, current applications are likely to come with exculpatory contractual paperwork regarding AI where their work is 'supervised' by a doctor in the loop.

[47] *Gregg v Scott* [2005] UKHL 2.

diagnostic cases where 'there is no weighing of risks and benefits, only misreporting which may or may not be negligent', the fixed standard 'of reasonable skill and care, fixed by law' intervenes.[48] In summary, for a human healthcare professional to be negligent in a case of a missed diagnosis, the misdiagnosis must have altered the patient's chance of survival from above 50 per cent to below 50 per cent. This is an objective standard and will not take into account differing opinions. This 'standard of a reasonable radiologist' remains for the AI radiological application. There is an exact correlation between the two, and whether or not the diagnosis was missed by a human or an AI is more or less irrelevant.

This does, however, alter the 'standard of a reasonable provider' as compared with a human practitioner. If the challenging party can show that a non-negligent provider would indeed have caught the diagnosis, whether or not the individual's treatment would have substantially changed, the provider must show through their training, testing and standards data that this was not a known error, *and* that training, testing and standards were carried out with due diligence. If the error was known, such as the continued difficulty of Uber's identification of pedestrians walking bicycles, then the provider has shown negligence in failing to address the error. If the error was not known, then the provider's process will be examined in the same fashion as outlined above for the vehicle, whether their process was carried out in good faith; to the best knowledge of the field at the time; and with defensible choices in training, testing and XAI processes. This will provide a narrow possibility for the producer to prove due diligence –narrower than the AI's human counterpart.

This slight difference in liability level is for two reasons: first, it reflects the higher standard of diagnostic negligence present for human medical practitioners. Second, it reflects the characteristics of AI: the ability to fix errors across a multitude of functioning AI at once; and that the system with which the AI must contend is more fixed – scans are a two-dimensional grid with limited and well-understood inputs. There is a far greater level of foreseeability of what the AI is likely to encounter: bones, different types of tissue, polyps, cancer and accidental scans of jewellery or other body parts. Recall the AI quadrant:

Figure 8 Input and consequences of AI (see also above ch 1, Figure 1)

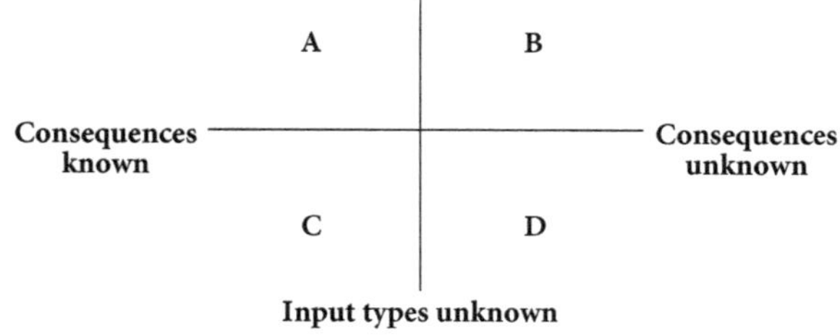

[48] *Muller* (n 42).

Radiological input types are known, and so are their consequences – they fall solidly into quadrant A. The ways in which harm will occur are well known, and as predictable as possible, yet the consequences are potentially severe. Finding the balance between making AI as safe as possible and not blocking innovation need not bow to accidents purely for the sake of novelty, and testing for medical applications has always been strict. Additionally, in order for this examination of the provider to occur, they still must have fallen below the standard of negligence in missing the diagnosis in the first place.

4.4. AI Specific Liability Issues

Across the examination of AI and negligence, there are a few additional characteristics to keep in mind. First, regular tort applications account for the statistical likelihood of a harm occurring and balance the cost of preventing that harm against the likelihood. This is a fundamentally interesting point for AI, because for humans, a 'one in a million' chance is minimal enough to avoid for all but the cheapest remedies. An AI, however, may be replicating an action across countless embodied applications a million times an hour. In balancing likelihood against prevention cost, does the likelihood of the occurrence stack, or is it statistically independent? In other words, will this potential act occur once in every million occurrences, such as winning a 'lucky cap' pop bottle contest wherein there are a guaranteed number of winners per million, or will it occur with a probability of one in a million each time, such as playing a lottery terminal?[49] If the result is the latter, assuming the potential harm is not horrendously high or the cost of prevention incredibly low, the risk may be acceptable even with an AI. However, given the repeatable nature of AI 'reasoning' and actions, a one per million chance may no longer be acceptable, depending on the level of potential harm per million. Furthermore, because an AI causing accidental death has an inherently high potential for harm, the acceptable level of cost to fix an issue is correspondingly also high.

Second, AI standards must deal with reasonably foreseeable use *and* misuse. Different justifications have different levels of accepted exculpatory literature and disclaimers, but for AI causing bodily harm, it is clear that providers should examine not only the ways the AI is intended to be used, but also how it will foreseeably be misused. For example, an AI escalator would certainly have a person run up or down it the wrong way. An autonomous forklift will certainly have its prongs sat or stood on to lift the occupier. An autonomous dog-walker will be put to walking other animals.[50] Because the decisions of what is foreseeable and how to deal with it remain with the human, the question of foreseeability need not be adapted, but may rest heavier on producers than many applications given the lack of failsafe provided by a human user.

[49] There are predetermined settings for lottery machine probabilities.
[50] But it may not be foreseeable that someone might try to walk a bear or a moose with it.

Third, AI is particularly vulnerable to edge cases. As alluded to in our stilt-walker example, there will be cases on which the AI simply cannot be trained – the 'all possible worlds' problem. Hard-coded software is insufficient to respond to all possible scenarios, and for applications such as automated vehicles 'machine-learning algorithms are mostly used along with some pre-determined rules'.[51] However, it is paradoxically 'known' that the AI will encounter the 'unknown' – that which it will not be able to classify or predict. Given this reality, it is crucial that AI of dangerous application – certainly those causing accidental death – be capable of dealing with scenarios in which they encounter the unexpected. For example, an autonomous vehicle driving through Regina, Saskatchewan might encounter 'Chewbacca the Alpaca', an alpaca who enjoys riding around in his owner's vehicle with his head stuck out of the window.

Figure 9 Chewbacca the Alpaca[52]

While Chewbacca delights many human road users, he may confound AI, as he substantially alters the shape of the vehicle while the AI tries to classify said vehicle in order to predict its road movement. Producers are not required to test the car on alpacas riding shotgun, but it is crucial that the autonomous vehicle be capable of reacting safely to unusual scenarios.

Fourth, AI does not share the inherent frailties of humanity. This is particularly evident in the analysis of human driver liability. Humans have undiagnosed ailments, such as blood glucose issues, that can unexpectedly cause driving issues.

[51] Kasap (n 36) 30.

[52] Cally Stephanow, 'Sask. Alpaca Becomes Internet Sensation after Road Trip through Regina' *CTV News Regina* (15 May 2020): regina.ctvnews.ca/sask-alpaca-becomes-internet-sensation-after-road-trip-through-regina-1.4942137.

Humans may only see in one direction at once and must focus on the direction of concern for the vehicle at the time, ie, forwards during a difficult turn, and not at a bollard partly behind the vehicle. AI does not have these frailties, nor should it. While cars may not be required to 'see' in 360 degrees at all times, there is an expectation that they be able to detect in all major avenues of driving: while a human cannot look backwards and forwards at the same time, AI must be capable of looking both backwards and forwards at given times – the AI has multiple potential directions of focus, and both can and should take multiple information inputs into account. Such adaptations are particularly important given the lack of particular types of information peculiarities that humans do have access to, such as body language and signalling to, for example, show acceptance of pedestrian movement by the driver. AI is capable of being tested on a variety of scenarios and will react without the imposition of human factors such as stress or surprise impacting the result, and so should be capable of performing in a generally predictable fashion.

Fifth, there are a variety of expectations set by the AI provider. As mentioned, the AI provider is likely to try to contract out of a variety of liabilities. And while it is important to note that providers cannot contract out of liability for personal injury resulting from negligence, there will certainly be conditions imposed on using the AI, such as 'must have both hands on the wheel' for semi-autonomous vehicles. In determining negligence and reasonable expectations, the court should, as it is in other areas, be guided by the expectations set by the company: in other words, its marketing and accompanying literature, possibly in conflict. A company advertising a vehicle that is fully and safely autonomous at all times, but which requires in the literature accompanying sale that a human driver be able to take over control that all times, is an expectation in direct conflict. There is a great deal of temptation for companies to overhype AI,[53] to the potential detriment of their users. Companies found making conflicting statements about the actual capabilities of their products, particularly those causing accidental death, will be held to the stricter standard provided, ie, if a vehicle is advertised as perfectly autonomous, the buyer or user has a reasonable expectation that said vehicle is suitable for that purpose. Additionally, while regular products have the defence that a product was as safe as known standards at the time in which it was provided for sale, AI products do not: once an issue is known, the producer has the recursive duty to update.

4.5. Conclusion

In summary, the use of AI in life-saving, and thus life-taking, applications is attractive enough to warrant consideration. While the applications must certainly be tested before allowed onto the market,[54] the law must be capable of examining a

[53] K Walch, 'Is AI Overhyped?' (*Forbes*, 4 June 2020): forbes.com/sites/cognitiveworld/2020/06/04/is-ai-overhyped/.

[54] To be discussed in section 7.1.1.

situation in which an AI has caused bodily harm. The examination of negligence for AI capable of causing accidental death does not differ entirely from its human counterparts; it simply adds further dimensions to account for the existence of a decision-making entity between humans. The first standard for the AI is that of a reasonable professional human in that capacity: where a human would not be judged to be negligent in its actions, neither will the AI. However, where a comparison is unavailable or a human would not be negligent (or the case is around a diagnosis), the court must look at the AI and its producers to examine the standard of care and its breach. This examination will look at both the moments of the accident, and the training of the AI throughout its lifecycle: what did the producer know? What ought the producer to have known? What ought the producer to have tested for? There will be a rebuttable presumption of liability where the producer can provide explanations of the building, training and testing process, showing the process can be favourably compared with the known standards in the field. In the case of a misdiagnosis, the court will examine the AI in question along the above lines but will probably not accept the exculpatory defence that the missed diagnosis would not have substantially changed the patient's outcome, a defence of liability available to human practitioners in negligence cases.

In the examination of the AI, several aspects should be kept in mind: the potential repeatable nature of AI decisions; the additionally foreseeable use and misuse without an intervening human; the known necessity of training for edge cases; the lack of defence of human frailties, known or unknown; and the expectations as set by the AI provider. Explanations provided by and to the courts should reflect those best practices discussed in section 3.6, particularly by the producers in their attempts to prove due diligence. Explanations must not only be truthful, but the XAI methods used to obtain them defensible as a choice of tool.

With the participation of expert witnesses and AI producers desiring their own exculpation, it seems likely that courts could reasonably examine AI and its use with a view to determining the necessary elements of negligence for liability: duty of care, standard of care and breach of the standard of care. This is, however, only half the puzzle. While it is necessary that the courts be capable of dealing with AI where harm has occurred, it is societally desirable that AI causes as minimal harm as possible. While providers are of course incentivised to minimise harm for fear of being liable, it is often necessary to provide regulation in advance of an issue occurring in order to minimise harm in the first place. This leads us to the second question of importance: how can we reduce the number of people AI kills?

5

Current Regulatory Approaches

The ultimate goal of regulation is to provide an ecosystem that encourages beneficial AI while ensuring it is as safe as possible. To achieve this requires two necessary components: establishing a regulatory structure within which producers can operate; and dealing with consequences when an incident arises. The previous chapters have examined how consequences can be addressed in the case of an incident, but it is equally important to establish a system in which satisfactorily safe AI will be produced. Such systems are necessary to implement a level of safeguards prior to the AI's provision to the market. Productive regulation does not merely spring into place after an incident has occurred; it needs to be designed so that appropriate safeguards are put in place, while creating a predictable environment for AI development and use. How these systems are designed depends on the jurisdiction and its particular goals.

5.1. Introduction

In taking steps to regulate, states and other powers have a set of tools at their disposal. While their goals determine what tools will be used, existing regulation and socio-political makeup of the state will have some influence as to how those tools might be used. For example, a pure dictatorship would want a form of regulation that cedes no power to other parties and might regulate very heavily how an activity might be done or a product produced. How regulatory tools are used can be referred to as regulatory theory – how states approach their regulatory goals. While reality may not reflect the exact designations of theories, regulatory theory nonetheless provides a range of choices in how states approach an issue. This chapter proceeds by discussing the range of available regulatory theory approaches, then investigates how selected states have applied their own approaches to regulating AI thus far.

5.2. Regulatory Theory

> 'Regulation' is not a concept that travels well, in either a centred or 'decentred' form. As any who have attempted to study 'regulation' outside of English-speaking countries will be aware, there is often no parallel word or even concept.[1]

[1] J Black, 'Critical Reflections on Regulation' (2002) 27 *Australasian Journal of Legal Philosophy* 1, 2.

The concept of regulation is a tricky one. As renowned regulatory theorist Julia Black notes above, it is not a universal concept. It involves, rather, the interplay 'between structural and systemic conditions and actors and agencies over time and at different levels'.[2] Rather than defining regulation, it is perhaps more efficient to frame it through its intended goal: the establishment of a flourishing system. That system may be a market system, a healthcare system, a financial system, or perhaps a digital ecosystem, but the intention is the same: to establish a compromise in power such that the system can continue to greatest possible benefit. The saying that 'a true compromise occurs when each party is unhappy' may indeed be applicable here – parties with power do not wish to cede it, and parties without it may wish the rules to be more suited to their aims, or their positions better protected. This is a definition that well suits the 'regulation of AI', as the goal is not to allow AI developers to proceed as they wish with no regard for the public, nor to stifle innovation in the pursuit of an immediately perfect product.

Regulation can be understood as involving at minimum three different parties: the regulator; the regulated; and those experiencing effects of those regulations. In UK financial regulation, for example, this would be the Financial Conduct Authority (FCA), the finance sector and those engaging with the finance sectors – businesses and individuals. The FCA's role 'includes protecting consumers, keeping industry stable, and promoting healthy competition between financial service providers'.[3] This aligns well with framing regulation through intended goals: the establishment of a flourishing system by keeping a balance between allowing industry to grow, protecting consumers, ensuring stability, and encouraging innovation through competition. This is not to say that maintaining the balance is easy, or necessarily achieved through regulation ahead of the stormy seas of a financial crisis.

Of the three parties at play in regulation, the regulator and the regulated must generally have a balance that maintains the inclusion of the third party: the consumer, recipient, or user. Broadly, there are three ways in which regulatory power can occur: entirely in the hands of the regulator; entirely in the hands of the regulated; or somewhere in between the two.[4] An entirely 'top-down' or regulator approach is called 'command and control'. The balance of power rests entirely with the regulator, at least in theory, and there is no dialogue between the regulator and other parties.[5] There are numerous examples of such regulatory approaches, such as tax collection and EU competition law.[6] While Black points out that much

[2] I Losoncz, 'Methodological Approaches and Considerations in Regulatory Research' in P Drahos (ed), *Regulatory Theory* (ANU Press 2017): jstor.org/stable/j.ctt1q1crtm.12.

[3] 'Financial Conduct Authority' (GOV.UK): gov.uk/government/organisations/financial-conduct-authority.

[4] While it could be argued that the public does indeed control through regulation through its votes, this is indirect. A direct form of regulation via the affected public would be more akin to Robin Hood.

[5] J Black, 'Decentring Regulation: Understanding the Role of Regulation and Self-Regulation in a "Post-Regulatory" World' (2001) 54 *Current Legal Problems* 103.

[6] ibid.

description of command and control regulation is more of a caricature than an acknowledgment of the approach as a whole, the downsides are in large supply: 'poorly targeted rules, rigidity, ossification, under- or over-enforcement, unintended consequences'.[7] Command and control legislation in general can mean that regulatory instruments are unsophisticated, as the regulating party has an insufficiently fine-tuned grasp of the core of the issue intended to be regulated.[8] As an example of an insufficiently tuned grasp of the concept at issue, consider former Australian Prime Minister Malcolm Turnbull's statement that 'the laws of mathematics are very commendable, but the only law that applies in Australia is the law of Australia'.[9] The regulatory process for command and control is assumed to be linear, unilateral and have a clear cause and effect, with a progression from policy formation through implementation.[10]

On the other side of the balance of power is an entirely self-regulated group, such as Canadian law societies; while 'other professional regulators move toward smaller, skill-based boards and other regulatory models', Canadian law societies remain almost entirely self-governed.[11] While it could be argued that this is merely command and control on a smaller scale, the fact remains that there is minimal if any barrier or differentiation between the governing and the governed, the regulator and the regulated, all while aiming to protect a third group: those interacting with lawyers, ie, the public. Arguments in favour of such a system, at least for lawyers, are that '[i]t would pose a conflict of interest if the organization that regulated lawyers was directly or indirectly controlled by the government'.[12] Justice is always a concern, and with the state often a party to legal affairs, lawyers need to be separate. Additionally, though, is that the actors in the system best placed to regulate it are those who understand its workings on a granular, and arguably personal, level. There is of course a clear argument against this: that the party intended to be regulated has a clear motivation to reduce barriers to their trade; to protect themselves and fellow practitioners; and to diminish competition with other potential players.[13] A counter-argument somewhere between these two is that lawyers can be trusted to recognise the inherent importance in fostering public trust in their governing system, with the implicit threat of losing the protected status of being self-governed if they do not operate their self-governance accordingly.

[7] ibid.

[8] ibid.

[9] Rachel Roberts, 'Laws of Maths Don't Apply Here, Says Australian Prime Minister' *Independent* (15 July 2017): independent.co.uk/news/malcolm-turnbull-prime-minister-laws-mathematics-do-not-apply-australia-encryption-l-a7842946.html.

[10] Black, 'Critical Reflections on Regulation' (n 1).

[11] 'Self-Regulation: The End of an Era? Lawyer Discipline and the Role of Law Societies' (*Canadian Lawyer*, 14 November 2019): canadianlawyermag.com/resources/professional-regulation/self-regulation-the-end-of-an-era-lawyer-discipline-and-the-role-of-law-societies/321919.

[12] ibid.

[13] There are specific requirements for who is allowed to practise law in Canada, eg, they must, among other requirements, be a member in good standing of a Canadian law society.

Self-governance is not, justice concerns aside, an appropriate approach for AI: while AI experts may be those best placed to understand it and may indeed wish to level the playing field for beneficial competition, AI does not share the same overarching concerns that law does for protecting the public interest. While not every lawyer may promote this concern, there is a clear understanding that the field of law relies implicitly on public interest, and that the field must and must be seen to be protecting its clients. Where there may certainly be public-interest AI actors, it is far less of a rights-based field inherently, although it is certainly rights-impacting.

Most common are regulatory systems that share a discussion between the regulator and the regulated. This is for good reason. There are many aspects of a system that may be important to influence or control, such as safety, stability, or protection of individual rights and health. No company is likely to voluntarily pay taxes, for example. However, there are considerable potential benefits from taking input from those most intimately familiar with the system, ie, the regulated. It is in the best interests of the regulated or system player (business, institution, etc) to have a playing field that does not unduly benefit another player, nor expose the system to criticism, scepticism, or fear from the public. There were few commercial zeppelins after Hindenburg, regulated or not. System players have a vested interest in attempting to achieve a playing field wherein rivals must play by the same rules, and who better to know the loopholes?

The balance of power and discussions between regulators and the regulated can occur in any variety of ways. Black remarks that 'regulation is being seen as "decentred" from the state, and even from the well recognised forums of self-regulation'.[14] While command and control legislation may have techniques backed by sanctions, decentred regulation has five central points: 'complexity, fragmentation, interdependencies, ungovernability, and the rejection of a clear distinction between public and private'.[15]

Complexity refers to both causal complexity – having multiple causal paths – and the interactions between actors in the system. While the potential for multiple causal paths may have an appealing parallel with the Rashomon Effect,[16] it is also a necessary recognition of the intricate nature of the system. AI developers are influenced not only by individuals' work, but by the data they hold, the permissions they have, the skills available to them, the influence of regulators, and the ever-expanding nature of the field. The understanding of the field is inherently shaped by its development: while it may be conceptually simple to anticipate whether a type of fuel might explode disadvantageously in a rocket, it may be more conceptually complex to anticipate how an algorithm might 'trip' itself when employed. Problems are more likely to be identified after they occur, and robust testing, as discussed in section 4.4, cannot anticipate all possible worlds.

[14] Black, 'Critical Reflections on Regulation' (n 1) 1.
[15] ibid, 4.
[16] The existence of multiple solutions, all potentially plausible – see section 3.3.

Relationships between actors are by nature complex as producers must navigate between the potential and the possible, the public and the private, the ethical and the unknown. Regulators must balance societal needs – safety, reliability, trust, human rights – with market concerns such as fostering innovation, keeping key market producers in their jurisdiction, and solving the problems of other fields – transportation, green initiatives, healthcare, etc. The public, on an individual level, is concerned with safety, their own rights, others' rights and access to innovation.

Fragmentation for decentred regulation is fragmentation of knowledge, power and control.[17] In essence, 'no single actor has all knowledge required to solve complex, diverse and dynamic problems, and no single actor has the overview necessary to employ all the instruments needed to make regulation effective'.[18] The industry knows more about itself than does the government.[19] Fragmentation of power means that there is no single centric point from which regulatory power flows, meaning that multiple positions have the ability to exert control or influence on the system as a whole.[20] There is a fundamental interdependency between regulator and regulated: the allocation of regulatory responsibilities lies between the two, and the principles for that allocation are formalised in a co-regulatory structure.

Ungovernability refers to the idea that 'actors will continue to develop or act in their own way in the absence of intervention. Actors or systems are self[-] regulating, and regulation cannot take their behaviour as a constant'.[21] This has several implications: unintended behaviour and outcomes will arise; the form of regulation may vary based on the relationship of the regulated and the form of compliance; the process cannot be dominated by a single actor; autonomy of different actors renders entirely external regulation very difficult; and the traditionally regulated parties have the capacity to self-regulate to a significant extent.[22] This is a critical point for regulation of AI. Formal, top-down regulation is inherently reactionary, in that it would be extremely difficult for an external regulator to predict the immediate future of an inventive sector more quickly than the sector itself. Few sectors demonstrate this better than AI, for two reasons: pace of growth, and nature of the technology. The field of AI can grow exceptionally quickly and is experiencing a boom. There is, and has been since the 1980s, a debate over whether general AI is possible.[23] This debate is not a debate within regulators, it is occurring within the field itself. To attempt a regulatory structure before general AI is realised could mean pouring time, resources and speculative confusion into a technology that may never exist. AI as a field is technology and research led,

[17] Black, 'Critical Reflections on Regulation' (n 1).
[18] ibid, 5.
[19] ibid.
[20] Regulatory control rather than, say, buying power on the part of the consumer.
[21] Black, 'Critical Reflections on Regulation' (n 1) 6.
[22] ibid.
[23] R Fjelland, 'Why General Artificial Intelligence Will Not Be Realized' (2020) 7(1) *Humanities and Social Sciences Communications*: nature.com/articles/s41599-020-0494-4.

not regulation led. Therefore, for any suitable/appropriate/effective governance to exist in an early stage, the field must be at least to some extent self-governing. This is supported by the many non-governmental consortia, some run by corporate partnerships such as Google and Microsoft, some by non-corporates such as the Future of Life Institute and OpenAI.

Ungovernability might best be framed for AI as the necessity for internal standard-setting.[24] Internal refers to inside the industry, rather than inside a particular provider. The field of AI faces numerous hurdles, both technical and societal. Technical expertise may be shared through journals, conferences, papers, websites, or simply over coffee. This is not to say that deep industry secrets are bandied about like business cards, but that AI like any field of science shares approaches, techniques and discoveries. Technical expertise in solving a problem may emerge from a long-used, stringently tested formulation, or from an entirely new approach. Governability or standard setting in this regard is the sharing, formally and informally, of the evolution of techniques. Standards here change without the impact or influence of regulatory route-setting. One parallel example is the 2020 SARS-CoV-2 vaccines: the fastest vaccine previously developed took four years, and yet multiple vaccines were developed using new mRNA techniques in under a year.[25] Such advances have changed medical research as we know it, yet were not governed by new legislation. Rules and regulations were those structured around defining the safety of previous efforts. This is not to say that mRNA vaccines are untrustworthy – quite the contrary – but to underline that standard setting in such industries is and must be led by innovation.

The second hurdle of standard setting is for societal reasons. The public is rightly concerned with the potential negative impacts of AI. This can come from any one of innumerable bases: surveillance,[26] criminal sentencing,[27] immigration,[28] weapons,[29] etc. Where the intricacies of industries such as finance have potentially deep impacts on individuals, the general lack of understanding of AI coupled with pop-culture fed fears multiply the well-founded concerns regarding AI.

[24] See also medical devices regulation, which focuses on standards for production, rather than, for example, the device itself. K Alexander and PJ Clarkson, 'Good design practice for medical devices and equipment, Part I: a review of current literature' (2009) 24 *Journal of Medical Engineering & Technology* 1: tandfonline.com/doi/abs/10.1080/030919000293987.

[25] P Ball, 'The Lightning-Fast Quest for COVID Vaccines – and What It Means for Other Diseases' (2020) 589 *Nature* 16: nature.com/articles/d41586-020-03626-1.

[26] S Feldstein, 'The Global Expansion of AI Surveillance' (Carnegie Endowment for International Peace, 2019): jstor.org/stable/resrep20995.1.

[27] R Piccolo, 'AI in Criminal Sentencing: A Risk to Our Human Rights?' (Law Society of South Australia, 2018): Bulletin search.informit.org/doi/abs/10.3316/agispt.20190121005803.

[28] B Ajana, 'Augmented Borders: Big Data and the Ethics of Immigration Control' (2015) 13 Journal of Information, Communication and Ethics in Society 58: doi.org/10.1108/JICES-01-2014-0005.

[29] HM Roff and R Moyes, 'Meaningful Human Control, Artificial Intelligence and Autonomous Weapons', Informal Meeting of Experts on Lethal Autonomous Weapons Systems: article36.org/wp-content/uploads/2016/04/MHC-AI-and-AWS-FINAL.pdf.

While the ethics of data gathering, use and assessment are not the key focus of this chapter, they are nonetheless a crucial point for the industry as a whole. As discussed in chapter one, bias is one of if not the most important point for safe, fair and ethical use. The AI industry has an uphill battle not just to develop AI that is unbiased, or at bare minimum quantifiably less biased than humans, but to convince the public that it has done so. Because AI has the potential to shape nearly every aspect of human life,[30] it is absolutely crucial that the industry engenders, and more importantly earns, the public's trust. The industry knows this, and this is what self-regulating bodies aim to achieve. Internal standard-setting arises at all levels: from broad industry coalitions, to individual companies, to individual projects. Google's 'Objectives for AI applications' are a good example of this:

1. Be socially beneficial.
2. Avoid creating or reinforcing unfair bias.
3. Be built and tested for safety.
4. Be accountable to people.
5. Incorporate privacy design principles.
6. Uphold high standards of scientific excellence.
7. Be made available for uses that accord with these principles.[31]

Google as a highly visible corporation is aware of the tightrope it walks between rolling out new technologies ahead of competition, and being found discriminating, creating bias, or otherwise disadvantaging its users. Yet society cannot trust internal debate to resolve these issues, for example, noted AI ethics researcher Timnit Gebru was forced out of the company, allegedly due to her co-authorship of a paper showing facial recognition's inaccuracy 'at identifying women and people of colour, which means its use can end up discriminating against them'.[32] Regulating at any level is not easy, and fractured needs and approaches provide ample evidence for the ungovernability of AI as a field.

Lastly, decentred regulation is founded on the rejection of a clear distinction between public and private, wherein regulation occurs via both state and non-state actors, both separately and together.[33] Static, pre-ordained divisions are eschewed and '[r]egulators focus not on detailed compliance but on whether the [regulated's] internal systems and processes can deliver the outcome which the regulator seeks'.[34] The variable regulator/regulated relationship can also include middle parties such as trade associations, brought in for expertise on interpretation

[30] Hairdressing perhaps an exception; see section 1.1.3.

[31] 'Our Principles' (*Google AI*): ai.google/principles/.

[32] K Hao, 'We Read the Paper That Forced Timnit Gebru out of Google. Here's What It Says' (*MIT Technology Review*): technologyreview.com/2020/12/04/1013294/google-ai-ethics-research-paper-forced-out-timnit-gebru/.

[33] J Black, 'Forms and Paradoxes of Principles Based Regulation' (2008) LSE Studies Working Paper No 13: ssrn.com/abstract=1267722.

[34] ibid.

and meaning.[35] This too is an interesting point for AI regulation. Certainly, it is a strategy pursued by Singapore, whose AI regulation is found in the Model AI Governance Framework,[36] linked closely to the 'Compendium of Use Cases' and the 'Implementation and Self Assessment Guide for Organisations'. Clearly there were in-depth discussions back and forth between the Personal Data Protection Commission (PDPC) and major AI developers being regulated. However, where other jurisdictions such as the European Union may suggest a more 'command and control' presence, there is also a degree of co-regulation through calls for consultation on the EU AI Act.

How, then, do these approaches to regulatory theory play out in practice? Where jurisdictions may espouse a certain regulatory aim, their regulatory approach and structure must not only match, but be integratable into existing legislation and govern the 'ungovernable' aspects of AI.

In brief, command and control regulatory theory provides that the state has the capacity to be the sole commander and controller of regulation, is effective at doing so, and there is no back and forth between the regulating body and other stakeholders.[37] It was also demonstrated in the EU's report detailing how liability was proposed to function under EU regulation,[38] though a greater degree of discussion did take place regarding the EU AI Act.

Conversational regulation occurs where there is an ongoing discussion between the regulated and the regulator, providing 'their interpretation and appropriate application or waiver in the [regulatee's] circumstances', consisting of elements of commitment, access, authority, trust and accountability.[39] This sort of back and forth conversational regulation is demonstrated by Singapore's ongoing conversations and adaptations between government and private industry, as detailed below. Co-regulation shares some of these characteristics, occurring when 'industry enjoys considerable flexibility in shaping self-regulatory guidelines, consumer advocacy groups have a seat at the table and government sets default requirements and retains general oversight'.[40] Co-regulatory models rely on corporations or associations to perform some regulatory functions, while conversational regulation is generally influenced and informed by the industry but does not necessarily provide bilateral governance power. Both conversational and co-regulation are shown to relative degrees by the creation of the new US National Artificial Intelligence Initiative Office, which serves in various capacities as a contact point for different branches of government and provides funding

[35] ibid.

[36] 'Model Artificial Intelligence Governance Framework Second Edition': pdpc.gov.sg/-/media/files/pdpc/pdf-files/resource-for-organisation/ai/sgmodelaigovframework2.pdf.

[37] J Black, 'Talking about Regulation' [1988)] *Practical Law* 77.

[38] European Parliament, 'Report with Recommendations to the Commission on a Civil Liability Regime for Artificial Intelligence (2020/2014(INL))'.

[39] ibid.

[40] I Rubinstein, 'The Future of Self-Regulation Is Co-Regulation' (2016) Social Science Research Network SSRN Scholarly Paper ID 2848513: papers.ssrn.com/abstract=2848513.

and skill-training within the industry. The degree to which regulation is in parts conversational or co-regulatory will become clearer as the department establishes itself and its guidelines.

Responsive regulation is premised on a personal relationship of regulatory interaction, and provides that regulators work closely with regulatees '[choosing] between punishment and persuasion, recognizing that neither approach works all the time'.[41] Essentially, it is predicated on direct involvement by the regulator who knows 'what behaviours constitute compliance and non-compliance, [is] able to interpret accurately signals from industry, and [is] able to calibrate appropriate responses'.[42] It has further been proposed that 'really responsive' regulation should respond not only to the regulated group or firm, 'but also to the operating and cognitive frameworks of firms; the institutional environment and performance of the regulatory regime; the different logics of regulatory tools and strategies; and to changes in each of these elements'.[43] While this approach is evidenced in part by the Singapore approach in terms of its responsive calibration, the importance of responding to these expanded elements will be expanded upon below as a fundamental step in regulating AI as a new technology.

5.3. State Approaches

The legislative jurisdictions of Singapore, the European Union, the United States and the United Kingdom are examined here because of their vastly different approaches to the regulation of AI, and their progress relative to many other jurisdictions. Singapore as a city-state has unilateral dexterity to move quickly, work directly with partners and delve into specifics. The European Union as a legislative conglomerate must work with a variety of government stakeholders and a variety of existing legislation. The United States has a legacy of facilitating rather than framing AI construction and must contend with the varying approaches of its changing administrations. The United Kingdom has structured around facilitating business interests, such as the National AI Strategy. Each of these jurisdictions offers something by their approach, and it seems likely that AI governance globally will be influenced by these initial attempts – both their successes and their failures.

Because the focus of this book is ultimately on AI causing accidental rather than intentional death, there will broadly be an exclusion of military-specific AI governance. It should also be noted that a great deal of traction has been gained by non-governmental consortia, many of whom have established principles, guidelines and frameworks of their own. In corporate governance this includes

[41] C Ford, 'Prospects for Scalability: Relationships and Uncertainty in Responsive Regulation: Prospects for Scalability' (2013) 7 *Regulation & Governance* 14: doi.wiley.com/10.1111/j.1748-5991.2012.01166.x.

[42] ibid.

[43] R Baldwin and J Black, 'Really Responsive Regulation' (2008) 71 *Modern Law Review* 59: onlinelibrary.wiley.com/doi/abs/10.1111/j.1468-2230.2008.00681.x.

both Google and Microsoft, and in not-for-profit organisations the Future of Life Institute; the MIT Media Lab; the Machine Intelligence Research Institute; and the United Nations, to name a few. Even sector-specific organisations such as the American College of Radiology have begun to develop their own rules or guidelines. However, as all of these groups and organisations are self-governing or compliance is optional, they do not share the same effects as government-produced legislation.

Examined in this chapter are the approaches that the sample states have taken in regulating AI en masse: the specific pieces of legislation and their effects. The approaches described and analysed are from a purely functionalist perspective. There is of course more to the regulatory story: why these states (and others) have approached regulation in this way comes from a particular outlook on how regulation should occur, and what it should aim to achieve.

The theories discussed in section 5.5.2 give some insight into not only how regulatory bodies can interact with those regulated, but also how responsive actions such as liability and punitive allocation can be effectively managed in a changing technological landscape. The need for compliance is predicated on the need to understand how to comply, an exceedingly difficult requirement in a turmoil of technological advancement if regulation is a one-way, command and control approach. Conversely, an adaptive approach to regulation such as conversational regulation can cause uncertainty to regulatees, making compliance difficult in another way.[44] This chapter will focus on explaining the current state of regulatory affairs.

It should be briefly noted that the AI creation process inherently conflicts with the fundamental principles of data protection to which all four jurisdictions subscribe, albeit in varying ways. Any AI that is even slightly complex requires vast amounts of data, and while there are many AI applications that do not interact directly with humans – those mapping the solar system, observing natural environments, creating products in factories – there are many more that do interact directly, and therefore need data based on humans. Any AI that has basic speech recognition needs untold terabytes of personal data, a medical AI far more. Where data protection espouses that controllers should 'limit the collection of personal information to what is directly relevant and necessary to accomplish a specified purpose [and] retain the data only for as long as is necessary to fulfil that purpose',[45] areas of AI such as unsupervised or semi-supervised learning are provided with all possible data for such cases where the AI might make previously unconsidered connections. While classification distinctions between data controllers and data processors, and technical approaches such as anonymisation and pseudonymisation are beyond the scope of this examination, it is worthwhile to note that while

[44] Black, 'Talking about Regulation' (n 37).

[45] European Union, 'European Data Protection Supervisor Glossary': edps.europa.eu/data-protection/data-protection/glossary/d_en.

all four jurisdictions begin to address the governance of AI, the ramifications of the data involved must be kept in mind. Data protection will not be analysed in depth in this book given that it does not directly relate to high-level physical harms but will be noted with regard to collection practices in section 7.2.

5.3.1. Singapore

Singapore, like many Commonwealth jurisdictions, has a parliamentary system of government with a legal tradition rooted in the English system.[46] Sources of law include the Singapore Constitution, legislation, subsidiary legislation such as rules and regulations, and judge-made law.[47] The legislature, executive and judiciary each act within their own sphere of power, and laws passed by Parliament must be consistent with the Singapore Constitution.[48] The Personal Data Protection Commission (PDPC) was established in 2013 to serve as Singapore's 'main authority' on data protection.[49] The PDPC's remit includes the governance of AI, and it has collaborated with other entities to create governance guidelines.[50]

Singapore established the Advisory Council on the Ethical Use of AI and Data in 2018, with the purpose of:

(a) advising the Government on ethical, policy and governance issues arising from the use of data-driven technologies in the private sector; and
(b) supporting the Government in providing general guidance to businesses to minimise ethical, governance and sustainability risks, and to mitigate adverse impact on consumers from the use of data-driven technologies.[51]

This Advisory Council is still in place.

In 2018, the PDPC published its Discussion Paper on Artificial Intelligence and Personal Data, which presented the Commission's 'preliminary analysis of some of the issues pertinent to the commercial development and adoption of AI solutions', with the objective of proposing 'an accountability-based framework for discussing ethical, governance and consumer protection issues related to the commercial development of AI in a systematic and structured manner'.[52] The PDPC then released the first edition of the 'Model AI Governance Framework' or

[46] 'Our Legal System' (Singapore Ministry of Law): mlaw.gov.sg/about-us/our-legal-system/.

[47] ibid.

[48] SS Gill, 'Legal Systems in Singapore: Overview' *Thomson Reuters Practical Law*: uk.practicallaw.thomsonreuters.com/w-008-9647?transitionType=Default&contextData=(sc.Default)&firstPage=true.

[49] Personal Data Protection Commission Singapore, 'PDPC/Who We Are' (*Who we are*): pdpc.gov.sg/Who-We-Are.

[50] Such as the Infocomm Media Development Authority of Singapore in the 'Companion to the Model AI Governance Framework – Implementation and Self-Assessment Guide for Organizations' and the Model Framework.

[51] 'Singapore's Approach to AI Governance', Personal Data Protection Commission Singapore: pdpc.gov.sg/help-and-resources/2020/01/model-ai-governance-framework.

[52] Personal Data Protection Commission Singapore, 'Discussion Paper on Artificial Intelligence (AI) and Personal Data – Fostering Responsible Development and Adoption of AI' (5 June 2018).

'Model Framework' in 2019 for 'broader consultation, adoption, and feedback', providing 'detailed and readily-implementable guidance to private sector organisations to address key ethical and governance issues when deploying AI solutions'.[53] This was furthered in the second edition of the 'Model Framework', which was released in January 2020, adding industry examples to show implementation; updated section titles; and minor clarifications.[54] The second edition also provided additional considerations including robustness and reproducibility, while sharing the 'sector- and technology-agnostic approach' of the first edition.[55]

The Model Framework follows two principles: that decisions made by AI systems should be 'explainable, transparent, and fair'; and that AI systems should be human-centric.[56] It also provides four ways in which these principles should be achieved: through internal governance structures and measures; in determining the appropriate level of human involvement to minimise the risk of harm; operations management in minimising bias and taking a risk-based approach including 'explainability, robustness and regular tuning'; and stakeholder interaction and communication in making AI policies known, providing feedback, and ensuring understandable communication.[57]

Parallel with and complementary to the Model Framework are the 'Companion to the Model AI Governance Framework – Implementation and Self Assessment Guide for Organisations',[58] as well as the 'Compendium of Use Cases', volumes I and II. The Implementation and Self Assessment Guide for Organisations is intended to help organisations in aligning their internal governance practices with the Model Framework, and provides a list of industry examples doing so.[59] The Compendium of Use Cases, conversely, '[demonstrates] how local and international organisations across different sectors and sizes implemented or aligned their governance practices with all sections of the Model Framework'.[60] Between volumes I and II the Compendium of Use Cases includes cases from Callsign, DBS Bank, HSBC, MSD, Ngee Ann Polytechnic, Omada Health, UCARE.ai, Visa Asia Pacific, the City of Darwin (Australia), Google, Microsoft, Taiger, IBM, RenalTeam, Sompo Asia Holdings, and Versafleet.[61] The Infocomm Media

[53] Personal Data Protection Commission Singapore, 'PDPC/Singapore's Approach to AI Governance': pdpc.gov.sg/Help-and-Resources/2020/01/Model-AI-Governance-Framework.

[54] 'Model Artificial Intelligence Governance Framework Second Edition' (n 36).

[55] ibid.

[56] ibid.

[57] Personal Data Protection Commission Singapore, 'PDPC/Singapore's Approach to AI Governance' (n 53).

[58] 'Companion to the Model AI Governance Framework – Implementation and Self-Assessment Guide for Organizations' pdpc.gov.sg/-/media/Files/PDPC/PDF-Files/Resource-for-Organisation/AI/SGIsago.pdf.

[59] ibid.

[60] Personal Data Protection Commission Singapore, 'PDPC/Singapore's Approach to AI Governance' (n 53).

[61] 'Compendium of Use Cases: Practical Illustrations of the Model AI Governance Framework (Volume I)': pdpc.gov.sg/-/media/Files/PDPC/PDF-Files/Resource-for-Organisation/AI/SGAIGovUseCases.pdf.

Development Authority of Singapore and the PDPC have with other partners also created a guide that 'helps organisations and employees understand how existing job roles can be redesigned to harness the potential of AI, so that the value of their work is increased'.[62] This too is technologically agnostic,[63] and provides guidance in terms of job transformation; charting pathways between jobs; dealing with barriers to digital transformation; and 'enabling effective communication between employers and employees'.[64]

The Model Framework is a flexible, base-level considerations structure for stakeholders in the AI arena. The Model Framework 'focuses primarily on four broad areas: internal governance structures and measures, human involvement in AI-augmented decision-making, operations management and stakeholder interaction and communication'.[65] The multiple levels of guidance are intended to provide 'regulatory clarity' for a variety of reasons, including market competition.[66] This is shown in the broad focus, for example, how companies can structure internal governance and operations management, but also in the documents that accompany the Model Framework. The Implementation and Self Assessment Guide for Organisations is clearly designed to help companies apply the Model Framework Guidance in an actionable way; the Compendium of Use Cases shows how governing bodies have structured to align their governance practices. While the Compendium of Use Cases is of course useful for governments to assess levels of alignment, it is equally if not more useful for the AI producers who will be governed by those methods. Regulatory clarity not only allows companies to structure in governance-desired ways, but also to legitimate claims of due care and appropriate steps being taken.

Clarity is an underlying theme for another reason, however, building consumer trust in AI deployment.[67] This is reflected in the overarching principles of explainability, transparency and fairness, as well as, of course, human-centricity. The Model Framework is not only structured towards companies but written in such a way to be accessible to consumers as well – assuring them that there is an approved, verifiably process of care undertaken when creating the AI with which they interact. While such trust may or may not be earned, depending on the adherence to the guidelines and their practicality, it is a very foresighted approach to take in engendering consumer trust.

Interestingly, the Singapore governance approach does not differentiate between types of AI applications.[68] While the Compendium of Use Cases includes

[62] Personal Data Protection Commission Singapore, 'PDPC/Singapore's Approach to AI Governance' (n 53).

[63] ie, refers to AI generally rather than specific types of AI applications.

[64] 'A Guide to Job Redesign in the Age of AI': file.go.gov.sg/ai-guide-to-jobredesign.pdf.

[65] 'Model Artificial Intelligence Governance Framework Second Edition' (n 36).

[66] Personal Data Protection Commission Singapore, 'Discussion Paper on Artificial Intelligence' (n 52).

[67] ibid.

[68] Besides the obvious fact that it is aimed at AI.

examples from different sectors, the overall thrust of the mechanisms are intended not to focus on particular types or uses: it is algorithm-agnostic, technology agnostic, sector-agnostic, scale-agnostic and business-model-agnostic.[69] This is not to say that the potential need for sector-specific legislation has been ignored, but that it is to

> *[serve] as a baseline set* of considerations and measures for organisations operating in any sector to adopt. Specific sectors or organisations may choose to include additional considerations and measures or adapt this baseline set to meet their needs. The PDPC encourages and will collaborate with public agencies adapting the Model Framework for their sectors.[70]

The Model Framework also explicitly notes that it does not address ethical principles for AI; issues around data sharing; issues relating to legal liabilities, 'intellectual property rights, and societal impacts of AI (eg on employment competition, unequal access to AI)'.[71] In terms of ethical principles, the Model Framework states that these are being discussed by other groups and partnerships, and that the Framework 'uses existing and common AI ethical principles … [converting] them into implementable practices'.[72]

In June 2023, Singapore launched the AI Verify Foundation and the AI Verify Toolkit.[73] The Foundation itself 'look[s] to boost AI testing capabilities and assurance to meet the needs of companies and regulators globally'.[74] It has seven 'pioneer premium members': the Infocomm Media Development Authority (IMDA); Aicadium (Temasek's AI Centre of Excellence); IBM; Microsof; Google; Red Hat; and Salesforce, with 60 general members being added. AI Verify as a whole appears to be a combination of a testing framework and a software toolkit. The Framework comprises 11 AI governance principles, namely,

- Transparency
- Explainability
- Repeatability/reproducibility
- Safety
- Security
- Robustness
- Fairness

[69] 'Model Artificial Intelligence Governance Framework Second Edition' (n 36).
[70] ibid.
[71] ibid.
[72] ibid.
[73] 'Singapore launches AI Verify Foundation to shape the future of international AI standards through collaboration', Infocomm Media Development Authority (7 June 2023): imda.gov.sg/resources/press-releases-factsheets-and-speeches/press-releases/2023/singapore-launches-ai-verify-foundation-to-shape-the-future-of-international-ai-standards-through-collaboration.
[74] ibid.

- Data governance
- Accountability
- Human agency and oversight
- Inclusive growth, social and environmental well-being.[75]

The software toolkit 'operates within the user's enterprise environment … enabl[ing] users to conduct technical tests on their AI models and record process checks. The toolkit then generates testing reports for the AI model under test'.[76] Users are then able to share their test reports. The tests are currently possible for 'common supervised-learning classification and regression models for most tabular and image datasets', although the testing does not look at ethical standards, and does not 'guarantee [that] AI systems tested will be completely safe or be free from risks or biases'.[77]

The AI Verify Foundation, in partnership with IMDA, also created a draft Model AI Governance Framework for Generative AI. This is an expansion on the second edition of the Model Governance Framework and works to address those issues specific to Generative AI. The announcement of its launch also notes that 'it draws on practical insights from ongoing evaluation tests, conducted within [the] Generative AI Evaluation Sandbox'.[78] The principles of this framework are:

1. Accountability: putting in place the right incentive structure for different players in the AI system development life-cycle to be responsible to end-users.
2. Data: ensuring data quality and addressing potentially contentious training data in a pragmatic way, as data is core to model development.
3. Trusted Development and Deployment: enhancing transparency around baseline safety and hygiene measures based on industry best practices in development, evaluation and disclosure.
4. Incident Reporting: implementing an incident management system for timely notification, remediation and continuous improvements, as no AI system is foolproof.
5. Testing and Assurance: providing external validation and added trust through third-party testing and developing common AI testing standards for consistency.
6. Security: addressing new threat vectors that arise through generative AI models.
7. Content Provenance: transparency about where content comes from as useful signals for end-users.

[75] 'Annex A Fact Sheet – Open sourcing of AI Verify and set up of AI Verify Foundation': imda.gov.sg/-/media/imda/files/news-and-events/media-room/media-releases/2023/06/7-jun---ai-annoucements---annex-a.pdf.

[76] ibid.

[77] ibid.

[78] 'Singapore proposes framework to foster trusted Generative AI development', Infocomm Media Development Authority (16 January 2024): imda.gov.sg/resources/press-releases-factsheets-and-speeches/press-releases/2024/public-consult-model-ai-governance-framework-genai.

8. Safety and Alignment R&D: accelerating R&D through global cooperation among AI Safety Institutes to improve model alignment with human intention and values.
9. AI for Public Good: responsible AI includes harnessing AI to benefit the public by democratising access, improving public sector adoption, upskilling workers and developing AI systems sustainably.[79]

Of these, 'accountability' is particularly interesting. The draft Model notes that

> players along the AI development chain need to be responsible towards end-users, and the structural incentives should align with this need … To do this comprehensively, there should be consideration for how responsibility is allocated both *upfront* in the development process (ex-ante) as best practice, and guidance on how redress can be obtained if issues are discovered *thereafter* (ex-post).[80]

In terms of *ex ante* allocation, the model states that '[r]esponsibility can be allocated based on the level of control that each stakeholder has in the generative AI development chain', and further notes that '[t]here is value in extending this approach to AI development … Being the most knowledgeable about their own models and how they are deployed, model developers are well placed to lead this development in a concerted manner'.[81] In terms of *ex post* approaches, the draft Model notes that there may be cases where shared responsibility models do not cover all possible scenarios; where additional redress is needed, such as in where it is clear that developers are 'implicitly acknowledging' responsibility for model training data and use; and that there will be other areas that are not yet well covered. The draft Model explicitly notes that it is 'useful to consider **updating legal frameworks** to make them more flexible, and to allow emerging risks to be easily and fairly addressed',[82] referring to the EU's draft Liability Directive and revised Product Liability Directive, with the aim of ensuring that 'no party is unfairly disadvantaged by the compensation process'.[83] Lastly, the draft Model notes that there will be 'residual issues that fall through the cracks'.[84]

Singapore Analysis

Essentially, the Singapore approach – via the Model Framework and accompanying documents – has many positive attributes. It is flexible, in that its approach can be applied no matter the type of AI in question or its development. It provides a general baseline for building a business approach of AI and prioritises cooperation

[79] 'Proposed Model AI Governance Framework for Generative AI', AI Verify Foundation and Infocomm Media Development Authority: aiverifyfoundation.sg/downloads/Proposed_MGF_Gen_AI_2024.pdf.
[80] ibid (emphasis in original).
[81] ibid.
[82] Emphasis in original, further detail on EU legislation in section 5.3.2.
[83] 'Proposed Model AI Governance Framework for Generative AI' (n 79).
[84] ibid.

through partnerships. There is a proactive approach to risk management,[85] without over-emphasising either potential risk or unrealistically low risk. The Model Framework provides a broad basis for technical considerations such as robustness and reproducibility of AI, and proper data sourcing to build the AI and its infrastructure. The accompanying documents provide actionable examples for companies to follow and lay out to a civilian-accessible level what steps have been taken to address concerns. Focusing on the need for AI decisions to be explainable, transparent and fair provides a solid basis for how companies must frame their AI usage. Ultimately, the governance ecosystem is aimed at building trust between all parties that AI is safe and reliable and is buoyed by AI Verify as a technical tool.

There are areas in which the Singapore approach could helpfully be expanded.[86] Some of these are explicitly noted within the Model Framework, such as the lack of discussion on data sharing, and on sector-specific needs. First, while the Model Framework provides a flexible, base-level set of questions to frame developer approaches, it could usefully acknowledge differentiation of baseline concerns between sectors to a greater extent. Promoting considerations such as whether a human should be in, over or out of the loop is helpful, but does not delve into the intricacies of how layered and diverse these questions may be for different industries. Harm is addressed, as are trade-offs relating to it, but the depth of the discussion generally only reaches probability and severity of harm.

Second, the Model Framework is by nature non-specific. This is intentional, and not a failure of design, but this does moderate its usability in some ways. A company that is using the Model Framework to guide decision-making will have no concrete benchmark on which to build. While this may come from sector-specific legislation, further discussion would be helpful. For example, the Model Framework states that:

> Documenting how the model training and selection process are conducted, the reasons for which decisions are made, and measures taken to address identified risks will enable the organisation to provide an account of the decisions subsequently … In this regard, the field of Automated Machine Learning aims to automate a significant portion of machine learning workflows, including feature engineering, feature selection, model selection and hyper-parameter tuning. Organisations using these types of tools can consider the transparency, explainability, and traceability of the automated machine learning approach, as well as the models selected.[87]

While such considerations are no doubt helpful, they are so broad as to be difficult to apply.

Third, the Model Framework and accompanying documents do not address liability. The Model Framework itself notes its lack of '[d]iscussing issues relating

[85] Such as encouraging producers to examine the trade-offs between severity of harm and probability of harm.

[86] And likely will be.

[87] 'Model Artificial Intelligence Governance Framework Second Edition' (n 36).

to the legal liabilities associated with AI'.[88] Obviously the authoring agencies are aware of this lack of inclusion. Yet where the Framework benefits from its flexibility and broad applicability, it falters in providing assurances to companies by way of defining liability, or steps to avoid it. The guiding principle that AI should be explainable, transparent and fair is an important one, but the Model Framework itself notes that even '[t]echnical explainability may not always be enlightening, especially to the man on the street. Implicit explanations of how the AI models' algorithms function may be more useful than explicit descriptions of the models' logic'.[89] The Model Framework accurately notes that '[m]easures such as explainability, repeatability, robustness, regular tuning, reproducibility, traceability, and auditability can enhance the transparency of algorithms found in AI models', and that '[e]xplainability features could focus on why the AI model had a certain level of confidence',[90] but it does not provide explicitly what such features should be. Building understanding and trust are admirable goals, as is the twin guiding principle of AI being human-centric, but the lack of specificity in regard to concrete guidelines is compounded by lack of assurance on liability. Even the inclusion of AI Verify, which may add a level of trust, does not add any clarity as to liability aspects.

This is not to say that the Model Framework should have provided a checklist of what AI producers should do to avoid liability; that is not what the Model Framework was intended to accomplish. This is merely to note that companies will be cautious about AI creation and use as regards liability, because there are no concrete steps to take to avoid being liable. There is no official agreement that taking the steps and approaches in the Model Framework and accompanying documents, nor undertaking the AI Verify tests, will avoid liability, and it would be difficult for a court which was determining liability to determine how closely these guidelines were actually followed.

The proposed expansion of the Model Framework, via the proposed Model AI Governance Framework for Generative AI, goes some way towards bridging these gaps. It is not entirely clear whether the proposed expansions apply exclusively to generative AI, or to all AI covered by the Model Framework so far. Accountability in particular is an interesting heading for expansion of liability: while the draft Model focuses primarily on the allocation of responsibility rather than its circumstances – the who rather than the why – this is nonetheless a usefully concrete advancement, if passed. It also explicitly notes that developers are best placed to minimise risks within their models. Moreover, the draft Model update notes what it lacks: that there are scenarios that may not yet be covered; that residual issues will occur; and that updates to the legal framework should be considered, particularly given that AI has 'risks that have disproportionate impact on society as a

[88] ibid.
[89] ibid.
[90] ibid.

whole, which may only emerge as AI is used'.[91] The fact that the draft Model explicitly references the EU Product Liability update is particularly interesting, given that Singapore itself does not have specific product liability legislation.

In summary: the Singaporean approach focuses on incentivising innovation, grouping AI applications under one umbrella. Prevention of harms is provided for through two approaches: the potential risk of liability claims, which are not clarified in the Guidelines; and the implicit threat that not following the Guidelines will lead to regulation. Neither depends explicitly on black-letter law terms. While the updates to the Model Framework aimed at generative AI may or may not apply to all AI, there is nonetheless promising consideration being given to the potential need for re-examining law in terms of accountability for AI.

5.3.2. European Union

The European Union is a union of European Member States that has a variety of institutions, bodies and agencies, producing its own legislation that affects its Member States in a variety of ways. EU legislation can be split into primary legislation in the form of treaties, which form the ground rules for EU actions, and secondary legislation, including regulations, directives and decisions.[92] Regulations are binding and are applied across EU Member States; a directive is a 'legislative act that sets out a goal that all EU countries must achieve', although the specifics are up to the Member States; decisions are 'binding on those to whom it is addressed (eg an EU country or an individual company) and [are] directly applicable'; recommendations are not binding but make the body's views known; and opinions '[allow] the institutions to make a statement in a non-binding fashion'.[93]

The EU approach to AI regulation has, understandably, been historically more piecemeal than the Singaporean approach, given the multi-state nature of its makeup. There have been assertions that existing directives, such as the 2006 Machinery Directive[94] would have an impact on the governance of AI use in robotics with the idea that 'robots in general are considered machinery',[95] even if the Machinery Directive does not explicitly mention robots. Certain types of AI applications would fall under sector-specific legislation such as the 2014 Radio

[91] 'Proposed Model AI Governance Framework for Generative AI' (n 79).

[92] European Union, 'Types of Legislation': european-union.europa.eu/institutions-law-budget/law/types-legislation_en.

[93] ibid.

[94] Council Directive 2006/42/EC of the European Parliament and of the Council of 17 May 2006 on machinery, and amending Directive 95/16/EC (Machinery Directive).

[95] A Santuosuosso, C Boscarato, F Caroleo, R Labruto and C Leroux, 'Robots, Market and Civil Liability: A European Perspective' (The 21st IEEE International Symposium on Robot and Human Interactive Communication 2012) 1051 as cited in Y Gheraibia et al, 'Review of Legal Frameworks, Standards and Best Practices in Verification and Assurance for Infrastructure Inspection Robotics' (2020) SSRN Electronic Journal: papers.ssrn.com/sol3/papers.cfm?abstract_id=3645997.

Equipment Directive,[96] which could include AI applications such as automated drones;[97] or the 2014 Electromagnetic Compatibility Directive,[98] which could include applications such as GPS (global positioning system) AI.[99] Other EU implications include considerations such as choice of law and jurisdiction regarding tort and delict laws.[100] Most notably, the General Data Protection Regulation (GDPR) provides that a data subject has the right 'not to be subject to a decision based solely on automated processing, including profiling, which produces legal effects concerning him or her or similarly significantly affects him or her',[101] which could certainly include AI applications such as loan review.[102]

Of the directives and relevant legislation which came about prior to the recent emergence of AI but which are likely to have the largest direct impact on AI which might cause death, the foremost is the Product Liability Directive (PLD). The 1985 PLD – reviewed in section 2.5.1 – was passed in 1985, and provides strict liability for damage caused by defective products.[103] The proposed revision to the PLD, which had passed the Committee Vote as of December 2023, would apply, if passed, to the current EU Member States.[104] The update addresses AI specifically, including whether or not the PLD itself applies to AI. The revised PLD (which will now simply be referred to as the PLD) states that AI and AI-enabled goods and software are to be considered products.[105] How can defectiveness be assessed, and what defences does the PLD provide?

The PLD defines defect thusly: '[a] product is defective when it does not provide the safety which a person is entitled to expect, taking all circumstances into account'.[106] While the level of safety one is entitled to expect becomes better

[96] Directive 2014/53/EU of the European Parliament and of the Council of 16 April 2014 on the harmonisation of the laws of the Member States relating to the making available on the market of radio equipment and repealing Directive 1999/5/EC (Radio Equipment Directive).

[97] Y Gheraibia et al, 'Review of Legal Frameworks, Standards and Best Practices in Verification and Assurance for Infrastructure Inspection Robotics' (2020) SSRN Electronic Journal: papers.ssrn.com/sol3/papers.cfm?abstract_id=3645997.

[98] Directive 2014/30/EU of the European Parliament and of the Council of 26 February 2014 on the harmonisation of the laws of the Member States relating to electromagnetic compatibility (Electromagnetic Compatibility Directive).

[99] Gheraibia et al (n 97).

[100] ibid.

[101] EU General Data Protection Regulation (GDPR): Regulation (EU) 2016/679 of the European Parliament and of the Council of 27 April 2016 on the protection of natural persons with regard to the processing of personal data and on the free movement of such data, and repealing Directive 95/46/EC (General Data Protection Regulation) [2016] OJ L119/1, article 22.

[102] AI-specific legislation has, however, been overall siloed from data protection-specific legislation. See, eg, the UNIO EU Law Journal's statement that 'The proposal for an AI Act should not be considered a GDPR for AI for one singular reason: there is already a GDPR for AI, and it is called the GDPR': officialblogofunio.com/2021/06/08/editorial-of-june-2021/.

[103] Council Directive 85/374/EEC on the approximation of the laws, regulations and administrative provisions of the Member States concerning liability for defective products [1985] OJ L210/29 (Product Liability Directive).

[104] And not to the UK, as the current PLD does.

[105] European Commission, 'Proposal for a Directive of the European Parliament and of the Council on liability for defective products 2022'.

[106] Product Liability Directive (n 103) Art 6(1).

defined over time, what is reasonable to expect from an AI is a more difficult question in AI's infancy.[107] While there may be areas where an AI is clearly defective, including where it does not function at all, there are many further grey areas which are likely to be fought on contextual detail. These could include cases where the AI performed the correct action, but not to the desired degree of accuracy, or where external factors contributed to an unsuccessful action, such as an AI robot slipping on a patch of mud and thereby failing to scale a hill.

Lastly, there are potential producer defences to strict liability, included or disincluded by the enacting Member State.[108] First, the 'development risks' defence: the defence is provided for in cases where 'the producer could not reasonably have been expected to discover the defect given the state of scientific and technical knowledge at the time'.[109] Second, the producer may cite compliance with mandatory requirements: that '[t]he defect is due to compliance of the product with mandatory regulations issued by public authorities'.[110] Third, Article 7(e) provides the state of the art defence, whereby a producer is not liable if the defect in question was not discoverable at the time of putting into circulation.[111] This is an obvious point of interest, as it brings into question what might reasonably be deemed 'discoverable' as a defect in AI. Clearly there are some issues which would be obvious defects, such as an autonomous car that runs into walls, but some which may be so circumstantially specific that their discoverability would be difficult if not unlikely, such as an English-designed autonomous car that is unable to classify and thus deal with a Canadian moose (see, eg, section 1.1.2). Given that obstacle classification can be a safety issue for non-human drivers,[112] this may in fact be a deadly issue, but one which would be very difficult to uncover in advance.

The second defence is the Article 7(b) latent defect defence,

> that, having regard to the circumstances, it is probable that the defect which caused the damage did not exist at the time when the product was put into circulation by [the producer] or that this defect came into being afterwards.[113]

[107] This could include, for example, 'the manner in which, and purposes for which, the product has been marketed, its get-up … or warnings with respect to, doing or refraining from doing anything with or in relation to the product' as per the UK Consumer Protection Act 1987 as regards determining whether a product is defective in respect to its safety not being 'what persons are generally entitled to expect'. As discussed in ch 3, 'Explainable AI (XAI)', while we can ask sensible questions about how a human producer or user of AI might be expected to behave, it is harder to define our expectations about the AI's functioning itself.

[108] The adoption of some defences is optional for Member States. The developmental risk defence, also known as the state-of-the-art defence, is one of these. AO Gbade, 'Reflection on Development Risk Defence Under Product Liability Law' (2017) 10:9 *OIDA International Journal of Sustainable Development* 29–38: ssrn.com/link/OIDA-Intl-Journal-Sustainable-Dev.html.

[109] Product Liability Directive (n 103) Art 7(e).

[110] ibid, Art 7(d).

[111] ibid, Art 7(e).

[112] Sam Levin and Julia Carrie Wong, 'Self-Driving Uber Kills Arizona Woman in First Fatal Crash Involving Pedestrian' *Guardian* (19 March 2018): theguardian.com/technology/2018/mar/19/uber-self-driving-car-kills-woman-arizona-tempe.

[113] Product Liability Directive (n 103) Art 7(b).

This would clearly be an issue, if unaddressed, for AI that learns, and likely for AI that is updated.

In the past few years there have been a series of EU reports, studies, white papers, and draft legislation which address questions of liability.[114] These raise several key issues: whether AI should be governed using an overarching model, and if so how such a model should be structured; what standards should be used and what information required to show compliance with those standards; and how liability should be addressed.

One of the first in the series of concentrated addresses of AI in the European Union can be seen in the European Commission's White Paper 'On Artificial Intelligence – A European approach to excellence and trust'. The White Paper focused on the idea of an overarching AI governance model to protect from both physical and rights-based harms. The White Paper had several well-considered areas of focus: the difficulties of regulating machines that learn; the problems of interpreting opaque AI; and how national and transnational governance would be needed for AI across the European Union. The White Paper introduced the EU's 'risk-based' approach to AI, but was relatively vague in doing so, for example the White Paper identified 'parts of the public sector' to be high risk, but not in the ways in which those high-risk elements would be identified (or how risks should be dealt with).[115] High-risk status was shown to take into account the field in which the AI would be employed, but addressed to a much lesser extent concerns such as opacity. Key requirement features noted in the White Paper include training data; data and record-keeping; information to be provided; robustness and accuracy; human oversight and specific requirements for certain AI applications. This included the note that training data should '[meet] the standards set in the applicable EU safety rules (existing as well as possible complementary ones) … [including] ensuring that all systems are trained on data sets that are sufficiently broad and cover all relevant scenarios'.[116]

These concerns were addressed in greater depth in later legislative documents, as will be explained below, but many of the key concepts of the White Paper are adopted and expanded upon in the later AI Act. The White Paper noted that '[d]evelopers and deployers of AI [were] already subject to European legislation [including] liability rules',[117] suggesting that grand developments in liability were not inherently included at this stage of the regulatory evolution, although it did note that it might be potentially difficult 'for persons having suffered harm to obtain compensation under the [then] current EU and national liability legislation' and that it would be necessary to assess whether legislation 'adequately [addressed] the risks that AI systems create, or whether adjustments [would be]

[114] Or, similarly, other policy documents with future legislation proposals.

[115] European Commission, 'White Paper on Artificial Intelligence: A European Approach to Excellence and Trust': commission.europa.eu/publications/white-paper-artificial-intelligence-european-approach-excellence-and-trust_en.

[116] ibid.

[117] ibid.

needed to specific legal instruments'.[118] Product liability law and the Product Liability Directive are referenced extensively. Lastly, the White Paper notes only very minimally the role of sectoral legislation, though in a key role: 'those aspects that are already addressed by existing horizontal or sectoral legislation … [would] continue to be governed by this legislation'.[119]

The October 2020 European Parliament 'Report with Recommendations to the Commission on a Civil Liability Regime for AI Operators' provided a more robust starting point for liability discussions. The report reflects the initial stage of the EU thought processes. The report is focused on dealing with liability of AI applications, and noted,

> whereas the concept of 'liability' plays an important double role in our daily life: on the one hand, it ensures that a person who has suffered harm or damage is entitled to claim and receive compensation from the party proven to be liable for that harm or damage, and on the other hand, it provides the economic incentives for natural and legal person to avoid causing harm or damage in the first place or price into their behaviour the risk of having to pay compensation.

The report further considered the importance of enabling small and medium enterprises; providing regulatory clarity; avoidance of regulatory fragmentation; the need for future-proof legislation; and the ultimate need for sector-specific legislation.[120] Most notably, however, are the regime split between applications' risk, and the compensation cap.

Initially, the report identified that its scope included 'where a physical or virtual activity, device or process driven by an AI-system has caused harm or damage to the life, health, physical integrity of a natural person, to the property of a natural or legal person or has caused significant immaterial harm resulting in a verifiable economic loss'.[121] In other words, it resolved the product/service dilemma of the PLD while still carving out a space for the PLD as existing legislation,[122] and forecast a focus on damage from a post-hoc lens going forward.[123] It also introduced a change that would later be reflected in the EU AI Act, namely splitting liability into high-risk and low-risk AI applications. Operators of high-risk AI systems were to be 'strictly liable for any harm or damage that was caused by a physical or virtual activity, device

[118] ibid.
[119] ibid.
[120] European Parliament, 'Report with Recommendations' (n 38).
[121] ibid.
[122] It also notes that 'the Product Liability Directive (PLD) has for over 30 years proven to be an effective means of getting compensation for harm triggered by a defective product, but should nevertheless be revised to adapt it to the digital world', and 'urges the Commission to assess whether the PLD should be transformed into a regulation, to clarify the definition of "products" by determining whether digital content and devices fall under its scope and to consider adapting concepts such as "damage", "defect" and "producer"'. In other words, the PLD may have an appropriately framed approach, but there is an acknowledgment that there have been certain applicational difficulties.
[123] This is furthered with the definition in Article 3(a), that '"AI-system" means a system that is either software-based or embedded in hardware devices, and that displays behaviour simulating intelligence by, inter alia, collecting and processing data, analysing and interpreting its environment, and by taking action, with some degree of autonomy, to achieve specific goals'.

or process driven by that AI-system'.[124] The report also recommended, although did not provide, an exhaustive (and amendable) list of '[a]ll high-risk AI-systems and all critical sectors where they are used'.[125] Amendments to the exhaustive list were to be based on criteria for high-risk applications, including 'a significant potential in an autonomously operating AI-system to cause harm or damage … that is random and goes beyond what can be reasonably expected'.[126] This strict liability explicitly excluded the ability for operators 'to exonerate themselves from liability by arguing that they acted with due diligence or that the harm or damage was caused by an autonomous activity, device or process driven by their AI-system'.[127]

'Low-risk AI-systems' were not independently defined and were explicitly categorised by dint of not being 'high risk AI-systems' noted in the exhaustive list.[128] Low-risk AI-system operators were presumed at fault in the event of damage caused by the AI,[129] but defendants could plead that all reasonable measures and due diligence were taken.

The report also included the concept of front end and back-end operators: front-end operator referring to 'the natural or legal person who exercises a degree of control over a risk connected with the operation and functioning of the AI-system and benefits from its operation';[130] back-end operator referring to

> the natural or legal person who, on a continuous basis, defines the features of the technology, provides data and essential backend support service and therefore also exercises a degree of control over the risk connected with the operation and functioning of the AI system.[131]

This dichotomy considered the difference between a producer and a user, which later legislative tools changed to a 'distributor' and a user, in order to reflect obligations on those importing AI to the European market.[132]

The report also proposed a cap for amounts of compensation which can be claimed, which further reflected the high-risk/low-risk designation.

What the report helpfully began to explain is how the European Union might start to conceptualise liability of operators of AI applications. Liability is naturally of concern to producers, and clarity is a much-needed step in both compliance and technical viability. Splitting liability into high-risk and low-risk applications provided recognition of the different potential risks that AI applications provide: one should not regulate the AI smoothie-maker to the same level of liability as the AI nuclear reactor. Much like the Singapore Model Framework (Second Edition), the report was not intended to be all things to all stakeholders, but it still managed

[124] European Parliament, 'Report with Recommendations' (n 38).
[125] ibid.
[126] ibid.
[127] ibid, although force majeure can be pleaded.
[128] ibid.
[129] Causation to be discussed in more detail below.
[130] European Parliament, 'Report with Recommendations' (n 38).
[131] ibid.
[132] Effectively stepping into the shoes of the producer in the EU market.

to integrate concerns such as compensation of victims and the need for inclusion of small and medium enterprises into the AI ecosystem. The report also provided helpful notes on its integration with other regulatory tools such as the Product Liability Directive, attempting to resolve arguments that still plague the EU's AI legislation.

While the report focused on liability and when it would be applied, it is clearly addressed entirely from a post-hoc lens. Rather than addressing what producers can do to avoid liability, it discusses the times at which it cannot be avoided. While the application of strict liability reduces questions around responsibility – or would do so with the promised list – there is no attention given to what responsible development looks like. This report portrays fault in a very responsive manner: one is guilty if caught, but irresponsible AI builds are of no regulatory concern unless they cause detectable damage. The approach taken does not incentivise thoughtful and measured production; it promotes either intentionally avoiding high-risk AI, even if it is beneficial – potentially depriving society of its use – or of building for profit and calculating for damage costs and putting to market if the former is even marginally higher than the latter. The case of the Ford Pinto[133] is an excellent example of why this approach may not be societally desirable. Further, particularly for high-risk applications such as transport and medical AI, there is a grey area between 'correct' and 'incorrect' decisions. It is unclear whether a producer's prioritising of certain outcomes will be rewarded or punished, for example whether to prioritise the reduction of human harm over the reduction of property harm.[134] Lastly, although the report set out an initial approach rather than proposing a complete set of regulations, it was relatively unclear how it would have related to other areas of the law in standard terms such as what due diligence would look like, or what constitutes reasonableness – all relevant aspects when liability is in question.

The two most crucial developments in the EU's AI regulatory regime are both recent. While their direct impacts as enacted legislation have not yet been seen, they represent some of the most significant steps seen in AI regulation: general regulation for AI writ large, and a liability regime to match. The two pieces are the EU AI Act, which has passed, and the EU AI Liability Directive, which has not yet passed. The EU AI Act (the Act) text was provisionally agreed in February 2024, and finalised May 2024. Although long anticipated and heralded by both the White Paper and the report, the Act is distinct in its attempt to address the challenges of regulating AI. It is first important to note that the regulation applies to:

> (a) providers placing on the market or putting into service AI systems or placing on the market general-purpose AI models in the Union, irrespective of whether those providers are established or located within the Union or in a third country;

[133] MM Helms and BA Hutchins, 'Poor Quality Products: Is Their Production Unethical?' (1992) 30 *Management Decision* 5: doi.org/10.1108/00251749210015661; in which Ford knew of the Pinto's defective fuel system but performed a cost–benefit analysis that indicated that the liability costs of consumer deaths would cost less than fixing the problem with the vehicle.

[134] K Grieman, 'Hard Drive Crash' (2019) 9 *Journal of Intellectual Property, Information Technology and Electronic Commerce Law* 294: jipitec.eu/issues/jipitec-9-3-2018/at_download/CompleteIssue.

(b) deployers of AI systems that have their place of establishment or are located within the Union;
(c) providers and deployers of AI systems that have their place of establishment or are located in a third country, where the output produced by the AI system is used in the Union;
(d) importers and distributors of AI systems;
(e) product manufacturers placing on the market or putting into service an AI system together with their product and under their own name or trademark;
(f) authorised representatives of providers, which are not established in the Union;
(g) affected persons that are located in the Union.[135]

In other words, while the Act does place obligations on users, 'providers' as a term has the potential to include not just those who produce AI, but also distributors or importers.[136] This is a broader definition than in the report and provides more focus on producers rather than the previously defined 'operators'.

The Act is risk-based, assigning AI to one of four categories (though there can be overlap between categories):

1. Unacceptable risk – prohibited.
2. High risk – permitted with conditions.
3. Limited risk – transparency requirements.
4. Minimal risk.

The Act also has certain areas aimed specifically at General Purpose AI models or GPAI:

> AI systems that have a wide range of possible uses, both intended and unintended by the developers … Current general purpose AI systems are characterised by their scale … as well as their reliance on transfer learning (applying knowledge from one task to another).[137]

The term also used to refer to such systems is 'foundation models', on which generative models are built, with generative models being designed for a particular task.

Unacceptable Risk AI

Article 5 provides a specific, though not unchangeable, list of prohibited AI. These prohibited practices are those considered unacceptable by virtue of contravening Union values, for instance by violating fundamental rights. The prohibition includes practices that deploy 'subliminal techniques beyond a person's consciousness or

[135] Regulation (EU) 2024/… of the European Parliament and of the Council of … laying down harmonised rules on artificial intelligence and amending Regulations (EC) No 300/2008, (EU) No 167/2013, (EU) No 168/2013, (EU) 2018/858, (EU) 2018/1139 and (EU) 2019/2144 and Directives 2014/90/EU, (EU) 2016/797 and (EU) 2020/1828 (Artificial Intelligence Act).

[136] ibid, 28.

[137] 'General Purpose AI and the AI Act (Future of Life Institute, May 2022): artificialintelligenceact.eu/wp-content/uploads/2022/05/General-Purpose-AI-and-the-AI-Act.pdf.

purposefully manipulative or deceptive techniques', as well as AI-based social scoring that leads to 'detrimental or unfavourable treatment' and '"real time" remote biometric identification systems in publicly accessible spaces for the purposes of law enforcement'[138], with caveats.

General Purpose AI

The Act further classifies general purpose AI as any 'general-purpose AI model with systemic risk' if it meets any of the following criteria:

> (a) it has high impact capabilities evaluated on the basis of appropriate technical tools and methodologies, including indicators and benchmarks;
> (b) based on a decision of the Commission, ex officio or following a qualified alert by the scientific panel, it has capabilities or an impact equivalent to those set out in point (a) having regard to the criteria set out in Annex XIII.[139]

The Act specifies that these benchmarks will include 'when the cumulative amount of computation used for its training measured in floating point operations is greater than 10^25', but may also include supplemental criteria as the field develops.[140] Providers of GPAI fitting these standards must notify the Commission, but may be able to show that the GPAI 'does not present, due to its specific characteristics, systemic risks and therefore should not be classified as a general-purpose AI model with systemic risk'.[141] The Commission will keep current a published list of general purpose AI models with systemic risk.[142] There are also further obligations on providers, such as with technical documentation, that align with the requirements on high-risk AI listed below, alongside distinct requirements such as for intellectual property rights in datasets.[143]

High-Risk AI

High-risk AI systems are those which fulfil both the criteria below, 'whether or not they are placed on the market or put into service independently':

> (a) the AI system is intended to be used as a safety component of a product, or the AI system is itself a product, covered by the Union harmonisation legislation listed in Annex I;
> (b) the product whose safety component pursuant to point (a) is the AI system, or the AI system itself as a product, is required to undergo a third-party conformity assessment, with a view to the placing on the market or the putting into service of that product pursuant to the Union harmonisation legislation listed in Annex I.[144]

[138] ibid, 5(1).
[139] EU AI Act (n 135) Chapter V, Art 51(1).
[140] ibid, Art 51(2).
[141] ibid, Art 52(2).
[142] ibid, Art 52(6).
[143] ibid, Art 53(1)(b).
[144] ibid, Chapter III, Art 6(1)(a)–(b).

Additionally, AI systems listed in Annex III are considered high risk, and include AI used for biometrics; critical infrastructure; educational and vocational training; employment, workers management and access to self-employment; essential private and public services and benefits; law enforcement; migration, asylum and border control management; and administration of justice and democratic process.[145] While high-risk AI are to be permitted, they will have certain pre-market requirements, for which providers must take into account the 'intended purposes as well as the generally acknowledged state of the art on AI and AI-related technologies'.[146] Providers must establish a risk management system, which 'shall be established, implemented, documented and maintained in relation to high-risk AI systems', and which will be an 'iterative process planned and run throughout the entire lifecycle of a high-risk AI'.[147] This risk management system will include the following steps:

> (a) the identification and analysis of the known and the reasonably foreseeable risks that the high-risk AI system can pose to health, safety or fundamental rights when the high-risk AI system is used in accordance with its intended purpose;
> (b) the estimation and evaluation of the risks that may emerge when the high-risk AI system is used in accordance with its intended purpose and under conditions of reasonably foreseeable misuse;
> (c) the evaluation of other risks possibly arising based on the analysis of data gathered from the post-market monitoring system referred to in Article 72;
> (d) the adoption of appropriate and targeted risk management measures designed to address the risks identified pursuant to point (a).[148]

The risks mentioned in (a)–(d) 'shall concern only those which may be reasonably mitigated or eliminated through the development or design of the high-risk AI system, or the provision of adequate technical information'.[149] Risks should be eliminated or reduced 'as far as technically feasible through adequate design and development of the high-risk AI system'; mitigated and controlled where risks cannot be abolished, and information on risks must be provided to deployers.[150] Systems will be tested, and testing may include real-world conditions, and may occur at any point in the development process: '[t]esting shall be carried out against prior defined metrics and probabilistic thresholds that are appropriate to the intended purpose of the high-risk AI system'.[151]

High-risk AI systems also have specific data requirements, including that the '[t]raining, validation and testing data sets shall be subject to data governance

[145] EU AI Act (n 135) Annex III.
[146] ibid, Chapter III, Art 8(1).
[147] ibid, Chapter III, Art 9(2) (emphasis removed).
[148] ibid.
[149] ibid, Chapter III, Art 9(3).
[150] ibid, Art 9(5)(a).
[151] ibid, Art 9(8).

and management practices appropriate for the intended purpose of the high-risk AI system',[152] and that said datasets shall be

> relevant, sufficiently representative, and to the best extent possible, free of errors and complete in view of the intended purpose … hav[ing] the appropriate statistical properties, including as regards the persons or groups of persons in relation to whom the high-risk AI system is intended to be used.[153]

Interestingly, the data requirements also provide an exception for the processing of special categories of personal data, referred to in other legislative instruments, if that data is 'strictly necessary for the purpose of ensuring bias detection and correction in relation to the high-risk AI systems'.[154]

High-risk AI systems must also include technical documentation,

> drawn up in such a way to demonstrate that the high-risk AI system complies with the requirements set out … and to provide national competent authorities and notified bodies with the necessary information in a clear and comprehensive form to assess the compliance of the AI system with those requirements.[155]

Annex IV contains many of these requirements, including a general description, such as the intended purpose, relevant versions of software, a description of the forms in which the AI is put into service; a 'detailed description of the elements of the AI system and of the process for its development', including, among other things, the 'methods and steps performed for the development of the AI system', 'the key design choices including the rationale and assumptions made', and 'the validation and testing procedures used, including information about the validation and testing data used and their main characteristics[, and] metrics used to measure accuracy, robustness and compliance'.[156]

Other general requirements for high-risk AI include record-keeping, transparency and provision of information to deployers; human oversight; and provisions relating to accuracy, robustness and cybersecurity.[157]

Limited Risk: AI with Specific Transparency Obligations

Specific transparency obligations apply for a wide variety of AI systems. First, these include AI systems that are intended to interact directly with natural persons, unless it would be reasonably obvious to the person without being informed.[158] Second, providers of AI systems that generate 'synthetic audio, image, video or text content, shall ensure that the outputs of the AI system are marked in a

[152] ibid, Art 10(2).
[153] ibid, Art 10(3).
[154] ibid, Art 10(5).
[155] ibid, Art 11(1).
[156] EU AI Act (n 135) Annex IV 2(g).
[157] EU AI Act (n 135) Chapter III, Arts 12–15.
[158] ibid, Chapter IV, Art 50(1).

machine-readable format and detectable as artificially generated or manipulated'.[159] This clause notes specifically the inclusion of general purpose AI models. Third and fourth, deployers of emotion recognition AI, biometric categorisation and 'deep fakes' must 'inform the natural persons exposed thereto' and 'disclose that the content has been artificially generated or manipulated', respectively.[160]

Minimal Risk

Minimal risk AI, such as 'AI-enabled video games or spam filters', is allowed with no restrictions. These applications will still fall under other legislation but are allowed 'free use' by the AI Act.[161]

Lastly, the EU Commission established the European AI Office in February 2024, to oversee 'the AI Act's enforcement and implementation with the member states', as well as to participate in 'international dialogue and cooperation on AI issues, acknowledging the need for global alignment on AI governance'.[162]

Draft AI Liability Directive

The draft AI Liability Directive (the Directive)'s full title is 'for a Directive of the European Parliament and of the Council on adapting non-contractual civil liability rules to artificial intelligence'. The Directive employs similar reasoning to prior work in the AI regulatory arena (ie, the draft AI Act), planning

> to promote the rollout of trustworthy AI … by ensuring victims of damage caused by AI obtain equivalent protection to victims of damage caused by products in general. It also reduces legal uncertainty of businesses developing or using AI regarding their possible exposure to liability and prevents the emergence of fragmented AI-specific adaptations of national civil liability rules.[163]

The Explanatory Memorandum provides that the European Union is continuing its co-regulatory approach, surveying key stakeholders, and identifying liability as one of the 'top three barriers to the use of AI by European countries'.[164] The Directive notes that with several Member States striking out with their own approaches to civil liability for AI, there is a risk of 'further fragmentation and increased costs for businesses active throughout the EU', with a great risk of legal uncertainty to businesses operating in multiple Member States.[165] This is notable given that Member States employ their own civil liability systems in other regards.

[159] ibid, Art 50(2).
[160] ibid, Art 50(3–4).
[161] European Commission 'AI Act' (*Shaping Europe's digital future*): digital-strategy.ec.europa.eu/en/policies/regulatory-framework-ai#:~:text=The%20European%20AI%20Office%2C%20established,dignity%2C%20rights%2C%20and%20trust.
[162] ibid.
[163] 'Proposal for a directive of the European Parliament and of the Council on adapting non-contractual civil liability rules to artificial intelligence (AI Liability Directive)' (2022) COM.
[164] ibid, Explanatory Memorandum 1.
[165] ibid.

The Directive is proposed as part of a three-pronged approach to AI regulation: the draft AI Act noted above, and 'a [forthcoming] revision of sectoral and horizontal product safety rules' form the other two prongs.[166] The use of sectoral legislation is critical, though potentially at odds with the AI Act as a broader regulatory tool and will be discussed in chapter six.

The Liability Directive itself proposes adaptations directly to the PLD discussed above: where the PLD covers 'producers' no-fault liability for defective products … This covers national liability claims mainly based on the fault of any person with a view of compensating any type of damage and any type of victim'.[167] This is proposed to occur in two stages; the first focusing on burden-of-proof issues specific to AI. The second stage is to assess the effects of the first stage, examining whether it has been effective 'in terms of victim protection and uptake of AI', considering 'future technological, regulatory and jurisprudential measurements when assessing the need to harmonise additional elements such as, potentially, mandatory insurance'.[168]

The Directive splits the first stage into five substantive portions:[169] subject matter and scope; definitions; disclosure of evidence and rebuttable presumption of non-compliance; rebuttable presumption of a causal link in the case of fault; and evaluation and targeted review. There are a few notable points for subject matter and scope: first, that the Directive focuses on 'the disclosure of evidence on high-risk artificial intelligence (AI) systems to enable a claimant to substantiate a non-contractual fault-based civil law claim for damages; [and] the burden of proof in the case of non-contractual fault-based civil law claims'.[170]

Second, the Directive does not apply to criminal liability, and does not affect, among other things, 'rules of Union law regarding conditions of liability in the field of transport; any rights which an injured person may have under national rules …; and the exemptions from liability and the due diligence obligations as laid down in [the Digital Services Act]'.[171] In other words, transportation liability schemes already pre-empt the Liability Directive, as do, potentially, additional rights under national rules. Definitions refer in many cases to the AI Act (eg, 'AI system', 'high-risk AI system'). Others are more classical references to civil claims – 'claimant', 'defendant', etc.

Article 3, 'Disclosure of evidence and rebuttable presumption of non-compliance', is where the Directive proposes expansion in areas that may be newer to civil than common law systems. Member States must ensure that courts are empowered to require providers to 'disclose relevant evidence at [their] disposal about a specific high-risk AI system that is suspected of having caused damage'.[172]

[166] ibid.
[167] ibid.
[168] ibid, Explanatory Memorandum 2.
[169] ibid. Arts 6–9 address administrative concerns such as amendments, transposition, entry into force, and addressees (Member States).
[170] ibid, 1(1).
[171] ibid, 1(3)(c).
[172] ibid, 3(1).

This will only be done if the claimant has taken 'all proportionate attempts' to gather the evidence from the defendant, and the court order will be limited to 'the disclosure of evidence to that which is necessary and proportionate to support a potential claim or a claim for damages and the preservation to that which is necessary and proportionate to support such a claim for damages'.[173] Common law systems already go through a similar approach through the discovery process, but it is not inherently native to civil law jurisdictions.[174]

However, for a court to make such an order 'the potential claimant must present facts and evidence sufficient to support the plausibility of a claim for damages'.[175] What is unclear is how courts will interpret this statement and what 'plausibility' will be taken to mean with regard to AI.

Article 4, or 'Rebuttable presumption of a causal link in the case of fault', is more or less what it appears to be: 'national courts shall presume, for the purposes of applying liability rules to a claim for damages, the causal link between the fault of the defendant and the output produced by the AI system or the failure of the AI system to produce an output',[176] where certain conditions are met. Conditions include a demonstrated non-compliance with duty of care,[177] the reasonable likelihood based on circumstance that 'the fault has influenced the output produced by the AI system or the failure of the AI system to produce an output', that the claimant 'has demonstrated that the output produced by the AI system or the failure of the AI system to produce an output gave rise to the damage'.[178] This presumption is also rebuttable by the defendant.[179] However, and most interestingly, in a claim against a high-risk AI provider, the presumption of a causal link between a defendant producer's fault and the harm to the complainant will only apply where the producer failed to follow certain sections of the AI Act:

(a) the AI system is a system which makes use of techniques involving the training of models with data and which was not developed on the basis of training, validation and testing data sets that meet the quality criteria referred to in [Article 10(2) to (4) of the AI Act];
(b) the AI system was not designed and developed in a way that meets the transparency requirements laid down in [Article 13 of the AI Act];
(c) the AI system was not designed and developed in a way that allows for an effective oversight by natural persons during the period in which the AI system is in use pursuant to [Article 14 of the AI Act];

[173] ibid, 3(4). Trade secrets are also accounted for. For failure to comply with such an order 'national court[s] shall presume the defendant's non-compliance with a relevant duty of care', with the defendant 'hav[ing] the right to rebut that presumption'. Explanatory Memorandum 3.

[174] GC Hazard, 'Discovery and the Role of the Judge in Civil Law Jurisdictions' (1998) 73 *Notre Dame Law Review* 1017.

[175] 'Proposal for a directive of the European Parliament and of the Council on adapting non-contractual civil liability rules to artificial intelligence' (n 163).

[176] ibid, 2(6)(a).

[177] The duty of care presumption also only applies where, in a claim against a high-risk AI producer, 'the defendant demonstrates that sufficient evidence and expertise is reasonably accessible for the claimant to prove the causal link', ibid, 4(4).

[178] ibid, 4(2).

[179] ibid, 4(7).

(d) the AI system was not designed and developed so as to achieve, in the light of its intended purpose, an appropriate level of accuracy, robustness and cybersecurity pursuant to [Article 15 and Article 16, point (a), of the AI Act]; or
(e) the necessary corrective actions were not immediately taken to bring the AI system in conformity with the obligations laid down in [Title III, Chapter 2 of the AI Act] or to withdraw or recall the system, as appropriate, pursuant to [Article 16, point (g), and Article 21 of the AI Act].[180]

As restated by a practitioner:

> Under the proposed new AI Liability Directive, the presumption of causality will apply only if claimants can satisfy three core conditions: first, that the fault of an AI system provider or user has been demonstrated, or at least presumed to have been so by a court; second, that it can be considered reasonably likely, based on the circumstances of the case, that the fault has influenced the output produced by the AI system or the failure of the AI system to produce an output; and third, that the claimant has demonstrated that the output produced by the AI system or the failure of the AI system to produce an output gave rise to the damage.[181]

This is an interesting legislative choice from the first hurdle, because proving fault requires proof of causality. Recall from section 2.1 that the steps in establishing fault are to establish a duty of care, a breach in the standard of that duty of care, and that the breach causing the harm was not too remote. What the legislation appears to propose is that if a claimant can show fault (duty of care + breach of care + not too remote), then the claimant can demand detailed information from the producer to substantiate the claim. This relies on the idea that it is feasible to prove fault on the part of the defendant without that information and suggests that the major barrier to AI claims is proving causality, rather than proving fault, even though fault in all likelihood includes major causality elements.

Consider a common law jurisdiction scenario in which there are complications after a surgery undertaken by an AI. The surgical AI removes a section of the bowel from a patient with bowel cancer. After the surgery, the patient has an unusual amount of nerve damage in the pelvic area, decreasing the patient's quality of life. In attempting to claim for damage allegedly caused by the AI, the fault of the provider (or user) must be demonstrated or presumed by the court. The court is unlikely to assume that surgical complications provide an inherent presumption of fault, particularly where the type – nerve damage – is known, even if the level – unexpectedly high – is not. The patient or claimant must then prove fault (a concept the Directive leaves to Member States) on behalf of either the producer or user. The patient has no particular medical nor AI knowledge. The patient has no access to any of the AI's training, testing, or validation data in order

[180] 'Proposal for a directive of the European Parliament and of the Council on adapting non-contractual civil liability rules to artificial intelligence' (n 163), square brackets in original text.
[181] S Cameron and W Seinen, 'AI Liability Addressed in Fresh EU Proposals', Pinsent Masons: pinsentmasons.com/out-law/news/ai-liability-addressed-eu-proposals.

to show fault. The patient cannot access the AI's performance records, XAI data, nor any sort of guide as to whether the surgery was performed correctly, including the AI's own visual data records, such as a video of the surgery. The patient must convince the court as best they can, without any inside knowledge, that fault has in fact occurred – fault that is not inherent just because the surgery did not result in a perfect outcome for the patient. Even if the patient were able to overcome this nigh insurmountable barrier, they would still have to show that, under the circumstances, the fault that occurred influenced the AI's output in undertaking the surgery. If successful, the patient must then show that the output change caused the issue itself, potentially all still without any access to knowledge of the AI's working or explanations. Then, and only then, does the Directive provide a presumption of causality.

Concepts such as *res ipsa loquitur* – a common law doctrine stating that 'the thing speaks for itself', through which (common law) courts can infer negligence by nature of the harm – are well placed to take the place of this first hurdle. Ireland's *Hanrahan v Merck, Sharp & Dohme (Ireland) Ltd* states the focus of the doctrine well:[182]

> [I]n the tort of negligence, where damage has been caused to the plaintiff in circumstances in which such damage … would not usually be caused without negligence on the part of the defendant, the rule of res ipsa loquitur will allow the act relied on to be evidence of negligence in the absence of proof by the defendant that it occurred without want of due care on his part. The rationale behind the shifting of the onus of proof to the defendant in such cases would appear to lie in the fact that it would be palpably unfair to require a plaintiff to prove something which is beyond his reach and which is peculiarly within the range of the defendant's capacity of proof.

However, the Directive does not use *res ipsa loquitur* principles. It does provide in 3(1) that 'a court may order the disclosure of relevant evidence about specific high-risk AI systems that are suspected of causing damage', but 'requests should be supported by facts and evidence sufficient to establish the plausibility of the contemplated claim for damages'.[183] The Directive further notes that disclosure may (not must) be ordered 'only to the extent necessary to sustain the claim'.[184] It will be difficult if not impossible for the injured party to know what information would be necessary to sustain the claim, given that they have no knowledge of the inner workings of the AI. Additionally, even if granted access to all information pertaining to the AI, the claiming party is unlikely to possess or have access to the kind of expertise required to interpret the evidence. The European Union acknowledges that under existing liability rules 'victims need to prove a wrongful action or omission by a person who caused the damage[; and t]he specific characteristics of AI, including complexity, autonomy and opacity (the so-called 'black

[182] *Hanrahan v Merck, Sharp & Dohme* (Ireland) Ltd [1988] ILRM 629.

[183] 'Proposal for a directive of the European Parliament and of the Council on adapting non-contractual civil liability rules to artificial intelligence' (n 163) 3.

[184] ibid.

box' effect), may make it difficult or prohibitively expensive for victims',[185] yet fails completely to address this difficulty. This lack of address is not only troubling, but thus far entirely unexplained.

The regulatory system must redress the power imbalance earlier than causation – if a pedestrian is hit by a self-driving vehicle or has a spleen rather than a liver removed by an AI surgeon, the nature of the injury speaks to the onus of proof. What the legislation seems to be prioritising, however, are non-physical harms – cases where an output of an AI is not so direct nor concrete. Yet in this arena, too, the legislation attempts to resolve the wrong issue – fault implies that a level of causation has already been found. Moreover, fault will be the harder element to prove: in granting a bank loan, the system is not necessarily faulty if the answer to a loan request is 'no'. This does not mean that the system cannot be faulty, but that proving fault will be more difficult. This is where elements of XAI should be used – the injured party should have the right to an explanation.[186] This explanation should be supplied for the perspective of a lay audience, providing key reasons for the decision given. This is what can be used to show a presumption of fault, from which causality can then be assumed. In both physical and non-physical harm cases, when looking at fault the court will ask: what should the producer have predicted? Tested for? Foreseen? Fault is difficult if not impossible to address in the abstract, and all the more so when the case is fact-dependent: whether it was reasonable to make a wide right turn with a trailer, or leave a certain margin of tissue in a surgical procedure.

Additionally, the Directive's provision to assist potential victims is even more restrictive in its allowances for claims against producers than it first appears: causal fault can only be proven where the producer had also deviated from the AI Act requirements. At the time of writing, the EU AI Act has been updated, but the proposed AI Liability Directive does not inherently reflect these changes, and it is unclear if similar pivots in content will be made.

If the non-contractual duty of care cannot be shown, then the Liability Directive does not offer any additional help to claimants, leaving all potential claims to the Product Liability Directive, as before, and with all the previously examined questions thereof. If the compliance with the duty of care can only be shown with a level of adhesion to the AI Act that cannot possibly be shown by producers, then '[t]he underpinning vision … to have AI systems and services that seek to support the economy, society, and the environment'[187] cannot be fulfilled.[188]

[185] ibid, 'Context of the proposal' section 1.

[186] Not unlike the GDPR's requirement that the subject of an automated decision be able to require an explanation. 'General Data Protection Regulation'.

[187] FF Liza, 'Challenges of Enforcing Regulations in Artificial Intelligence Act – Analyzing Quantity Requirement in Data and Data Governance' (2022) 1st International Workshop on Imagining the AI Landscape After the AI Act (In conjunction with the First International Conference on Hybrid Human-Artificial Intelligence) 10: ueaeprints.uea.ac.uk/id/eprint/85717/1/IAIL2022.pdf.

[188] The Directive further breaks down cases where claims for damages against a user of a high-risk AI system may be made, but for reasons of scope the producer to complainant pipeline will be assumed to be two parties here.

The draft Directive also provides a checkpoint for its own objectives: five years after the Directive has been transposed, a report will review and examine the effects it has achieved, and whether additional changes are needed such as insurance coverage. This appears to be a sensible approach to the ongoing difficulty of regulating a developing technology. While five years may be a long time in such a fast-moving area, it at least avoids the legislative pitfalls and headaches associated with a potential full review and discard if the legislation proves unfit for purpose.

Analysis

The EU AI Act and draft AI Liability Directive form two integral parts of the EU's approach to liability regulation, with the third being more targeted sectoral legislation (to be discussed in chapter six). While certain areas such as transportation liability are deliberately excluded, the two regulations still form a relatively comprehensive backdrop to AI as a bloc concept. They are the product of incremental legislative approach: as demonstrated, neither sprung to life unheralded. While preceding acts and reports have been updated and tweaked to reflect new information, the newest legislative additions are a reflection of the work that has come before rather than a vast departure. The European Union is also the only jurisdiction of the four discussed that has taken on AI liability so explicitly. This is particularly noteworthy given that the European Union must contend with individual Member States' approaches to liability nationally. This is not dissimilar to the United States, wherein states have jurisdiction over liability.

Furthermore, the AI Act went through a great deal of discussion and debate before ending up in its current stage. Its current stage reflects a more thoughtful evolution than the initially released, reflecting, in all likelihood, the many consultations and debate sessions that it went through between and passing. These steps include an address of particular criticisms, such as the initial's requirement for 'error free' datasets, but also the inclusion of sensible steps in the development and licensing process such as requiring risk management address of reasonably foreseeable risks, and the inclusion of technical documentation. This does not mean that the Act is free of criticism – far from it[189] – but that certain elements are much more practical than in the initial. While the Act itself does not address liability directly,[190] it does set the stage for necessary requirements prior to high-risk AI being placed on the market.

One potential area still at issue is that design must provide for both transparency and human oversight: that: '[h]igh-risk AI systems shall be designed and developed in such a way, including with appropriate human-machine interface tools, that they can be effectively overseen by natural persons during the period in which they are in use', with the oversight levels being suitably coordinated

[189] One area of note being the definition of AI, which is broad enough to catch a number of software programs.

[190] With the exception of very specific areas, such as in relation to notified bodies.

with risk.[191] As discussed in chapter three, transparency can be difficult to both design and achieve. Human oversight is perhaps even more nebulous. This oversight is frequently alluded to as a protective measure for human rights. Oversight is problematic for several reasons: first, it means that with any sort of depth to said oversight, the application will not scale well. Second, humans over trust technology, for example,

> [o]vertrust of a robot happens in scenarios where (1) a person accepts a risk because that person believes the robot can perform a function that it cannot or (2) the person accepts too much risk because the expectation is that the system will mitigate the risk.[192]

Third, a human overseeing a complex AI is unlikely to have a meaningful understanding of how the AI is making its decision, particularly in the moment – see section 4.2.2.

While there have been many criticisms levelled at the Act, its relative recency and the lack of standards, cases and individual Member State responses mean that much of the Act's potential impacts are unclear. Much analysis, therefore, rests on the decisions around the AI labelled high-risk: the criteria regarding whether an AI is high-risk, how such AI is to be governed, and movement of AI in and out of the category based on use. The Act has a clear and stated focus on fundamental rights and the protection thereof. Rights to physical safety and freedom from harm are clearly essential rights, yet physical safety standards require, broadly speaking, differing protections from those less physics-oriented harms. The Act intermingles physical and non-physical harms, to an extent that has the potential to minimise clarity for not only providers, but for governance overall. Technical decisions are being made to govern fundamental rights, with what may prove to be insufficient regard as to whether the requirements are technically feasible, such as human oversight.

The effects of the Liability Directive depend heavily on the Act. Not only do the two share definitions and an overall approach, but the Liability Directive states conditions taken directly from the Act. The aims of the Liability Directive are well considered: the recompense of victims is an important consideration, as is the level of certainty for AI producers. The Directive addresses key concerns, such as access to data as a potential imbalance, and where the lack of output of an AI might be as much of a concern as a false or harmful output. However, in placing a great deal of focus on the causal link rather than proving fault, the Directive does not provide the key piece of the puzzle to common law approaches to liability: the concepts of reasonableness and foreseeability. Instead, it anchors reasonableness to the concepts found in the AI Act: potentially concrete but currently immeasurable concepts. The Directive notes in its Preamble that

> [c]urrent national rules, in particular based on fault, are not suited to handling liability claims for damage caused by AI-enabled products and services … victims need to prove

[191] EU AI Act (n 135) Art 14(1)–14(2).

[192] P Lin, K Abney and R Jenkins, *Robot Ethics 2.0: New Challenges in Philosophy, Law, and Society* (Oxford University Press 2017): philarchive.org/rec/LINRE-3.

> a wrongful action or omission by a person who caused the damage. The specific characteristics of AI, including complexity, autonomy and opacity … may make it difficult or prohibitively expensive for victims to identify the liable person.[193]

The Directive attempts to leverage around the concept of fault by altering the burden of proof of causation, but not only cuts this off by limiting it to where it can be shown that the producer deviated from the AI Act, but states that 'this Directive does not harmonise the conditions under which national courts establish fault'.[194] In fact,

> [f]or the presumption of causality under this Directive to apply, the fault of the defendant should be established as a human act or omission which does not meet a duty of care under Union law or national law that is directly intended to protect against the damage that occurred.[195]

The causal link is not the crucial issue: the pressing question is whether the harm resulted from something unreasonable. Recall the unfortunate woman in *Ahanonu* who was squashed against a bollard by a bus: the bus driver was not liable because his actions were reasonable in having to look forward when making a physical turn.

The personal injury principle, *res ipsa loquitur*, states that 'the thing speaks for itself' – that the injury itself is evidence of negligence. There are cases where this is true, but it is not universal. For the very reasons that porting the Driving Code to AI is not an overnight action, the Directive misses the crucial point for many jurisdictions: they still depend on concepts of reasonableness. Demanding that aspects such as potentially continuous human oversight may not be practicable, and in setting these as requirements both the Act and the Directive set themselves up as barriers to their own intended use: to induce and encourage high-societal value AI while ensuring victims are compensated.

While it is difficult to predict the impact of, for example, Article 3 of the AI Liability Directive in stating that claims must be 'plausible', what the examination throughout other chapters of this book show is that the concept of fault in common law systems relies on certain ingrained concepts: foreseeability, and reasonableness. The AI Liability Directive does not even begin to address these concepts, deferring instead to national courts and attempting an easing of showing a causal link as a stopgap. Yet this removal is ineffective: showing fault requires a measure of causality to begin with, and fault is where the difficulty with raising a case against a producer will lie. AI producers will have the advantage in a variety of aspects: not just resources, but knowledge, data and evidence. This is not to say that AI producers should be barred from showing innocence of fault, but the law should recognise the realistic difficulty of the plaintiff in doing so.

This book endeavours to show that not only are foreseeability and reasonableness key components of non-AI liability, but that they should not be abandoned in regulating AI liability. This is supported by the Act's own statements regarding

[193] EU AI Act (n 135) Explanatory Memorandum 1.
[194] ibid, Preamble (22).
[195] ibid.

risk assessments: the 'identification and analysis of the known and the reasonably foreseeable risks that the AI system can pose'; as well as foreseeable misuse.[196] The realities of situations such as the power and data-access advantage of AI producers should not be ignored, but they can be overcome by measures that address contextual factors such as burdens of proof and reasonable inference of harm. The European Union has the pressure of not only building a regulatory system that works with its other regulatory architectures, but one which must contend with each Member State's arrangements as well, in both common and civil law jurisdictions. However, the AI Liability Directive does not, in and of itself, go any particular distance in resolving AI liability questions: it affirms those endeavours shown in the then-draft AI Act, such as the conformity assessment, but does not resolve the serious concerns that both producers and the public will have about AI. This does not mean that the structure of the AI Liability Directive is useless, but that it may represent more of a building point for the liability conversation. For example, if one were to keep the emphasis on conformity assessment, but add an inquisitorial body capable of delving into whether conformity was sufficient, this would allow for the types of due diligence discussions shown in section 3.5 – having stated in their conformity assessment what their process should be, producers would have the possibility and requirement to show what their process actually was – decisions made, factors optimised for, etc. This means that rather than consumers being forced to rely on what producers said they would do, that the process can be defensibly shown to have occurred – or not – depending on the case. This model and process will be expanded on in chapter seven.

5.3.3. United States

The United States as a federal republic has legislative ability and traditions both at a state and federal level. While the European Union has encouraged Member States to develop AI legislation, the United States has seen states try to encourage it at a federal level.[197] While states have taken the lead in developing sector-specific legislation,[198] legislation at the federal level has started gaining traction. This direction, however, has varied somewhat in the presidential leadership of the moment. Under Barack Obama's presidency, reports on AI emphasised AI for public good, as fairness, safety and governance.[199] The 2016–20 presidency, however,

[196] EU AI Act (n 135) Chapter II, Art 9(2).

[197] 'Legislation Related to Artificial Intelligence', National Conference of State Legislatures (31 January 2023): ncsl.org/research/telecommunications-and-information-technology/2020-legislation-related-to-artificial-intelligence.aspx.

[198] Such as, eg, California and Nevada with self-driving vehicles. C Pinto, 'How Autonomous Vehicle Policy in California and Nevada Addresses Technological and Non-Technological Liabilities' (2012) 5 *Intersect* 1, 1.

[199] S Gerke, T Minssen and G Cohen, 'Ethical and Legal Challenges of Artificial-Intelligence-Driven Healthcare' (2020) *Artificial Intelligence in Healthcare* 295: ncbi.nlm.nih.gov/pmc/articles/PMC7332220/, citing 'Preparing for the future of artificial intelligence' (Executive Office of the President

saw US AI strategy shift 'to a more free-market approach'.[200] In May 2018, the US-hosted 'AI for Industry' summit typified this approach with the takeaway that the Administration's key aim was to remove barriers to AI innovation, rather than structure its approach.[201] The Executive Office of the President announced later that year that AI would be one of the top R&D budget priority areas for 2020.[202]

February 2019 saw a step further towards governing legislation with the 'Executive Order on Maintaining American Leadership in Artificial Intelligence'. This order provided 'five high level principles … to be implemented by the National Science and Technology Council (NSTC) Select Committee on Artificial Intelligence'.[203] Daly et al note that the order provided that

> agencies are to receive a memorandum from the Office of Management and Budget within 180 days to inform their regulatory and non-regulatory approaches to AI which 'advance American innovation while upholding civil liberties, privacy, and American values' and shall 'consider ways to reduce barriers to the use of AI technologies in order to promote their innovative application while protecting civil liberties, privacy, American values, and United States economic and national security'.[204]

However, the draft of the memorandum was (and appears to remain) unavailable. Further, the Order directed that

> within 180 days of the date of this order, the Secretary of Commerce, through the Director of the National Institute of Standards of Technology (NIST), shall issue a plan for Federal engagement in the development of technical standards and related tools in support of reliable, robust, and trustworthy systems that use AI technologies.[205]

In May 2019, the National Institute of Standards of Technology (NIST) issued a Request for Information regarding this plan and in August issued 'A Plan for

National Science and Technology Council Committee on Technology): obamawhitehouse.archives.gov/sites/default/files/whitehouse_files/microsites/ostp/NSTC/preparing_for_the_future_of_ai.pdf; US Government, 'The National Artificial Intelligence Research and Development Strategic Plan' (National Science and Technology Council; Networking and Information Technology Research and Development Subcommittee): obamawhitehouse.archives.gov/sites/default/files/whitehouse_files/microsites/ostp/NSTC/national_ai_rd_strategic_plan.pdf; and 'Artificial Intelligence, Automation, and the Economy' (Executive Office of the President) obamawhitehouse.archives.gov/sites/whitehouse.gov/files/documents/Artificial-Intelligence-Automation-Economy.PDF.

[200] ibid, citing T Dutton, 'An overview of national AI strategies' (2018): medium.com/politics-ai/an-overview-of-national-ai-strategies-2a70ec6edfd.

[201] ibid, citing 'Summary of the 2018 White House summit on artificial intelligence for American Industry' (Office of Science and Technology Policy, 2018): trumpwhitehouse.archives.gov/wp-content/uploads/2018/05/Summary-Report-of-White-House-AI-Summit.pdf.

[202] ibid, citing 'Memorandum for the Heads of Executive Departments and Agencies' (Executive Office of the President, 2018) M-18-22: whitehouse.gov/wp-content/uploads/2018/10/m10-32.pdf.

[203] A Daly et al, 'Artificial Intelligence, Governance and Ethics: Global Perspectives' (2019) SSRN Electronic Journal: ssrn.com/abstract=3414805.

[204] ibid, citing 'Executive Order 13859: Maintaining American Leadership in Artificial Intelligence' (White House, 11 February 2019): trumpwhitehouse.archives.gov/presidential-actions/executive-order-maintaining-american-leadership-artificial-intelligence/.

[205] 'Executive Order 12859: Maintaining American Leadership in Artificial Intelligence' (White House, 11 February 2019) web.archive.org/web/20190212000146: www.whitehouse.gov/presidential-actions/executive-order-maintaining-american-leadership-artificial-intelligence/.

Federal Engagement in Developing Technical Standards and Related Tools'.[206] Lastly, the Order launched the American AI initiative, which set out five principles:

> (a) The United States must drive technological breakthroughs in AI across the Federal Government, industry, and academia in order to promote scientific discovery, economic competitiveness, and national security.
> (b) The United States must drive development of appropriate technical standards and reduce barriers to the safe testing and deployment of AI technologies in order to enable the creation of new AI-related industries and the adoption of AI by today's industries.
> (c) The United States must train current and future generations of American workers with the skills to develop and apply AI technologies to prepare them for today's economy and jobs of the future.
> (d) The United States must foster public trust and confidence in AI technologies and protect civil liberties, privacy, and American values in their application in order to fully realize the potential of AI technologies for the American people.
> (e) The United States must promote an international environment that supports American AI research and innovation and opens markets for American AI industries, while protecting our technological advantage in AI and protecting our critical AI technologies from acquisition by strategic competitors and adversarial nations.[207]

In January 2020, the White House published draft guidance for the regulation of AI applications, which contained 10 principles that agencies should consider when formulating AI approaches: public trust in AI, public participation, scientific integrity and information quality, risk assessment and management, benefits and costs, flexibility, fairness and non-discrimination, disclosure and transparency, safety and security, and interagency coordination.[208] In February 2020, a White House Report on the AI Initiative highlighted progress made since the Executive Order on Maintaining American Leadership in Artificial Intelligence was signed, including the 'US-led efforts' on the Organization for Economic Co-operation and Development (OECD) principles of AI.[209]

February 2021 saw the introduction of the National Defense Authorization Act.[210] While the focus of this book is not intended to include national defence nor military,[211] this Act is necessarily included for reasons of being

> the most substantial legislation addressing the artificial intelligence (AI) approved by Congress to [that] date, including landmark legislation setting national policy on

[206] The Plan called for 'deeper, consistent, long-term' engagement at the federal level. National Institute of Standards and Technology, 'US Leadership in AI: A Plan for Federal Engagement in Developing Technical Standards and Related Tools' (US Department of Commerce 2019) nist.gov/system/files/documents/2019/08/10/ai_standards_fedengagement_plan_9aug2019.pdf.

[207] 'Maintaining American Leadership in Artificial Intelligence' (n 205).

[208] RT Vought, 'Memorandum for the Heads of Executive Departments and Agencies' whitehouse.gov/wp-content/uploads/2020/01/Draft-OMB-Memo-on-Regulation-of-AI-1-7-19.pdf.

[209] Gerke, Minssen and Cohen (n 199).

[210] US Congress, 116th Congress (2019–2020): National Defense Authorization Act for Fiscal Year 2021.

[211] ie, AI causing intentional rather than accidental death.

> the emerging technology already shaping and transforming virtually every aspect of military and civilian life.[212]

The Act includes Division E, also known as the 'National Artificial Intelligence Initiative Act of 2020 … [which draws on previous legislative initiatives] to establish a coordinated, civilian-led federal initiative to accelerate research and development to encourage investments in trustworthy AI'.[213] The bill includes the creation of a new National Artificial Intelligence Initiative Office under the White House Office of Science and Technology Policy (OSTP) 'to lead US global leadership in the development and use of trustworthy AI systems' and to serve as the contact point for both federal and executive branch departments; funding to support research and skill-training; department of energy research; and the writ for NIST to 'expand its mission to include advancing collaborative frameworks, standards, guidelines for AI, supporting the development of a risk-mitigation framework for AI systems, and supporting the development of technical standards and guidelines to promote trustworthy AI systems'.[214] Needless to say, it is a bill of broad application.

The National Defense Authorization Act was followed up by the (introduced, but not passed) Algorithmic Accountability Act 2022. While the Algorithmic Accountability Act is far less broad than the National Defense Authorization Act, it would have required entities using AI that 'deploys any augmented critical decision process' to have a level of significant income and/or customer base and employ automated decision-making 'in an augmented critical decision process' to conduct critical impact assessments of the automated system.[215] One of the bill's sponsors, Senator Cory Booker, stated: 'This bill requires companies to regularly evaluate their tools for accuracy, fairness, bias and discrimination. It's a key step toward ensuring more accountability from the entities using software to make decisions that can change lives'.[216] Senator Booker explicitly notes the potential impacts of algorithms in employment, housing and financing.[217] The bill states that entities falling under the criteria must:

> Evaluate the rights of consumers, such as … by assessing the transparency and explainability of such system or process and the degree to which a consumer may contest, correct, or appeal a decision or opt out of such a system or process.[218]

The explainability measures focused on include information about the system or process, 'such as any relevant factors that contribute to a particular decision,

[212] T Samp et al, 'Landmark Artificial Intelligence Legislation Advances toward Becoming Law/ Insights/ DLA Piper Global Law Firm', DLA Piper: dlapiper.com/en/us/insights/publications/2020/12/ landmark-artificial-intelligence-legislation-advances-toward-becoming-law/.

[213] ibid.

[214] ibid.

[215] 'Algorithmic Accountability Act of 2022' (2 April 2022) H.R.6580 – 117th Congress (2021–2022).

[216] M Shacklett, 'Algorithmic Accountability Act: What Tech Leaders Need to Know and Do Now' (*TechRepublic*, 28 July 2022): techrepublic.com/article/know-algorithmic-accountability-act/.

[217] ibid.

[218] YD Clarke, 'Text – H.R.6580 – 117th Congress (2021–2022): Algorithmic Accountability Act of 2022' (2 April 2022).

including an explanation of which contributing factors, if changed, would cause the system or process to reach a different decision',[219] as well as documentation and remediation measures. Essentially, the requirements do edge slightly into XAI techniques – local explanations and important variables. However, it does so only to a similar extent to the GDPR – the requirement of an explanation for an automated decision. While the functional application of the bill may prove more impactful, the GDPR precedent does not yet suggest that this will be a radical redesign of such systems.

At the federal level, the White House released in early October 2022 the 'Blueprint for an AI Bill of Rights: Making automated Systems Work for the American People'. The Blueprint was created by the Office of Science and Technology, and notes the potential dangers of AI particularly with regard to civil rights and democratic values.[220] The Blueprint identifies 'five principles that should guide the design, use and deployment of automated systems to protect the American public', those principles being: safe and effective systems; algorithmic discrimination protections; data privacy; notice and explanation; and human alternatives, consideration, and fallback.[221] Essentially, systems should be safe and effective at their intended purpose; no party should face discrimination by algorithm; AI should include data protection practices by default; parties should be informed that an automated system is being used to make a decision about them and how that decision might be used; and parties should be able to opt out of automated decision-making in favour of human decision-making. While these areas all seem reasonable and thought through, it is important to note that the Blueprint is completely non-binding: it is an advisory tool only, and its principles remain at a very broad level.

The US address of AI as a whole expanded considerably in 2023, likely in response to a greater public awareness of AI generally, coming off the publicity of generative AI models. This included a number of reports, statements and hearings, such as those from the US Chamber of Commerce;[222] a variety of federal agencies,[223] and the Senate Judiciary.[224] It also resulted in a number of proposed AI bills and frameworks: the National AI Commission Act; the Bipartisan AI Framework for US Act; the Algorithmic Accountability Act; the Bipartisan AI Bill to Strengthen Accountability and Boost Innovation; and the AI Risk Management Act. These numerous proposed approaches are both at a very early stage and not necessarily indicative of a particular direction for US AI Policy.

[219] ibid.

[220] 'Blueprint for an AI Bill of Rights/OSTP': whitehouse.gov/ostp/ai-bill-of-rights/.

[221] ibid.

[222] 'Artificial Intelligence Commission Report' (US Chamber of Commerce, 9 March 2023) uschamber.com/technology/artificial-intelligence-commission-report.

[223] 'FTC Chair Khan and Officials from DOJ, CFPB and EEOC Release Joint Statement on AI' (Federal Trade Commission, 25 April 2023): ftc.gov/news-events/news/press-releases/2023/04/ftc-chair-khan-officials-doj-cfpb-eeoc-release-joint-statement-ai.

[224] 'Oversight of AI: Rules for Artificial Intelligence' (US Senate Committee on the Judiciary, 16 March 2023): judiciary.senate.gov/committee-activity/hearings/oversight-of-ai-rules-for-artificial-intelligence.

While the National AI Commission Act proposes the establishment of, unsurprisingly, a National AI Commission, the others focus on more broad headings. The Bipartisan AI Framework for US AI Act appears, at this stage, to consist of a one-page outline.[225] The Algorithmic Accountability Act is intended to 'direct the Federal Trade Commission to require impact assessments of automated decision systems and augmented critical decision processes',[226] though it does not mention liability, and was introduced in 2022 with no progress by 2024. The Bipartisan AI Bill to Strengthen Accountability and Boost Innovation, introduced November 2023, ostensibly focuses on 'transparency, accountability, and security [for] the development and operation of the highest-impact applications of AI',[227] although the text appears to be limited in availability to those portions posted on Senator Klobuchar's home site.[228] The AI Risk Management Act is in support of the most recent federal-level intercession so far, and perhaps the most impactful: the 2023 Executive Order on Safe, Secure, and Trustworthy Artificial Intelligence.

The 2023 Executive Order addresses AI on a number of levels, including the establishment of new standards; protecting against a range of AI-created or 'AI-assisted harms' and ensuring the protection of rights and vulnerable persons.[229] Of particular interest are the Executive Order's requirement

> that developers of the most powerful AI systems share their safety test results and other critical information with the [US] government … companies developing any foundation model that poses a serious risk to national security, national economic security, or national public health and safety must notify the federal government when training the model, and must share the results.[230]

Because Executive Orders are not bound by the same process as legislative bills or similar legislative approaches, and are instead official documents 'through which the President of the United States manages the operations of the Federal Government', the Executive Order has a higher level of immediacy and impact than the proposed bills listed above, even though it may be revoked at any time.[231]

[225] R Blumenthal and J Hawley, 'Bipartisan Framework for U.S. AI Act': blumenthal.senate.gov/imo/media/doc/09072023bipartisanaiframework.pdf.

[226] H.R.6580 – Algorithmic Accountability Act of 2022.

[227] 'Klobuchar, Thune, Commerce Committee Colleagues Introduce Bipartisan AI Bill to Strengthen Accountability and Boost Innovation' (United States Senator Amy Klobuchar, 15 November 2023): klobuchar.senate.gov/public/index.cfm/2023/11/klobuchar-thune-commerce-committee-colleagues-introduce-bipartisan-ai-bill-to-strengthen-accountability-and-boost-innovation#:~:text=The%20bipartisan%20legislation%20establishes%20a,highest%2Dimpact%20applications%20of%20AI.

[228] ibid.

[229] 'FACT SHEET: President Biden Issues Executive Order on Safe, Secure, and Trustworthy Artificial Intelligence' (White House, 30 October 2023): whitehouse.gov/briefing-room/statements-releases/2023/10/30/fact-sheet-president-biden-issues-executive-order-on-safe-secure-and-trustworthy-artificial-intelligence/.

[230] ibid.

[231] 'Executive Orders', Bureau of Justice Assistance, US Department of Justice: bja.ojp.gov/program/it/privacy-civil-liberties/authorities/executive-orders#:~:text=%E2%80%9CExecutive%20Orders%20(EOs)%20are,and%20statute%20(sometimes%20specified).

While the Executive Order does not yet provide sufficient detail of how exactly these aims will be carried out in practice, it does nonetheless provide specific mandates to agencies such as the NIST to '[d]evelop standards, tools, and tests to help ensure that AI systems are safe, secure, and trustworthy'.[232] Lastly, at the federal level, is the Federal Trade Commission's authorisation of 'compulsory process' for AI-related products and services. While this is investigation rather than strict rules around AI creation or liability, it may well play an important part in the US AI ecosystem, particularly given that it applies to 'investigations involving products and services that use or claim to be produced using artificial intelligence (AI) or claim to detect its use'.[233]

States have also started the process of enacting or considering enacting AI legislation.[234] As of February 2024, these include a variety of laws with a particular focus such as on various aspects of privacy;[235] prohibition of bots in sales or services without making the other party aware of the bot;[236] restrictions and prohibitions on using AI in video interviews;[237] permission for licensed practitioners to use a certain 'assessment mechanisms', including those based on AI, for ophthalmological exams;[238] and a city-specific requirement for bias audits by employers using AI for employment decisions.[239] Many other pieces of AI-specific legislation are in process.

Lastly, the United States has a thus far unique source of information on AI governance: a case on its use, *State v Loomis* of Wisconsin saw a criminal defendant's sentencing by a judge who took into account the results of COMPAS (Correctional Offender Management Profiling for Alternative Sanctions), an AI risk-assessment application.[240] The use of the tool was challenged by the defence, who 'demanded access to the coding of its algorithm'.[241] The proprietary nature of COMPAS' makeup prevented other parties from assessing its use and accuracy.[242] Ultimately the use of COMPAS by the judge was upheld, based in large part 'on the fact that it was the judge who sentenced the defendant – not the AI'.[243] However, it is demonstrative that courts are at the very least receptive to use of AI in making

[232] 'FACT SHEET' (n 229).
[233] 'FTC Authorizes Compulsory Process for AI-related Products and Services' (Federal Trade Commission, 21 November 2023): ftc.gov/news-events/news/press-releases/2023/11/ftc-authorizes-compulsory-process-ai-related-products-services.
[234] 'US State-by-state AI legislation snapshot', BCLP: bclplaw.com/en-US/events-insights-news/2023-state-by-state-artificial-intelligence-legislation-snapshot.html.
[235] California Consumer Privacy Act; Indiana SB5; Texas Data Privacy and Security Act HB4; Connecticut Privacy Act; New Jersey S332.
[236] California SB 1001.
[237] Illinois AI Video Interview Act.
[238] Georgia HB 203.
[239] New York City specifically; Local Law 144.
[240] *State v Loomis* 881 NW 2d 749 (Wis 2016).
[241] I Giuffrida, 'Liability for AI Decision-Making: Some Legal and Ethical Considerations' (2019) 88 *Fordham Law Review* 439.
[242] ibid.
[243] ibid.

decisions about humans whether or not AI decisions can be explained – a position not necessarily shared by the governance approaches of the European Union.[244]

US Analysis

Ultimately, the US governance approach to regulation of AI appears to be in its early days. That said, there are still signposts and lessons to be learned from its approach thus far. While American AI consortia and companies have certainly had an effect on the self-regulatory side, the federal approach has been slower to provide concrete provisions. The state-level approach has in many ways furthered the use of AI in sector-specific legislation, such as explicitly banning or allowing self-driving vehicles, whereas the federal-level legislation focused initially on removing barriers and facilitating creation of AI, rather than guiding its application or creation.

At the federal level, AI has clearly been made a priority, although the governing approaches have swung with the pendulum of the White House. The Obama Administration's focus on AI for public good did not establish a concrete level of governance for AI, but did focus on ways it might be beneficial, such as its use for the public good, and the need for fairness and safety. This approach was not followed by the subsequent administration, which focused instead on establishing dominance in the use of AI, particularly in areas such as R&D.[245] The 2020 draft guidance's provision of 10 principles for agencies to consider in formulating AI approaches comes closest to the principles-based approach of Singapore, but there is limited evidence as to its application and effect on AI producers. While the 2020 White House Report on the AI Initiative rightly pointed out progress made in the AI governance arena, initiatives included those such as the OECD principles, which are not enshrined as legislation. The National AI Initiative Act of 2020 also called for the establishment of the National Artificial Intelligence Advisory Committee (NAIAC), 'tasked with advising the President and the National AI Initiative Office on topics related to the AI Initiative', focusing on topics such as the US market's relative competitiveness, leveraging of resources, funding, coordination, etc, and, interestingly, 'issues related to accountability and legal rights', although the latter has not yet been expanded upon.[246]

The impact of 2023's greater public awareness of AI, brought on by the publicity of generative models, seems to have ushered AI into the arena of political capital, a point on which politicians can show that they are attuned to public concern. It is difficult to tell from the flurry of proposed bills what exactly will be enshrined in law, but the focus on the need for, at base level, guidelines on development and testing requirements is heartening. This is buoyed too by intergovernmental organisations, such as the promotion of NIST to provide collaborative frameworks,

[244] See, eg, the GDPR requirement for decisions about humans to be explained.

[245] 'Summary of the 2018 White House summit on artificial intelligence for American Industry' (n 201).

[246] 'National Artificial Intelligence Advisory Committee (NAIAC)' (*NIST*, 1 March 2024): nist.gov/itl/national-artificial-intelligence-advisory-committee-naiac.

standards technical and otherwise, and guidelines. While it is still very early days, the 2023 Executive Order on Safe, Secure, and Trustworthy Artificial Intelligence is likely the most impactful so far in terms of the governance of civil applications. It too provides a level of focus on standards, alongside societal-level concerns such as bias. While many details are ultimately an extension of other concerns, such as data privacy, civil rights and cyber security, there are also the first formal forays into demanding transparency elements from AI companies, such as safety test results and critical information for companies developing foundation models posing a potentially serious risk. There is a distinct lack of address, however, of liability or the relationship between the standards proposed and harm that occurs.

5.3.4. United Kingdom

The UK address of artificial intelligence began comparatively early but has not yet produced direct legislative action. Starting in 2016, the United Kingdom has produced a series of studies, reports and calls for evidence on AI and its regulation. The earliest recent address[247] could be stated to be the October 2016 House of Commons Science and Technology Committee Report, *Robotics and Artificial Intelligence*, which recommended greater emphasis on relevant skills for those creating robots and AI.[248] It suggested a standing commission on AI to examine its implications and establish relevant principles, but also concluded that it was too early to regulate AI specifically.[249] This was followed in April 2017 by the Royal Society Report, *Machine learning: the power and promise of computers that learn by example*. The report recommended promotion of open data standards, the improvement of education in machine learning, targeting immigration needs in line with the sector, and the facilitation of public dialogue on what machine learning might mean, but ultimately 'argued in favour of specific sectoral approaches to regulating AI, rather than a more overarching, cross-sector approach'.[250] Following soon after, the June 2017 British Academy and Royal Science Joint Report, *Data management and use: Governance in the 21st century* focused primarily but broadly on data management, including its importance and relevance to AI. While not aimed at AI specifically, it did recommend 'the establishment of a new body to steward the data governance landscape as a whole'.[251] October 2017 saw the review 'Growing the artificial intelligence industry in the UK' – produced as part of the

[247] The UK government did engage with state-sponsored R&D in the 1980s, but '[d]espite overall funding of £350 million … it failed in its central objective of improving the competitiveness of UK information technology (IT) business'. Select Committee on Artificial Intelligence, *AI in the UK: Ready, Willing and Able* (HL 2017–19) 183.

[248] Science and Technology Committee, *Robotics and Artificial Intelligence* (HC, 2016–17).

[249] ibid.

[250] *AI in the UK: Ready, Willing and Able* (n 247) citing Royal Society, *Machine learning: the power and promise of computers that learn by example*: royalsociety.org/~/media/policy/projects/machine-learning/publications/machine-learning-report.pdf.

[251] British Academy and the Royal Society, *Data management and use: Governance in the 21st century*: royalsociety.org/-/media/policy/projects/data-governance/data-management-governance.pdf, 3.

UK government's Digital Strategy, it provided 18 recommendations on making the United Kingdom a world-leading place for AI businesses, focusing on areas such as increased adoption, secure data storage and building research capacity.[252]

Defining AI as integral to the UK's long-term strategic goals was certainly cemented in 2017, with some balance between its presence in the UK government's Digital Strategy and the November 2017 UK White Paper on the UK's four 'Grand Challenges', one of the grand challenges being AI. Where the Digital Strategy review provided policy-oriented recommendations for attracting AI business and investment, the White Paper responded to the October Review in detailing AI policies and new institutions. The White Paper provided for the 2018 £950 million AI Sector Deal, and established the Office for AI, operating jointly under the Department for Digital, Culture, Media & Sport, and the Department for Business, Energy & Industrial Strategy. Where other jurisdictions asked existing ministries to coordinate an office dedicated to AI, this joint unit represents a more unusual approach.[253] The White Paper noted the key role of ethics in AI adoption, thus establishing the Centre for Data Ethics and Innovation (CDEI), but also concluded 'that there should not be a new AI-specific regulator for the UK, but rather that all existing regulators must meet the challenges AI poses to their sector'.[254] The CDEI would, with the AI Council, go on to take point in establishing AI working principles and broader governance.[255]

In 2018, the House of Lords Select Committee on Artificial Intelligence conducted a far-reaching inquiry 'to consider the economic, ethical, and social implications of advances in artificial intelligence', asking five questions:

- How does AI affect people in their everyday lives, and how is this likely to change?
- What are the potential opportunities presented by artificial intelligence for the United Kingdom? How can these be realised?
- What are the possible risks and implications of artificial intelligence? How can these be avoided?
- How should the public be engaged with in a responsible manner about AI?
- What are the ethical issues presented by the development and use of artificial intelligence?[256]

This call for responses heralded 223 pieces of written evidence; 57 accounts of oral evidence; visits with industrial stakeholders including DeepMind,

[252] W Hall and J Presenti 'Growing the artificial intelligence industry in the UK' (2017): assets.publishing.service.gov.uk/media/5a824465e5274a2e87dc2079/Growing_the_artificial_intelligence_industry_in_the_UK.pdf.

[253] R Radu, 'Steering the Governance of Artificial Intelligence: National Strategies in Perspective' (2021) 40 Policy and Society 178: doi.org/10.1080/14494035.2021.1929728.

[254] *AI in the UK: Ready, Willing and Able* (n 247).

[255] Radu (n 253).

[256] *AI in the UK: Ready, Willing and Able* (n 247).

the Microsoft Research Lab, and several startups; and a variety of civil society groups. Where previous reports had considered ethical implications and responses, such as establishing the CDEI, this inquiry and report was a deeper look at public trust and AI integration. This is not to say that the report was insensible to business interests; for example, concluding that 'industry should take the lead in establishing voluntary mechanisms for informing the public when artificial intelligence is being used for significant or sensitive decisions in relation to consumers'.[257]

In engaging with the five above questions, the report was structured (beyond an introduction to AI and notes on everyday engagement) into several categories: designing artificial intelligence; developing artificial intelligence; working with artificial intelligence; living with artificial intelligence; healthcare and artificial intelligence; mitigating the risks of artificial intelligence; and shaping artificial intelligence.

Design covers access to and control of AI data; transparency and explainability; addressing prejudice; and data monopolies. Developing AI focuses on investment; commercial potential; improving access to AI talent; and 'maintaining innovation'. Working with artificial intelligence focuses on productivity; government adoption and procurement; labour market impact; and a national retraining scheme. Living with artificial intelligence covers education; impact on social and political cohesion; and inequality.

While healthcare and artificial intelligence might seem self explanatory, this section covers 'the opportunity', and the value of using data, but also cases where public trust in data usage has been damaged, such as the partnership between DeepMind and the Royal Free London NHS Foundation Trust. Mitigating the risks of AI is perhaps the most legislatively focused of the sections, covering legal liability; criminal misuse of AI and data; and autonomous weaponry.

Lastly, shaping AI covers the areas of regulatory control: the AI Council and the Government Office for AI; the CDEI; regulation and regulators; assessing policy outcomes; and an AI Code. This list of categories is wide, but not without purpose. It engages on a variety of levels: technical questions such as the control and protection of data, and transparency and explainability; social questions such as inequality and social impact; legal questions such as liability and criminal misuse; regulatory structure governance bodies. However, its primary focus is clearly business: how to educate, attract and maintain talent; avoid misuse of public trust that might damage practices engaging with AI; investment; productivity; a National Retraining Scheme. This is supported within the report itself, which engages business concerns within other areas, such as 'urg[ing] the Government to consider further substantial public investment to ensure [ultrafast internet]', 'endorsing the recommendation … aimed at encouraging greater use of AI in the public sector', etc.[258]

[257] ibid.
[258] ibid.

The report is not merely supporting a home-grown industry of AI, but actively fostering it in the long term with specific recommendations such as 'improv[ing] digital understanding and digital literacy across society' and recognising 'an urgent need to analyse or assess, on an ongoing basis, the evolution of AI in the UK, and develop policy responses' with regard to the impact on the labour market.[259]

The report also makes some directly practical suggestions, such as a cross-sectoral ethical code of conduct for AI producers, efforts to make publicly held data available and portable, and recognising the need for intelligible AI, '[w]hether this takes the form of technical transparency, explainability, or indeed both … but in most cases we believe explainability will be a more useful approach for the citizen and consumer', even going so far as to suggest that where explanations of decisions producing a substantial impact on an individual's life cannot be explained, this 'may mean delaying [AI] deployment for [such] uses until alternative solutions are found'.[260] This reflects the EU approach shown in the GDPR, which requires that explanations be possible and providable.

The report does not drastically disengage with previous UK assessments of AI legislation, continuing the stance that '[b]lanket AI-specific regulation, at this stage, would be inappropriate. [They] believe that existing sector-specific regulators are best placed to consider the impact on their sectors of any subsequent regulation which may be needed', with the Government Office for AI and the CDEI identifying gaps 'where existing regulation may not be adequate'.[261] It also drives home the stance that 'it is essential that the policies towards artificial intelligence are suitable for the rapidly changing environment which they are meant to support'.[262]

Where the report does not make definitive statements is in recommending how liability, for businesses or others, should play out in practice. The report notes the seriousness of the issue, for both embodied or non-embodied AI, and directly quotes the Royal College of Radiologists that 'legal liability is often stated as a major societal hurdle to overcome before widespread adoption of AI becomes a reality'.[263] The report suggests that the adequacy of existing liability legislation be considered by the Law Commission in order to, at the very least, 'establish clear principles for accountability and intelligibility'.[264] The report does suggest that the aforementioned cross-sectoral ethical code of conduct or AI Code could be the basis for eventual regulation, but does so tepidly with the caveat that it should do so 'if and when this is determined to be necessary'.[265]

[259] ibid.
[260] ibid.
[261] ibid.
[262] ibid.
[263] ibid.
[264] ibid.
[265] ibid.

In less widely impactful engagement, January 2020 saw the publication of 'A guide to using artificial intelligence in the public sector'. Being both sector-specific and a continuation of current policies in the governance of the public sector, the guide did not provide or produce the same sort of impact as the 2018 Report. December 2021, however, saw the release of 'The Roadmap to an Effective AI Assurance Ecosystem' or AI Roadmap, as part of the Plan for Digital Regulation.[266] Published by the CDEI, the Roadmap is in many ways a continuation or expansion of the House of Lords report, and focuses on a roadmap to growing the AI industry, though with considered acknowledgment of the essential nature of public trust.[267] The Roadmap refers to the 'UK AI ecosystem', and opens with the potential financial benefits of AI – moving then to the idea that 'consumer and citizen' trust in AI is crucial for accomplishing such goals. The guide's Depiction of trust, or rather justified trust, is captured as being between the responsible party, such as a developer, and a second party, such as a party procuring an AI for use.[268]

The Roadmap categorises three layers of AI stakeholders: supporting structures in the way of Government, Regulators, Standards Bodies, and Accreditation/professional bodies; AI assurance service providers and independent research; and AI developers, executives deploying AI systems, frontline users, and affected individuals.[269] The Roadmap envisions AI assurance service providers – independent assurance providers such as auditors and certification bodies, as well as internal assurance teams – influencing AI developers and deploying executives directly.[270] The Roadmap depicts AI assurance as being a necessary step to 'understand[ing] and commmunicat[ing] whether AI systems are trustworthy and compliant with regulation', while also stating that 'AI assurance will also become a significant economic activity in its own right, with the potential for the UK to be a global leader in a new multi-billion pound industry'.[271] The former is interesting in that little regulation has in fact been conceived, although the latter is not necessarily dependent on this idea. The Roadmap also provides a 'spectrum of mechanisms for assuring AI systems', ranging from least to most known: impact assessment; impact evaluation; bias audit; compliance audit, certification; conformity assessment; performance testing; and formal verification.[272] This in some ways mirrors the EU's CE marking approach, although it does not yet explicitly provide such a programme. It does provide examples of regulatory initiatives for AI assurance such as the Information Commissioner's Office (ICO)'s AI Auditing Framework, the combination ICO/Alan Turing Institute's guidance on explaining AI decisions,

[266] 'Digital Regulation: Driving Growth and Unlocking Innovation' (GOV.UK, 10 October 2023): gov.uk/government/publications/digital-regulation-driving-growth-and-unlocking-innovation.
[267] 'The Roadmap to an Effective AI Assurance Ecosystem' (GOV.UK, 8 December 2021): gov.uk/government/publications/the-roadmap-to-an-effective-ai-assurance-ecosystem, 4.
[268] ibid.
[269] ibid.
[270] ibid.
[271] ibid.
[272] ibid.

and the Medicines & Healthcare products Regulatory Agency's work programme to update regulations involving AI and medical devices.[273] Lastly, the Roadmap breaks down its statements into three categories: vision; current challenges; and what needs to happen. For example, a vision of 'reliable and defective assurance across the supply chain, and across the range of risks', faces the current challenge of limited demand, requiring '[a]ctors in the AI supply chain to have a clearer understanding of AI risks', among other things.[274]

In 2021, the Department for Digital, Culture, Media & Sport released the 'Digital Regulation Plan', a summary theme policy paper on the regulation of digital technologies, AI among them, providing 'high-level considerations, including the establishment of three principles that should guide future plans for the regulation of digital technologies',[275] these principles being the active promotion of innovation, the achievement of forward-looking, coherent outcomes, and the exploitation of opportunities and address of challenges internationally. This too, perhaps unsurprisingly, begins with the contributions both so far and forthcoming, of digital technologies to the UK's economy.

The policy paper does look at digital regulation: 'the range of regulatory tools that government, regulators, businesses, and other bodies use to manage the impact that digital technologies and activities can have on individuals, companies, the economy and society … [including] norms, self-regulation, statutory codes of conduct, and rules in primary legislation'.[276] It further notes the importance of distinct regulation of digital applications, stating that governance based on the three measures is intended 'to create proportionate, agile, flexible measures'.[277] The paper is largely prospective, stating that the government 'will take action', 'will examine the case for a new mechanism', 'will work closely with key regulators', 'will explore further ways to ensure regulators are able to share resources', etc.[278] More than most of the aforementioned engagement, this paper does provide some focus on the international approach – the UK's then G7 presidency, and the relationship between the United Kingdom and several other jurisdictions.[279] The report does not, however, lay down any set of regulation in and of itself.

Continuing through 2021 did not break the governmental trend of economy-oriented publications, with September 2021 seeing the publication of the 'National AI Strategy', this time with the slightly different wording of 'recognising the power of AI to increase resilience, productivity, growth and innovation across the private

[273] ibid.
[274] ibid.
[275] 'Regulate to Innovate' (Ada Lovelace Institute, 2021): adalovelaceinstitute.org/report/regulate-innovate/.
[276] 'Digital Regulation: Driving Growth and Unlocking Innovation' (n 266).
[277] ibid.
[278] ibid.
[279] Including Singapore, with whom the UK had 'set out intentions to negotiate a Digital Economy Agreement, [seeking] to further enhance [their] relationship and cooperation on digital trade'. ibid.

and public sectors'.[280] Slightly more inward-facing than the Digital Regulation Plan, the National AI Strategy lauded the success of measures until that point, stating that '[t]he UK is a global superpower in AI'.[281] An additional continuation on prior themes, the Strategy aims to

1. Invest and plan for the long-term needs of the AI ecosystem to continue [UK] leadership as a science and AI superpower;
2. Support the transition to an AI-enabled economy, capturing the benefits of innovation in the UK, and ensuring AI benefits all sectors and regions;
3. Ensure the UK gets the national and international governance of AI technologies right to encourage innovation, investment, and protect the public and [UK] fundamental values.[282]

The Strategy splits its actions into terms of the next three months; 6–12 months; and 12 plus months in the areas of investing in the long-term needs of the AI ecosystem, ensuring AI benefits all sectors and regions, and governing AI effectively. While the first two are largely reflected in previous reports and approaches, focus on governance continued. The first three months foresaw the publication of the Centre for Data Ethics Assurance Roadmap, determination of the role of data protection in wider AI governance, publication of details of the Ministry of Defence approach when using AI, and the development of an all-of-government approach to international AI activity. Governance in the 6–12 month range involved the publication of a White Paper on a national position on governing and regulating AI, an analysis on algorithmic transparency 'with a view to develop a cross-government standard', the pilot of an AI standards hub, and the establishment of a medium and long-term scanning operation to increase government awareness of AI safety.[283] Lastly, the 12 months and beyond activities included the exploration of AI technical standards with stakeholders, work with global partners on shared research and development standards, work with the Alan Turing Institute on updating guidance regarding AI ethics and safety in the public sector, and working with national security, defence and researchers on using public sector action to mitigate catastrophic risk.[284]

The National AI Strategy references, albeit briefly, values including 'fairness, openness, liberty, security, democracy, the rule of law and respect for human rights'.[285] With this strategy, the United Kingdom appears to be attempting to leverage strengths in regulatory standards, such as by partnering with the Alan Turing Institute to provide technical standards, though commentators have expressed doubt that the United Kingdom would be successful in competition

[280] 'National AI Strategy' (GOV.UK, 18 December 2022): gov.uk/government/publications/national-ai-strategy.
[281] ibid.
[282] ibid.
[283] ibid.
[284] ibid.
[285] ibid.

with regulatory blocs such as the European Union on regulatory substance looking at AI specifically, particularly given the comparatively small UK market.[286]

Relatedly, the United Kingdom has kept up with its 2021 promised initiative to create a global standards hub via the Alan Turing Institute, supported by the British Standards Institution (BSI) and the National Physics Laboratory.[287] The hub itself is backed by the Department for Digital, Culture, Media & Sport and the Office for AI.[288] In its initial stage, the hub will focus on:

- Growing UK engagement to develop global AI standards by bringing together information about technical standards and development initiatives in an accessible, user-friendly and inclusive way.
- Bringing the AI community together through workshops, events and a new online platform to encourage more coordinated engagement in the development of standards around the world.
- Creating tools and guidance for education, training and professional development to help businesses and other organisations engage with creating AI technical standards, and collaborate globally to develop these standards.
- Exploring international collaboration with similar initiatives to ensure the development of technical standards are shaped by a wide range of AI experts, in line with shared values.[289]

The launch itself aligns with the CDEI's aforementioned Roadmap, which itself is part of the National AI Strategy.[290]

The March 2023 White Paper 'A pro-innovation approach to AI regulation', updated August 2023, focuses yet again on the UK's investment into AI – '£2.5 billion in AI since 2014'[291] – but does so within the context of enabling that investment to pay off by 'providing a framework to ensure risks are identified and addressed'.[292] The White Paper attempts to balance the desire not to introduce new legislation with the need to manage risks, which it tackles by proposing to set expectations. It simultaneously highlights the UK's aim and desire 'to continue to lead the international conversion on AI governance and demonstrate the value of [the UK's] pragmatic, proportionate regulatory approach'.[293] The 'pro-innovation framework' itself has five principles: safety, security and robustness; appropriate transparency and explainability; fairness; accountability and governance; and contestability

[286] ibid.
[287] 'New UK Initiative to Shape Global Standards for Artificial Intelligence' (GOV.UK, 12 January 2022): gov.uk/government/news/new-uk-initiative-to-shape-global-standards-for-artificial-intelligence.
[288] Which is itself set between DCMS and BEIS.
[289] 'New UK Initiative to Shape Global Standards for Artificial Intelligence' (n 287).
[290] ibid.
[291] 'Policy paper: A pro-innovation approach to AI regulation' (GOV.UK, 3 August 2023): www.gov.uk/government/publications/ai-regulation-a-pro-innovation-approach/white-paper.
[292] ibid.
[293] ibid.

and redress.[294] The White Paper suggests that these principles 'will be issued on a non-statutory basis and implemented by existing legislators', alongside a period of collaboration 'to identify any barriers to the proportionate application of the principles', and ultimately the introduction of 'a statutory duty on regulators requiring them to have due regard to the principles'.[295]

In early November 2023, the United Kingdom played host to the AI Safety Summit at Bletchley Park, which brought together 'international governments, leading AI companies, civil society groups and experts in research to consider the risks of AI, especially at the frontier of development, and discuss how they can be mitigated through internationally coordinated action'.[296]

The Summit's objectives were largely focused on alignment: shared understanding of risk; various measures on safety; areas of collaboration on AI safety research; and to 'showcase how ensuring the safe development of AI will enable AI to be used for good globally'.[297] In terms of the wide range of AI, discussions focused prominently on 'frontier AI', which the UK Summit documentation describes as '[h]ighly capable general purpose AI models that can perform a wide variety of tasks and match or exceed the capabilities present in today's most advanced models'.[298] Given the public focus on generative AI models at the time, this seems to be an effort to include not only generative models, but similar apparent leaps in capability that might not be caught by defining AI by current abilities. This future-proofing focus is mirrored in the Government Office for Science's 'Future Risks of Frontier AI', which asks '[w]hich capabilities and risks could emerge at the cutting edge of AI in the future'.[299]

Late 2023 saw the introduction of the Artificial Intelligence (Regulation) Bill to the House of Lords, on its second reading at the time of writing. The bill proposes the creation of an AI Authority; a series of regulatory principles; the creation of regulatory sandboxes; the requirement for businesses developing, using, or deploying AI to have an AI officer;[300] the introduction of transparency, intellectual property, and labelling requirements; a public engagement requirement; and the specific regulatory inclusion of generative AI. The AI Authority is intended to, among other things, 'ensure alignment of approach across relevant regulators

[294] ibid.
[295] ibid.
[296] 'About the AI Safety Summit 2023' (GOV.UK): gov.uk/government/topical-events/ai-safety-summit-2023/about.
[297] ibid.
[298] 'Safety and Security Risks of Generative Artificial Intelligence to 2025', HM Government: assets.publishing.service.gov.uk/media/653932db80884d0013f71b15/generative-ai-safety-security-risks-2025-annex-b.pdf.
[299] 'Future Risks of Frontier AI' (Government Office for Science, October 2023): assets.publishing.service.gov.uk/media/653bc393d10f3500139a6ac5/future-risks-of-frontier-ai-annex-a.pdf.
[300] Not dissimilar to the GDPR's data protection officer, although in this case 'to ensure the safe, ethical, unbiased and non-discriminatory use of AI by the business … [and that] so far as reasonably practicable, that data used by the business in any AI technology is unbiased'. Artificial Intelligence (Regulation) Bill [HL] 4 (1–2).

in respect of AI', 'coordinate a review of relevant legislation, including product safety', 'accredit independent AI auditors', and 'promote interoperability with international regulatory frameworks'.[301] Regulatory principles include that AI should deliver:

(i) safety, security and robustness;
(ii) appropriate transparency and explainability;
(iii) fairness;
(iv) accountability and governance;
(v) contestability and redress.[302]

While the proposed bill itself is not particularly long, its major principles align with many of those called for by international agreements. If adopted, the bill would prove to be a departure for UK AI policy, particularly given its explicit call for a centralised AI regulator.

UK Analysis

The UK's approach to overall AI governance has been an interesting example of a tentative legislative approach. Sensibly, reports and studies are far more prevalent than actual legislation, showing a measured and considered response, rather than legislating too far too quickly. However, there is also a clear and prevalent focus on the economic potential of AI, and what resources are required to achieve this: human, non-human, and enabling legislation. The engagement clearly pushes the human factor of business-building: a bedrock of skilled actors to create the desired AI powerhouse of economy. The 2016 House of Commons Science and Technology Committee Report, 'Robots and artificial intelligence' emphasises relevant skill-sets to AI and robotics; 'Machine learning: the power and promise of computers that learn by example' provides for education and targeted skill-sets. Six out of the 18 recommendations in 'Growing the AI industry in the UK' are directed at improving the UK's supply of AI skills: broadening participation; industry-sponsored masters-level courses; exploration of demand for conversion courses at the masters level; a minimum 200 PhD places dedicated to AI; credit-bearing massive open online courses on AI alongside Continuing Professional Development courses for those with master of science degrees; and an international fellowship programme for AI in the UK (partnered with the Alan Turing Institute). The 2018 House of Lords report has a particular focus on skill: retraining schemes, strategies to attract talent, etc. The National AI Strategy devotes a section to 'skills and talent' as part of Pillar 1: Investing in the long-term needs of the AI ecosystem.

While resources of course include access to funding, which the documents provide for in abundance, AI requires and is therefore provided another asset: data.

[301] Artificial Intelligence (Regulation) Bill [HL] 1(2).
[302] Artificial Intelligence (Regulation) Bill [HL] 2(1)(a).

'Machine learning: the power and promise of computers that learn by example' begins to address open data standards and access to data. The British Academy and Royal Science Joint Report, 'Data management and use: Governance in the 21st century' is focused nearly exclusively on data management, including very clearly its availability and usability. 'Growing the AI industry in the UK' provides three of 18 recommendations on data: access to data; facilitation of data; availability of data. While data is not explicitly one of the five questions in the House of Lords *AI in the UK: Ready, Willing and Able* Report, it is a clear theme in how AI might affect everyday lives, and in how to realise potential opportunities.

Third, there is a clear thread of hesitancy to legislate unnecessarily. This could be derided as being overly supportive of businesses, or lauded as promoting innovation, but the thread remains uncut, at least until the proposed House of Lords bill in late 2023. Overarching AI legislation has not been a governmental priority, so far, even as building the AI ecosystem clearly has been. 'Robots and artificial intelligence' explicitly notes that it is too early to regulate AI. 'Machine learning: the power and promise of computers that learn by example' states that specific sectoral approaches are preferable to cross-sectoral, overarching legislation. The UK's 'Grand Challenges' note 'that there should not be a new AI-specific regulator for the UK, but rather that all existing regulators must meet the new challenges AI poses to their sector'.[303]

The House of Lords notes both that 'blanket AI-specific regulation, at this stage, would be inappropriate', but also recognises liability as a potential hurdle for growing AI.[304] The 'Roadmap to an Effective AI Assurance Ecosystem' notes that government, regulators and standards bodies are supporting structures of the AI ecosystem, but only goes so far as to suggest that a necessary component is that '[r]egulators make active efforts to translate their concerns with AI into assurable guidelines for the AI supply chain', with the CDEI's role being to '[a]dvise regulators and policy teams to ensure that approaches to AI regulation support, and are supported by, a thriving AI assurance ecosystem'.[305] The National AI Strategy provides that it must '[e]nsure the UK gets the national and international governance of AI technologies right to encourage innovation, investment, and protect the public and [UK] fundamental values'.[306] The March 2023 White Paper on 'A pro-innovation approach to AI regulation' again notes hesitancy to introduce new legislation, and proposes to introduce principles on a non-statutory basis. Overall, the concept of black-letter legislation is far more a suggestion than black-letter law.

However, there have been no brakes applied in creating governance bodies. While this may seem at first blush surprising, there has been a clear distinction

[303] *AI in the UK: Ready, Willing and Able* (n 247).
[304] ibid.
[305] 'The Roadmap to an Effective AI Assurance Ecosystem' (n 267).
[306] 'National AI Strategy' (n 280).

between governance bodies and defined cross-sectoral legislation. Bodies such as the Office for AI, placed between two government ministries, the CDEI, and the Alan Turing Institute, are clearly set in place to aid and solidify a potential set of governance bodies. In the creation of standards with the British Standards Institute, the Alan Turing Institute does not provide a clear-cut right/wrong, liable/not liable dynamic, but does provide potential industry-specific practices, informed by both industry and research. The proposed House of Lords bill on AI would establish an overarching, cross-sectoral regulator, in terms that suggest that it would create overarching legislation, but this would again be a departure from government policy statements thus far. The impacts of this bill remain to be seen.

While the UK approach is particularly focused on economy building, this does not mean that it ignores the human side of AI. It may do so on the basis that public trust is necessary to build a positive AI ecosystem, and that, among other things, harm to humans would damage this trust, but it does so nonetheless. The cornerstone of the promised 'world-leading', 'global super-power' AI ecosystem that the documents so clearly promote is the human side of AI: in training, importing and hiring skilled workers, but also in providing societal support for such an approach. While the name of the game may be facilitation over regulation, the United Kingdom is clearly alive to the necessity of social buy-in.

5.4. Summary Analysis

> 'At present, AI governance is an unorganised area'.[307]

Notwithstanding the above initiatives, AI governance is clearly in its nascence. This is not the slow, incremental progression of an existing set of regulation, but a sandpit of creation: not insurance law as it exists in the 2020s, but Lloyds Insurance growing out of a coffeehouse in the 1680s. If any legislation in history has been perfect, it has certainly not been in relation to AI, nor should we expect it to be – our understanding of the technology is imperfect, and while a legislative balance is important, so too is the realisation that adjustments may be needed.

Between the four jurisdictions, there are a series of questions that are covered to varying degrees. These questions attempt to address AI governance both prior to the AI being put to market, and after an incident has occurred. First, the principles of regulation. What is the regulation trying to achieve? How should regulation be structured? What approach should the regulation take? In terms of regulation regarding incidents, we have the questions of how best to prevent harm, to punish in the case of liability, and how to apportion that punishment.

[307] J Butcher and I Beridze, 'What is the State of Artificial Intelligence Governance Globally?' (2019) 164 *RUSI Journal* 88: tandfonline.com/doi/full/10.1080/03071847.2019.1694260.

Singapore, as a more principles-based regulation, provides that the Model AI Governance Framework is intended to provide guidance for ethical and governance issues when deploying AI. It is structured around a close partnership between industry and governance. Regulation is structured to facilitate internal governance rather than top-down regulation, as evidenced by the Companion to the Model AI Governance Framework, which is intended to help producers align their internal governance. Legislation approaches AI in an agnostic fashion – addressing AI as a whole, rather than differing AI applications. Harm prevention is treated, if anything, as a by-product of the base-level foci on 'internal governance structures and measures, human-involvement in AI-augmented decision-making, operations management and stakeholder interaction and communication'.[308] It avoids the question of liability and post-hoc governance altogether. While the Personal Data Protection Commission's remit includes the governance of AI, it is not an AI-exclusive regulator.

The EU AI Act and draft Liability Directive suggest that the European Union has taken a very different approach. Regulation is more clearly trying to achieve human-rights oriented goals, seen directly in the outright banning (albeit very specifically) of certain AI applications. The EU approach to regulation includes a clearer risk/benefit analysis, which takes on more of a consideration of the harms specific to certain kinds of AI applications. There is more view to the creation of a distinct regulatory entity, albeit one that utilises existing structures for activities such as approval processes. In this sense there is an adoption of co-regulatory processes, with the recognition that even 'high level only' approval must be widespread in order to be at all practicable. Differentiating AI into unacceptable, high risk, transparency obligations, and minimal risk creates a certain level of stability for providers, particularly with the closed – although expandable – list of high-risk applications. The draft Liability Directive expands directly on these approaches, tackling the establishment of a causal link, but only where the producer has otherwise varied in their following of the Act. In this way, the Directive attempts to overcome the concept of reasonableness as the build-up of expectations over time, and to focus its attention on an area it deems to be more quantifiable: the status of datasets and other technical measures in the approval process.[309]

The United States has taken an overall light-touch approach to the regulation of AI as a category, particularly at the federal level. The 'free market' approach has been cited, and while draft guidance for AI has been produced, it does not as yet appear to have had a significant impact on regulation of AI as a whole. While the National Artificial Intelligence Initiative Act includes the creation of a National Artificial Intelligence Initiative Office, its focus appears to have been more on those efforts of allied departments such as the Department of Defence (DoD), the

[308] 'Singapore's Approach to AI Governance' (n 51).
[309] 'Draft AI Liability Directive' (n 180).

Nuclear Regulatory Commission (NRC), and the Office of Science and Technology (OSTP).[310] There does not appear to be overall focus on what regulation might look like at the federal level particularly given that the Executive Order appears to be a stopgap to focus on large, immediate threats. Additionally, regulation varies in both intensity and approach at state levels.[311]

The UK approach falls somewhere between the EU and US approaches: while it concentrates on the economic potential of AI, it also puts a great deal of focus on what is needed to achieve this, including enabling legislation. The United Kingdom appears to share the US fears of regulating unnecessarily and has noted that blanket AI legislation may not serve its needs. While the United Kingdom has not focused on what the structure of AI regulation might look like, it has created a relatively strong network of co-regulation: between standards bodies, advisory roles and examination into sectoral regulation,[312] it has focused on regulatory approach rather than regulatory structure. In terms of post-hoc address, liability has been noted as a potential hurdle to the industry, but not been addressed in detail.

These approaches to regulatory aims, regulatory structures, regulatory approach, and post-hoc dealings lead to further questions: how well will these approaches function in practice? How well will they withstand future developments? What do the approaches say about these jurisdictions' goals? How well do they truly address risk?

First, how will these approaches function in practice? Functionality can be examined from two aspects: buy-in from stakeholders and technical workability. An ideal system clearly needs both buy-in from a social perspective, which can come from, for example, public trust in an institution, or in the processes around AI; and a regulatory system that takes into account how AI actually works. There has been a split approach to these two sides of functionality. Singapore has clearly considered both areas, working with partners both within the government and private parties. This is evident in both its structuring and its technical suggestions. The European Union is forced to look to buy-in by its Member States, and while it has clearly consulted with private parties, there is less evidence of a direct and ongoing relationship with outside stakeholders. The European Union has engaged in some technical guidance and standard setting and has gone so far as to provide the initial list of high-risk AI. The United States has, up until the National Defense Authorization Act 2021, clearly been most concerned with its stakeholder functionality: facilitating workable and enticing conditions for AI producers. The United States has started to address other stakeholders with the National Defense Authorization Act 2021, primarily in other areas of government, but has yet to

[310] As of 10 July 2022, the National Artificial Intelligence Initiative Office's list of recent publications is from the NRC, OSTP, DoD and the Consumer Financial Protection Bureau; three out of five of which are requests for information.

[311] Including sectorally, as seen in ch 6.

[312] Expanded upon in ch 6.

provide specific standards for technical workability. The UK's focus on the creation pipeline has not been mirrored by regulatory growth, but its partnerships focus more clearly on standard setting, including functional technical approaches.

Future-proofing is not unique to AI legislation but is certainly a greater concern for AI than many other legislative initiatives. This is largely informed by each governing body's ability to act and update legislation, and cohesiveness with existing legislation. Best-case regulation is both reactive to updates in the field, while preventing as many incidents as possible, and providing compensation to victims. Singapore enjoys a distinct advantage in terms of updating and cohesiveness for several reasons. First, its ability as a city-state to act quickly and unilaterally. Second, it has had fewer integration hiccups in terms of existing legislation.[313] Third, its structure of both technical and governance requirements as minimally specific and ultimately flexible means that while case law may fill in the gaps, the legislation itself will not be mired in ageing definitions.

The European Union, while at a disadvantage for integrating with existing legislation, has nonetheless made concrete efforts to engage in future-proofing, such as clarifying the fit between upcoming and existing legislation,[314] excluding potential defences from existing areas of law, and requiring a five-year review of the directive if passed. The United States may have the stumbling block of contending with both state and federal levels, but there is reason to be optimistic about future application for two reasons. First, the surprisingly successful integration of conflicting legislation on the use of marijuana: illegal at the federal level, but legal in several states. This shows that the US system is capable of coping with differential legislation in a mix of separate and overlapping jurisdictions. Second, the pendulum nature of successive federal administrations: priorities may be conflicting between one administration and the next, which means that conflicts may be resolved simply by sweeping previous requirements and frameworks under the carpet.[315] While this may be detrimental to cohesiveness, it means less of a commitment to strategies that may become outdated. The UK's use of non-binding standards over black-letter law means that there is less clarity as to how the law may treat AI, but that standards can change and be improved more quickly.[316]

Where these jurisdictions differ most greatly is in their goals and treatment of risk. While the goal is clearly to regulate AI in a cohesive, intelligible manner that promotes safety, the 'why' or 'how' of the approach differs. Singapore's approach suggests that its goal is to induce trust from the business side: to provide stakeholders with useful information that will encourage buy-in from consumers. The EU approach is clearly to uphold existing human rights approaches, both in terms

[313] Or at least fewer have come to light than issues such as the Product Liability Directive or have been smoothed over in consultation with multiparty stakeholders.

[314] eg, the Product Liability Directive (n 103).

[315] eg, the 2016–20 Administration's treatment of the previous fairness, governance and public good priorities.

[316] See greater discussion in ch 7.

of ensuring fair decisions are made and that victims will be compensated. The US approach has so far been to induce business, though further goals may become apparent when NIST frameworks are provided. The United Kingdom has focused on its co-regulatory advantages such as standards-building.

Risk has been split into three different approaches. The European Union most clearly divides its approach into areas it believes will have greatest versus lesser risk and relies on a licensing approach. Singapore takes a more minimalist approach, suggesting that '[b]efore deploying AI solutions, organisations should decide on their commercial objectives of using AI, and then weigh them against the risk of using AI in the organisation's decision making'.[317] At the federal level, the United States has not clearly approached a risk division; and neither has the United Kingdom.

Ultimately, where do these approaches leave us? Singapore provides guidance on how AI producers should work. The European Union provides that operators of AI will be liable where they deviate from licensing processes and focuses on damage from a post-hoc lens. The United States has largely provided what AI producers should do, made evident in terms of incentives in funding and market openness. The United Kingdom provides functional, expert-produced standards that do not rely on drawn-out legislative updates. While each approach is informative, it is the relationship between these approaches that is missing: producers need the connection between what to do, what not to do, and a source to clarify the difference. Society needs incentives and clarity for producers to create valuable technology. Governments need to clarify the relationship that AI has with other pieces of the puzzle: with other product areas (sectoral); with other concepts in law (foreseeability); and with its own technical parallels (explainability). The next chapter therefore examines sectoral regulation of AI liability, and the similarities and differences in the approaches of the four jurisdictions.

[317] 'Model Artificial Intelligence Governance Framework Second Edition' (n 36).

6

Sectoral Regulation

Although the four jurisdictions analysed in the previous chapter differ in their approach to AI legislation, a common core is identifiable: they all provide a focus on risk identification and mitigation, and all engage, to a greater or lesser extent, in co-regulation. The differences between their approaches are explained by their different approaches to economics considerations and the need to protect individuals. While the European Union expresses the most strongly that sectoral regulation is a part of its AI approach scheme, interesting advances have been made sectorally in all the aforementioned jurisdictions.

AI causing accidental death will occur in a variety of sectors but is likely to occur most often in transportation and medical applications given their promises on saving lives – where deaths can be prevented, there is an implicit acknowledgement that they are otherwise happening, and although an AI approach has the potential to reduce such deaths, it will not completely eliminate them overnight, if ever.

Sectoral advancements are important for two reasons: first, broad AI legislation must still contend with (or deliberately exclude) existing legislation. Second, sectoral regulation has the advantage of specificity in what technology it addresses, but also expertise. While it is difficult for blanket legislation to inform the governance of specific technologies, blanket legislation can and should learn from the address of specific technologies: a bottom-up approach where expertise informs the larger field.

Sectoral regulation also has the potential benefit of being cross jurisdictional: the United States and Singapore, for example, are exploring opportunities for cooperation in areas including digital economy and healthcare, 'identifying ways to collaborate on common technical standards and build more trustworthy and interoperable systems'.[1] Similar already existing partnerships include the Asia-Pacific Economic Cooperation (APEC)'s Cross Border Privacy Rules system that aims to facilitate interoperability of privacy regimes.[2]

[1] 'Joint Press Release: New Collaboration Under the U.S.–Singapore Partnership for Growth and Innovation (PGI)' US Department of Commerce: commerce.gov/news/press-releases/2022/03/joint-press-release-new-collaboration-under-us-singapore-partnership.

[2] ibid.

6.1. Sectoral Regulation: Self-Driving

Self-driving vehicles provide a new quadrant of expansion for sectoral legislation. While medical legislation is designed to deal with practical advances in medical fields, driving legislation has faced relatively static challenges: cars still drive on roads, and in some cases the same roads, as a hundred years before. Incremental changes have been added, such as laws regarding seat belts and appropriate headlights, but they have not required a fundamental examination of the practice of driving.

Many jurisdictions have made advancements towards sectoral legislation aimed at self-driving or automated vehicles, including the European Union, Singapore, certain US states and the United Kingdom. One key and perhaps surprising similarity between these and other jurisdictions' approaches is the use of the categorisations of six levels of automation of the Society of Automotive Engineers (SAE International). Levels 0–2 provide only 'driver support features', wherein the human is 'driving whenever these driver support features are engaged – even if [their] feet are off the pedals and [they] are not steering'; whereas levels 3–6 are considered 'automated driving features', wherein the human is 'not driving when these automated driving features are engaged – if [they] are seated in 'the driver's seat'.[3] Level 0 features 'are limited to providing warnings and momentary assistance', level 1 to 'provide steering OR brake/acceleration support to the driver', and level 3 'features provide steering AND brake/acceleration support to the driver'.[4] Levels 3 and 4 provide that the 'features can drive the vehicle under limited conditions and will not operate unless all required conditions are met', whereas level 5 states that '[t]his feature can drive the vehicle under all conditions'.[5]

Unsurprisingly, the jurisdictions discussed here have taken largely different approaches to self-driving legislation outside the automation levels. The European Union has taken an approach intended to integrate with its other areas of legislation with the strategy paper 'On the road to automated mobility: An EU strategy for mobility of the future'. The United Kingdom through the Law Commission of England and Wales has undertaken a 'far-reaching review to enable the safe and responsible introduction of automated vehicles on GB roads and public places', publishing a joint report on 26 January 2022 with the Scottish Law Commission, 'with recommendations for legal reform'.[6] Singapore has taken a very business-oriented approach, creating legislative sandpits and collaborative testing programmes partnered with industry, as well as introducing specific self-driving technical standards. The United States has so far made targeted minor expansions

[3] 'SAE Levels of Driving Automation™ Refined for Clarity and International Audience': sae.org/site/blog/sae-j3016-update.

[4] ibid.

[5] ibid.

[6] 'Automated Vehicles', Law Commission: lawcom.gov.uk/project/automated-vehicles/.

in legislation at the federal level, but has as yet left major changes to states, with whom the majority of driving-related legislation rests.

These four approaches, while varying greatly in some respects, illustrate one of the most important aspects of sectoral legislation – the ability to institute incremental progression of regulation, based on specific expertise. This is evident in two respects: what regulation is present; and what is missing and/or instituted at a later point. In terms of what regulation is present, all four jurisdictions have instituted three types of progression approaches, albeit through different means: approval systems,[7] safety regulations[8] and classifications. Exact approaches differ, but in essence, they each have a way for companies' vehicles to be approved for use on roadways, certain specific guidelines companies must follow, and how different features/vehicles will be classified. In terms of what regulation is missing and/or lacking, liability is notable in its absence: while the EU has produced the draft liability directive for AI writ large, only the UK has laid down specific guidance as to which party is liable when in terms of self-driving vehicles, even going so far as to note that it will 'require self-driving vehicles to achieve a level of safety at least as high as careful and competent human drivers.'[9] While the UK has identified the potential parties bearing risk at certain stages, there is no particular definition as to what standard is required or might look like, beyond that of a careful and competent human driver. Each jurisdiction has prudently required liability insurance, some to a great deal of specificity,[10] but other than the UK have left liability as a later piece of the regulatory puzzle in fear of cementing an unworkable system. These are the sorts of benefits that sectoral regulation enjoys over broad-type regulation: where broad regulation must take a macro approach to technologies of varying use, more micro regulation can contend with the realities of lessons learned in specific use of AI, such as requiring insurance. In the same way that, for example, the UK Driving Code is greatly supplemented by case law that acknowledges certain realities such as the difficulties in making a turn with a tractor-trailer, the knowledge of the specific use cases for AI supplement its informed regulation.

6.1.1. EU Self-Driving

The European Union has taken the approach of referring to the category of 'connected and automated' driving, putting the potentially connective aspect of

[7] Such as EU Regulation 2018/858, Singapore's Road Traffic Act, the American (federal) Model State Policy, and the UK required listing via the Automated and Electric Vehicles Act 2018, all to be discussed shortly.

[8] EU Draft ADS Legislation, the Singapore Road Traffic Act, the (American) Federal Automated Vehicles Comprehensive Plan, and the UK (voluntary) Code of Practice.

[9] 'Self-driving vehicles set to be on roads by 2026 as Automated Vehicles Act becomes law' (GOV.UK, 20 May 2024): https://www.gov.uk/government/news/self-driving-vehicles-set-to-be-on-roads-by-2026-as-automated-vehicles-act-becomes-law#:~:text=The%20act%20delivers%20the%20most,for%20how%20the%20vehicle%20drives.

[10] See, eg, Singapore in section 6.1.2 of this chapter.

self-driving vehicles at an equal forefront with autonomy. As a group of Member States, the EU's approach is naturally different from other jurisdictions, including that of the other group of 'United States'. This is likely due to two reasons: first, that the US states do still cede some level of influence to the federal system that includes several elements of regulation crucial to self-driving; and second, that the European Union has a series of other legislation that it is required to match, including that integrating a multitude of Member States and those with more varying legal traditions such as common law and civil law. EU Member States also have a mix of approaches for liability for vehicles, for example with the Netherlands employing a 'semi-strict' liability system, and France with a 'very strict' liability system.[11]

Currently, the EU legislation in force 'for current vehicles is only on the European level, and restricted to SAE Level 3 and 3 use cases in SAE Level 4 (Robot-taxi, Shuttles and Valet Parking)'.[12] This has not, however, been a direct route. Automation in vehicles was initially barred by the Vienna Convention on Road Traffic 1968, which required that '[e]very moving vehicle or combination of vehicles … have a driver'.[13] This was amended in 2016 by the United Nations Economic Commission for Europe with the 'Report of the Global of the Global Forum for Road Traffic Safety', which deemed an automated system acceptable so long as it complied with other domestic and international regulations.[14]

Directive 2007/46/EC of the European Parliament and of the Council of 5 September 2007 'Establishing a framework for the approval of motor vehicles and their trailers, and of systems, components and separate technical units intended for such vehicles' naturally formed the core of EU legislation on approval for vehicle types and components, and was amended by Regulation 2018/858.[15] The European Union saw testing via the L3Pilot, co-funded by the European Commission, in 10 different Member States starting in 2017,[16] and produced the strategy paper 'On the road to automated mobility: An EU strategy for mobility of the future', which formed part of the Commission's third mobility package and stated that '[e]xisting EU legislation [was] to a large extent already suitable for the placing on the market of automated and connected vehicles'.[17] In October 2018, the European Commission

[11] T Evas, 'A common EU approach to liability rules and insurance for connected and automated vehicles' (European Parliamentary Research Service, 2018): europarl.europa.eu/RegData/etudes/STUD/2018/615635/EPRS_STU(2018)615635_EN.pdf.

[12] 'Connected Automated Driving/Regulations and Policies' (*Connected automated driving.eu*, 12 December 2023): connectedautomateddriving.eu/regulation-and-policies/.

[13] Vienna Convention on Road Traffic 1968.

[14] 'Report of the Global Forum for Road Traffic Safety on Its Eighty-First Session' (UNECE, 12 January 2021): unece.org/transport/documents/2021/01/reports/report-global-forum-road-traffic-safety-its-eighty-first a.

[15] Regulation (EU) 2018/858 of the European Parliament and of the Council of 30 May 2018 on the approval and market surveillance of motor vehicles and their trailers, and of systems, components and separate technical units intended for such vehicles, amending Regulations (EC) No 715/2007 and (EC) No 595/2009 and repealing Directive 2007/46/EC (Text with EEA relevance) [2018] OJ L858.

[16] A Nestoras (ed), *EU Policy Review Volume 1* (*European Policy Review* 2021) 1: liberalforum.eu/wp-content/uploads/2022/01/ELF-POLICY-REVIEW-Vol-1-2021.pdf.

[17] 'On the road to automated mobility: An EU strategy for mobility of the future 2018' (Communication from the Commission to the European Parliament, The Council, The European Economic and Social Committee, The Committee of the Regions, 2018).

built on the third mobility package, introducing 'new level[s] of co-operation between road users'.[18] The World Forum for Harmonization of Vehicle Regulations set out a framework in 2019 to 'guide the regulatory work of the United Nations Economic Commission for Europe (UNECE) in autonomous/automated vehicle levels 3–5', prioritising safety in development;[19] and the European Commission adopted the Regulation on 'Cooperative Intelligent Transport Systems (C-ITS) on Europe's roads', focusing on vehicle-to-vehicle communication, and aligning rules with proposals on clean mobility and zero fatalities and serious injuries.[20] Also in 2019, the Technical Committee on Motor Vehicles published guidelines regarding the exemption procedure for EU approval of automated vehicles, aimed at harmonising Member State practices for SAE levels 3 and 4. Member States were thereby granted the ability to provisionally approve a vehicle type, though valid only in its own jurisdiction.[21] While the national level provides scope for Member States to enact their own measures, there is no EU-level coordination between Member State jurisdictional governments.[22]

While the overhaul for automated vehicle approval began in 2018, it did not enter into effect until 1 September 2020, and is now provided by Regulation 2018/858, which allows new automation technology to be validated under the new framework under Article 39.[23] The Article provides that manufacturers may apply 'in respect of a type of vehicle, system, component or separate technical unit that incorporates new technologies or new concepts that are incompatible with one or more regulatory acts', and that approval will be granted where

a. the application for the EU type-approval states the reasons why the new technologies or new concepts make the vehicles, systems, components or separate technical units incompatible with one or more regulatory acts listed in Annex II;
b. the application for the EU type-approval describes the safety and environmental implications of the new technology or new concept and the measures taken in order to ensure at least an equivalent level of safety and environmental protection to that provided by the requirements in respect of which an exemption is sought;
c. test descriptions and results are presented proving that the condition in point (b) is met.

[18] 'Europe on the Move: Questions & Answers on the Commission's initiatives' (European Commission, 17 May 2018): ec.europa.eu/commission/presscorner/detail/pt/MEMO_18_3681.

[19] Nestoras (15).

[20] 'European Commission Adopts the "Delegated Act" for the Deployment of C-ITS' (*InterCor*, 14 March 2019): intercor-project.eu/european-commission-adopts-the-delegated-act-for-the-deployment-of-c-its/.

[21] 'The Legal Framework for Autonomous Vehicles in the European Union' (*Business Going Digital*, 12 February 2020): www.businessgoing.digital/the-legal-framework-for-autonomous-vehicles-in-the-european-union/.

[22] ibid.

[23] Regulation (EU) 2018/858 (n 14).

In essence, this provides for type approval for systems that regulators may not have foreseen in existing legislation. EU- type approvals are still subject to authorisation by the EU Commission.[24]

April 2021 saw the European Commission's 'Proposal for a Regulation on a European approach for Artificial Intelligence' (AI Act), previously discussed in section 5.5.3. The EU's Proposal has now passed, and self-driving vehicles are included in class specification, but are done so deliberately to assign them to more sectoral legislation. This has begun to occur through the EU Draft ADS Regulation. The initial EU Draft ADS Regulation came out in 2021, amending Directive 2006/1/EC 'On the use of vehicles hired without drivers for the carriage of goods by road'. The Regulation provides type-approval rules for self-driving vehicles at SAE levels 4 and 5, as well as specifying certain types of technical responses, such as providing 'sufficient time and space in lateral manoeuvres'. The Regulation draft was criticised by stakeholders, for reasons including the lack of technical definitions such as 'harsh braking/steering', which could 'result in overly conservative worst behaviour [by the vehicle], failing to conform with any definition of what is reasonably foreseeable'.[25] The lack of defined boundaries were felt to be detrimental to knowing 'what is reasonably foreseeable vs. what is unexpected, and this may require an emergency evasive manoeuvre is needed in order for ADS-equipped vehicles to be able to drive in a predictable manner that conforms with societal expectation'.[26] Comments on the second draft were not dissimilar, asking for further definition on the scope of a 'fully automated vehicle … with regard to their automated driving system', and noting that the draft still does not clarify how it interacts with Member States with jurisdiction-specific legislation such as Germany, which already has SAE level 4 legislation in place for certain activities.[27]

Most recently, the European Union has released a draft of its ADS legislation, which applies to fully automated vehicles, 'hub-to-hub' vehicles which operate 'on a predefined route with fixed start and end points', and 'automated valet parking' vehicles which are fully automated in the case of parking 'within predefined facilities'.[28] The ADS draft focuses in particular on performance requirements and compliance assessments: it provides performance requirements for certain traffic scenarios, clarifies technical definitions such as 'automated driving system', 'dynamic driving task' and 'time to collision', as well as summary information on compliance assessment – document information is to be submitted according to EU Regulation 2018/858, as discussed below, and in accordance with the technical specification in the ADS draft itself.[29]

[24] ibid.

[25] MS Elli and J Weast, 'Analysis of Draft EU ADS Performance Requirements' (2021): arxiv.org/abs/2106.02148.

[26] ibid.

[27] 'Automated Cars – Technical Specifications' (European Commission, 5 May 2022): ec.europa.eu/info/law/better-regulation/have-your-say/initiatives/12152-Automated-cars-technical-specifications_en.

[28] ibid.

[29] ibid.

For all that these many increments add to the whole of EU self-driving sectoral legislation, legislation can be broadly grouped into five areas: the type approval framework; safety regulations; connectivity; privacy; and data protection,[30] and broad AI legislation. The type approval framework is broadly covered by Directive 2007/46/EC, which establishes a framework for the approval of motor vehicles and their systems, components and separate technical units (aka the Framework Directive) and is not aimed specifically at self-driving vehicles but by necessity includes them; by Regulation (EU) 2018/858 on the approval and market surveillance of the aforementioned motor vehicles, their systems, and components; and by Regulation (EC) No 78/2009 on the type approval of motor vehicles with regard to the protection of pedestrians and other vulnerable road users, which amended Directive 2007/46/EC and repealed Directives 2003/102/EC and 2005/66/EC.[31]

General safety regulations include Regulation (EC) No 661/2009 concerning type-approval requirements for the general safety of motor vehicles, components and technical units, as well as the current proposal for a regulation on type-approval as regards the general safety of the aforementioned and the protection of vehicle occupants and vulnerable road users, which is to amend Regulation (EU) 2018 and repeal Regulations (EC) No 78/2009, (EC) No 79/2009 and (EC) No 661/2009.[32] Connectivity is covered under Directive 2010/40/EU on the framework for the deployment of Intelligent Transport Systems in the field of road transport and interfaces with other modes of transport; and by the Commission Delegated Regulation supplementing Directive 2010/40/EU. Privacy and data protection are covered under the General Data Protection Regulation (aka Regulation (EU) 2016/670). Broad AI legislation is covered under the previously discussed EU AI Act.

How, then, does liability fall under this many categories? Broadly, it does not. Liability was examined in the 2018 EC communication, which states that:

> Liability for motor vehicles is addressed through various instruments at EU level such as [the] Motor Insurance Directive or Product Liability Directive as well as the different liability regimes in the Member States (eg traffic law, civil law, specific strict liability regimes, and national implementation of the EU Product Liability Directive).[33]

The Communication further provides that

> the actual cause of events that lead to damage or incident is decisive for the attribution of liability, [so] the Commission is proposing that automated vehicles are fitted with data recorders to clarify who was driving (the vehicle's autonomous systems or the driver) during an accident.[34]

[30] Not included in the aforementioned legislation.
[31] Regulation (EU) 2018/858 (n 14).
[32] 'Connected Automated Driving/Regulations and Policies' (n 11).
[33] 'On the road to automated mobility' (n 16) 10.
[34] ibid.

As for compensation of victims, the insurers 'can take legal action against a manufacturer under the Product Liability Directive if there is a malfunction/defect of the automated driving system'.[35] The Commission has evaluated the Motor Insurance Directive, concluding that while self-driving vehicles will be required to have third-party liability insurance as the Directive already requires, no changes are necessary to fit the Directive to self-driving vehicles.[36] The Commission has recently proposed an update to the Product Liability Directive. Changes include 'allowing compensation for damage when products like robots, drones or smart-home systems are made unsafe by software updates, AI or digital services that are needed to operate the product, as well as when manufacturers fail to address cybersecurity vulnerabilities',[37] and 'eas[ing] the burden of proof in complex cases and ease restrictions on making claims'.[38] However, the Proposal upholds the division that liability regulations are the jurisdiction of Member States. Lastly, though not liability-specific, the Commission has established the European Artificial Intelligence (AI) Alliance to draft AI ethical guidelines, 'which will produce an approach on ethical issues for autonomous systems with relevance also for autonomous vehicles'.[39]

6.1.2. Singapore Self-Driving

Singapore's initial address of self-driving began in 2013, with an invitation to private industry to 'tap into Singapore's business friendly environment to implement AVs'.[40] This was formalised in 2014 with the establishment of the Committee on Autonomous Road Transport for Singapore (CARTS), which included public and private sector stakeholders.[41] Since that point, the Singaporean Land Transport Authority (LTA) has focused in particular on deployment, beginning with small-scale test-beds with the plan to eventually deploy island wide.[42] The current state of testing appears to be the pilot of bus and shuttle deployment across three districts, which the LTA states will be through the early 2020s.[43]

[35] ibid.
[36] ibid.
[37] 'New Liability Rules on Products and AI to Protect Consumers' (European Commission, 22 September 2022): ec.europa.eu/commission/presscorner/detail/en/ip_22_580.
[38] 'Proposal for a directive of the European Parliament and of the Council on adapting non-contractual civil liability rules to artificial intelligence (AI Liability Directive)' (2022) COM.
[39] On the road to automated mobility' (n 16).
[40] SY Tan and A Taeihagh, 'Adaptive Governance of Autonomous Vehicles: Accelerating the Adoption of Disruptive Technologies in Singapore' (2021) 38 *Government Information Quarterly* 101546: sciencedirect.com/science/article/pii/S0740624X20303257.
[41] Land Transport Authority, 'Autonomous Vehicles': lta.gov.sg/content/ltagov/en/industry_innovations/technologies/autonomous_vehicles.html.
[42] ibid.
[43] ibid.

The Road Traffic Act (Autonomous Motor Vehicles) Rules came into effect August 2017, and is the most specific piece of legislation regarding self-driving vehicles. It covers in detail the need for authorisation to trial an autonomous vehicle, what is needed for the application to trial an automated vehicle technology or autonomous motor vehicle, and what authorisation entails.[44] It also covers liability insurance for said trials, stating that:

> (1) The specified person for an approved trial or approved special use must
>
> (a) before the approved trial or special use starts, have in place liability insurance; and
>
> (b) ensure that the liability insurance is in force at all times for the duration stated in the authorisation
>
> ...
>
> (2) The specified person for an approved trial or approved special use must ensure that the liability insurance is issued by an insurer who, at the time liability insurance is issued, is lawfully carrying on an insurance business in Singapore.
>
> (3) A specified person who contravenes (1) or (2) shall be guilty of an offence and shall be liable on conviction to a fine not exceeding $1,000 and, in the case of a second or subsequent conviction, to a fine not exceeding $2,000.[45]

In lieu of liability insurance, the Authority may in some cases accept a security deposit 'of not less than $1.5 million'.[46] The Act also specifies 'duties of a specified person' with regard to trial vehicles:

> (1) The specified person for an approved trial or approved special use must ensure that –
>
> (a) any autonomous motor vehicle used in the approved trial or approved special use, and any accessory, sensor or equipment forming part of the vehicle, is at all times maintained in a state of good condition; and
>
> (b) the autonomous system of any autonomous motor vehicle used in the approved trial or approved special use is at all times functioning properly,
>
> such that no harm or damage is caused, or likely to be caused, to any person in the vehicle or any other person, or to any property.
>
> (2) A specified person who contravenes paragraph (1) shall be guilty of an offence and shall be liable on conviction to a fine not exceeding $2,000 and, in the case of a second or subsequent conviction, to a fine not exceeding $5,000.[47]

Lastly, the Act includes the requirement to collect and keep data from the data recorder; to keep records; to notify of incidents and accidents; and the power of the Authority to require vehicles to undergo tests.[48] The road traffic rules were

[44] 'Road Traffic (Autonomous Motor Vehicles) Rules 2017 – Singapore Statutes Online': sso.agc.gov.sg/SL/RTA1961-S464-2017?ValidDate=20170824&ProvIds=av-.

[45] ibid.

[46] ibid.

[47] ibid.

[48] ibid.

primarily intended to be regulatory sandboxes, effective for five years, after which they could be amended or made permanent.[49]

The majority of Singaporean self-driving legislation is aimed at testing and deployment, both via clarification and cooperative testing. The formal standard Technical Reference (TR) 68 was developed as a provisional standard by the Singapore Standards Council's Manufacturing Standards Committee in cooperation with four working groups including stakeholders from the self-driving industry, research institutions, higher education and government agencies, and covers areas such as 'vehicle behaviour, vehicle functional safety, cyber security, and data formats'.[50] More specifically, these include

> conduct of autonomous driving, including but not limited to, vehicle-to-vehicle interactions; interpretation of road signs, markings, and traffic signals; management of non-transferrable rules; the functions between an AV and any occupants; and communication flows between an AV, an occupants and external stakeholders, including but not limited to, pedestrians and other drivers.[51]

It explicitly does not include

> interface design elements, hardware or software between an AV and any occupants including the human safety driver; rules relating to non-driving tasks and longer term tactical cognitive functions such as route planning; communication or signalling software or hardware between the AV and external stakeholders, including but not limited to, pedestrians and other drivers, which extends beyond the use of standard equipment, including lighting and horn, as described in the existing road rules.[52]

The standard was published in 2019 and is intended to be continually reviewed as technologies advance.

In terms of liability outside self-driving vehicles, Singapore follows a fault-based negligence framework,[53] much like many other common law countries. However, there is still uncertainty as to what approach Singapore will take with liability for self-driving vehicles, as it has a 'adopted a "wait and see" approach to wholesale legal and regulatory reform'.[54] This means that until otherwise addressed that accidents will continue to be governed by common law,[55] although what exactly this means is left to many points discussed in chapter seven – negligence,

[49] Tan and Taeihagh (n 40).
[50] 'Joint Media Release by the Land Transport Authority, Enterprise Singapore, Standards Development Organisation & Singapore Standards Council – Singapore Develops Provisional National Standards to Guide Development of Fully Autonomous Vehicles', Land Transport Authority: lta.gov.sg/content/ltagov/en/newsroom/2019/1/2/joint-media-release-by-the-land-transport-authority-lta-enterprise-singapore-standards-development-organisation-singapo.html.
[51] 'Autonomous vehicles – Part 1: Basic behaviour' (Singapore Standards): singaporestandardseshop.sg/Product/SSPdtDetail/df6492de-c92b-435c-a979-d9ad211621c3.
[52] ibid.
[53] Tan and Taeihagh (n 40).
[54] ibid.
[55] S Chen, JHS Lim and BKL Lim, 'Attribution of Civil Liability for Accidents Involving Automated Cars' (2020) Research Collection School of Law 1: ink.library.smu.edu.sg/sol_research/3369.

product liability and no-fault liability – under the corresponding Singaporean legal tradition. While commentators have identified potential parties for liability to be the car's manufacturer, component(s') manufacturers, the car owner and the car driver,[56] such attributions may raise other issues.[57]

Singapore's overall policy approach has been very light-touch and focuses on the promotion of innovation and the framework for testing rather than introducing widespread, individual customer use.[58] The city state's 'adaptation-oriented' strategy is juridically nimble, and able to adapt policy changes to changing circumstance, as evidenced by TR 68 – though it is a technical-specific standard, it is intended to be updated as technological advances warrant. Tan and Taeihagh point to Singapore's 'proven track record in accelerating the nation's socio-economic development … show[ing] institutional capacity in strategically steering the adoption of self-driving vehicles as a predominant mode of transport in the next decade'.[59] This approach has been considered to have placed them in a favourable position with regard to self-driving roll-out: the KPMG Automated Vehicle Readiness Index, which ranks 30 jurisdictions on their self-driving ecosystem in four categories – policy and legislation; technology and innovation; infrastructure; and consumer acceptance – rated Singapore second in 2019 and first in 2020, the most recently available data as of January 2023.[60]

6.1.3. US Self-Driving

At a federal level of jurisdiction, the United States has the Department for Transportation. The Department for Transportation or 'USDOT' purports to act 'as a convenor and facilitator, partnering with a broad coalition of industry, academic, states and local, safety advocacy, and transportation stakeholders to support the safe development, testing, and integration of automated vehicle technologies'.[61] USDOT's 'Automated Vehicles Comprehensive Plan 4.0' defines the three goals of automated driving systems (ADS) to be promotion of collaboration and transparency, modernisation of the regulatory environment, and preparation of the transportation system.[62] This (Federal) Automated Vehicles Comprehensive Plan (FAVP) adopts the SAE automated vehicle levels; provides a vehicle performance guide for automated vehicles with 15 safety assessments that manufacturers

[56] ibid.

[57] K Grieman, 'Hard Drive Crash' (2019) 9 *Journal of Intellectual Property, Information Technology and Electronic Commerce Law* 294: jipitec.eu/issues/jipitec-9-3-2018/at_download/CompleteIssue.

[58] Chen, Lim and Lim (n 55).

[59] Tan and Taeihagh (n 40).

[60] '2020 Autonomous Vehicles Readiness Index', KPMG International 70: kpmg.com/xx/en/home/insights/2020/06/autonomous-vehicles-readiness-index.html#download.

[61] 'USDOT Automated Vehicles Activities', USDOT Automated Vehicles Activities: transportation.gov/AV.

[62] ibid.

should address prior to testing or deploying; a model state policy; a summary of the current regulatory tools; and a discussion of potential new tools and authorities.[63] The 'Model State Policy' confirms that 'States retain their traditional responsibilities for vehicle licensing and registration, traffic laws and enforcement, and motor vehicle insurance and liability regimes while outlining the Federal role for [highly automated vehicles]'.[64] It provides that:

> Federal responsibilities include:
>
> - Setting safety standards for new motor vehicles and motor vehicle equipment;
> - Enforcing compliance with the safety standards;
> - Investigating and managing the recall and remedy of non-compliances and safety-related motor vehicle defects on a nationwide basis;
> - Communicating with and educating the public about motor vehicle safety issues; and
> - When necessary, issuing guidance to achieve national safety goals
>
> State responsibilities include:
>
> - Licensing (human) drivers and registering motor vehicles in their jurisdictions;
> - Enacting and enforcing traffic laws and regulations;
> - Conducting safety inspections, when States choose to do so; and
> - Regulating motor vehicle insurance and liability.[65]

The Model Framework itself covers administrative structure, applications by manufacturers to test on roads, testing specifics, driver specifics, registration and titling, law enforcement considerations, and liability and insurance.[66]

Since the FAVP's publication in 2016, two federal bills have been introduced in the form of the SELF DRIVE and AV START Acts of 2018. Although both have made a certain amount of headway in Congress, neither had been passed as of January 2024.[67] States have progressed in their legislation of automated vehicles, albeit with reference to federal levels. This level of governance covers licensing and registration, as well as insurance and liability, and is thus a key level of AV governance, at bare minimum before a continuation of legislation at the federal level. Since 2012, at least 41 states have considered AV legislation.[68] As of March 2022, 29 states have enacted various – and varying – legislation of automated vehicles.[69]

[63] Tools range from record keeping and data collection to a pre-market approval process.

[64] 'Fact Sheet: AV Policy Section II: Model State Policy', US Department of Transportation: transportation.gov/AV/av-fact-sheet-model-state-policy.

[65] ibid.

[66] ibid.

[67] The SELF DRIVE Act 'includes automated driving systems from SAE Levels 2-5, while the AV START Act includes only HAVs at levels 3–5 … neither bill requires a fallback for human control or manual override' in H Westbrook, 'Look Ma, No Hands: Providing Automated Vehicle Regulations and Precedents Inclusive of Disabled Individuals' (2018) 19 *Texas Tech Administrative Law Journal* 385.

[68] 'Autonomous Vehicles/Self-Driving Vehicles Enacted Legislation' (National Conference of State Legislatures, 18 February 2020): ncsl.org/research/transportation/autonomous-vehicles-self-driving-vehicles-enacted-legislation.aspx.

[69] ibid.

Approaches to legislation tend to target three areas: whether or not a licence is required; regulation of vehicle design; and the testing of vehicles on roadways.[70]

While earlier military and academic applications may have started the modern conception of the self-driving car, and other efforts such as mining applications[71] Google (now spin-out Waymo) was one of the most publicly visible companies to test on public roads. The then Google car 'passed the first U.S. State Self-Driving Test' as early as May 2012 in Nevada, though passing the test included Google choosing the test route, setting limits on road and weather conditions, and taking control of the car twice.[72] The two most populous American states, California and Texas, were the first and second testing grounds for Google cars,[73] and became the testing grounds for many others under the USDOT designation of 10 sites to serve as testing grounds,[74] and later efforts.[75] They also provide an interesting comparative dynamic: one state being heavily Democratic and on the political left; one being Republican and on the political right; and found at opposite ends of many policy issues.[76]

California

California's regulatory approach to self-driving vehicles began in 2012 with Senate Bill No 1298. The bill defines 'autonomous technology' as 'a technology that has the capability to drive a vehicle without the active physical control or continuous monitoring by a human operator', and 'autonomous vehicle' as 'any vehicle equipped with autonomous technology that has been integrated into the vehicle', but explicitly excluding vehicles that automate by category:

> An autonomous vehicle does not include a vehicle that is equipped with one or more collision avoidance systems, including, but not limited to, electronic blind spot assistance, automated emergency braking systems, park assist, adaptive cruise control, lane

[70] Westbrook (n 67).

[71] C Brown, 'Autonomous Vehicle Technology in Mining' (2012) 213 *Engineering and Mining Journal* 30: proquest.com/openview/ae4f7afb678c263bfe38727071f82d30/1?pq-origsite=gscholar&cbl=39 2024.

[72] 'How Google's Autonomous Car Passed the First U.S. State Self-Driving Test' (*IEEE Spectrum*, 10 September 2014): spectrum.ieee.org/how-googles-autonomous-car-passed-the-first-us-state-selfdriving-test.

[73] Lance Whitney, 'Google's Self-Driving Cars Hit the Roads in Austin, Texas' (*Roadshow*): cnet.com/roadshow/news/googles-self-driving-cars-hit-the-roads-in-austin-texas/.

[74] Andrew J Hawkins, 'These Nine States Will Serve as Testing Grounds for Self-Driving Cars' (*The Verge*, 23 January 2017): theverge.com/2017/1/23/14357564/dot-self-driving-car-testing-sites-nine-states.

[75] 'Autonomous Vehicle Testing Permit Holders' (California DMV): dmv.ca.gov/portal/vehicle-industry-services/autonomous-vehicles/autonomous-vehicle-testing-permit-holders/; Josh Fisher, 'Autonomous Truck Testing Heats up under the Texas Sun' (*FleetOwner*, 27 May 2021): fleetowner.com/perspectives/trucks-at-work/blog/21165424/autonomous-truck-testing-heats-up-under-the-texas-sun.

[76] Kenneth P Miller, 'America's political future is a California-Texas duel' (2023) *USA Today* eu.usatoday.com/story/opinion/2020/11/01/how-california-and-texas-u-s-s-great-rivals-policy-column/6060779002/.

> keep assist, lane departure warning, traffic jam and queuing assist, or other similar systems that enhance safety or provide driver assistance, but are not capable, collectively or singularly, of driving the vehicle without the active control or monitoring of a human operator.[77]

'Operator' refers to either a person in the driver's seat *or* the person who 'causes the autonomous technology to engage'.[78] The bill prohibits a self-driving vehicle from being operated on public roads unless the manufacturer's application is approved by the California Department of Motor Vehicles (DMV), satisfying questions such as: whether the vehicle 'has a mechanism to engage and disengage the autonomous technology that is easily accessible to the operator'; whether the vehicle's autonomous technology meets Federal Motor Vehicle Safety Standards; whether it captures and stores autonomous sensor data surrounding a crash; that the vehicle 'has been tested on public roads and complies with any DMV testing standards'; and that the manufacturer will 'maintain a surety bond, or proof of self-insurance, in an amount of $5 million' (USD).[79] Successful application provides the manufacturer a Manufacturer's Testing Permit.[80]

Bill 1298 also requires the DMV to hold public hearings with regard to regulation applications, allows the DMV to notify the legislature when it receives an application for an autonomous vehicle to operate, and '[p]rovides that federal regulations promulgated by the National Traffic Safety Administration will supersede this bill's provision when found to be in conflict'.[81]

Draft deployment regulations were released in 2015, with revised regulations released in 2016.[82] In 2017, the pilot project for the testing of autonomous vehicles was launched, without previously required safety equipment such as manual braking, steering, or accelerating, though with the requirement for a remote backup driver. The 'Autonomous Vehicle Express Terms' are administered by the DMV, and while it was initially unclear whether the terms were expected to enter into force,[83] such a route remains the current approach for manufacturers to test and deploy self-driving vehicles on public roads in California.[84] Manufacturers can apply to test either with or without a safety driver, and must certify that 'the vehicle will be operated for testing purposes only'.[85] Manufacturers are also required to

[77] Senate Bill 1298 – An Act to add Division 16.6.

[78] ibid.

[79] California Senate Senate Floor Analyses, 'Vehicles: autonomous vehicles: safety and performance requirements' (2011–2012) SB-1298: leginfo.legislature.ca.gov/faces/billAnalysisClient.xhtml?bill_id=201120120SB1298.

[80] NE Vellinga, 'From the Testing to the Deployment of Self-Driving Cars: Legal Challenges to Policymakers on the Road Ahead' (2017) 33 *Computer Law & Security Review* 847: sciencedirect.com/science/article/pii/S0267364917301334.

[81] California Senate Floor Analyses (n 79).

[82] 'Driverless Testing of Autonomous Vehicles': dmv.ca.gov/portal/dmv/detail/vr/autonomous/auto.

[83] Vellinga (n 80).

[84] 'Driverless Testing of Autonomous Vehicles' (n 82).

[85] ibid.

'report any collision that results in property damage, bodily injury, or death within 10 days of the incident'.[86]

Effective 2019, California provided legislation via Assembly Bill No 87, Chapter 667,[87] allowing 'a peace officer or public employee engaged in directing traffic or enforcing parking laws [to] remove a vehicle' if:

- The registered owner or person in control of the vehicle does not have a valid Autonomous Vehicle (AV) Permit (Manufacturer Testing Permit, Driverless or Deployment, issued by the [California] DMV.
- The vehicle is operating with autonomous technology after the registered owner or person in control of the vehicle received notice that their AV Permit is suspended, terminated, or revoked.[88]

In terms of liability, California considered but did not pass legislation in 2018 that would have allowed manufacturers not to be liable if a self-driving vehicle had not been maintained to manufacturer specifications, such as by failing to clean the car's sensors.[89] This abandonment was celebrated by consumer advocates, particularly as it could have helped manufacturers evade liability where the maintenance failure did not contribute to the actual cause.[90]

Texas

The initial approach of Texas to AV legislation occurred via failed Senate Bill No 1167 in 2015. The bill gave definition to the term 'autonomous motor vehicle', and provided that the department of motor vehicles would 'establish a program to provide an autonomous motor vehicle operation designation either on the face of a driver's license or on the reverse of the driver's license issued to a person who is authorised to operate an autonomous motor vehicle'.[91] The bill was alleged to be 'very restrictive to manufacturers who were experimenting with [AVs]' and ultimately did not pass.[92] While other bills aimed at AVs for specific uses such as border security or construction were forwarded,[93] it was not until 2017 that Senate Bill No 2205 passed in regulation of AVs more generally.

The bill mirrors federal language around automation levels and adopts SAE levels 0–5; provides definitions for the AV sector and for governance exclusivity; defines the role of the 'operator' of an AV; addresses duties following accidents;

[86] ibid.
[87] Amending § 22651 of the California Vehicle Code.
[88] State of California Department of Motor Vehicles, 'New Autonomous Vehicle Laws' (2018) AB 87.
[89] 'California Regulators Nix Rules Limiting Carmaker Liability' *AP NEWS* (6 May 2021): apnews.com/article/north-america-technology-business-california-mi-state-wire-ce707c88718446c5b9b93b3180c70e6e.
[90] 'California Axes Self-Driving Car Rule Limiting Liability for Crashes' (*Engadget*): engadget.com/2017-12-02-california-axes-self-driving-car-rule-limiting-liability.html.
[91] (Texas Senate) An Act relating to autonomous motor vehicles SB 1167.
[92] Westbrook (n 67).
[93] ibid.

provides for optional vehicle classification; and addresses the 'request to intervene' by an AV.[94] More specifically,

> '[a]utomated driving system' means hardware and software that, when installed on a motor vehicle and engaged, are collectively capable of performing, without any intervention or supervision by a human operator:
>
> (A) all aspects of the entire dynamic driving task for the vehicle on a sustained basis; and
>
> (B) any fallback manoeuvres necessary to respond to a failure of the system.[95]

In turn, '"automated motor vehicle" means a motor vehicle on which an automated driving system is installed'.[96] The bill clarifies that the owner 'is considered the operator for the purpose of complying with traffic and motor vehicle laws'.[97] The owner of the vehicle is considered the operator

> solely for the purpose of assessing compliance with applicable traffic or motor vehicle laws, regardless of whether the person is physically present in the vehicle while the vehicle is operating; and … the automated vehicle system is considered to be licensed to operate the vehicle.[98]

The AV may only operate on a highway with the automated system driving if it is:

> (1) capable of operating in compliance with applicable traffic and motor vehicle laws of this state; subject to this subchapter;
>
> (2) equipped with a recording device, as defined by Section 547.615(a), installed by the manufacturer of the automated motor vehicle or automated driving system;
>
> (3) equipped with an automated driving system in compliance with applicable federal law and federal motor vehicle safety standards;
>
> (4) registered and titled in accordance with the laws of this state; and
>
> (5) covered by motor vehicle liability coverage or self-insurance in an amount equal to the amount of coverage that is required under the laws of this state.[99]

Point (3) refers to the Federal Motor Vehicle Safety Standards and Regulations (FMVSS), which is administered by the National Highway Traffic Safety Administration. The FMVSS has relatively recently been amended,

> to account for future vehicles that do not have the traditional manual controls associated with a human driver because they are equipped with Automated Driving Systems (ADS)[; making] clear that, despite their innovative designs, vehicles with ADS technology must continue to provide the same high levels of occupant protection that current passenger vehicles provide.[100]

[94] Texas Transportation Code (2021) TRANSP § 545.451.
[95] ibid.
[96] ibid.
[97] (Texas) Senate Research Center, 'Bill Analysis' (2017) SB 2205.
[98] Texas Transportation Code (2017) TRANSP § 545.453.
[99] (Texas) Senate Research Center (n 97).
[100] National Highway Traffic Safety Administration, 'Occupant Protection for Vehicles with Automated Driving Systems' (2022).

The FMVSS – Occupant Protection for Vehicles with Automated Driving Systems – also clarifies existing terminology, particularly in relation to terms such as 'driver's seat', and provides that 'children should not occupy the "driver's" position when the vehicle is operating in ADS mode and steering controls are present, given that the driver's seating position has not been designed to protect children in a crash', though the federal standard shied away from requiring that the vehicle refrain from driving at all with a child in the 'driver's' seat, a position it did consider.[101] The new rules also drop the requirement for automated vehicles to equip vehicles with manual driving controls if they are capable of complete automation.[102]

While AVs are in development, the National Highway Traffic Safety Administration's 2017 'Vehicle Performance Guidance for Automated Vehicles' also provides a set of *voluntary* guidance points relating to system safety, operational design domain, object and event detection and response, fallback, validation methods, human machine interface, vehicle cybersecurity, crashworthiness, post-crash ADS behaviour, data recording, consumer education and training, and federal, state and local laws.[103]

In terms of liability, the bill provides that the manufacturer of an AV is not liable for damage arising from modifications made by another party without the consent of the manufacturer except for potential contractual obligations where a vehicle is modified by installing a system to convert it to an AV.[104] Broadly speaking, however, 'the manufacturer will be liable in the event that a crash or accident occurs'.[105]

California/Texas Comparison

Even with the differences between the California and Texas approaches to self-driving regulation, it is important to note that they are both subject to certain federal competencies, including the March 2022 'Occupant Protection for Vehicles with Automated Driving Systems' FMVSS update.[106] Beyond the current USDOT Automated Comprehensive Plan 4.0, it is unclear what federal action may include in future, though US Transportation Secretary Pete Buttigieg remarked in March 2022 that 'federal policy on autonomous vehicles will undergo "meaningful"

[101] ibid.

[102] D Shepardson, 'U.S. Eliminates Human Controls Requirement for Fully Automated Vehicles' *Reuters* (11 March 2022): reuters.com/business/autos-transportation/us-eliminates-human-controls-requirement-fully-automated-vehicles-2022-03-11/.

[103] US Department of Transportation, 'Automated Driving Systems: A Vision for Safety' 36: www.transportation.gov/policy-initiatives/automated-vehicles/automated-driving-systems-vision-safety; www.nhtsa.gov/sites/nhtsa.gov/files/documents/13069a-ads2.0_090617_v9a_tag.pdf.

[104] (Texas) Senate Research Center (n 97).

[105] Westbrook (n 67).

[106] National Highway Traffic Safety Administration, 'Occupant Protection for Vehicles with Automated Driving Systems' (n 100).

developments in the coming years … [including] meaningful developments here in the 2020s'.[107]

While the federal government powers include setting and enforcing safety standards and investigating non-compliance with those standards, it also, via the Interstate Commerce Act, includes more generally the power 'to [r]egulate [c]ommerce with foreign Nations, and among the several states'.[108] In other words, the federal government can exercise power in certain ways relating to inter-state commerce, which includes a great deal of driving. In terms of liability, while states rather than the federal government are responsible for liability regimes,[109] some commentators have argued that the Supreme Court's decision in *Geier v American Honda Motor Company, Inc* – holding that federal objectives can pre-empt product liability claims – may mean that federal involvement in AVs may ultimately pre-empt that of states. However, such pre-emption has not yet occurred.[110] Under the US Constitution, there is also what is called the 'Supremacy Clause', by which state law conflicting with federal law is pre-empted: this clause has been tested through the federal Medical Devices Amendment which 'expressly preempts state common-law tort claims',[111] although the extent to which this would be effective for AI is as yet untested.

Neither state has adopted the federal Model State Policy. While the differences in initial policy may reflect the different stages of development during which legislation originated – California's as early as 2012, Texas as recently as 2017 – the foci of the legislation have differed. California's initial focus on licensing has since been updated but was a clear indication that the state was focusing on safety-critical aspects. Texas' first bill attempt would have gone a step further in requiring the autonomous vehicle to be designated *on* a driver's licence, but was ultimately vetoed, and the legislation that did pass does not include such restrictions. Because California now includes the option to test without a driver this has less impact now than it likely did in intervening years but was a much more top-down approach to regulation. Conversely, Texas' inclusion that the automated vehicle system is considered to be licensed to operate the vehicle is potentially a more industry-friendly approach.

The states differ slightly in their approach to definitions: where California defines 'autonomous technology', Texas defines the 'automated driving system'. California refers to the 'autonomous vehicle', Texas the 'automated motor vehicle'. Again, such differences may more broadly represent their contextual time periods

[107] Tina Bellon, 'U.S. Will See "meaningful" Autonomous Vehicle Policy in 2020s – U.S. Transportation Secretary' *Reuters* (17 March 2022): reuters.com/world/us/us-will-see-meaningful-autonomous-vehicle-policy-2020s-us-transportation-2022-03-16/.

[108] 'U.S. Senate: The Interstate Commerce Act Is Passed': www.senate.gov/artandhistory/history/minute/Interstate_Commerce_Act_Is_Passed.htm.

[109] Vellinga (n 80).

[110] Westbrook (n 67).

[111] SA Mota, 'Federal Preemption after Medtronic, Altia Group, and Wyeth' (2010) *Oklahoma City University Law Review* 23.

but are interesting nonetheless; while the clinical differences between 'autonomous' and 'automated' may be minimal, the practical differences may be wider: 'autonomous' seems to imply an entirely separate functioning entity, whereas 'automated' is more familiar to the consumer mind in smaller, discrete functions, such as the automated lane keeping system which many modern cars have as a feature. Texas' definition of 'automated driving system' reflects this understanding, stating explicitly that it means 'hardware and software that, when installed on a motor vehicle and engaged are **collectively capable of performing, without any intervention or supervision** … (a) **all aspects** of the entire dynamic driving task'.[112] California is potentially slightly less restrictive, referring purely to 'a **technology** that has the capability to drive … without the active **physical control** or **continuous monitoring** by a human operator', with 'autonomous vehicle' referring to 'any vehicle equipped with autonomous technology that has been integrated into the vehicle'.

While it is difficult to imagine a technology that would not fairly be referred to as hardware and software but that could nonetheless substantively be considered to be 'driving' the vehicle, such specificities can matter. For example, both sets of regulations provide that an autonomous vehicle (or a motor vehicle on which an automated driving system is installed) does not include those aspects of automation which cannot collectively pilot the vehicle themselves; that do not include 'all aspects of the entire dynamic driving task for the vehicle on a sustained basis'.[113] This makes sense from the perspective that legislators do not want to allow manufacturers the ability to call their vehicle autonomous/automated/self-driving if it is not in fact capable of such.

However, manufacturers are aware of this, and are currently (March 2022) attempting to use this to their own advantage. Tesla's Full Self Driving vehicles are in beta, having been slowly rolled out since October 2020: '[t]he software enables the vehicle to drive autonomously to a destination entered in the car's navigation system, but the driver needs to remain vigilant and ready to take control at all times'.[114] Updates to the Full Self Driving or FSD system appear to only be available to drivers obtaining a certain safety score, but Tesla also states they may lower the score currently required if the update performs well.[115] By maintaining that drivers must be ready and able to take control at all times, Tesla keeps their FSD beta at an SAE level 2, and by doing so, 'Tesla hopes that FST beta avoids meaningful regulation',[116] even having named the system 'Full Self Driving'. This is a mismatch

[112] Texas Transportation Code (2021) (n 94) (emphasis added).
[113] ibid.
[114] Fred Lambert, 'Tesla Starts Releasing Big Full Self-Driving Beta Update' (*Electrek*, 14 March 2022): electrek.co/2022/03/14/tesla-full-self-driving-fsd-beta-update-10-11/.
[115] ibid. From article: 'CEO Elon Musk says that if this update "performs well", Tesla will "probably" lower the access to drivers who scored "95" on the driver safety score. This should give a lot more FSD buyers access to the beta'.
[116] WH Widen and P Koopman, 'Autonomous Vehicle Regulation, Does Tesla's Full Self-Driving Beta Release Comply with Law?' (2021) SSRN Scholarly Paper ID 3931341: papers.ssrn.com/abstract=3931341.

in marketing versus regulation; to wit, 'Tesla's description of its FSD capability matches the SAE … requirements for level 4'.[117] In California, for example, Tesla maintains that the vehicle is merely an amalgamation of those features excluded from the definition of an autonomous vehicle, and that it lacks the 'capability to drive [the] vehicle without the active physical control or monitoring by a human operator'.[118] Texas' legislation approach is likely to be similarly sidestepped. While this classification is certain to be challenged, perhaps under marketing legislation, it nonetheless sidesteps the legislation specific to self-driving vehicles by dint of categorisation choices.[119]

In practice, it is difficult to see how the two legislative approaches will play out, due first and foremost to the aforementioned federal factor. Second, both now provide for more human hands-off testing, which evens out some of their original differences, and may continue to trend towards one another. Third, the states might handle an identical case differently even outside the sectorally specific self-driving legislation, as they have different liability regimes. While California may not have allowed companies to evade liability if the vehicle was not maintained to the manufacturer's specifications, Texas excludes liability only where the vehicle has been modified without the consent of the manufacturer. Neither state has indicated that liability would fall on a party other than the manufacturer in a non-tampering case, particularly given that both require an autonomous vehicle not to require intervention. Lastly, both states require self-driving vehicles to be insured: a requirement unlikely to change as it falls under state competency and has been confirmed to be so in the (Federal) Model State Policy, is repeated under the self-driving vehicle specific legislation in addition to non-self-driving vehicle legislation and responds to the practical need to compensate victims.

6.1.4. UK Self-Driving

The UK's self-driving legislation journey began with the Automated and Electric Vehicles Act in 2018. The Act required the listing of automated vehicles by the Secretary of State, a list which must be updated to include those vehicles which 'are in the Secretary of State's opinion designed or adapted to be capable, in at least some circumstances or situations, of safely driving themselves, and … may lawfully be used when driving themselves'.[120] The Act defined the liability of insurers where an accident is caused by an electric vehicle; where an accident results from unauthorised software alterations or failure to update software;

[117] ibid.

[118] Senate Bill 1298 (n 77).

[119] Consumer groups have also started to protest Tesla's specific 'full self-driving' classification. Ramishah Maruf, 'Super Bowl ad slams Tesla's 'Full Self-Driving' tech' (*CNN Business*, 12 February 2023): edition.cnn.com/2023/02/12/business/super-bowl-ad-tesla-full-self-driving/index.html.

[120] Automated and Electric Vehicles Act 2018.

and where the insurer may claim against a person responsible for an accident. Notably,

> (1) Where –
> (a) an accident is caused by an automated vehicle when driving itself on a road or other public place in Great Britain,
> (b) the vehicle is insured at the time of the accident, and
> (c) an insured person or any other person suffers damage as a result of the accident, the insurer is liable for that damage.[121]

The Act also adds that if the vehicle is not insured at the time of accident, in accordance with the Road Traffic Act 1988, the owner of the vehicle would be liable for damage caused.[122] Contributory negligence is similarly addressed, being divided along the lines of contributory negligence of human drivers. The Act does provide, however, that where an accident results from software alterations or failure to update the vehicle software, an insurance policy may in fact 'exclude or limit the insurer's liability', but the limitation 'applies only in relation to software alterations which, at the time of the accident, the person knows are prohibited under the policy'; where the accident occurred as a result of alterations made by the insured individual, with their knowledge; or where they 'knew, or ought to have reasonably known', that the alterations or failure to update 'were safety-critical'.[123] While the Act has not seen in-depth litigation directed at self-driving vehicles, it was nonetheless an interesting starting point of liability legislation – defining explicitly the relationship between self-driving vehicles and insurance, even to the extent of including the neglect of software updates. This was a comparatively early, though ultimately narrow, address of liability issues specific to automated vehicles. Its focii and considerations can be seen in follow-up legislation, though taken to greater extents – see, for example, the depth of the Law Commission's focus on technical issues such as the handover problem.

Following the Automated and Electric Vehicles Act was the Centre for Connected and Automated Vehicles' 2019 Code of Practice, a non-statutory and non-binding set of practice outlines dealing with areas such as failure warnings, privacy and cybersecurity, alongside requirements that the test driver be licensed and supervising at all times.[124] The Code states that those undergoing autonomous vehicle trials would be expected to publish related information regarding safety, trial performance and pre-trial risk assessments.[125]

Overlapping the Code of Practice was the Law Commission Report on Automated Vehicles, based on three rounds of consultation between November

[121] ibid.
[122] ibid.
[123] ibid.
[124] Vellinga (n 80).
[125] 'UK Government Issues New Autonomous Testing Code of Practice' (*ITS United Kingdom: Better Transport Through Technology*, 7 February 2019): its-uk.org.uk/uk-government-issues-new-autonomous-testing-code-of-practice/.

2018 and December 2020, with 404 responses.[126] The major recommendations for legislation include:

- Writing the test for self-driving into law, with a bright line distinguishing it from driver support features, a transparent process for setting a safety standard, and new offences to prevent misleading marketing.
- A two-stage approval and authorisation process building on current international and domestic technical vehicle approval schemes and adding a new second stage to authorise vehicles for use as self-driving on GB roads.
- A new in-use safety assurance scheme to provide regulatory oversight of automated vehicles throughout their lifetimes to ensure they continue to be safe and comply with road rules.
- New legal roles for users, manufacturers and service operators, with removal of criminal responsibility for the person in the passenger seat.
- Holding manufacturers and service operators criminally responsible for misrepresentation or non-disclosure of safety-relevant information.[127]

As the most exhaustive examination of self-driving vehicles to date, the Law Commission did go into much more depth along these lines, recommending a new Automated Vehicle Act to enshrine a new regulatory regime and actors.[128] This Act, which will be discussed shortly, passed in May 2024. The report raises several areas of interest: first, the notable difficulty in human handovers. Second, the changeover in legal accountability during a handover. Third, several new legal entities with regard to different levels of automation. Fourth, the recommendation of a new criminal offence. The article also addresses new avenues for vehicle type and approval.

While the handover problem has previously been addressed on technical grounds,[129] the Law Commission is among the first to address it on a liability level, calling it the 'problem of passivity'. The problem of passivity is that

> people find it more difficult to monitor a task passively than to be actively engaged in it … Once their eyes and minds wander away from the road, they have limited ability to respond appropriately to events. They should not be held accountable for failure to notice problems. The law therefore needs a clear-cut distinction setting out when the user is no longer responsible for the dynamic driving task.[130]

While the need for 'bright line' divisions is not unique to the Law Commission Report, nor indeed to this section of the report, it is nonetheless a stand-out address of a technical issue in need of a legal response.

[126] 'Automated Vehicles' (n 6).

[127] ibid.

[128] ibid.

[129] DA Drexler and T Haidegger, 'Handover Process of Autonomous Vehicles – Technology and Application Challenges' (2019) 16 *Acta Polytechnica Hungarica* 235.

[130] 'Automated Vehicles' Summary of joint report: s3-eu-west-2.amazonaws.com/cloud-platform-e218f50a4812967ba1215eaecede923f/uploads/sites/30/2022/01/AV-Summary-25-01-22-2.pdf 2024.

Second, the changeover in legal accountability during a handover. While closely related to the passivity problem, the report delineates between having a '"self-driving" ADS feature' and being capable of having 'no user-in-charge'. The report provides that '[o]nce a vehicle is authorised as having "self-driving" ADS features, and a self-driving ADS feature is engaged, the system of legal accountability will change'[131] from a 'user-in-charge' to 'no user-in-charge'. A user-in-charge will 'have immunity from a wide range of offences relating to the way the vehicle drives, ranging from dangerous or careless driving, to exceeding the speed limit or running a red light', but will still have obligations regarding non in-the-moment duties such as insurance, and 'may be also required to take over driving in response to a "transition demand" if the vehicle encounters a problem it cannot handle'.[132] Where the vehicle is driven by an Authorised Self-Driving Entity (ASDE) and drives in a way that would be considered criminal by a human driver, it will be considered a regulatory matter to 'be resolved between the in-use regulator and the ASDE'.[133] Where a feature is authorised for 'no user-in-charge' (NUIC) any vehicle occupants are purely passengers, and any responsibilities for overseeing driving are undertaken by a licensed NUIC operator.[134] The report also imports the provisions of the Automated and Electric Vehicle Act relating to insurers and compensation. Because of the overall change in liability, the report recommends a statutory test for 'self-driving', differentiating between the aforementioned 'user-in-charge', who must be in and capable of occupying the driver's seat; the licensed NUIC operator who can oversee a vehicle with no capacity for an internal driver; and an ASDE, as the 'manufacturer or developer that puts the vehicle forward for authorisation and takes responsibility for its actions'.[135]

Lastly and perhaps most interestingly, the report recommends a new criminal offence with regard to marketing, prohibiting any commercial practice which

> (1) uses certain terms ('self-drive', 'self-driving', 'drive itself', 'driverless' and 'automated vehicle') in connection with driving automation technology that is:
>
> (a) not authorised under our recommended scheme; and
> (b) designed for use on roads or in public places; or
>
> (2) is likely to confuse drivers into thinking that an unauthorised vehicle does not need to be monitored when used on a public road or place.[136]

This recommendation is particularly interesting in light of the aforementioned Tesla argument with regard to SAE levels versus their own marketing.

[131] ibid.
[132] ibid.
[133] Automated and Electric Vehicles Act 2018.
[134] ibid.
[135] 'Automated Vehicles' (n 6).
[136] ibid.

Partially alongside the Law Commission Report is the Department for Transport and Centre for Connected and Autonomous Vehicles' 2020 'Call for evidence on the safe use of Automated Lane Keeping Systems', with regard to authorising automated lane keeping systems as an automated driving technology. Automated Lane Keeping Systems '[enable] a vehicle to drive itself in a single lane, while maintaining the ability to easily and safely return control to the driver when required'.[137] While the 2017 House of Commons Session saw the introduction of the 'Vehicle Technology and Aviation' bill,[138] which proposed updates to compulsory insurance frameworks, including those regarding self-driving vehicles, this bill only passed the House of Lords in 2023. However, 2021 did include the publication of the Department for Transport's consultation on automated vehicles, authorising automated lane keeping systems as 'the first approved system designed to perform the dynamic driving task instead of the driver, under certain conditions'.[139] It also proposed an amendment to the Highway Code, which was updated July 2022 to define automated vehicles, and clarify that '[w]hile a self-driving vehicle is driving itself in a valid situation, [the human is] not responsible for how it drives [and] many turn [their] attention away from the road', and includes the possibility of using a built-in infotainment system at such times.[140] However, it further clarifies that the human user must still be fit to drive and ready to take control, the vehicle road-legal, and restrictions on all illegal activities – including hand-held phone use – remain in place.[141] Lastly, it reaffirms that all vehicles considered 'self-driving' in Great Britain will be listed.

The Act passed on 20 May 2024, and is a clear follow-up from the research and lessons from the Law Commission Report. The Act has seven parts: a regulatory scheme for automated vehicles; criminal liability for vehicle use; police and investigation; marketing restrictions; permits for automated passenger services; adaptation of existing regimes; and general provisions.[142] The regulatory scheme covers licensing for self-driving vehicles, cementing the concepts of the ASDE and NUIC introduced in the Law Commission report. Criminal liability defines 'user-in-charge' cases, looking at the liability and circumstances under which they might be liable. Policing and investigation allows for stop and seizure. The marketing restrictions section is aimed very particularly to restrict the use of certain terms in relation to authorised automated vehicles, and includes sections on 'communication likely to confuse as to autonomous capability,' as well as providing for the liability of corporate officers. The section on permits allows for authorities to grant permits, while also exempting autonomous vehicles from other specific legislation,

[137] 'Government Paves the Way for Self-Driving Vehicles on UK Roads' (GOV.UK): gov.uk/government/news/government-paves-the-way-for-self-driving-vehicles-on-uk-roads.

[138] Vehicle Technology and Aviation Bill 2021.

[139] 'Rules on Safe Use of Automated Vehicles on GB Roads' (GOV.UK): gov.uk/government/consultations/safe-use-rules-for-automated-vehicles-av/rules-on-safe-use-of-automated-vehicles-on-gb-roads.

[140] Highway Code 2015.

[141] ibid.

[142] Automated Vehicles Act 2024.

such as that applying to taxis. The section on adapting existing regimes enables the secretary of state to make amendments where necessary to allow for automated vehicles. Lastly, the section on general provisions provides definitions, disclosure of information, and other details such as the Act's scope.

The Act's points of interest are primarily those heralded by the Law Commission Report. First, it clearly shows that the co-regulatory discussion between stakeholders was weighed heavily in its impact on the ultimate legislation. Second, there is a tacit acknowledgment of where issues have occurred elsewhere, such as by addressing the misuse of terms in marketing where confusion is likely. Third, it addresses practical and technical issues, such as which part is expected to have control, when, and how this handover can happen, alongside other specific contexts such as remote operation which are under addressed in other discussions on automated vehicles. Fourth, it puts in place certain licensing conditions, such as the power to authorise automated vehicles, and what requirements may be put in place for a vehicle to be authorised. Ultimately, the Act provides that self-driving vehicles may be on public roads by 2026, and affirms to drivers that 'while their vehicle is in self-driving mode, they will not be held responsible for how the vehicle drives'.[143]

As regards liability, the 2018 Automated and Electric Vehicles Act affirms that insurers are liable where 'an accident is caused by an automated vehicle when driving itself on a road or other public place in Great Britain'.[144] The government has also not changed the statement that motor insurance is required to drive on UK roads, and there are currently no cars approved for purely autonomous driving.[145]

In summary, the United Kingdom has been looking at regulating since 2017 and has engaged in intense consultation on how to go about legislating. This has the benefit of providing informed commentary vis-a-vis on-the-ground issues, such as the passivity problem. It has also provided a more granular look at potential legal actors, such as the user-in-charge, NUIC, and ASDE, and their varying states and potential for liability. It maintains the necessary relationship of insurers, adjusting only for new technical issues such as tampering and updates. The regard to specific technologies such as automated lane keeping signals a willingness to engage with automated technologies on a more individual/type level than purely automated vehicles.

While there may of course be changes and updates in due time, particularly by the promised potential roll-out of automated vehicles in 2026,[146] the UK has

[143] 'Self-driving vehicles set to be on roads by 2026 as Automated Vehicles Act becomes law' (GOV.UK, 20 May 2024): https://www.gov.uk/government/news/self-driving-vehicles-set-to-be-on-roads-by-2026-as-automated-vehicles-act-becomes-law#:~:text=The%20act%20delivers%20the%20most,for%20how%20the%20vehicle%20drives.

[144] Automated and Electric Vehicles Act 2018.

[145] See, bare minimum, the list of 'Self-driving vehicles listed for use in Great Britain', which is as of 3 March 2024 empty: gov.uk/guidance/self-driving-vehicles-listed-for-use-in-great-britain.

[146] 'Self-driving vehicles set to be on roads by 2026 as Automated Vehicles Act becomes law' (n 143).

taken a very focused and pragmatic approach to automated vehicles. Consultations and ultimately legislation have taken on a variety of considerations, ranging from small semi-automated function to 'part-time' self-driving and remote operation, attempting to cover contingencies in as broad a range of scenarios as possible. Regulation has also taken into account a level of personal liability within companies, examining contingencies such as the hiding or lack of provision of information, alongside the need for *post-hoc* actions such as accident investigation. While the efficacy of the measures taken or promised remain to be seen, such as what the approval process to be created through secondary legislation will look like in practice, or what the requirement to 'achieve a level of safety at least as high as careful and competent human drivers might look like,'[147] regulation of automated vehicles in the UK has been particularly proactive.

6.1.5. Self-Driving Overall

Sectoral self-driving legislation is a particularly interesting point of comparison for several reasons. First, while some jurisdictions, such as the United States with Waymo, had a slight advantage in terms of home-grown products, the proliferation of global tech news means that all jurisdictions had a similar level of advance warning of the potential for self-driving vehicles to become a reality. Second, each jurisdiction discussed has a different type of liability system, which includes vehicles: even California and Texas are able to set their own liability legislation, as has the United Kingdom despite formerly being part of the European Union. Third, driving law applies to a large, mostly inexpert percentage of each jurisdiction's population and thus requires more detail compared with, say, medical regulation as we will see. Fourth, while the concept of driving a motor vehicle is relatively universal, there are a variety of different driving practices – EU Member States may differ from one another; Singapore and the United Kingdom drive on the opposite side of the road from the United States and the European Union; and even California and Texas differ in detailed elements such as roads running parallel to freeways, and bits of driving etiquette such as the 'wave acknowledgment'.[148] All of these help explain the differences between jurisdictional approaches, but also the underlying difficulties for self-driving producers in serving different jurisdictions, not to mention climates.

Despite the aforementioned variety, there are two points on which the jurisdictions overlap. First, there appears to be near universal acceptance of the SAE categorisations of six levels of automation. This is particularly helpful as a point of relative harmonisation, despite other differences in driving worlds. It also provides a certain commonality in technical language, at the very least in relation

[147] ibid.
[148] 'What Is It Like Driving in Texas Compared to California? – AIS Insurance' (*AIS Insurance Specialists Blog*, 28 August 2020): blog.aisinsurance.com/2020/08/27/driving-in-texas-compared-to-california/.

to comparative automation. Second, it seems reasonable to say that all legislation previously discussed that is aimed at self-driving vehicles is first and foremost aimed at human safety. While each attempts to do so in different ways, such as focusing on testing or type approval, safety is a clear priority. This is heartening, though perhaps unsurprising – any government in favour of self-driving has the clear need to balance public buy-in with technical capacity. All jurisdictions also included, at some point in their legislative process, reference to data security of vehicles and to recording.[149]

While the jurisdictions share safety as a first priority, they differ greatly in their approaches to fostering safe self-driving, and indeed their second priorities. While the European Union has included definitions for both connectivity and autonomy, there is an overarching concern about integration of specific, self-driving sectoral legislation with legislation in a multitude of other areas. This integration comes both with the international community, such as working with the UN Economic Commission for Europe, but also with the broad swathes of legislation that touch on self-driving vehicles. Areas of focus include the type of approval framework, general safety regulations, connectivity, privacy and data protection, and AI legislation more broadly, but all under an overarching strategy – 'On the road to automated mobility, an EU strategy for mobility of the future'. This in essence explains why connectivity is included deliberately with automation: while many if not all automated vehicles will be connected, there is a potential need for broader integration between vehicles and other infrastructure.

Keeping with the EU's desire to both combine existing legislation and harmonise new efforts, the liability regime for motor vehicles remains unchanged. The European Commission proposes that vehicles have data recorders to clarify accident details, and that insurers 'can take legal action against a manufacturer under the Product Liability Directive if there is a malfunction/defect of the automated driving system'.[150] The Commission maintains that the Motor Insurance Directive already requires third-party liability insurance, and no changes are necessary.

Singapore, very similarly to its general AI legislation, had a very business-friendly start to self-driving vehicles and has continued with light-touch legislation promoting testing and innovation. It has so far focused on widespread testing rather than individual customer availability, which suggests both high levels of government to business cooperation, and a high level of concern for safety buy-in. As Tan and Taeihagh suggest, the Singapore government seems to be '[s]trategically steering the adoption of self-driving vehicles as a predominant mode of transport in the next decade'.[151] The Committee on Autonomous Road Transport for Singapore (CARTS) has both public and private stakeholders, and the Road Traffic

[149] eg, Singapore's requirements for data recording.
[150] AI Liability Directive (n 38).
[151] Tan and Taeihagh (n 40).

Act is very clear on how commercial enterprises can apply for testing authorisation, going so far as offering alternatives to liability insurance. Technical Reference 68 is both enshrined in law and acknowledged to be mandatorily updated as technological advances arise – while this might not be achievable for jurisdictions' slower legislative processes, Singapore is the most likely jurisdiction to be able to update such a reference given both its private sector cooperation and its adaptive legislation. As to liability, however, it is not yet clear upon whom or exactly how liability would fall.

Given the complex political interplay between the state and federal governments in the United States, it is perhaps unsurprising that it has the most fractured set of regulations. The two most populous states have taken differing – though not dynamically opposed – approaches, yet are simultaneously dependent on updated Federal Motor Vehicle Safety Standards and Regulations (FMVSS), an area over which the federal government has distinct jurisdiction. The FMVSS are the definite safety standards to which vehicles across the United States must perform and would take precedence over any internally imposed state standards. However, states have separate jurisdiction over liability, including liability for motor vehicle accidents. California has not yet passed legislation regarding self-driving specific vehicles, but Texas has stated that 'the manufacturer will be liable in the event that a crash or accident occurs'. As previously mentioned, case law may act to give federal jurisdiction slightly more input on liability issues, but it is unlikely that the power will shift to federal jurisdiction entirely.

The United Kingdom started its journey with the Automated and Electric Vehicles Act, which, uniquely, gave very specific guidance on automated vehicle liability, including, among others:

- Liability of insurers etc where accident caused by automated vehicle.
- Contributory negligence etc.
- Accident resulting from unauthorised software alterations or failure to update software.
- Right of insurer to claim against person responsible for accident.[152]

The Law Commission followed this up with a range of practical and technical elements, many of which were ultimately put into practice through the Automated Vehicles Act 2024, including criminal-level prohibitions and marketing restrictions, alongside innovations such as information requirements and accident investigation requirements. While the UK is certainly the jurisdiction that has addressed liability in its greatest detail, including which parties might be liable under broad circumstances, its requirement that self-driving vehicles be at least as safe as their human counterparts could be fleshed out in greater detail: what tests might look like, further standards, etc.

[152] Automated and Electric Vehicles Act 2018.

In consequence, these approaches leave manufacturers and other stakeholders in a variety of positions with regard to predictability about liability and other concerns. Singapore, with its specific technical recommendations, clear legislation regarding authorisation, and multitude of government–partnership testing entities is highly predictable in most aspects, but nebulous in terms of liability. The United States is not particularly predictable in either category, as its 50(+) jurisdictions have separate liability legislation, and the federal government both has recently changed and has signalled its likelihood to change in the near future sector-specific safety regulations (FMVSS). The European Union has arguably provided a high level of predictability by stating that the liability rules will not change and will continue to relate to product liability,[153] but has not provided guidance as to the interaction between specific legislation and Member State specific legislation.[154] The United Kingdom has provided a level of guidance with relation to self-driving vehicle liability, but has not committed a general idea as to what constitutes liability for AI, or what depth of requirements might look like where the Law Commission has not yet ventured.

Lastly, it is interesting to note the different approaches in terminology. While an exact comparison is not necessarily useful, as interpretation may depend on other jurisdictional specificities,[155] it is informative that multiple jurisdictions have taken the time to clarify or define new terms. The EU's involvement in changing the Vienna Convention definitional requirement of a (human, present) driver; the FMVSS' clarification of functional terminology such as 'driver's seat'; the UK's creation of several new legal entities and their terms, and to define a new potential offence to avoid such situations as aiming for one SAE classification and marketing as another. Singapore has also produced definitions as part of its initial legislation, but more interestingly has pledged to keep its Technical Reference up to date to cover technical realities and corresponding definitions.

6.2. Sectoral Regulation: Medical

Regulation of medical activities versus driving practices differs notably in that while there is a significant risk of harm in both, in medical practice the party without specific training is strictly a bystander. In other words: there may be professional drivers, but there are no non-professional doctors.[156] Medical patients are not required to have a knowledge of the field for which they are seeking care. Medical professionals must meet a high standard of training and education in order to be licensed, whereas driver training is comparatively less stringent, even though drivers must also contend with other parties – drivers or otherwise – in their space of practice.

[153] Although they have not addressed what exactly 'defective' might mean, as per 2.5.
[154] See, eg, France and Germany which have both passed self-driving specific legislation.
[155] See, eg, the use of 'reasonable'.
[156] Although there may be unprofessional doctors if they are acting with insufficient decorum.

However, both practices have the capacity to cause accidental death, and their devices are thus highly regulated. In transportation, this regulation is aimed at vehicles: transport[157] person A, B, and/or C to place X, Y and/or Z. In medicine, this regulation is aimed at a multitude of devices used in a multitude of ways: everything from tongue depressors – simple – to ventricular assist devices, which assist in moving blood about the body – complex. While one could fairly contend that vehicles – even those without AI – are complex, their use is not as complicated as that of complex medical devices. For example, there is no requirement that cars be sterile prior to use, a requirement common to medical devices.

Unsurprisingly, all four jurisdictions regulate medical devices stringently. Each has a regulatory body that concerns itself with the regulation of such devices, from the simple to the complex. Each jurisdiction has the exact same aim as their regulation: to provide as safe medical care as possible. While there are still slight differences in the attempts to realise this goal, the arc of each is similar. Where they begin to differ is in their approach to medical devices which use AI.

Medical regulation is another example of why sectoral regulation is important: the needs and specificities of the profession are inherently complex, must apply to an incredible level of circumstantial nuance, and must react to changing standards as specific knowledge of the field continuously improves. The focus on patient care and safety is of utmost concern, and determinations of liability specific to AI uses have taken a back seat to determining its workability as a reliable tool of the profession.

In addition to regulation of medical devices, there are of course various levels of regulation of medical personnel. This can be through established professional bodies such as, in the United Kingdom, the General Medical Council, regulating doctors; the Nursing and Midwifery Council; and the General Optical Council, regulating optometrists, opticians and optical businesses.[158] These bodies 'aim to ensure that proper standards are maintained by health and social care professionals and act when they are not', although they will generally only investigate (in accordance with selection criteria) 'where other regulators do not have such powers'.[159] Other regulators such as the English Care Quality Commission (CQC) act as the independent regulator for the 'quality and safety of care', regulating:[160]

- Providers of healthcare services to people of all ages, including hospitals, ambulance services, clinics, community services, mental health services and other registered locations, including dental and GP practices.
- Providers of social care services for adults in care homes (where nursing or personal care is provided), in the community and in people's own homes.

[157] Or contribute to a vehicle which does, such as the regulation of gas pumps.
[158] 'Who Regulates Health Care' (Health and Safety Executive): hse.gov.uk/healthservices/arrangements.htm.
[159] ibid.
[160] ibid.

- Providers of services for people whose rights are restricted under the Mental Health Act.

Jurisdictions such as Singapore have a singular act for licensing and registration of medical practitioners, with a medical Council that issues an ethical code for doctors.[161] While the specifics of regulation may vary, medical professionals are very much considered the core of the medical system and are regulated as such regardless of jurisdiction. While each jurisdiction has a different approach to standards of practice, many if not all share the concept of medical negligence or medical malpractice: three European Union Member States, the United Kingdom and the United States all rank in the top 10 countries contributing to medical negligence publications.[162] Singapore also uses the concept of medical negligence, and in fact uses the *Bolam v Friern* standard discussed in depth in section 2.2.1.[163] Broadly speaking, 'medical negligence occurs when a healthcare professional selects the wrong method or procedure', although '[t]here is no clear definition of medical negligence [cross-jurisdictionally] due to lack of nomenclature, overlapping of definitions, and lack of a standard[s]ed method to measure it'.[164]

6.2.1. EU Medical Devices

As of 1 January 2021, there are three directives applicable to medical devices: Directive 90/385/EEC on active implantable medical devices; Directive 93/42/EEC on medical devices; and Directive 98/79/EC on in vitro diagnostic medical devices. Medical devices in the European Union are regulated at the Member State level, but the European Medicines Agency (EMA) also plays a role in certain types of assessment, and in 'evaluating the quality, safety and efficacy of marketing authorisation applications … including the safety and performance of a medical device in relation to its use with a medicinal product'.[165] The EMA also issues guidelines on quality documentation.[166] Legislatively, Regulation 2017/745 on medical devices

> [l]ays down rules concerning the placing on the market, making available on the market or putting into service of medical devices for human use and accessories for such

[161] E Barre and YE Jin, 'In Brief: Regulation of Healthcare M&A in Singapore' (*Lexology*, 30 June 2021): lexology.com/library/detail.aspx?g=84157a29-02a2-4755-a472-3cc0705aeb49.

[162] S Dahlawi et al, 'Medical Negligence in Healthcare Organizations and Its Impact on Patient Safety and Public Health: A Bibliometric Study' (2021) 10 F1000 Research 174: ncbi.nlm.nih.gov/pmc/articles/PMC8156516/.

[163] K Amirthalingam, 'Medical Negligence and Patient Autonomy – Bolam Rules in Singapore and Malaysia – Revisited' (2015) 27 *Singapore Academy of Law Journal* 666: journalsonline.academypublishing.org.sg/Journals/Singapore-Academy-of-Law-Journal-Special-Issue/e-Archive/ctl/eFirstSALPDFJournalView/mid/513/ArticleId/1067/Citation/JournalsOnlinePDF.

[164] Dahlawi et al (n 165).

[165] Where medical products include a medical device; medical devices with ancillary medical substances; in-vitro diagnostics; medical devices where substances are systematically absorbed, and borderline products.

[166] 'Regulating Medical Devices in the UK' (GOV.UK, 31 December 2020): gov.uk/guidance/regulating-medical-devices-in-the-uk.

> devices in the Union. This Regulation also applies to clinical investigations concerning such medical devices and accessories conducted in the Union.

Manufacturers must comply with the Regulation to place new devices on the market, doing so by undergoing a conformity assessment by a notified body within a Member State which is itself regulated by the EMA. Conformity assessments usually involve 'an audit of the manufacturer's quality system and, depending on the type of device, a review of technical documentation from the manufacturer on the safety and performance of the device'.[167]

With regard to AI medical devices specifically, the European Commission conducted a study on AI in medical device legislation in 2020. The report specifically examines the potential and varying responsibilities of the AI developer and user, as well as the deployer/operator.[168] It is important to note that this report was published prior to the EU AI Act but does nonetheless provide interesting insight into the thought process on AI medical devices. In terms of transparency, the report notes that: (1) the key question in interpretability is 'interpretable to whom?'; (2) the current regulations do not 'require devices to explain or render transparent their decisions to the user, nor does it preclude manufacturers from placing "inexplicable" devices on the market … requir[ing instead] that manufacturers demonstrate that the safety and performance of their devices *reaches state of the art considering its intended use*';[169] (3) that the GDPR requires meaningful information about the system's internal rules; and (4) that while the European Parliament Committee on Legal Affairs does not require decisions be explained to the user, it does propose that AI be 'developed, deployed and used in an easily explainable manner so as to ensure that there can be a review of the technical processes of the technology'.[170]

In terms of performance, the European Commission study notes that manufacturers are required to

> describe in the instructions for use, if applicable, the intended purpose with a clear specification of indications, contra-indications, patient target group or groups, intended users and operating parameters and limitations of their device. If applicable, manufacturers must also include the performance characteristics, accuracy, precision and stability, the limits of accuracy and the analytical performance. From the perspective of describing performance there are similarities between an in-vitro diagnostic device analyzing samples and a device analyzing data, in that software can

[167] 'Medical Devices' (European Medicines Agency, 26 November 2018): ema.europa.eu/en/human-regulatory/overview/medical-devices.

[168] European Commission Joint Research Centre, *Artificial Intelligence in EU Medical Device Legislation* (Publications Office, 2020): data.europa.eu/doi/10.2760/382730.

[169] Emphasis added.

[170] Council Regulation (EC) 2017/745 of 26 May 2021 on medical devices, amending Directive 2001/83/EC, Regulation (EC) No 178/2002 and Regulation (EC) No 1223/2009 and repealing Council Directives 90/385/EEC and 93/42/EEC.

> be described, as applicable, in terms of analytical sensitivity, analytical specificity, trueness, precision, etc.[171]

The Medical Devices Regulations also require that the device in question 'achieves state-of-the-art safety and performance in terms of its intended use' before it can be marketed.[172] Existing regulations also require follow-up and post-market surveillance, robustness of the system, and minimisation of bias.[173] The Commission also maintains a periodically updated list of medical devices using AI that have already been approved.

6.2.2. UK Medical Devices

Given the United Kingdom's history as part of the European Union, it is unsurprising that both share a similar initial approach. In the United Kingdom, the body responsible for regulation of medical devices is the Medicines and Healthcare Products Regulatory Agency (MHRA).[174] The three directives applicable to medical devices – Directive 90/385/EEC on active implantable medical devices, Directive 93/42/EEC on medical devices, and Directive 98/79/EC on in vitro diagnostic medical devices – were all imported into UK legislation after the UK's exit from the European Union, although the Medical Devices Regulation has since been updated.[175] The MHRA is responsible for performing market surveillance and the designating and monitoring of conformity and assessment bodies in the United Kingdom.[176]

In order to place a device on the market in the United Kingdom, manufacturers need to register with the MHRA, complying with 'relevant product marking and conformity assessment requirements', conforming to medical devices regulations according to date.[177] This includes a risk classification. UK conformity assessment markings are explicitly not recognised in the European Union, EEA, or Northern Ireland markets, and (EU) notified bodies in the United Kingdom must become UK Approved Bodies.[178] While these are clear moves to remove the UK's approval process from the EU's, they maintain significant parallels in the approval process, such as the mark and conformity assessment bodies.

With the introduction of more AI equipment into the field of medicine, '[t]he Medicines and Healthcare products Regulatory Agency (MHRA) has embarked

[171] ibid.
[172] ibid.
[173] ibid.
[174] With the exception of Northern Ireland.
[175] 'Regulating Medical Devices in the UK' (n 169).
[176] ibid.
[177] Conforming to the UK Medical Devices Regulation after 30 June 2023.
[178] 'Regulating Medical Devices in the UK' (n 169).

on a reform program to ensure that medical device regulation is fit for purpose for software, including artificial intelligence'.[179] This is a work in progress, but the Roadmap aims to ensure that:

A. The requirements for software and AI as a medical device provide assurance that these devices are acceptably safe and function as intended, thereby protecting patients and public.
B. The requirements for manufacturers are clear, supported by both clarificatory guidance and streamlined processes that work for software, as well as bolstered with the tools to demonstrate compliance, for instance, via the designation of standards.
C. The friction is taken out of the market by working with key partners such as the National Institute for Health and Care Excellence (NICE) and NHS England to align domestically, de-duplicate, and combine requirements, ultimately providing a joined-up offer for digital health within the UK. Internationally, we will work with other regulators both bilaterally, and multilaterally through the International Medical Device Regulators Forum (IMDRF) to strengthen international convergence and consensus on software and AI products.[180]

This will be done through 11 work packages in two workstreams. Stream one focuses on key reforms across for 'software as a medical device' (SaMD), and stream two focuses on 'challenges that AI as a medical device (AIaMD) can pose over and above classically programmed software'.[181] The Roadmap also explicitly notes that many of its aims 'require the development of standards and tools to help manufacturers clearly demonstrate that their device meets the requirements set', and are therefore working with the British Standards Institute and 'groups in the wider setting of standards' in order to create reporting and assurance frameworks.[182]

Lastly, the United Kingdom intends to provide a regulatory advice and approval service, or Multi-agency advisory service (MAAS).[183] MAAS is intended to streamline AIaMD review by coordinating and simplifying the review process, ultimately 'clear[ing] the regulatory pathway for safely scaling technologies'.[184]

6.2.3. US Medical Devices

The United States regulates medical devices through the federal Food and Drug Administration (FDA). Within the FDA is the Centre for Devices and Radiological

[179] 'Software and AI As a Medical Device Change Programme' (GOV.UK, 14 June 2023): gov.uk/government/publications/software-and-ai-as-a-medical-device-change-programme.

[180] 'Software and AI as a Medical Device Change Programme – Roadmap' (GOV.UK, 14 June 2023): gov.uk/government/publications/software-and-ai-as-a-medical-device-change-programme/software-and-ai-as-a-medical-device-change-programme-roadmap.

[181] ibid.

[182] ibid.

[183] 'Regulating the AI Ecosystem' (NHS Transformation Directorate): www.nhsx.nhs.uk/ai-lab/ai-lab-programmes/regulating-the-ai-ecosystem/.

[184] ibid.

Health, which is 'responsible for regulating firms who manufacture, repackage, relabel, and/or import medical devices sold in the United States'.[185] Manufacturers must comply with a variety of regulatory requirements, including establishment registration, medical device listing, pre-market notification or approval,[186] labelling requirements, medical device reporting and, for clinical studies, investigational device exemption.[187]

While pandemic-era vaccination approval may prove an outlier, commentators note that while 'new drug approval takes an average of 10 to 15 years, moving a new medical device from concept to market takes an average of [3 to7] years'.[188] The device must be classified under, be selected for the appropriate regulatory pathway, then registered and listed.[189] There are three classifications, based on both intended use and indications for use – the lower the class, the lower the risk posed to the patient.[190] Different classes may also require different pre-market applications or potentials for exemption, for example Class I devices such as examination gloves may be exempt from certain regulation requirements.[191] The FDA has pre-existing classifications for around 1,700 'different generic types of devices', sorted into 16 medical specialties, which are then designated Class I, Class II or Class III.[192] In terms of sub-uses, the FDA provides the rather helpful example that:

> Device classification depends on the intended use of the device and also upon indications for use. For example, a scalpel's intended use is to cut tissue. A subset of intended use arises when a more specialized indication is added in the device's labeling such as, 'for making incisions in the cornea'. Indications for use can be found in the device's labeling, but may also be conveyed orally during sale of the product.[193]

Where a product represents an entirely new medical device, the device will be assessed to determine whether it is low/moderate or high risk.[194]

[185] Center for Devices and Radiological Health, 'Overview of Device Regulation' (US Food and Drug Administration, 9 April 2020): www.fda.gov/medical-devices/device-advice-comprehensive-regulatory-assistance/overview-device-regulation. Interestingly, the CDRH also regulates 'radiation-emitting electronic products (medical and non-medical) such as lasers, x-ray systems, ultrasound equipment, microwave ovens and color televisions'.

[186] Unless exempt.

[187] Allowing a device to be used in a clinical study.

[188] A Purnama and D Drago, 'FDA Regulatory Pathways for Medical Devices' (Organisation for Professionals in Regulatory Affairs): topra.org/topra/topra_member/pdfs/CPD-May-2019-Medical-Devices-and-FDA.pdf.

[189] ibid.

[190] Center for Devices and Radiological Health, 'Overview of Medical Device Classification and Reclassification' (US Food and Drug Administration, 2018): fda.gov/about-fda/cdrh-transparency/overview-medical-device-classification-and-reclassification.

[191] Purnama and Drago (n 191).

[192] Center for Devices and Radiological Health, 'Classify Your Medical Device' (US Food and Drug Administration, 22 October 2020): fda.gov/medical-devices/overview-device-regulation/classify-your-medical-device.

[193] ibid.

[194] Purnama and Drago (n 191).

The United States has also begun to delve into questioning AI-specific medical devices. In April 2019, the FDA produced the 'Proposed Regulatory Framework for Modifications to Artificial Intelligence/Machine Learning (AI/ML)-Based Software as a Medical Device (SaMD) – Discussion Paper and Request for Feedback'. This work was then updated with the 'Artificial Intelligence/Machine Learning (AI/ML)-Based Software as a Medical Device (SaMD) Action Plan' (Action Plan) which promises to '[u]pdate the proposed framework for AI/ML-based SaMD, including through issuance of Draft Guidance on the Predetermined Change Control Plan'.[195] The Action Plan notes the FDA's plan to engage with stakeholders through a public workshop on device labelling to support transparency; support efforts to develop evaluation methodology including that on bias; and support those piloting real-world performance monitoring.[196] The Action Plan's actions and goals include an update to the regulatory framework proposed in the original SaMD paper, further harmonisation of machine learning practices in building consensus standards, hosting discussions on the role of transparency, and 'support[ing] regulatory science efforts on the development of methodology for the evaluation and improvement of machine learning algorithms, including for the identification and elimination of bias, and on the robustness and resilience of these algorithms'.[197] Similarly to the European Union, the FDA also provides a list of AI devices currently licensed and available.[198]

6.2.4. Singapore Medical Devices

Singapore's medical devices are regulated under the Health Products Act (HPA) and the Health Products (Medical Devices) Regulations 2010.[199] Companies are required to register for a dealer's licence to manufacture, import, or supply medical devices, and devices must be registered to import, manufacturer, or wholesale.[200] Registration requirements depend on the device's risk classification, and the Health Sciences Authority – Singapore's statutory board under the Ministry of Health of the Government of Singapore – must be notified prior to the implementation of any changes to medical devices, including 'technical changes, review changes, administrative changes, notification changes and changes arising from

[195] 'Artificial Intelligence/Machine Learning (AI/ML)-Based Software as a Medical Device (SaMD) Action Plan' (US Food and Drug Administration, January 2021): fda.gov/media/145022/download.

[196] ibid.

[197] ibid.

[198] Center for Devices and Radiological Health, 'Artificial Intelligence and Machine Learning (AI/ML)-Enabled Medical Devices' (US Food and Drug Adminsitration, 2021): fda.gov/medical-devices/software-medical-device-samd/artificial-intelligence-and-machine-learning-aiml-enabled-medical-devices.

[199] Singapore Health Sciences Authority, 'Regulatory Overview of Medical Devices' (HSA): hsa.gov.sg/medical-devices/regulatory-overview.

[200] ibid.

Field Safety Corrective Actions'.[201] Singapore also requires that the applicant for a manufacturer or importer licence be

> able to provide and maintain, or ensure the provision and maintenance of, such staff, premises, equipment and facilities for the handling, storage and distribution of the medical device as are necessary to prevent the deterioration of the medical device while it is in the applicant's ownership, possession, or control.[202]

The Health Products Act shares a few similarities with other broader liability schemes, namely that a medical product falls short,[203] if

> (i) it is not in conformity as regards strength, quality or purity with the specifications of its manufacturer;
> (ii) it has a strength which differs from, or a standard of quality or purity which falls below, that which is represented on its label.[204]

A product may also fall short for other failings such as contamination, compromisation or expiration.[205]

In 2017, Singapore launched its 'Digital Health' guidance, which is aimed at helping manufacturers, developers and importers 'determine if their device, software or app are regulated medical devices under HSA and … understand the relevant regulatory requirements'.[206] This includes broad categories of new technologies including wearable devices, personalised medicine, apps and AI.[207] This guidance was further specialised in 2022 with the Ministry of Health, the Health Science Authority, and the Integrated Health Information Systems co-developing the MOH Artificial Intelligence in Healthcase Guidelines (AIHGle). AIHGle's purposes are to share practices between stakeholders, including manufacturers, implementers and healthcare institutions, and to complement the HSA's regulation of AI medical devices. AIHGle provides a set of recommendations on self-development, including guiding principles of fairness, transparency, explainability and patient centricity.[208] On explainability in particular, AIHGle provides that:

> The decisions or recommendations from an AI-MD should endeavor to be explainable and reproducible. The level of explainability is dependent on the varying expectations of the end-user and the risks of the AI-MD. End-users should be consulted during the development or adoption of the AI-MD to ensure the explainability meets their

[201] ibid.
[202] Health Products Act 2007.
[203] In the Health Products Act, 'unwholesome'.
[204] Health Products Act 2007.
[205] ibid.
[206] Singapore Health Sciences Authority, 'Digital Health' (HSA): hsa.gov.sg/medical-devices/digital-health, 4.
[207] ibid.
[208] Singapore Ministry of Health, 'Artificial Intelligence in Healthcare Guidelines (AIHGle)' moh.gov.sg/docs/librariesprovider5/eguides/1-0-artificial-in-healthcare-guidelines-(aihgle)_publishedoct21.pdf.

> expectations. For example, this can include, but are not limited to, end-users knowing the data sets, testing protocols, and algorithmic model uses.[209]

AIHGle splits responsibility and recommendations into two distinct categories: developers and implementers. Developers refers 'to organisations or individuals who plan, fund, develop and/or maintain AI [medical devices], including standalone software medical devices that can interact with patients directly, or [which are] intended to be used as part of healthcare service provision by organisations or individual healthcare professionals'.[210] Implementers, conversely, refers to 'organisations or individuals who use AI [medical devices] to deliver healthcare services'.[211] AIHGle recommends that given the gaps and lack of clarity over responsibilities, service level agreements between developers and implementers are an optimal way to cover uncertainty, and should cover design, build, testing, use, monitoring, reviewing and intellectual property.[212]

AIHGle's categories of guidance for developers include design, building and testing. The design guidance includes areas such as seeking clinical inputs when developing the device: clinical guidance is to include the clinical problem statement; the representatives of training and testing datasets; and the algorithm testing approach.[213] Biases and limitations should be documented and reflected in the user manual.[214]

The report also includes relative standards guidance such as the recommendation to '[d]etermine the current clinical practice baseline to ensure that the AI [medical device's] performance is minimally no worse off than current practice'.[215] Testing guidance includes that the developers should '[e]valuate and validate periodically … to ensure it minimally meets the clinical practical baseline'.[216]

AIHGle also provides a particular focus on explainability, noting its importance in fostering end-user trust, as well as during the testing and deployment stages. It is not overly optimistic, however, in its assessment, noting that 'current techniques to interpret and explain algorithmic decisions are uneven and may hinder complete AI explainability. Developers should therefore demonstrate effectiveness of the AI [medical device] and endeavour to ensure a sufficient level of explainability based on what their intended end-user requires'.[217] It further delineates this classification into explanations for medical practitioners – clarity in recommendations, algorithmic decisions involved, concurrence with current practices – and patients – engendering trust that the device is safe and that their standard of care

[209] ibid.
[210] ibid.
[211] ibid.
[212] ibid.
[213] ibid.
[214] ibid.
[215] ibid.
[216] ibid.
[217] ibid.

is no worse.[218] AIHGle also addresses testing, such as through self-validation and risk assessment.

For implementers, AIHGle specifically addresses use, monitoring and review. Use covers clinical governance and oversight; organisational approval; tracking the device from the point of deployment; cybersecurity policies; staff training; and ensuring patient trust and comfort with the device. However, the report also notes the importance of the decision to implement the AI medical device, and focuses on organisational leadership review, which is to consider the intended use and purpose of the device, as well as expected clinical impact, alignment with clinical services, existing regulatory approval, any known patient safety issues, and identified risks of the device, among others.[219] Appropriate oversight also focuses primarily on staff education, awareness and communication of the use of the device.[220]

The report re-combines recommendations to developers and implementers in the case of continuous learning AI medical devices, stating that '[i]mplementers should ensure that the risk of deploying AI [medical devices] with continuous learning capabilities are identified and reasonably mitigated beforehand', including risks such as biased or unrepresentative data, inability to validate model updates, and abnormal behaviour – maliciously introduced data 'and/ or end-user manipulations'.[221] Both developers and implementers are encouraged to consider the alternative of deploying locked or non-learning AI 'at user facilities while allowing the AI to learn in parallel'.[222]

6.2.5. Medical Devices Analysis

Medical devices are an obvious point of regulation. They must conform to highly specific standards, in many cases be produced and provided sterilely, and be potentially compatible with other high-harm potential devices and procedures. While one could propose that the dangers of medical devices are reduced because they are wielded by the highly trained, there is a perhaps equal counter-proposal that medical professionals must be able to rely on their tools, particularly where those tools have a high potential to cause harm. Each jurisdiction discussed takes a clear and cautious view of the regulation of medical devices, albeit through different approaches. The European Union and the United Kingdom share clear initial parallels, given that the UK's system was indeed originally attached to the European Union. While the European Commission has expanded its scope of examination into AI, the United Kingdom has perhaps delved more specifically

[218] ibid.
[219] ibid.
[220] ibid.
[221] ibid.
[222] ibid.

into adaptation within the approval bodies. The United States continues its approach of supplying safety standards at the federal level,[223] with the FDA as the dominant regulatory body. While the United States has begun to regulate in the AI-specific medical device case, it appears to be largely in the stage of actions and planning, such as updating the proposed regulatory framework. Singapore is, as with AI generally, more integrated in partnership and testing guidelines. The guidelines in particular are clearly informed by and cohesive with the Singapore AI Governance Framework. While multiple jurisdictions do refer to the need for checks on the AI's function and use throughout its life-cycle, Singapore is the only jurisdiction to explicitly state that the manufacturer or importer must 'provide and maintain' the device, or otherwise ensure its maintenance, including staff, premises and equipment.

All states queried engaged in risk classification for medical devices, which informed the path taken for registration. The states also focus on the 'state of the art' and 'current clinical practice', which are both used to define a minimum standard to which the medical device must conform, which is also notable given the UK defence of 'state of the art' for information unknown at the time of creation, as discussed in chapter two. 'Intended use' is a phrase which has no doubt been used for medical devices for decades if not centuries, but becomes particularly interesting in light of AI: many AI models are open source, meaning that it may not be obvious to what use an AI derived from such a model will be put, and marketing and presentation will be relevant to that question as well – consider Tesla's marketing strategy regarding 'full self-driving'.

Particularly interesting is the mismatch in focus on aspects of understanding the AI and its design. The EU's AI Report notes the importance of interpretability, and the importance of designing the format of the explanation to the intended audience. The United Kingdom refers to the need for interpretability, albeit in a potentially overlapping manner. The US Action Plan discusses the need for and role of transparency. Singapore engages the most explicitly, stating the decisions should be both explainable and reproducible, with a focus on what the intended audience requires. While the focus on who the explanations must reach is appropriate, none of the states address what explainability should look like: rather than addressing how it can be achieved, they look at what it must achieve. Even if one is to assume that all jurisdictions' references are to refer to the interplay of interpretability and explainability via XAI, the 'how' is critically under-addressed: how explanations should be produced, what methods are acceptable, and the roles the explanations themselves will play.

[223] See, eg, safety standards for cars.

7

Blueprint for Liability Regulation

Ultimately, AI needs a regulatory system that combines both *ex ante* and *ex post* approaches: what safeguards AI should have to go through to reach the market, and what will be done when an accident occurs. In order to incentivise both safe and innovative AI, a regulatory system must take into account legal, technical and sociological factors: how the law will examine actors; what tools are available to build and dissect AI; and, critically, how to build and maintain public trust. Aspects of this system already exist: low harm applications do not require tailored legislative changes. This chapter acknowledges the influences and current approaches to building such systems, then proposes a novel blueprint encompassing AI regulation with regard to liability.

As discussed in section 5.2, there are many potential avenues through which to regulate, from public/private partnerships to international bodies and internal forces. Development of AI is not limited to any one jurisdiction: every jurisdiction has producers, and many producers have contributors in multiple jurisdictions. This means, however, the regulators need to consider the socio-political factors of more than one jurisdiction. In regulating new technologies, governments must factor in not only crucial realities such as public trust, both in the technology and its regulation, but how to integrate new regulation with existing regimes. In regulating synthetic biology, for example, the US 'reliance on courts to resolve regulatory disputes may complicate or disincentivize efforts to develop a multi-stakeholder approach to … governance'.[1] The European Union, however '[exhibits] a cooperational nature with a greater willingness of governments, industry and non-governmental organizations to develop shared best practices', with Singapore showing a 'soft authoritarian nature [generally ensuring] a cooperational style of legalism where industry and academic stakeholders work[ing] with the government to inform the state of [the art]'.[2] None of these approaches is wrong, but each has its risks. There are also commonalities between regulatory regimes: each aims for compliance, both in outcome and in process – whether the regulated party did

[1] BD Trump, 'Synthetic Biology Regulation and Governance: Lessons from TAPIC for the United States, European Union, and Singapore' (2017) 121 *Health Policy* 1139: sciencedirect.com/science/article/pii/S0168851017301999.

[2] ibid.

what was required or desired, and whether compliance as a broader process within that group was achieved.[3]

As evidenced by the flurry of regulatory activity, all four regimes examined and many more besides are regulating, or preparing to regulate, for an increasing influx of AI. None have moved to ban it, beyond specific uses such as, for the European Union, emotion recognition applications in work or education.[4] While there will no doubt be a series of cases on what is acceptable use or even style of creation of an AI, governments are moving in ways to promote AI while establishing public trust, see, for example, the UK's 'National AI Strategy'.[5] Governance regimes see AI as a great potential benefit, particularly economically, as evidenced by the clear statements in the legislation itself: two of the three pillars of the UK AI strategy are investment and planning, and supporting the diffusion of AI across the economy. There will, of course, be AI systems that are deemed too dangerous or too damaging to human rights to employ, and it is crucial that there be an ongoing conversation as to what these systems might be. A risk/benefit analysis is part of nearly any regulation: which harms are unacceptable, and which risks are tolerable in pursuit of particular benefits.

While risk/benefit assessments must be undertaken on an application-by-application basis, there is a strong case for allowing, if not encouraging, the field of life-saving AI to grow. The jurisdictions already examined have all noted the potential benefits of AI and set out to maximise these properties. How they have chosen to do so varies, and while all four jurisdictions are to an extent co-regulatory, their level of interoperability with non-government actors varies – all four benefit from targeted industry knowledge, with the tacit acknowledgment that 'no single actor has all knowledge required to solve complex, diverse and dynamic problems, and no single actor has the overview necessary to employ all the instruments needed to make regulation effective'.[6] This acknowledgement may be shown through industrial partnerships (Singapore), extensive consultation (UK, EU), or even a less overarching approach to regulation (US), but no jurisdiction has shown a top-down, command-and-control approach to AI – it is simply too complex, and too broad a question of how to regulate, to do so.

In providing trust, stability and predictability with a regulatory system for AI, the four jurisdictions have all taken different approaches. However, what none have yet established is exactly how AI will be dealt with in terms

[3] V Braithwaite, 'Closing the Gap between Regulation and the Community' in P Drahos (ed), *Regulatory Theory* (ANU Press 2017): jstor.org/stable/j.ctt1q1crtm.9.

[4] Except for medical or safety reasons. EU AI Act.

[5] 'National AI Strategy' (GOV.UK, 18 December 2022) gov.uk/government/publications/national-ai-strategy.

[6] J Black, 'Critical Reflections on Regulation' (2002) 27 *Australasian Journal of Legal Philosophy* 1.

of liability: what to do, what not to do, and what the difference is. While case law and individual circumstance will add a great deal of nuance, the current status quo in all four systems means that the public does not enjoy a great deal of certainty on how liability will be dealt with. Producers cannot predict court reactions, and the relationship between sectoral and AI-specific regulation remains unclear. While sweeping legislation such as the EU AI Act provides some guidance, the accompanying draft EU AI Liability Directive maintains a high level of uncertainty: the core of liability is left to Member States, with no discussion of what fault might actually look like, leaving both producers and the public without a conceptual grounding of responsible practice, and what safety requirements can be expected.

This chapter therefore sets out my proposed blueprint for a regulatory system to deal with the liability of AI causing accidental death, with the aim of encouraging AI to grow, while mitigating the risks which it brings. While discussions on tort and its counterpart delict have taken common law as a starting point, this system should still be compatible with civil law systems, which will be discussed in more depth in chapter eight, and with the understanding that while civil and common law systems differ in structure between civil codes and legal precedent, 'the distinction between the common law "tort" model and the conceptual model of civil law systems such as in France, although true, has been somehow exaggerated'.[7]

Construction of this regulatory system must consider co-regulatory conversations, socio-political factors, and existing regulation (particularly for high harm systems). The first step is to create a new general regulator for AI liability – something already done by the European Union, de facto in practice in Singapore, and proposed in the United Kingdom. While this regulator will have AI writ large as its purview, there is particular emphasis on AI with high or unknown levels of harm. A high-level description of the proposed regulatory system is as follows:

- Where potential harm is known to be high, the general regulator will have the power to decide if an application has too high a risk/reward balance to be publicly acceptable.
- The regulator will also have the power to require certain disclosures and design choices from AI producers – model facts and scope control – which will be discussed in depth in section 7.2.
- Sectoral regulation:
  - Where sectoral regulation exists, sectoral regulators, in contact with industry, will have the power to set specific standards and expectations for the field.

[7] E Steiner, *French Law*, 2nd edn (Oxford University Press 2018) ch 14: 'The Law of Tort'.

   - Where sectoral regulators do not or do not yet exist, the general regulator will have the power, if appropriate, to set these standards.

- When an incident has occurred, an inquisitorial arm of the general regulator will have the mandate to investigate the producer's practices and records, in order to determine whether the producer has breached one or both of two necessary standards:
      - the standards of a reasonable human performing the same task, and
      - the standard of a reasonable producer of that sub-specialty.
   - A due diligence defence will be available to producers with regard to whether their conduct met the standard of a reasonable producer, though in all cases victims must be compensated.

- The inquisitorial arm of the regulator does not bar the consumer from other remedies, such as those under any available product liability or consumer protection headings.

While detail will be expanded upon, the system can be illustrated like so:

Model Blueprint

Figure 10 Pipeline for harm prevention

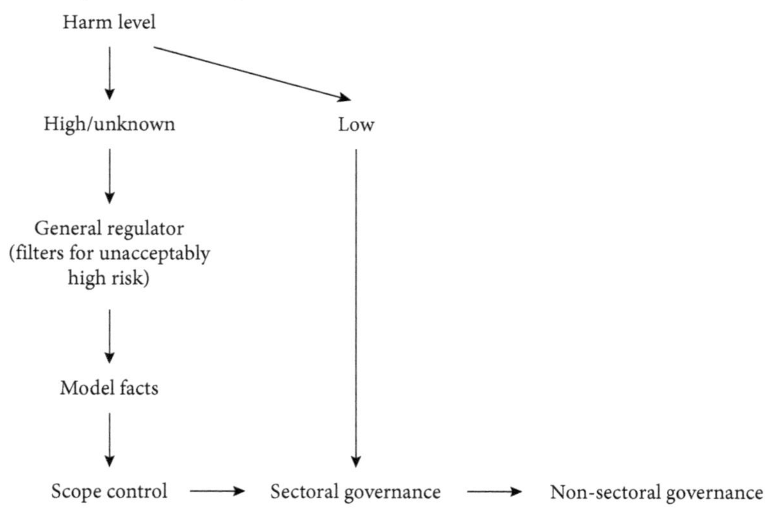

Figure 11 Deciding liability under the blueprint

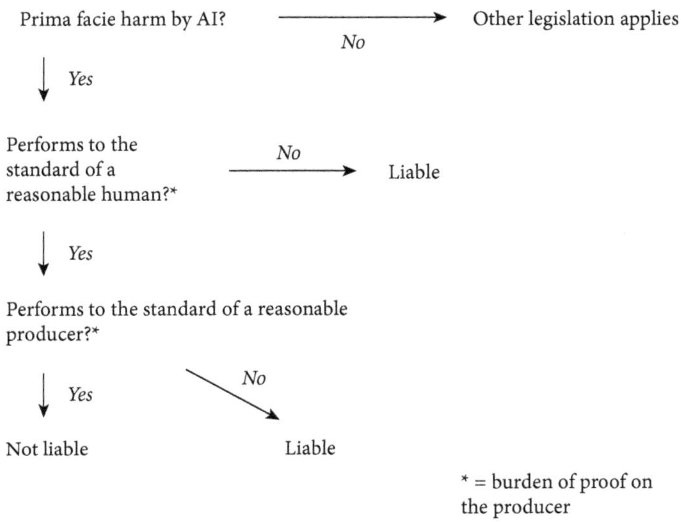

This novel system incentivises beneficial AI, while ensuring that it is as safe as possible. The AI regulatory ecosystem shown above must prioritise a variety of factors, including buy-in from stakeholders, technical workability, and suitability of the legislation in the long term. Without buy-in from stakeholders – trust from the public, innovation and growth from producers – AI will not be produced nor made use of. AI applications that damage trust disproportionate to the application's benefit will damage public trust and make new producers more wary to enter the field. Regulation that is not workable on a technical level will sink innovatory efforts. The ecosystem must account for future-proofing: the governing body's ability to act and how quickly; updatability of legislation; and cohesiveness with existing and future legislation. Some legislation, such as the draft EU AI Liability Directive, discussed in section 5.3, builds in timeline checks to ensure that regulation is achieving what it was implemented to achieve.

As will be discussed in chapter eight, product liability and consumer protection ultimately follow similar lines of questioning and end with similar answers to liability in Figure 11.

7.1. Principles for Regulation

The overarching question of regulation is, and always should be, what is it trying to achieve? For example, the goal of financial regulation is to provide a stable system in which undue risks to parties is minimised. While knowing the end goal is critical to the success of regulation, the inverse is also true: regulation without clear goals is inefficient at best, and an active hindrance at worst.[8]

The desired outcome of regulating AI causing accidental death is two-fold: to create a regulatory system that encourages the development of AI with great benefit, such as transportation and medical applications, while simultaneously incentivising the development thereof to be as safe and beneficial as possible. The system should create stability, reasonable expectations and predictability – neither producers nor the (reasonably well-informed) public should experience overarching gaps in how the system is to function.

While these are not simple goals, they are clear ones. How, then, to structure a regulatory system to achieve such a system?

7.1.1. Regulatory Aims

Key to a regulatory system is to prevent, as far as possible, high-stakes harm while allowing for high-stakes benefit. Prevention is a combination of outright bans on certain uses (eg, social credit AI in the EU), disincentivising disproportionately risky activity (eg, killer robots), and incentivising safety positive practices (eg, rigorous testing and training of AI). Preventing high-stakes harms is critical for many reasons, not least of which is that AI such as self-driving vehicles have already killed people in ways that should have been prevented,[9] which is actively damaging to public trust in both AI and regulation. Furthermore, AI has the potential to unleash high repeatability: a single trained AI system could be used for an uncountable number of applications. In other words, where a human making a mistake will make a potentially unique mistake, AI will make the same mistake in every application for which it is used, be that turning in front of traffic on a red light or denying job applicants for unlawful reasons. Prevention is key to block what could be mistakes multiplied by the million. Lastly, from a third-party perspective, prevention is a key outlook in examining foreseeable use *and misuse* of AI applications – while an AI application may have been designed with the best testing and training in the world, it may do an unpardonable amount of damage if its potentially disastrous uses are allowed to be realised.[10]

The first issue in devising AI regulation is to determine what AI should not be allowed into the field, and different cultures and jurisdictions will have different

[8] C Reed, 'How to Make Bad Law: Lessons from Cyberspace' (2010) 73 *Modern Law Review* 903: jstor.org/stable/40926555.

[9] See, eg, the Tempe Arizona crash, where the issue of identifying a walking cyclist and thereafter stopping was known.

[10] This is reflected in the EU AI Act's section on risk assessment: Regulation (EU) 2024/… of the European Parliament and of the Council of … laying down harmonised rules on artificial intelligence and amending Regulations (EC) No 300/2008, (EU) No 167/2013, (EU) No 168/2013, (EU) 2018/858, (EU) 2018/1139 and (EU) 2019/2144 and Directives 2014/90/EU, (EU) 2016/797 and (EU) 2020/1828 (Artificial Intelligence Act).Intelligence Act) Chapter III, Art 9(2).

answers as to what should be allowed. This response can take a variety of forms, but in essence the aim is to block unsafe AI from entering the marketplace. The European Union, for example, has approached this by being prescriptive: actively stating which AI purposes will not be allowed.[11] This is not the only method to disinclude AI, and similar ends could be achieved with broad principles as to what will be allowed: must not damage human rights, must be 'safe', etc, and then put into place with governing bodies to help the industry align with the principles. Such an approach could be co-regulatory, with governments communicating with the governed as to what is practicable and what is safe or unsafe. It could even be self-regulatory, with the industry itself creating standards, and governance mechanisms stepping in only when an accident has occurred. Yet the goal of each type of approach is the same: how can we block – on the basis of risk/benefit analysis – unacceptable AI from entering the market? Not only for safety reasons, but for the critical building of public trust in both the regulation and the technology. The practical and inherent follow-up question to this is, how can we create this filter on top of existing rules, and in light of the knowledge we have of AI?

A risk-based regulatory system requires that risks be identified and analysed, and this is a challenging task for complex AI. The XAI techniques examined in chapter three will play an important role here, as explained throughout this regulatory blueprint.

Regulatory regimes attempt to make certain behaviour either attractive or unattractive to actors in that realm: incentivising desirable behaviour, and disincentivising undesirable behaviour. Compensation for liability is one such disincentive. Regimes must thus provide for compensation: the acknowledgment that accidents will happen must be accompanied by the acknowledgment that victims of such accidents will be compensated. Compensation and liability as twin factors are also necessary to build trust: the public must be able to see producers 'putting their money where their mouth is' with regard to safety practices. Practices such as attempting to contract out of liability[12] will damage trust in the field and set back those actors trying to show a more responsible approach. While actors may be penalised by liability systems, they are not necessarily against its existence writ large. Industry is clear in its desire to know what regulation and liability look like. Companies have offered their willingness to be liable under appropriate circumstances,[13] but have asked regulators to make as clear as possible what those circumstances are. Companies must currently cope with a great deal of uncertainty surrounding liability, meaning

[11] ibid.

[12] It may be acceptable to allocate liability via contract between responsible parties, so long as overall there is one or more who remain responsible and can compensate.

[13] David Mullen, 'Mercedes to Accept Legal Responsibility for Accidents Involving Self-Driving Cars' (*Driving.co.uk from The Sunday Times*, 28 March 2022): driving.co.uk/news/technology/mercedes-to-accept-legal-responsibility-for-accidents-involving-self-driving-cars/.

that they must either woo insurers into new fields, or have a sufficient war-chest to weather new and likely lengthy litigation. While hard-and-fast rules on what choices should be made in AI development are unlikely – and, as discussed in chapter three, impractical – there must be some type of guidance given as to what liability looks like: how, when and most importantly *why* an entity will be liable.

Providing a compensation and liability regime for AI must not be divorced entirely from existing regimes. This is for two reasons: there is no need to create an entire system from scratch, and there are practicable parallels between the old and the new, taking into account the intricacies of AI. This is particularly so in that there is no 'reasonable AI': it cannot comprehend context and is not affected by human incentives or disincentives, and so we are left still to regulate the humans involved in the AI process. Human developers will lack the context of responsibilities in the moment: what pedestrians are in the roadway, what clot blocks the ventricle. Yet this is not particularly different from liability prior to AI: a toy producer does not know in advance how the toy might harm a child but will still be liable if their toy was negligently made – one does not escape liability simply because there has been a length of time between the negligent action and the harm. The elements of liability: duty of care, breach of the standard of care and resulting proximate harm, are not tied to an immediate effect. While there are limitations – in some cases by statute – there is not a separation of harm and liability merely by the unpredictability of what may happen, because of the choice in question, in the future. Foreseeability, duty of care and the resulting liability remain unchanged in their reliance on reasonableness.

While the concept of reasonableness itself does not change, it has come to rely on standards defined by case law: the build-up of expectations over time. With life-saving AI this is time we do not have, and so we must provide standards that are sufficiently definable to be communicated, yet adaptive and flexible enough not to hinder the field itself. Regulation therefore needs to set standards of reasonableness in two ways: first, in relation to the AI's actions in the moment as compared with a human practitioner of that activity – a driver, a radiologist, a pilot. Second, and perhaps more demandingly, in terms of the conduct expected of an AI producer.

In the former case, we consider whether the AI's actions would have been considered reasonable if done by a human. While this does not mean that the actions are required to be perfect, as human actions also are not, it does mean a level of predictability and acceptable behaviour. Achieving the standard of 'as good as a reasonable human' is contextual: even if AI failure rates statistically match or exceed human failure rates, if the AI malfunctions in a way that a human would not, it does not pass this standard. For example, in the Tesla crash mentioned in section 3.4, the vehicle mistook a tractor-trailer for a cloud, which a human would not. In some cases, a sectoral regulator might choose to lower the standard below that of a reasonable human if the technology is still adequately useful. The regulator may choose to do so where the AI offers the benefit of speed, rather than complete accuracy, and human oversight will still play a large part. For example, in using AI for diagnosing eye conditions, regulators may have producers err on the side of over-caution to ensure that every possible sign is caught, even where a human may not have flagged an issue. Here the AI would be used to triage and thus speed up care provision rather than complete the entire care process by itself.

As to whether the AI was produced to the standard of the reasonable producer, we must assess whether the development processes which led to those actions were reasonable, based on both the context of the decision/action pair taking place, and on what the AI producer knew or ought to have known about what the AI would encounter, and what they knew, or ought to have known, that they should have tested for. This relies heavily on the knowledge of the field at the time.

The knowledge of the field, or state of the art, is a crucial point for AI overall. This is where the regulatory regime must examine what was known about the potential dangers or indeed the intricacies of design. It also means that the high-water mark of the field represents best practices, and that there must be significant reason to deviate. For example, automated vehicle companies have used many sensors to enable the vehicle to drive itself. These have included cameras, sonar, LIDAR, RADAR, etc. A company may choose to remove one of these inputs that contribute to the sensing capacity of the vehicle. This may be done for a variety of reasons, including cost, but society would expect that the producer has determined that removing the sensor in question would not decrease the car's capacity to drive safely. In the case of an accident, the court would then need to engage in an analysis of that choice: would a knowledge of the field show that there was a reduction in the capacity of the vehicle with the removal of that sensor? Was there a proportionate loss of safety, and was the risk/benefit both proportionate and acceptable? Lastly, did the removal cause the accident, or, equally, cause the failure to prevent it? This level of investigation will also be necessary to deal with compensation claims, which will be expanded on in section 7.2.2.

7.1.2. Regulatory Structures

It seems a reasonable (or perhaps a modest) proposal that there will be activities that society finds exceed the bounds of the risk/benefit analysis. Where this is true without the injection of AI, it is equally the case with AI: not to over-regulate, not to under-regulate, and how best to leverage legislation to prevent disproportionate harms.

What harms will be considered disproportionate and therefore out of bounds will depend on the regulating group in question: where China has forged ahead with social credit systems,[14] the European Union has placed any similar activity in the realm of the entirely unacceptable.[15] Whatever the specifics of these blacklisted activities, it seems clear there will be some: murder by AI is still murder.[16] This is the first layer of the building blocks of regulation, and must come from a purely top-down, command-and-control perspective.[17] However, applying top-down, command-and-control legislation for each and every facet of AI use is clearly not feasible: to regulate that an AI vacuum cleaner must stay at least 3cm away from a drop of no less than 10cm, etc, extended ad nauseam to each and every aspect of each and every AI's existence, lends itself to new appreciations of the word 'infinite'. Moreover, strict levels of top-down control are inflexible, if not brittle. There are risks which we will fail to predict, and if we are to crystallise standards too early, we crystallise with known and understood dangers, but lock out potential benefits. For example, the (American) Federal Aviation Administration (FAA) has safety statistics back to the 1960s, a time that saw commercial aircraft eight to ten times more dangerous than those we enjoy today.[18] Were the FAA to have doubled down on control, those statistics would not have improved, or would have done so much more slowly.

It is clearly far too regulatorily intensive to specify in detail how an AI system should work. Yet to leave AI unregulated would allow for far more harm than would be acceptable to a populace, even with certain activities pre-banned. Insufficient regulation can kill a technology as surely as over-regulation by failing to establish trust in the technology's safety. What, then, to regulate?

Providing specific steps of a process to follow would not only be inefficient, but quickly outdated. Showing responsible practice processes is part of a due diligence process and can be left for the producer to show rather than the regulator to enumerate. The same applies to testing the AI; the required standard should be broadly defined, such as 'acceptable safety', while the producer is left to devise and, importantly, justify the testing.

Producers must justify their choices: justification and robustness of the datasets, the types of testing employed, the optimisation of certain effects. This is where XAI steps in. XAI must be used not just after the fact to explore what has gone wrong, but throughout the process: in examining the training data, in training the model, in debugging the model and training data.[19] Rather than specifying what the AI must consist of, regulation must demand the internal quality assurance of

[14] F Liang et al, 'Constructing a Data-Driven Society: China's Social Credit System as a State Surveillance Infrastructure' (2018) 10 *Policy & Internet* 415: onlinelibrary.wiley.com/doi/abs/10.1002/poi3.183.

[15] EU AI Act (n 10).

[16] Though not, necessarily, Murderbot: Martha Wells, *Murderbot* (Tor.com 2017).

[17] Many such cases will be inferred from existing legislation, such as not to hit a pedestrian with a vehicle – societies regulate driving, and do not simply rely on its citizens to sue for compensation.

[18] 'U.S. General Aviation Safety Data' (Bureau of Transportation Statistics, United States Department of Transportation): bts.gov/content/us-general-aviationa-safety-data.

[19] V Arya et al, 'One Explanation Does Not Fit All: A Toolkit and Taxonomy of AI Explainability Techniques' (2019): arxiv.org/abs/1909.03012.

the building process, not creating a specific test, as tests can be gamed,[20] but incentivising the building of internal cultures that develop AI to meet the *purpose* of the test rather than to the test itself. Building a procedural assessment can focus on the care and skill put into the design, development and testing of a robot, rather than cementing a particular, and potentially sub-optimal, process. At a general level, the AI must be safe enough for its intended use – this is what the idea of 'reasonable care' is intended to fulfil. What this means in specifics, however, will vary greatly, and the details of what this means for particular AI applications will be provided by sectoral regulators, who are best posed to address such questions – a concept which will be expanded on in section 7.2.3.

Some level of regulation is needed for AI causing high-impact harm. A distinct regulatory entity is a sensible choice to do so, so long as they do not extend to over-regulation, or in particular to regulate that which is not necessary to regulate, a discussion continuing in section 7.1.3. AI causing *de minimis* harm, such as only being a tripping hazard, is a good example of an AI that does not need direct regulatory address. This is not to say that any command and control – even beyond that of the basic ban – is not useful. There is an element of command and control to any system which employs compensation. There is, however, a great range between total command and control and zero top-down regulation. The optimal mix depends on the capacity and background of the jurisdiction, but in the case of a technology as potentially complex as AI, a range of actors are likely necessary to create this mix. This returns us to the discussion of regulatory theory: 'the state becomes part of a network of regulation in which the tasks of regulation are redistributed in various ways among actors within the network'.[21] Co-regulatory arrangements – by which the state or jurisdiction participates in regulation as part of the aforementioned network – allow governance to be more flexible and responsive. Responsive regulation in too close an arrangement has its risks, such as corruption[22] and regulatory capture, but a positive balance of co-regulation can increase regulatory capacity while motivating positive change. Multipart regulation beyond a state-to-industry actor relationship can help combat the potential risks, leading to ideas of polycentric or networked governance: the 'rising interconnectedness characterises the relationship among the many centres and sources of regulation in the modern world'.[23]

On the other side of the spectrum from command and control is a self-regulatory system, by which industry actors set the standards themselves. There are no sanctions imposed because there is no system set to impose them. This too can lead to a co-regulatory arrangement, such as Singapore: the test case pattern means that there is a close level of cooperation between industry and state actors, with the state proposing, through mechanisms such as Singapore's

[20] See again the VW diesel scandal in section 3.3.

[21] P Drahos and M Krygier, 'Regulation, Institutions and Networks' in P Drahos (ed), *Regulatory Theory* (ANU Press 2017): jstor.org/stable/j.ctt1q1crtm.7.

[22] ibid.

[23] ibid.

Model AI Governance Framework, broad regulatory ideals, with the actor demonstrating its internal standards to the state through a cooperative programme of communication regarding development and testing processes, etc. The European Union, conversely, proposes self-reporting of processes, and focuses on a more rights-driven co-regulatory process, closely tied to its approach to data protection. Both the United Kingdom and the United States focus on a business-driven co-regulatory process: removing obstacles to innovation and development, with both jurisdictions developing safety standards in discussion with stakeholders.[24] While this may look more like the Singaporean approach, it is important to note that the United Kingdom, for example, does not have the comparative capacity of Singapore to engage with each of its industry partners, and must rely to an extent on broader alliances such as industry groups. Overall, each of these jurisdictions has taken a co-regulatory approach, albeit through different balances of power and partnerships. The European Union, for example, engages with advanced certification through the CE mark, by which industry entities show that their processes have followed standards compliance relating to production and inspection – showing, to an extent, reasonable care.

In summary, the aim is to create a regulatory system that incentivises as-safe-as-possible development of AI that passes a risk/benefit analysis, particularly in the cases of high-impact harms.[25] Capacities and existing regulatory regimes are an inherent consideration of jurisdictions looking to create such a system, and each has different approaches and motivations to doing so. All regulatory systems aim for compliance, but what amounts to compliance may differ: adherence to a broad set of principles, or to minute and specific guidance. No system has banned AI outright, and it seems unlikely that any would do so, which leads to the question how regulation should be structured.

First, some AI applications will be banned – likely in some ways directly parallel to their human counterparts, given that anything illegal to do as a human would be illegal to do through the creation of an AI. Second, there need to be circumstances under which liability can be applied. While the effects of liability may and likely should be mitigated,[26] the concept of 'fault' allows for a line of what regulation accepts, and what it does not. Third, there needs to be a concept of what regulation is appropriate and when. It is appropriate to divide this along the lines of what harms the AI might cause. Fourth, regulation must tread the tightrope of regulating too early and cementing solvable problems, and regulating too late and allowing preventable harms to occur. This is best addressed through iterations of examination of harms, mitigating as knowledge increases. This is likely to be a non-legislative process, as legislation frequently moves at a glacial pace,

[24] Such as, in the UK, the Alan Turing Institute as a standards hub.

[25] As examined here, accidental death.

[26] Such as through insurance: insurance companies can build relationships with producers and provide their own specialists to examine the producers' practices far more easily than, say, a victim of an accident.

and might better take the form of broad care obligations supplemented by non-binding guidelines which might be clearer than binding legislation: legislation can also reference standards or classifications which move more quickly, such as the SAE International (formerly the Society of Automotive Engineers) classification of levels of self-driving automation. Fifth, AI regulation should focus on the process rather than the product: the care and skill taken to create, train and test AI, rather than those concerns best left to sectoral regulation. Sixth and finally, regulatory efforts have so far been co-regulatory: some level of cooperation between states and stakeholders. While the balance of conversation differs by jurisdiction, it is clear that no state has assumed the level of technical capacity and agility to regulate such a fast-paced technology without the input of, at the very least, standards bodies. What, then, are the regulatory structures that should be built in order to make this design a reality?

7.1.3. Regulatory Approaches

While one can use the term AI as a reduction for ease of discussion, it fits a nearly impossibly large field of applications. It is therefore easy to forget just how many fields it does or may impact – the list is huge, as is the range of complexities: a spectrum between interpretable (inherently understandable) and explainable (in need of additional tools to understand) AI. There is also the temptation to treat all AI as the same: the AI surgeon the same as the smart fridge. It is helpful to return to the input and harms distinction made in section 1.1.2: where the input types being acted upon are known or unknown, and the consequences of the AI's use are known or unknown. It is perhaps fair to say that even where the immediate effects are known, the knock-on effects are unknown and AI will continue to shape society in ways that we cannot predict. Yet this risk classification is helpful to demonstrate why not all AI should be regulated alike. At the deep and murky end of the AI harm spectrum are those complex practices which have or will take lives, purposefully or not, or whose harm is not clearly known. At the clear and more penetrable spectrum, we have those which are easily understood, and their harms well known: the autonomous zeppelin versus the autonomous vacuum. The types of harms are clearly different, and there is a hierarchy of risk. Additionally, as has been repeated throughout, the occurrence of physical harms is inherently simpler to find than non-physical harms – systemic harms are far more difficult to prove, to find, to track.

In treating all AI as the same, or in attaching the concerns of one range of dangers to another type of application, the temptation is great to either over-regulate or under-regulate. This brings us to the 'Collingridge Dilemma':

> When a technology is still at an early stage of development, it is still possible to influence the direction of its development, but we do not know yet how it will affect society. Yet, when the technology has become societally embedded, we do know its implications, but

> it is very difficult to influence its development. The dilemma is one of the biggest challenges for responsible design and innovation.[27]

This dilemma is easily seen for any modern society-level technological change. One could not possibly have regulated the internet in 1984, given a scant year of computer network communication. Early users could hardly have dreamed what such a technology would go on to do, to enable, to harm. When applications such as social media, e-commerce, e-banking, mass communication – and harms, psychological and illegal – became clearer, it was nearly unfathomably difficult to claw some semblance of control together, even where certain harms such as human trafficking were agreed upon as requiring control.

Yet regulating too early is also problematic. Over-regulation risks stifling innovation and is seen by designers and developers as 'an obstacle to the development of disruptive and creative approaches'.[28] For example, the EU 'Electronic Signatures Directive' of 2000 was replaced by the eIDAS Regulation, which specified the functional requirements for the technology rather than, as in the 2000 Directive, attempting to specify technology and processes which became outdated and excluded alternative technologies.[29]

There are different strategies that attempt to address this regulatory dilemma. Some focus on anticipation: trying to predict the types of impact a technology will have while it can still be addressed in the technology's infancy, approaching innovation as a 'variation' exposed to a 'selection environment' of markets and regulatory environments, to bring a 'nexus between variation and selection by anticipating the future implications of technologies during their development'.[30] If successful, such a strategy can tailor the technology in question to avoid, at least, the greatest harms thus posed. Examples are tricky, however, not knowing what harm may have occurred if the regulatory intervention had not happened. If unsuccessful, the intervention has cemented the wrong or at least less than ideal variation, skewing both regulation and market.

Conversely, other strategies focus on regulating the innovation process through socio-technical experimentation, treating innovations as 'social experiments'. Van der Poel proposes such an approach for dealing with uncertainties: when assessing a new technology, van der Poel proposes that

> it is to be judged in comparison with other approaches for dealing with uncertain or unknown hazards and benefits of new technology. This includes such approaches as risk-cost benefit analysis, risk standards, the precautionary principles and scenarios … Approaches based on the precautionary principle or approaches that focus on

[27] O Kudina and P-P Verbeek, 'Ethics from Within: Google Glass, the Collingridge Dilemma, and the Mediated Value of Privacy' (2019) 44 *Science, Technology, & Human Values* 291: doi.org/10.1177/0162243918793711.

[28] G Sgueo, 'Using technology to 'co-create' EU policies' (2020) European Parliamentary Research Service: europarl.europa.eu/RegData/etudes/BRIE/2020/646127/EPRS_BRI(2020)646127_EN.pdf.

[29] 'Overview of Standards: Specifying Formats of Advanced Electronic Signatures and Seals' (European Union Agency for Cybersecurity, 2019).

[30] Kudina and Verbeek (n 27).

> scenarios provide interesting alternatives but they still focus on the anticipation of consequences ... the technology-as-social experiment approach is the only one that recognizes that uncertainty and ignorance are partly irreducible and, in as far as they can be reduced, such reduction is an ongoing process.[31]

This approach places the 'traditional question about acceptability of a technology' after a certain period of experimentation,[32] while not quite 'wait and see' but placing the emphasis on a continuously adaptive assessment.

A further dynamic of over-regulation and under-regulation is whether the regulation is to be binding or non-binding. Binding legislation is time-intensive to construct, and is difficult to change given, at bare minimum, the lengthy process required to change it. Vellinga suggests that 'this makes non-binding regulation more suitable' for rapid innovation, provisioning exemptions whereby 'every exemption can be tailored to the testing of the newest technological capabilities'.[33] This can and has been taken as a spectrum of possibilities. While the Singaporean approach does not deem each entrant to the market an exception, it does treat each as a test case, closely partnered with the government institutions. The opposite approach would be to define each and every capacity a technology must have, and how to achieve it. There are also multitudes of international regulatory bodies, both sectorally and cross-sectorally, that produce non-binding, or internal-only binding, regulation for their members. One positive example of this is the SAE's taxonomy of autonomy levels – while not regulation in the legislative sense, they provide a helpful commonality in language which has been adopted by multiple regulators, including, for example, Texas' laws on automated vehicles. This means that while the SAE specifics of the definitions of autonomy levels can and has been updated, the regulation specific to jurisdictions need not be, and is updated simply by including reference to the predefined levels.

In summary, the difficulties of regulating AI are many, not only what to regulate, but how much, and by whom. Nuance is clearly necessary, lest we have surgical requirements on the fridge – producing, no doubt, a chilling effect.

7.2. Regulation Proposal

7.2.1. Regulation to Prevent Harms Arising

In advance of an incident, we look to prevention. These are the structures that are built into regulation to attempt to reduce incidents before they happen; to

[31] I van de Poel, 'Why New Technologies Should Be Conceived as Social Experiments' (2013) 16 *Ethics, Policy & Environment* 352: doi.org/10.1080/21550085.2013.844575.

[32] ibid.

[33] NE Vellinga, 'From the Testing to the Deployment of Self-Driving Cars: Legal Challenges to Policymakers on the Road Ahead' (2017) 33 *Computer Law & Security Review* 847: sciencedirect.com/science/article/pii/S0267364917301334.

incentivise a culture of safe practices. There is a hierarchy of regulation based on risk as we inherently regulate more those aspects of life which represent a great risk to life and health. A ventricular shunt that drains extra cerebrospinal fluid is going to be regulated far more carefully than a doorstop. Risk is also inherently comparative: all technologies have risk, but there are limited resources available to deal with risk, and so some assessment must go to whether or not the risk is worth addressing. This assessment must go to both what happens if the creation (here an AI) in question works exactly as expected, and what if it does not. Effects can be unpredictable, even if the creation works perfectly. AirBnB was astonishingly effective at enticing its consumer base yet has increased the housing crunch.[34] In many cases, those best placed to assess risks are in specific sectors – experts rather than judges. Sector-specific experts are better placed to assess what the likely risks are from the outset.[35] The draft EU AI Liability Directive, for example, provides that transportation liability schemes pre-empt the Directive, and will continue to do so once the Directive is in place.[36] While there may be lessons that can be exported to the whole of AI, those based on specific risks require the specificity of expertise. Regulators in high-risk fields must not be blocked from leveraging their expertise in creating sector-specific legislation, albeit with input from industry experts.

Standards are also a helpful mark of regulation, if not legislation. Standards are not limited to command and control centres, nor necessarily to central bodies – they can be produced within an industry, or even by an individual producer, such as Google's Machine Learning Universal Guidelines.[37] Another example is the Alan Turing Institute's pilot AI Standards Hub, supported by the British Standards Institute, the National Physics Laboratory, the Department for Digital, Culture, Media & Sport, and the Office for AI.[38] The Standards Hub is intended to focus on:

- Growing UK engagement to develop global AI standards by bringing together information about technical standards and development initiatives in an accessible, user-friendly and inclusive way.
- Bringing the AI community together through workshops, events and a new online platform to encourage more coordinated engagement in the development of standards around the world.

[34] Gary Barker, 'The Airbnb Effect On Housing And Rent' (*Forbes*, 21 February 2020): forbes.com/sites/garybarker/2020/02/21/the-airbnb-effect-on-housing-and-rent/.

[35] With the inquisition asking after the fact whether the producer technologically aligned with the processes the producer said they were using.

[36] European Commission, 'Proposal for a directive of the European Parliament and of the Council on adapting non-contractual civil liability rules to artificial intelligence (AI Liability Directive)' 2022 COM.

[37] Martin Zinkevich, 'Rules of Machine Learning' (*Google Developers*): developers.google.com/machine-learning/guides/rules-of-ml.

[38] 'New UK Initiative to Shape Global Standards for Artificial Intelligence' (GOV.UK, 12 January 2022): gov.uk/government/news/new-uk-initiative-to-shape-global-standards-for-artificial-intelligence.

- Creating tools and guidance for education, training and professional development to help businesses and other organisations engage with creating AI technical standards, and collaborate globally to develop these standards.
- Exploring international collaboration with similar initiatives to ensure the development of technical standards are shaped by a wide range of AI experts, in line with shared values.[39]

Standards can run where legislation can only walk, keeping closer pace with the field and its developments through regular updating. In interweaving industry and third-party standards with the idea of the 'reasonable producer', regulation can benefit from this on-the-ground knowledge without needing to wait for legislative debate. Sector-specific standards will be needed, and are beginning to be set, such as with the British Standards Institute draft standard for AI medical devices.[40] The EU AI Act also contains direct reference to sectoral legislation. The UK Law Commission Report on self-driving vehicles goes into industry-specific issues such as the 'passivity problem', or the difficulty of having a vehicle hand driving control back to a human – what timeline is appropriate and practicable?

Returning once again to the harms/quadrant division – known and unknown inputs and known and unknown outputs – we find two different types of harm. These are harms where the immediate effect is known or unknown. For example, as discussed in chapter one, if a self-driving vehicle malfunctions, there will be a crash. The harm is immediately apparent. If a mortgage-granting AI malfunctions, it may or may not be apparent that something has gone wrong. The application is not necessarily 'correct' or 'incorrect' in granting or not granting a mortgage – it can malfunction in either direction. The resulting harm may not be apparent for some time, if it is ever discovered. For both types, the inputs may be known or unknown, but the outputs, and thus the impacts, vary between the two: known outputs mean at least some known harms, unknown outputs always mean unknown harms. Indirect harms are more difficult to catch, as they must first be detected. The AI may be working on false assumptions, or indeed illegal ones such as protected characteristics, but harm may not immediately be realised because there is a far less binary output for 'correct' activity. Sectoral regulation is critical to continual oversight of such applications, on an expert basis, to ensure systemic errors are caught.

What goes Wrong?

It is crucially important to determine not just that the AI is successful at pattern matching, but to know what is going on internally in order to actually understand

[39] ibid.

[40] 'Consultation on New Guidelines for the Application of ISO 14971 to AI and ML' (*Compliance Navigator*, 21 June 2021): compliancenavigator.bsigroup.com/en/medicaldeviceblog/consultation-on-new-guidelines-for-the-application-of-iso-14971-to-artificial-intelligence-and-machine-learning/.

and prevent risk. If there is to be liability, there needs to be a workable understanding of what 'fault' means in relation to an AI system.

Strict Liability?

Applying strict liability would solve the problem of determining what level of fault or duty of care over the AI is necessary to incur or avoid liability. Strict liability does not require fault to be shown on a particular level, but provides that if an AI causes harm, then those with power over the actions of the AI are liable. As a solution, this looks, at first glance, to be tempting: it is comparably cheaper, as it needs minimal to no review of practices, testing, or training; it removes the burdens of proof; it spreads the economic burden through practices such as insurance; and victims are still compensated. However, this approach not only disincentivises potentially life-saving AI, but it also does not necessarily fit all AI accidental death scenarios. Strict liability may work where the burden can be shared through widespread insurance, such as the insurance that most jurisdictions have for cars, but this merely moves the fault conversation to between the manufacturer and the insurer and the question of level of duty remains. Spreading the burden means that the burden does not fall solely on the manufacturer, though without absolving them from risk. Strict liability could also work in a medical system like that in the United States where parties engaging in the medical system almost inevitably have insurance, yet would fail where there are public health systems: centralising liability in a shared health service that does not require insurance will disproportionately concentrate liability cost. Jurisdictions such as the United Kingdom which have a public health service without additional insurance would concentrate potential liability on its National Health Service. Strict liability is also not the most beneficial approach to inducing the potential social benefit that is medical AI. Additionally, strict liability represents the unique danger that companies will undertake a cost analysis comparing the requirements to fix the fault against the liability cost: the cost to, for example, recall an expensive piece of equipment that may function in limited cases, versus the liability cost of that failure causing harm.

Essentially, strict liability is a possible answer for some sectors and jurisdictions, but not all, and it does not ultimately address the question of what went wrong, why and how it can be fixed so as to avoid future issues.

Demonstrating Care and Skill

If strict liability is an insufficient solution, what provides a more satisfactory answer? There is no point in looking at fault on the part of the AI itself: as discussed in depth in section 2.7, the AI has no understanding of context, and thus of reasonableness. The AI does not 'care', and thus cannot be influenced by carrot or stick – beneficial or negative consequences. One must therefore look elsewhere to address issues with the AI. Instead of looking at fault in the AI, therefore, one must look for fault on the part of the humans who develop, train and test the AI. This does not mean that one does not look at the AI, but that the AI becomes evidence for the demonstration of due care and skill.

Due Diligence

Examination of liability involves looking at whether the AI acted to the standard of an analogous reasonable human in the field – a driver, a nurse, a surgeon – and if the producer acted to the standard of a reasonable producer in the field. For the analogous reasonable human, sectoral regulators may choose, in limited circumstances, to lower the standard if the AI is used in particular circumstances, such as the optical care triage mentioned in section 7.1.1. This would be done only in cases where the limitations on the use of the AI are well understood, and the potential risks will have sufficient oversight not to impact overall safety.

The 'standard of a reasonable producer' can be met and defended even if an AI has caused harm, if a case for due diligence can be made that the producer took 'all reasonable steps to avoid the particular event'. An examination of due diligence will require looking at what the AI did – the standard of a reasonable human – and how the AI was made – the standard of the reasonable producer. While the standard of a reasonable human does not inherently require XAI techniques, they will be incredibly useful. For complex AI such as a self-driving vehicle, it will be crucial to examine why the AI did what it did. For example, consider that a self-driving vehicle drove into a fire hydrant. While this is naturally undesirable, a producer could show, through an XAI tool like LIME (a local interpretable model agnostic application) that the car had swerved to avoid a child. This is exactly the action that a reasonable human driver would take under the same circumstances. XAI can be used to show why the AI did what it did, or perhaps more convincingly, why it did not do something else – such as staying in the road.

XAI will be required as part of the evidence of a due diligence defence in showing the standard of a reasonable producer. The standard of the reasonable producer requires that a producer acted to the standard of a reasonable member of their (sub)speciality – that they considered and acted upon the known state of the field: what did the producer know, ought to have known, and should have tested for? This requires an examination of the producer's production process: whether they showed due diligence in creation, training and testing of the AI, up to and including recurring obligations. The producer must lay bare their creation process: that datasets were appropriate and representative; that known harms were tested for; edge cases addressed; unidentifiable scenarios not causing a full shutdown. This brings us back to Arya et al's steps of the AI modelling pipeline:

Figure 12 Explanations in the AI creation process (see also above ch 3, Figure 6)[41]

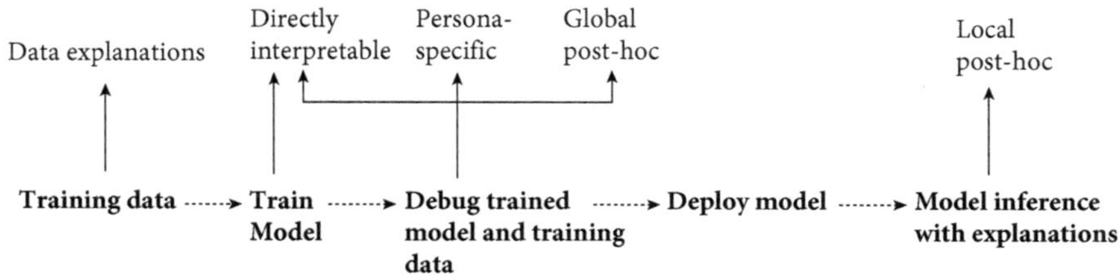

This shows what XAI tools might be used at different development stages. This is not to say that these exact tools should be used, but that the tools that have been used are defensible as the most appropriate: not those that show the best performance, but that reflect what the AI has been claimed to optimise for. For example, if a company were to claim that their AI had driven perfectly in all tested scenarios and its performance tools showed a mastery of driving, it would be indefensible if the car had not been tested at night, and only XAI tools appropriate to daylight and perfect conditions had been used. This also means that companies must keep a record of not only what training, testing and tools have been used, but why they were chosen. Requiring additional keeping of records as a prerequisite to market entry then means that producers will have this evidence available if needed. It is also an additional backstop to jurisdictions such as the European Union, whose requirements of high-risk AI producers pre-market are largely self-certification:[42] producers can show that they did what they said they would do.

Experts have already proposed the 'Model Facts' label for end users, originally developed for clinicians making machine-learning supported decisions.[43] Its purpose is to collate relevant, actionable information in a single page, 'in order to "standardize presentation of machine learning model information" to end users in high-risk applications'.[44] This is not dissimilar in purpose to the EU AI Act's requirements for technical documentation, which include the 'methods and steps performed for the development of the AI system', 'the key design choices including the rationale and assumptions made', and 'the validation and testing procedures used, including information about the validation and testing data used and their

[41] Arya et al (n 19).
[42] EU AI Act (n 10).
[43] MP Sendak et al, 'Presenting machine learning model information to clinical end users with model facts labels' (23 March 2020) *NPJ Digital Medicine*: semanticscholar.org/paper/Presenting-machine-learning-model-information-to-Sendak-Gao/15bab838342b7fc6897e8729e92697d705d8e2e1.
[44] ibid.

main characteristics [and] metrics used to measure accuracy, robustness and compliance'.[45]

The proposed label looks very much like a food label, and includes a brief summary, as well as notes on the mechanism, validation and performance, uses and directions, warnings (risks, inappropriate settings, clinical rationale, inappropriate decision support, generalisability, and 'discontinue use if'), and other information. The authors note that 'there has not been a systematic effort to ensure that front-line [medical users] actually know how, when, how not, and when not to incorporate model output into clinical decisions'.[46] While this lack of provision thus far is troubling in and of itself, it is clearly information needed not only for front-line users, but to assess the realistic capabilities of AI and the uses for which it is optimised.

Sendak et al's version of the Model Facts label, focused on medical users, includes a summary of the input data and where it is collected; a detailed bullet-point explanation of the mechanism (outcome, output, target population, time of prediction, input source data, input data type, training data location and time period, and model type); information on the validation and performance of the model, with associated statistics; notes on usage and directions (including benefits, target populations and use case, general use, appropriate decision support, instructions before using the model, and a safety and efficacy evaluation); warnings (risks, inappropriate settings, clinical rational, inappropriate decision support, generalisability, and 'discontinue use if'); and lastly, 'other information', including links to more information and where to direct enquiries.[47] Such a label could be expanded conceptually, though ideally not greatly in length, to include major decisions made: models used, approaches taken, other routes tried. Requiring such a label not only provides a well-needed amount of information for deployers, but also provides companies with a potential body of evidence for due diligence.

Keeping strict records of the producer's choices and the defences thereof, providing this information in a Model Facts style information sheet, expanded where necessary, will be essential to establish the due diligence defence for high-risk, high-value AI. The blueprint proposes that, in the case of an incident and subsequent litigation, the burden of proof will be on the producer and not a potential victim or sector. This reflects both the difficulty in sifting through such information, and the power imbalance in availability of information. It is absolutely critical that the alignment of the stated purpose of the AI and the documentation of choices align, including why a less interpretable model was chosen over a more interpretable model. These choices include the entire gamut of AI creation, testing and deployment: not just what tests were employed, but *why* they were employed

[45] EU AI Act (n 10) Annex IV, 2.
[46] ibid.
[47] Sendak et al (n 43).

and, more importantly, why they were employed *over other tests*. XAI are not a crystal ball into the workings of an AI, and producers must strive to show, to a high level, why their choices and tests were appropriate to show that the AI was sufficiently accurate to deploy.

Another important area of consideration is scope control. Scope control is a way of using a small measure of regulation to prevent greater and backdated regulation in future. I define scope control as a design approach that limits the design and data collection to what is necessary to accomplish the stated aim of the AI. This means not providing the AI with the ability to potentially accomplish aims outside its stated purpose, be they particular activities or data collection – so no rocket launcher on the toaster, but also no medical data collection from the smart shower. The stated purpose must be examined from a multitude of angles: what did the producers say they were making and how do their choices reflect this statement? Additionally, and possibly more importantly, how do the design and function reflect the marketing of the AI to the public? Producers must be able to defend their design choices as creating the AI to be as straightforward, explainable and minimalistic as possible – a controlled scope of activity.

Scope control is important in two respects. First, the AI should be as 'minimal' as possible to achieve its stated purpose. While this could be interpreted as a grand principle of design, it is often as simple as not adding unnecessary features. It should be exceptionally clear what the AI can and cannot do, even to a lay audience. The greater the additions to an AI, such as more types of data collection, more types of interaction, the greater chance it has to go wrong by combining these elements and the more difficult it is to understand.[48] This is not intended as a particular tightrope to walk – a feature is defensible if it adds to the stated purpose, such as 'safely navigating a vehicle'. An ideal example of this is the First World War era warplane synchronisation gear, or interrupter gear, which allowed the aircraft to fire bullets through its own propeller without hitting the propeller blades. While there are certainly reasons for doing so,[49] there is an incredible risk to hitting the plane's own propeller. If the gear worked perfectly nothing would necessarily go wrong, yet the potential for something to go wrong increased exponentially compared with putting the armament elsewhere on the plane.

The second portion of scope control ranges into data minimisation. This is in recognition of how entrenched the internet of things already is, and is likely

[48] Consider a self-driving vehicle: not only do XAI tools need to be used on each input/sensor source, but on how they are combined. The fewer the sources of input, the less correspondingly complex the assessment of how the AI works, and the fewer sources for error in understanding why decisions are made.

[49] These reasons being a trade-off between risk and purpose. While the plane was more dangerous to its pilot, it was also more effective at shooting down *other* planes. N Franks, *Sharks among Minnows: Germany's First Fighter Pilots and the Fokker Eindecker Period, July 1915 to September 1916* (London, Grub Street, 2001).

to become: devices have an increasing level of data on their users, and this level will only increase. As AI enables and devours even more data, the consumer becomes ever more entrenched in a system they are unlikely to understand. In keeping with scope control, producers must also justify data collection along the lines of the AI's stated purpose. For example, a smart fridge that has the stated purpose of aiding the user in bettering their diet, using their resources and planning their meals, would not defensibly have a feature to gather information about the user that could be used to infer, anonymously or not, a medical condition: the fridge might infer that a user prefers non-sugar cola, not that they are diabetic. The question that must be asked is: what information is it reasonable for the AI to collect based on what it is stated to have been developed to do?

Machine learning relies on over-collection: the initial machine 'wants' as much data as possible, because the connections have not been made as to what is relevant. But once a purpose is set, and the purpose is to be implemented, the producer must set hard lines on what data will be excluded on a need-to-know basis. This is data minimisation, but not necessarily for the same reasons as in data protection law (see below): extra data does not help *ex ante*, and it does create potential extra risks that could be avoided by collecting less information. A car does not need any health information on its passengers unless one is actively undergoing a health emergency, but if it has health information, it becomes a more valuable target for hacking. Minimisation of unjustified collection at a regulatory level will save a world of headaches in having to backtrack why the vacuum knew the user was of a protected characteristic.

These data choices include what input the AI is going to have. This includes a distinction between the intentional design inputs and the information that the AI may glean from its own data gathering and connections. What information will the AI be capable of reporting back, and why? How can that data be used? Producers will have a positive duty to protect users, particularly in cases where there was a lower barrier to entry for their products: where AI causing accidental death is likely to have a heavier burden in bringing their product to market, those with a lower burden in initial sale should have a correspondingly more difficult case to make in defence of their choices.

This scope control with regard to data aims deliberately to reassert a level of human autonomy: an avoidance of social control, to the benefit of social health; and to avoid unanticipated consequences by reducing types of data captured. That which is not caught cannot be misused, either against individuals or groups, or for unintended purposes. It is an acknowledgement that while the specific harms of various non-life-threatening AI may be difficult to predict, this is indeed an area where we have seen other harms. While an exact balance may be a nebulous thing, data protection provides a sufficiently analogous case study to attempt to disallow AI as yet another source of widespread data collection.

This approach has certain parallels with the concepts of data minimisation and privacy by design in data protection law. The concepts of privacy by design and privacy by default are not necessarily recent. Concepts of privacy by design were 'expressed in the 1970s and were incorporated in the 1990s into the RL 95/46/EC Data Protection Directive'.[50] GDPR Article 5 (Principles relating to processing of personal data) states that personal data shall be 'adequate, relevant and limited to what is necessary in relation to the purposes for which they are processed',[51] and Article 25 (Data protection by design and default) that:

> (1) Taking into account the state of the art, the cost of implementation and the nature, scope, context and purposes of processing as well as the risks of varying likelihood and severity for rights and freedoms of natural persons posed by the processing, the controller shall, both at the time of the determination of the means for processing and at the time of the processing itself, implement appropriate technical and organisational measures, such as pseudonymisation, which are designed to implement data-protection principles, such as data minimisation, in an effective manner and to integrate the necessary safeguards into the processing in order to meet the requirements of this Regulation and protect the rights of data subjects.
>
> (2) The controller shall implement appropriate technical and organisational measures for ensuring that, by default, only personal data which are necessary for each specific purpose of the processing are processed.{2} That obligation applies to the amount of personal data collected, the extent of their processing, the period of their storage and their accessibility.{3} In particular, such measures shall ensure that by default personal data are not made accessible without the individual's intervention to an indefinite number of natural persons.

The GDPR expands upon this in Recital 78 with what measures might be taken, such as 'minimising the processing of personal data, pseudonymising personal data as soon as possible, transparency with regard to the functions and processing of personal data',[52] among others.

However, these measures fall short of what AI scope minimisation proposes, for two reasons. First, the GDPR is primarily aimed at active collection of data: measures to minimise, anonymise and protect information that is gathered. A consumer filling out a form is actively being asked for information, whether private information or otherwise. Certainly, the GDPR does not disinclude the potential for passive collection, but the brunt of its efforts focus on purposeful collection. AI goes a step further by massively increasing passive collection: while one can imagine a CCTV camera in fringe cases picking up private medical details – perhaps someone marching with a sign disclosing a medical status – this type of collection will be in the minority. An autonomous AI, however, needs a great deal of information about its surroundings in order to function: a care home

[50] 'Privacy by Design' (General Data Protection Regulation (GDPR)): gdpr-info.eu/issues/privacy-by-design/.

[51] Regulation (EU) 2016/679 of the European Parliament and of the Council of 27 April 2016 on the protection of natural persons with regard to the processing of personal data and on the free movement of such data, and repealing Directive 95/46/EC (General Data Protection Regulation) [2016] OJ L119/1.

[52] ibid.

robot, for example, will almost inevitably pick up personal information, including but not limited to medications, facial recognition and personal habits. While some areas of concern between AI and non-AI data are the same, such as anonymisation and secure storage, the potential difference between active and passive collection must be noted. Where no sane person would install a camera in their bathroom, one might not think to warn a houseguest of a self-driving mop that patrols the bathroom floor.

Second, the data protection measures such as the GDPR fall short in AI cases because they are aimed primarily at controllers, not producers. The references to measures to be taken, such as pseudonymisation, are measures taken after information has already been collected. Bygrave notes that 'Article 25 measures are primarily imposed by data controllers only', and that '[e]xacerbating this shortcoming is that Article 25(1) formulates the design stage as the time when the controller assumes controller status – a phase that might not equate with the time when a particular data-processing device is actually designed and manufactured'.[53] Additionally, measures taken vis-a-vis producers are not as stringent; they 'should be encouraged', rather than, as controllers, required to take certain measures.[54]

Essentially, scope minimisation takes the concepts of data minimisation and privacy design a step further. AI, and particularly AI that learns, will take in more data than ever before, and while this data shares certain requirements with data protection, its increased collection and additional concerns are such that requirements must be placed further in the process – on the producer, rather than primarily on the controller. This is particularly so in cases where personal information is increasingly likely – in the home, in continual close contact, in medical settings. There must be a rebuttable presumption on producers that a data collection function is not required, unless its purpose can be reasonably shown to be required for the stated purpose of the AI, and the potential dangers thereof mitigated to a reasonable extent.

Burden of Proof (1)

In assessing defences to liability, two requirements arise. First, the injured party should have the right to a preliminary explanation – why the AI made the decisions that resulted in their injury (see further the discussion in section 5.3). Second, a reverse burden of proof should be put on the provider. This is for multiple reasons.

First, it would be unacceptably difficult for the claimant to show fault. They are extremely unlikely to have the expertise necessary to analyse the AI – particularly

[53] LA Bygrave, 'Data Protection by Design and by Default: Deciphering the EU's Legislative Requirements' (*Oslo Law Review*, 25 August 2017): idunn.no/doi/10.18261/issn.2387-3299-2017-02-03.

[54] ibid.

complex AI – and the production practices that produced it. This analysis will require a deep familiarity with the process, and the XAI tools used in training, testing and validating. Second, this assessment will be expensive, particularly without a previous familiarity with the AI and its production. Third, there is a vast imbalance in the access to the relevant data. Not only does the provider hold all access to the data, but they can easily overwhelm the claimant by providing unnecessary or undescribed data. The EU draft AI Liability Directive attempts to redress these imbalances by minimising the barrier of the claimant providing a causal link, but the crucial step is to prove fault in the first place – a step which inherently involves proving a causal link, and thus inherently requires proof that the AI should have acted differently. Burden of proof should proceed with the principles of *res ipsa loquitur*, or 'the thing speaks for itself'. If there is a clear factual connection between the AI and the incident, such as an individual being hit by a self-driving car, the initial assumption should be that the party who has produced the AI should shoulder a rebuttable burden of proof that they were not negligent, and acted with due diligence.

This initial burden should be put to the provider for the reasons previously mentioned – imbalance of access and complexity – but also in that the producer must defend their design choices, such as scope control. This is to an extent a chance for the producer to show Occam's razor: that testing showed that the simplest possible solution that did not result in a proportionate lowering of accuracy was the one employed. 'Simple' here is a key word. Not only must the producer show that they did not add functions that were unnecessary for the purported purpose of the AI, but also that the methods and builds chosen were as interpretable as possible, producing as complete and accurate explanations as possible. This is not to say that complex AI should be barred, but that there should not be complexity without purpose, or only for the purposes of obfuscation. Depending on the function, the producer may need to show alternative attempts at more interpretable models, against a sliding scale between interpretability and acceptable performance.

As mentioned in chapter two, there is a cross-section of jurisdictions, in the European Union in particular, that engage in strict liability for portions of activity that will engage AI causing accidental death. These include France's strict approach to liability for driving, and the Netherlands 'semi-strict' approach, Spain's strict liability for medical incidents, and elements of the Czech Republic's forms of strict contractual liability. These may generate some differences with their non-strict liability counterparts; yet as discussed in section 2.5, acts and regulations that purport to provide strict liability, such as the Product Liability Directive, in practice raise similar questions to negligence arguments. Theoretically objective standards in practice import a degree of subjectivity. Even if the same questions are ultimately being asked, such as what expectations society should have of AI and its level of function, the question with greater direct impact is effectively 'what recourse does someone who has suffered because of AI have?' This is why the reverse burden of proof is crucial.

7.2.2. Regulation to Compensate/Punish if Harms Arise

Conceptions of fault, liability and compensation still underscore the 'stick' aspect of regulatory carrot and stick. While inducing societally beneficial AI is certainly an aim, the harms are too great to ignore the potential consequences with no response. This is not to say that liability and associated cost should hang like a Sword of Damocles – there are many aspects to addressing liability, not least of which is, for many industries, arrangements with insurers. Negligence is assessed along the same lines as negligence for humans: that a duty of care exists; that the standard of care was breached; and that there was a proximate connection between the breach of the standard of care and a harm that occurred. For these, the law will look to the relationship between the parties, acknowledge the context of the incident, the imposition of obligations, and the foreseeability of the harm. A duty of care is not likely to pose much of a barrier: those that it is reasonably foreseeable that the AI will impact; those with whom the AI will interact. As discussed in chapter four, reasonably foreseeable harm means, for AI, the culmination of obligations on the party in advance – where humans have the benefit of context in the moment, producers are left to make educated assumptions about harms. Just as human actions in the moment are not expected to be perfect,[55] neither are those of the producer in producing the AI: it is 'all but impossible to specify, in advance, what kind of behaviour constitutes adequate caution or due care in given situations'.[56] When examining these assumptions after harm has occurred, the court should ask three questions with respect to reasonable foreseeability: what did the producer know? What ought they have known? What ought they have tested for?

Abbott's *The Reasonable Robot* provides as its central thesis that 'the law should not discriminate between AI and human behaviour', a default deviated from 'where there are good reasons for doing so'.[57] This is not an unreasonable starting point, and one which Abbott thoughtfully supports with details such as the idea that legal neutrality 'should not come at the expense of other principles such as transparency and accountability'.[58] We paradoxically expect AI to fail in unexpected ways, and must, therefore, plan accordingly. With AI that is so high-risk as to guarantee that lives will be lost, it is crucial to set the required standard to be as high as possible. This means that we must look to standards that would hold AI to be better than humans, both for the burdens AI imposes – high ecological cost, potential loss of traditional work patterns, etc – and for the lack of inherent human advantages – such as the ability to cope with differing context.

[55] Recall, eg, *Ahonanu* – standards are specific to context, including contextual factors such as drivers only being able to see in one direction.

[56] E Green, 'The Reasonable Man: Legal Fiction or Psychosocial Reality?' (1968) 2 *Law & Society Review* 241: jstor.org/stable/3052783.

[57] R Abbott, *The Reasonable Robot* (Cambridge University Press 2020).

[58] ibid.

This also means that the high water-mark of best practices will continue to rise, a view with which Abbott might align, stating that when AI are notably better than humans, that humans should be perhaps held to the standard of AI.[59]

The standard of care, as discussed in chapter four, has two stages: first, in comparison to the AI's human counterpart, given their expected level of expertise. If the AI's performance is not found to have met the standard of that reasonable human, the producer fails at the first hurdle.[60] The AI's production will then be examined to the standard of a reasonable producer. This standard is not dissimilar to that of medical practice: just because an approach is novel or unusual does not mean that its use is inherently negligent. Its employment must, however, be defensible to those skilled in the same art. The process must be found to have been tested on what the producer knew, ought to have known, and ought to have tested; their decisions and labelling found to match the evidence provided by their logs; and design choices around scope control defended. If a producer had asked for clarification from the inquisition prior to the accident occurring, information given to the producer that the producer then acted upon will not be considered to have contributed to negligent action, even if it is later found by the inquisition to be sub-optimal.

The practices of a reasonable producer capture the high-water practices of the field at the time. While recursive obligation requires a provider to update their practices and upgrade already deployed AI, the producer with the first accident of its kind may rely solely on providing evidence of due diligence: that they took all reasonable care and skill to investigate and prevent such accidents. This defence does not run to specificities of instance: just because one would not predict that an autonomous car in Beijing would encounter a giraffe does not mean that the state of the art defends the producer – it is clearly foreseeable that the car would encounter a range of potential obstacles, animal or otherwise. However, it would cover the producer in the case that a novel issue occurred, such as if it were unknown that, for example, communication between the sensors of two colliding autonomous cars was unexpectedly affected by radar guns.

XAI serves as a tool for producers to show due diligence, but also for an investigation to show negligence. The inquisition can use any range of tools in its arsenal, because the same tools were available, or potentially available, to the producer. This may seem a high standard, and indeed it is. Playing for the highest of stakes – human life – means a need to employ what instruments are available. This potential liability does raise the barrier to entry, at least initially: while broad AI legislation provides general standards, such as negligence, sectoral legislation is likely to be both more specific, and lower the barriers to entry by providing more

[59] US Case *The TJ Hooper*, 60 F.2d 737 (2d Cir 1932) held that failure to adopt an improved technology was negligent when a cost-benefit analysis was in its favour.

[60] Though may, as discussed in section 7.1.1, be saved if the sectoral regulator has specified a lower standard for a particular activity in advance.

exact guidance. Between the general and sectoral, the regime detailed herein aims to bridge the gap proposed by the Collingridge Dilemma: not regulating restrictively too early, but incentivising practices that are as safe as possible.

In a non-AI case of negligence, the burden of proof is on the harmed party to show that the accused party failed to act to the standard of reasonable care. This must be reversed for AI. There are significant imbalances in power, information and tools between the producer and the potential victim. First, an explanation must be produced by the provider to the injured party as to why an incident occurred. Second, the defence of due diligence is intended only to induce societally beneficial AI, and not to act as a shield for producers to engage in less than highly skilled practices. If a duty of care exists and a human has been harmed, then there will be a de facto assumption of negligence on the producer, which they have the potential to rebut. Rebuttal must be backed up by those elements previously mentioned: design choices, training and testing, with all decisions shown with proper records. Opacity therefore cannot be used as a barrier to a negligence claim but is rather an obstacle for the producer to defend: the producer will need to justify why the design allowed for that measure of opacity, and the exhaustiveness through which it was tested. The producer's evidence via explanations should consider those aspects which make explanations most expository: that they are contrastive, convincingly selected, social, and balance the reality of probabilities with the audience's ability to interpret them.[61] The harmed party need only bring an incident to the regulator with the details they themselves are aware of – a harm caused by the AI – and not needing a sufficient war-chest to bring litigation against the producer. The regulator will need certain capacities to address these incidents, including expertise in investigation as the next section explains.

7.2.3. Regulatory Structures

Once again, regulation should not be over-extended, particularly where it is not necessary or may otherwise overlap with existing legislation.[62] This is not, however, to ignore the critical role that regulation can and should play. The Collingridge Dilemma remains, and while over-regulation threatens the field and its promised benefits, under-regulation threatens trust in both the system and AI developments, and also direct harm to individuals.

While some AI applications that are forecast to cause accidental death are in highly sectorally regulated areas such as medical devices, it is entirely possible that unforeseen areas of AI will cause accidental death. This brings us back to the quadrant division: where inputs and impact are known/unknown. Areas that may not have predictable inputs as of the moment of action, such as self-driving vehicles,

[61] See, eg, Miller on explanations in section 3.6.

[62] Such as with minimal autonomy, wherein the AI does not represent an intermediary decision-maker.

may still have potentially predictable outputs, for example, dangerous activity on the road causing injury or death. There are applications that may have either known or unknown inputs, but which produce more unknown impacts in terms of harm. While new sectoral regulators may spring up as areas of AI that are not dealt with by existing sectoral regulators become more known, it is nonetheless a necessary interim step to have some sort of body to approve AI applications with high potential for harm. This could include, for example, AI management systems for resources such as utilities.

The general regulator has several key roles. First, to provide a broad regulatory filter for AI. This includes identifying and banning unacceptable AI, as well as identifying new problem areas and structuring appropriate regulations such as requirements for pre-approval of the riskiest AI applications or recommending the establishment of a new sectoral regulator. A second function of the regulator will be to receive the results of quasi-independent investigations where an AI causes serious harm, such as in cases of death. Third will be to impose sanctions for failure to comply with producer and user obligations, including, potentially, those laid down by sectoral regulators. Fourth, to issue guidelines and communicate with industry, government and the public.

What does the regulator need in order to satisfy these requirements? First, it needs the ability to levy consequences. The Information Commissioner's Office (ICO) is a positive entity for consumer protection but does not have the resources to wield its power effectively. While the potential fields of AI are endless, it is particularly important that the AI regulator be built around communication, and the ability to enforce clearly communicated responsibilities: what regulatory approval looks like; how problems can be addressed; and what investigations will entail. An investigatory arm of the regulator will be needed, to act as a reliable source of both guidance and consequence: incentivising consultation where necessary, but also assessing and publicising where an AI producer has not conformed to the necessary standard. Second, the entity needs to be quasi-judicial. This relates to its power, perhaps by way of passing its decisions on to courts, but also to its differentiation: the investigatory arm of the regulator must have the ability to move quickly, particularly where an incident has occurred. This is crucial for two reasons: to make knowledge gained from the incident public, raising the standard of the field immediately; and to engage and properly support public trust in both the regulation and the technology.[63] The public is not blind to such accidents, particularly where death is involved, and the media even less so. Although few cases have yet gone to the courts on the basis of AI causing accidental death, there has been substantial media coverage about such incidents. Moreover, it is necessary for the public to receive reports which are more than merely the AI producer stating that they have done X, Y or Z, perhaps in very technical language: having

[63] These objectives are similar to those of accident investigators in aviation and transport sectors, as discussed below.

a non-industry expert reporting increases trust in the idea that the regulation will be carried out without excusing, by the producer, their own mistakes. Third, the regulator needs a team of experts. This may seem self-evident, but such a team should be composed of, at minimum, technical and legal experts. Depending upon the level of co-regulation or cooperation, or indeed if the exchange occurs with or without an inciting incident, this may also include industry representatives. The need for technical experts comes from the need to examine the choices made by the AI producer on a technical level. The need for legal experts comes from the need to examine whether or not those decisions constitute negligence or a breach of regulation, or perhaps whether a due diligence defence might be available in cases where the producer has engaged in all possible mitigation for a not 'absolute liability' offence. These two groups should be represented both in pre-approval, and in investigation.

In terms of pre-approval for the deployment of high-risk AI, the regulator will need a body to give opinions, approve codes of practice, examine standards, and provide a level of oversight, such as, for example, interpreting a body of XAI explanations about the AI's architecture and key points of decision-making. This body could be within or separate from the regulator, depending on the jurisdiction's existing regulatory bodies. A specialist advisory entity is necessary not only to enhance public trust, but to provide co-regulatory interaction with AI producers: one where stakeholders ask for clarification or an assessment of their practices, such as inquiring direction from the ICO on difficult data protection issues.[64] This interaction is also not necessarily sectoral: while certain high-stakes sectors such as medicine are likely to furnish their venue for direct contact, and should not be blocked from doing so, having a general AI regulator is also a necessary tool to provide a level of standards cross-industry. The recent rise of AI foundation models, which can be adapted to a range of uses, makes this even more necessary. The regulator should act as a point of contact for both producers and sectoral regulators, although not to the exclusion of those stakeholders' other interaction.

Sectoral regulation is the most focused level of regulation and develops incrementally. As shown in chapter six, sectoral legislation has both the task and the benefit of moving at the pace of the field that it governs: while broad legislation must govern at the macro level, sectoral legislation can look at the micro, those specificities which cannot be defined in all fields, but which are crucial for certain parts of particular fields. Incrementality occurs in many fields, for example, financial services regulation in Britain went from formalised conceptions of barter markets in 1000 AD, to credit requirements on banks in the late 1600s and early 1700s, to the veritable thicket of regulation we see today.[65] Today, fields like

[64] Which allows for reports, enquiries, registration and complaints, as well as providing a dedicated advice service for small and medium enterprises.

[65] G Gilligan, 'The Origins of UK Financial Services Regulation' (26 March 1997): papers.ssrn.com/abstract=2213218.

driving, even for non-professionals, have developed specialised requirements for entry: acquiring a provisional licence, driving lessons and practice, a theory test, a driving test, insurance, eyesight, etc. Use of AI in certain fields will certainly not take quite as long to develop but can similarly be viewed as a process: there must be enough of the field present to regulate, and sufficient understanding to do so at a functional, practical level, but not so much that regulation chokes progress before the utility of AI in that field can be tested. This is reflected in chapter five. Even though the jurisdictions examined there take varying approaches, in, for example, regulating self-driving vehicles, they have shared similarities in creating approval systems, safety regulations and classification systems, before tackling liability specifics. Regulation at the micro level must be nimble enough to match the state of the art, but powerful enough to engage the attention of those regulated, thus leading to co-regulation. This process might be guided by the principle set out in *Bolam v Friern*: 'common law is open to risk taking, even if the new treatment is endorsed only by a sub-specialty (super-specialists) of a responsible body, and is not to be considered unreasonable'.[66]

At its most specific, AI regulation should primarily be imposed at a sectoral level where accidental death is a likelihood. The draft EU AI Liability Directive acknowledges this indirectly, stating that transportation liability schemes will take precedence over the Liability Directive itself.[67] While broad AI regulation should not reach to spelling out what AI producers should build and the steps taken to do so, sectoral legislation is well placed to do exactly this where those steps are identifiable, or at least to indicate some essential steps along the way. This is particularly pertinent for high-risk AI, where the types of dangers can be best expressed by the working reality: an autonomous aircraft must deal with a full sphere of possible hazards, whereas an autonomous car creates few risks above ground and none below it. This is also a way to act on the division of AI by consequence: life-threatening AI would benefit from targeted regulations, particularly in areas already so regulated such as medical devices, but there would be little or no need to target AI with minimal harms. For AI with minimal harms, there need not inherently be additional sectoral regulation: the smart fridge is likely sufficiently covered by broad AI legislation, whereas medical AI needs a strict path of testing and assurances to reassure the public of its safety and usability, a process which it already has for non-AI technologies. Sectoral legislation will need to onboard a certain quantum of AI specialists, and many already have – the American Food and Drug Administration (FDA) as well as the European Commission already provide a list of approved AI devices, suggesting that they have sufficient access to specialists to satisfy their concerns with such devices. While such direct testing may prove more difficult for other industries such as automobiles given the sheer number of entrants to the field,

[66] *Bolam v Friern Hospital Management Committee* [1957] 1 WLR 582.
[67] AI Liability Directive (n 36).

such industries are no stranger to regulating safety standards across a variety of applicants, for example see the American Federal Motor Vehicle Safety Standards (FMVSS).[68]

This sectoral approach may also involve co-regulatory cooperation with larger industry partners, as has been the case in data protection. Data protection authorities

> aim to assess the compliance of cloud providers with and enforce the relevant data protection laws … [potentially going] beyond checking whether a cloud provider complies with the relevant data protection laws and [into checking] whether the cloud provider is attempting to be in the 'best practice zone'.[69]

While different jurisdictions and authorities employ different methods, this can be a back-and-forth exchange on how best to achieve the desired results, for example the Irish Data Protection Authority (DPA) investigation of Facebook included the DPA

> directing the cloud provider to specific data protection resources; regular discussions between the Irish DPA and Facebook on various issues (eg product development); visits of the Irish DPA to Facebook's headquarters; and informal correspondence between the Irish DPA and Facebook on specific data protection queries.[70]

This involved a variety of actors on both sides, including 'Facebook's legal team, and the Irish DPA, the Norwegian consumer council, and … Norwegian Facebook users'.[71] This is not to say that the Irish DPA confines its investigations to these specific methods and groups, but that there is a level of sector-specific discussion ongoing, particularly where the field is new and guidelines are more prevalent than hard-and-fast rules. This brings us to the next question: how can and should co-regulation shape AI regulation more broadly?

The regulator must be capable of providing compensation to wronged parties. As discussed in chapter two, the compensation of victims is a key driver of a tort-based liability system. While normally imposed through the court system, this is undesirable writ large for AI for two reasons: first, this means that resolution for the case in question will be very drawn out, and as a result updates to the state of the field will of necessity wait for the resolution of the case. Second, it means that victims do not receive compensation in as fast a manner as practicable. This means that while a quasi-judicial process may be necessary to bring out arguments such as due skill and care, there are significant benefits to a leaner, more specialised

[68] 'Regulations – NHTSA issues Federal Motor Vehicle Safety Standards' (United States Department of Transportation): nhtsa.gov/laws-regulations/fmvss.

[69] A Vranaki and C Reed, 'The Rise of Investigations by European Data Protection Authorities in the Context of Cloud Computing' (2014) SSRN Electronic Journal: researchgate.net/publication/315336890_The_Rise_of_Investigations_by_European_Data_Protection_Authorities_in_the_Context_of_Cloud_Computing.

[70] ibid.

[71] ibid.

system. In order to achieve compensation and quasi-judicial outcomes, the regulator must be equipped to levy fines and costs upon parties, similar to sectoral regulators and courts themselves. This explains why there must be a specialist arm to examine processes and internal decisions – including XAI tools and their appropriateness to what is being examined – in order to help determine allocations of liability.

A specialist investigatory entity designed to interact directly with AI producers will be a required feature of the regulatory body. Where an accident has occurred, such an investigative body will need to provide evidence on which the regulator can make a decision. The level of specialist expertise required for this type of activity is thin on the ground, and concentrating it into a single investigatory entity means that not only will the system be more efficient, but that unnecessary cost in finding such experts may be avoided. This should be a specialist body for multiple reasons: first, such investigation will require specialist resources – there will not be an abundance of qualified witnesses for such cases, particularly in the early days of regulation. Second, if cases were to go directly to judicial proceedings, the time period of investigation would be extreme – a specialist, non-partisan investigation is able to move much more quickly. Third, the investigatory body should be able to produce not only evidence on the incident, but recommendations for the future to both the regulator and the other stakeholders in question. Fourth, this body will over time gain a wide range of experience of different AI – a luxury that would not be possible if expertise were to be split amongst a variety of bodies. Lastly, having the investigatory body separate from the regulatory body means that investigations can be used for public policy objectives rather than being limited strictly to liability investigations.

There are many parallels to this entity, such as, in the United Kingdom, the AAIB or Air Accident Investigation Branch, or in the United States, the National Transportation Safety Board. Such entities investigate where an incident has occurred and make recommendations to the relevant authority to reduce the risk that such incidents happen again. This type of role is not dissimilar to the Irish DPA previously discussed: there is a direct access of systems in question, and the authority has the power to go in and conduct audits that directly lead to regulatory changes in guidelines. This power is a combination of specialist knowledge and communicative access – in aviation, a cooperative effort to decrease accidents.

What the inquisition is to look at are the processes of AI development.[72] XAI is a tool to do so, and the inquisition must examine not only what they themselves can glean from the AI and its training and testing data, but also what tools the producer used, and their justification for that use. The inquisition looks at the process of creation, and how reasonable the decisions made therein are. The inquisition must be able to take information to the regulator – not, perhaps, to

[72] In detail, see ch 4.

set or state what liability looks like, but to state what accepted practice in the field looks like, and whether the producer has fallen short. This is a subtle but illustrative difference: negligence is the failure to match a standard of reasonable behaviour – the standard of a reasonable specialist. Liability is the application of that standard to a legal consequence. This is the difference between, for example, the contents of the UK Highway Code and the case law springing from it: while it may not be the correct action to bring a tractor-trailer onto the road in the off-lane rather than the on-lane, it does not mean that the driver is inherently liable for doing so. This is similar to a doctor failing to make a diagnosis, but where that failure did not cause damage to the patient on the balance of probabilities. A less than perfect action is not necessarily cause for liability, in AI use no less than in humans.

Lastly, and tied in with the need for the inquisition to have these powers, is mandatory reporting of the outcome of these investigations to the regulator. The regulator may then decide how much of the information should be released, in order that both the industry and the public might benefit from the investigation. The investigator needs a certain level of power to be able to do this, as evidenced by Waymo's current fight to restrict crash information.[73] This is supplemented by the power of the regulator itself, with the ability to, for example, wield GDPR-level fines, particularly where larger producers are concerned.

7.3. Conclusion

To conclude, there are many parts of the current legal system that will adequately serve the demands of AI. Where they do not, certain adjustments are needed: by establishing new regulatory bodies, such as a general regulator; providing necessary tweaks in liability such as the reversed evidential burden and the due diligence defence; and providing for specialist investigation. The system pictured above provides for novel bodies and powers, but not by disregarding functioning mechanisms and viable technolegal parallels such as XAI as evidence of due diligence. The system incentivises responsible innovation, providing a level playing field by requiring parties to hit a mandatory minimum level of responsible practice. It provides clarity to producers by explaining the steps they can take to avoid liability and helps to establish societal trust by holding producers to account. It supports novel applications by not needlessly punishing innovation but upholds the requirements of a quickly growing field by keeping its standards at the level of the field's knowledge. The framework is inherently informed by industry, in

[73] Andrew J Hawkins, 'Waymo Sues California DMV to Keep Driverless Crash Data under Wraps' (*The Verge*, 28 January 2022): theverge.com/2022/1/28/22906513/waymo-lawsuit-california-dmv-crash-data-foia.

co-regulatory discussions; by the regulator, in continual reassessment of applications and their risk/reward balance; by sectoral regulators who are best placed to assess on an individual application basis; and by the ever-growing toolkit of explainable and responsible practice. While the contexts that case law provides will help settle the minutiae, introducing a definition and defence of liability provides a necessary predictability that the field of AI desperately needs.

8

Test Case Study

8.1. Common Law versus Civil Law Liability

Of the four jurisdictions examined, three are common law jurisdictions – the United Kingdom, the United States and Singapore. The European Union also has two common law Member States – Ireland and Cyprus – but the majority of Member States employ civil law systems. This of course raises the question of how differently liability is treated between common law and civil law jurisdictions, particularly where legislation such as the Product Liability Directive has effect in both common and civil law areas.

Civil law systems originate in the Roman civil code and aim to create structure via 'a great number of general rules and principles … the court's main task is to apply and interpret the law in the code'.[1] Common law systems are not codified in the same way, and courts are to base their decisions on rulings from higher courts and earlier cases, ie, following precedent. Pejovic describes the difference from the perspective that

> [a] civil law lawyer usually starts from a legal norm contained in a legislation … [whereas] a lawyer in common law starts with the actual case and compares it with the same or similar legal issues that have been dealt with by courts in previously decided cases.[2]

This distinction may be more theoretical than borne out in practice. Common law authorities and materials such as textbooks consolidate legal norms from the combined matter of precedents, and common law judges undertake the same exercise when analysing precedents and attempting to identify the legal norm which they should apply to a case.

Given the rarity of two jurisdictions trying an identical case, it is difficult to compare exact, real-world outputs between either a common law and civil law or two different civil law countries. However, there is a country that employs both common and civil law systems under one banner: Canada has a civil law system in

[1] C Pejovic, 'Civil Law and Common Law: Two Different Paths Leading to the Same Goal' (2001) 155 *Poredbeno Pomorsko Pravo* 7, 9.

[2] ibid, 10.

Quebec, but a common law system in the rest of the country. The General Law of Delict in the Quebec Civil Code states that:

> Every person has a duty to abide by the rules of conduct which lie upon him, according to the circumstances, usage or law, so as not to cause injury to another. Where he or she is endowed with reason and fails in this duty, he is responsible for any injury he causes to another person and is liable to reparation for the injury, whether it be bodily, moral or material in nature. He is also liable, in certain cases, to reparation for injury caused to another by the act or fault of another person or by the act of things in his custody.

In examining the idea of injury in common law negligence and personal extra-contractual liability in civil law, within the Canadian context, Katsivela asserts that common law injury can be physical or mental, or be pure economic loss; whereas in civil law it can be bodily, moral, or material, with both civil and common law requiring that the injury be proven on the balance of probabilities.[3] Katsivela ultimately notes that 'despite the apparent nuances between the civil and common law, the two approaches may converge towards the same result'.[4]

Other authors have noted functional similarities between common and civil law systems more generally:

> [u]nder civil law the courts do not create the law, but only apply and interpret it. **In practice**, however, **the higher court decisions certainly have a certain influence on lower courts**, since judges of lower courts will usually take into account the risk that their decisions would probably be reversed by the higher court if they contradict the higher court decisions.[5]

This book does not attempt to reconcile or examine in depth the nuanced differences between common and civil law systems, and the brief discussion here is to serve only as a reminder that the two come from different traditions that may ultimately affect liability outcomes. However, there is one particular point worth noting – that civil law systems allegedly rely entirely on written codes to determine liability. The draft EU AI Liability Directive would appear to be the best match for such a code in the case of AI liability for Member States and was in fact drafted with purposes of harmonisation within the European Union in mind. However, it would be wrong to treat the Directive as a definitive statement of the law for several reasons.

First, this legislation must apply to both common law and civil law systems, and each Member State has individual jurisdiction over liability. Thus, the AI Liability Directive itself could be reasonably regarded as unspecific, at the very least if it were to form the only document regarding AI liability. EU Member States

[3] M Katsivela, 'The notion of injury in the tort of negligence (common law) and the personal extra-contractual liability (civil law) in Canada: A comparative study' (2018) *translation* 96 *Canadian Bar Review* 3: ssrn.com/abstract=3373986.

[4] ibid.

[5] Pejovic (n 1) 11 (emphasis added).

will have to determine individually how they will proceed: by explicitly providing more legislation, which would undermine the harmonisation measure of the Directive; or by following solely the Directive and having to 'reinvent the wheel' for each case; or ultimately to be informed by precedents as they come out, either in the Member State's own jurisdiction, or by other jurisdictions. The latter would be the most sensible approach, particularly given the lack of specific expertise in judicial application available to each Member State and given the novel nature of AI cases. Ultimately, this would start to look very like a common law approach: not that civil law states would take on a common law approach to negligence, but in practice their cases would ultimately begin to be influenced by precedent. This fits in well with the blueprint, and other areas of legislation that provide elements such as the development risks defence, providing for a rising standard based on the state of the field, a state that is shared not only internally to a jurisdiction, but worldwide, as knowledge in the field grows regardless of borders.

8.2. Test Application

To demonstrate how the blueprint in chapter seven might function in different jurisdictions, a test application would be helpful. For such purposes, let us assume that a manufacturer has produced an (as yet theoretical) AI chainsaw.[6] This is an AI application that can clearly produce a high level of harm, and is not intended to cause physical harm to humans.

This theoretical AI chainsaw has the ability to identify trees and to make calculations relating to their recorded density and width, modifying how it operates so as to cut most effectively. The AI company advertises this as a safety feature, because it allows the AI to calculate when the chainsaw should stop cutting, in order for the user to have plenty of time to vacate before the tree topples. The chainsaw also has a safety feature very similar to the company SawStop: the blade can sense electrical conduction that human skin provides and stops instantly when it comes into contact with this conduction.[7]

Alice, a consumer user, takes the chainsaw out to cut a tree. She has familiarised herself with the AI's promised safety features and engages the chainsaw's 'detect tree' function. At the time of use, there is snow on the trees at Alice's property, including the palm tree she intends to cut down. The AI's dataset does not contain palm trees in snow, and only contains evergreen data in conjunction with the presence of snow. The AI therefore misidentifies the palm tree as a pine tree.

[6] Thank you chronologically to Benjamin Hardin, Leah Madelaine Schmidt and Professor Chris Reed for their invaluable contributions to the AI chainsaw scenario. A very sharp bunch.

[7] M Simon, 'Despite Proven Technology, Attempts to Make Table Saws Safer Drag On' (NPR, 10 August 2017): npr.org/2017/08/10/542474093/despite-proven-technology-attempts-to-make-table-saws-safer-drag-on.

Palm wood is much tougher than pine, and as a result the AI fails to identify the right point to stop cutting, which causes the palm tree to fall onto Alice.

Bob, a consumer user, purchases an AI chainsaw with an additional safety feature. The chainsaw's AI is designed such that it will pause the chainsaw if it hits an air pocket in the wood, because the jerk as the chainsaw hits such an air pocket can startle the user and risk them touching the blade. The pause is initiated by a density detection system – if the density detection senses an air pocket, then the AI automatically 'checks' the electrical conduction sensor, restarting only if there is no input to the electrical conduction sensor. Bob is also working in very cold weather conditions. Bob's AI chainsaw encounters an air pocket, and he unthinkingly touches the edge of the chainsaw blade. Because Bob is suffering from frostbite – which affects the body's electrical conductivity[8] – the electrical conduction safety detection on the chainsaw does not work, and the chainsaw restarts and cuts Bob while he is still in contact with the chainsaw blade.

Both Alice and Bob have miraculous recoveries and bring their cases to the court.

First, there are two separate headings of law under which Alice and Bob may bring their cases: negligence liability; and consumer protection and product liability. The blueprint brings together the elements of negligence liability, proposing tests that unite the aims, requirements and utility in law with the functional realities of AI and its creation process. Consumer protection and product liability come directly from the governing law of the jurisdiction in which the case is brought.

Let us consider the application of the blueprint to Alice and Bob's cases. First, the principles of regulation, as in section 7.1: what is regulation trying to achieve? It attempts to prevent harm before it occurs and compensate where it does occur; both *ex ante* and *ex post* elements: what should happen before the AI is put on the market; and what will happen when an accident occurs. In terms of factors prior to the AI being put on the market, this sort of AI application is unlikely to be considered particularly objectionable. While damage clearly can occur, the application is more or less an extension of a device, rather than a distinct foray into new applications.

In terms of risk balancing and socio-political factors, public trust is unlikely to be unduly harmed if the product is allowed to enter the market, particularly given that the new AI features are safety-oriented, adding preventative elements to an already dangerous activity. While compliance for dangerous AI will be an important factor to all regions, there is no AI chainsaw-specific legislation at play. This does mean, however, that there is no specific build-up of expectations of what exact safety measures – what standard of care – one might expect from the producers of an AI chainsaw, even as compared with a non-AI chainsaw.

[8] Benjamin Wedro, 'Frostbite vs Hypothermia Differences in Symptoms and Stages' (emedicinehealth): emedicinehealth.com/frostbite_and_hypothermia_symptoms_and_stages/article_em.htm.

Second, we consider the factors known about the AI. Its inputs are likely relatively clear: machine vision to identify the tree and its width; a dataset of trees and their characteristics; a sensor for electrical conduction; a sensor for density. The type of potential harm is clearly high: chainsaws are already a dangerous piece of machinery. Legislating bodies are unlikely to ban the AI chainsaw as an unacceptable risk on the face of it, given that the AI portions are, as mentioned, safety-oriented rather than introducing the risk of new harms. Let us assume that the AI producers have provided a sufficiently robust set of model facts and have not allowed the AI to record information that it does not need to complete its task. Further, it is unlikely that there is considerable sector-specific regulation that applies to consumer-facing chainsaw use, and the industry is likely small enough that it has not engaged in a great deal of co-regulatory conversation. Lastly, let us assume that consumers would more than likely be enticed to buy the considerably more expensive AI chainsaw because of its AI safety features, and not other factors, and that subsequent to the accidents XAI tools have made clear exactly why the problem has occurred.

While there is, for example, health and safety guidance regarding working with chainsaws,[9] or workplace health and safety acts,[10] there is no specific legislation regarding chainsaws in the four jurisdictions. This means that there is no sectoral-specific law to apply, and we proceed to what non-AI specific legislation might apply to the AI in question: what, ultimately, reasonableness looks like for AI. This means a particular emphasis, as discussed in section 7.1.2, for producers to focus on internal quality insurance: that the AI has been built with all due diligence, particularly given its high-harm applications.

Inquisitorial Questions Regarding Harm and Development

1. Has harm been prima facie caused by an AI?

Relying on the AI safety measures of the chainsaw, which have failed in both cases, has directly caused direct harm to Alice and Bob.

2. Was the standard of action that was met by the AI equivalent to a(n analogous) reasonable human?

In Alice's case, a human in the place of the AI may not be an expert at identifying trees, but they would almost certainly have been able to distinguish between, say, an evergreen and a palm tree, even if either and/or both trees were covered in snow. The AI in Alice's case would not pass the 'at a standard of a reasonable human' part of the test.

[9] 'Working with chainsaws' (Health and Safety Executive): hse.gov.uk/treework/safety-topics/chainsaw-operator.htm.

[10] Singapore Workplace Safety and Health (Amendment) Act 2017 (Act 44 of 2017): sso.agc.gov.sg//SL/S766-2017?DocDate=20171227.

In Bob's case, a human in the position of the AI in question may not necessarily have identified that a lowered body temperature would affect a critical sensor. This could particularly be the case where the geographic location in question only rarely receives temperatures harsh enough to cause frostbite. While arguments could be raised that a human in the same position would be quicker to stop the blade, as they would have a greater variety of input, humans have also been known to injure themselves specifically because they cannot feel certain body parts.[11] A human in the same place as an AI would not necessarily have reacted differently in principle.

3. Were the standards in creating the AI those of a reasonable producer?

Applying the facts to Bob's case becomes inherently complex at this stage. What we are ultimately questioning is whether, even though a human may not have done better, societally, we should expect an AI to do so. This is not a simple question to answer and will depend on how far the court thinks that the AI producer should have anticipated, and guarded or warned against, the circumstances which led to Bob's accident. Additionally, it is important to remember that we are not questioning the AI's decision-making – as the AI cannot and does not think – we are questioning the decision-making of the humans that created the AI. In Bob's case, this involves the question of whether it was reasonably foreseeable that the combination of factors in question, taken together, would prevent the safety features from working. This takes us to questions such as the inherent likelihood of an occurrence, and the predictability of the failsafe's less than perfect function causing harm.

In this case, the AI correctly identified the tree that was being cut. This aspect has not introduced any additional harm, such as the tree falling on Bob. What becomes an issue, however, is the relation between the human-cutting electrical stop and the density detection stop: that the AI chainsaw did correctly stop when encountering the air pocket, but then restarted because the electrical sensor did not sense Bob's hand. The designers gave the human-cutting safety stop a higher measure of impact on the ultimate decision-making of the AI. While both the density detection and the human-cutting sensor provide weight to the 'decision' of whether or not to run the chainsaw, the electrical sensor has, between the two, more impact. This is not necessarily unreasonable: if the density-detection were to detect everything to be fine, but the electrical sensor sensed a person, the chainsaw should not restart. The question then becomes whether it was reasonable for the AI producing team to anticipate that AI would fail in such a specific way that it tripped the density detection, but *not* the electrical, human sensor.[12]

[11] See, eg, leprosy: 'Signs and Symptoms' (Centre for Disease Control and Prevention, 2017): cdc.gov/leprosy/symptoms/index.html.

[12] This sort of uncertainty is parallel to that in the Arizona incident in ch 4 – while the human response to uncertainty should clearly be stop, this is assuming a level of context AI does not have.

This brings us to an interesting point. Did the producers know, or ought they have known, that harm would arise from this or similar causes? If there were another AI chainsaw that had failed in a similar way, they should clearly have known. The electrical sensor operates similarly, but not identically, to safety measures employed on table saws. If such a sensor had failed in a similar way, then arguably the producers should have been aware of this as part of their due diligence. However, activities involving table saws and similarly heavy cutting machinery are generally conducted indoors, or at the very least under shelter, for a variety of reasons, the comfort and safety of users being a not immaterial reason – a reason including temperatures. Jurisdictionally specific assessments of general familiarity between indoor and outdoor heavy cutting may be relevant in assessing due diligence. Let us assume in this case that no similar sensor, indoor or outdoor, had failed in such a way, so the knowledge that it could do so was not a part of the knowledge of the field. Let us also assume that all other testing aspects of the AI chainsaw were robust: that the chainsaw was tested in a broad variety of temperatures, with a broad variety of trees, in a broad variety of lighting, by a broad variety of users.[13] The AI company would then need to justify their choices. While this step shows up last in the blueprint analysis, it is the most important first step from the producer's point of view: this is a step that needs to have been a key focus of the producer all along. They must show how and why certain metrics were chosen; how datasets were judged to be sufficiently robust; what the results of explainable techniques showed about their development process. They would need to show a level of understanding of what the AI was doing and when, which explainability tools were used when, and why. Their justification of these choices and steps is ultimately what must be judged to be due diligence, or not. This is likely to depend on the context of that jurisdiction: ultimately, would a landscape below zero be reasonably foreseeable? While this will be expanded upon below, ultimately for the United Kingdom, the single market of the European Union, and the United States, chilly conditions are predictable; for Singapore, they are likely not.

The emphasis on this due diligence and justification step is for key regulatory reasons: while liability law is intended to compensate for harm when it occurs, the regulatory system is intended to incentivise halting that harm before it can occur. This harm prevention is ultimately the focus of the blueprint: to reinforce to producers that while not every harm may be caught, the only potential redemption when harm is caught is to be able to credibly defend their design choices. This is one side of the coin of the duty of care.

The other side of that duty of care is a direct line between the product they produce and the consumer who is affected by it. This is drawn directly from duties of care that exist outside AI applications. In the case of AI chainsaws, there is no specific sectoral regulation, and so no codified standard of care, but the duty of

[13] See section 7.2.1.

care exists nonetheless, and so too can a corresponding breach of that duty. The standard of care, uncodified, defaults to the two-part test above: that of a reasonable corresponding human, and those of a reasonable producer, with an emphasis on what a breach looks like in context. As discussed in section 7.3.1, the burden of proof must be on the AI producer where *res ipsa loquitur* applies – where the harm has a clear inference of connection with the AI by nature of the accident – because of the imbalance of knowledge of the product. This would clearly be the case for Bob: he would not have the technical skills or background to ascertain why the AI did what it did, when it did, and from his perspective, the AI chainsaw stopped and started for no reason, directly counter to the advertised safety advantages. Putting the burden on the AI company means requiring the party with actual knowledge to speak to not only what the AI did, but what design choices resulted in that output: why they chose the tests and metrics that they did. In this case, their design choices are relatively defensible: the AI is not needlessly complex, and is likely capable of explanation, even when the wrong and harmful output occurred.

In terms of other design choices made about the AI chainsaw, there are several aspects in which the AI producer has succeeded, as detailed in section 7.2.1: the AI chainsaw is properly scope-controlled and does not contain mechanisms that do not go towards the direct function of the AI as advertised. They have not included additional methods of data collection, or over-collection. There is no indication that the AI is gleaning additional connections that it should not have from its use.

Let us then consider the other side of the coin: product liability and consumer protection law. While these do indeed fit in the blueprint under non-sectoral governance, they differ by jurisdiction and legal tradition.

8.2.1. Product Liability and Consumer Protection in the United Kingdom

For the United Kingdom, non-AI specific legislation would include the Consumer Protection Act 1987, implementing the Product Liability Directive; and the Consumer Rights Act 2015.

These pieces of legislation are discussed at length in section 2.5. The Consumer Protection Act 1987 provides that if a product is defective, the manufacturer is responsible, with defect defined as:

> (1) Subject to the following provisions of this section, there is a defect in a product for the purposes of this Part if the safety of the product is not such as persons generally are entitled to expect; and for those purposes 'safety', in relation to a product, shall include safety with respect to products comprised in that product and safety in the context of risks of damage to property, as well as in the context of risks of death or personal injury.

(2) In determining for the purposes of subsection (1) above what persons generally are entitled to expect in relation to a product all the circumstances shall be taken into account, including –

(a) the manner in which, and purposes for which, the product has been marketed, its get-up, the use of any mark in relation to the product and any instructions for, or warnings with respect to, doing or refraining from doing anything with or in relation to the product;

(b) what might reasonably be expected to be done with or in relation to the product; and

(c) the time when the product was supplied by its producer to another; and nothing in this section shall require a defect to be inferred from the fact alone that the safety of a product which is supplied after that time is greater than the safety of the product in question.[14]

The Consumer Rights Act 2015 provides, notably in this case, that:

> 65(1) A trader cannot by a term of consumer contract or by a consumer notice exclude or restrict liability for death or personal injury resulting from negligence.[15]

First, let us look to the United Kingdom itself. Although the United Kingdom comprises different national jurisdictions, the law of negligence is in practice identical[16] in all, and the other relevant legislation applies throughout.[17] All nations of the United Kingdom may be cold enough to receive snow at certain times, creating the risk of frostbite,[18] and the NHS notes that sufferers include 'people who take part in winter and high-altitude sports', 'people with conditions that cause blood vessel damage or circulation problems', and, notably, 'anyone who works outdoors in harsh conditions for long periods of time'.[19] The NHS also provides that frostbite can typically occur just below zero degrees celsius.[20] Chainsaws are typically used outdoors, and are likely to be marketed as such. Aligning with the Sale of Goods Act 1979 and the Consumer Rights Act 2015, a reasonable fit for purpose would seem to include the use of the chainsaw outdoors, for long periods of time – one is unlikely to pull out the chainsaw for one branch's worth of work at a time.

[14] Consumer Protection Act 1987, s 3 (1–2).

[15] Consumer Rights Act 2015, s 65(1).

[16] See, eg, Scotland: the University of Dundee notes that while there are differences in the Scottish delict system in terms of nuisance and defamation, '[t]he Scots law of delict (tort) is not significantly different [to the English and Welsh system] when it comes to negligence'. 'English Law of Obligations module' (University of Dundee): dundee.ac.uk/module/lw31026#:~:text=English%20law%20has%20a%20very,areas%20of%20nuisance%20and%20defamation.

[17] Although Northern Ireland's is in part enacted separately: Consumer Protection (Northern Ireland) Order 1987 No 2049 (NI 20).

[18] Though similar cold burns can occur through other means.'Prevention of Aerosol Col Burns ("Frosty")' (Australia & New Zealand Burn Association): anzba.org.au/assets/ANZBA-Factsheet-Aerosol-SC-v2.pdf.

[19] 'Frostbite' (NHS) nhs.uk/conditions/frostbite/.

[20] ibid. At –0. 55 degrees celsius.

In terms of the Consumer Protection Act 1987, implementing the Product Liability Directive, the 'safety of the product' must be 'such as persons are generally entitled to expect'.[21] Non-AI chainsaws do not have these safety features, so the chainsaw in question is safer than them. However, the new safety features are explicitly part of the AI chainsaw marketing, and the AI chainsaw might be reasonably expected to be used in conditions below freezing. From this a court might reasonably conclude that the AI chainsaw has not provided the safety level that persons would be generally entitled to expect.

Lastly, '[a] trader cannot by a term of consumer contract or by a consumer notice exclude or restrict liability for death or personal injury resulting from negligence'.[22] Even if the AI company excluded all liability as part of the AI chainsaw purchase, such exclusion would not hold up.

In summary, a reasonable producer, bringing a product to a market that includes sub-zero temperatures, with features that aim to increase safety by very specific measures, likely would not be able to mount a due diligence defence by failing to account for the impact of sub-zero temperatures on their safety mechanism. If Bob was in the United Kingdom, the AI chainsaw company would be liable.

8.2.2. Product Liability and Consumer Protection in the United States

The United States is a federal republic and, as discussed in section 5.3.3, leaves liability specifics to each state – there is no federal law on product liability.[23] However, treatises such as the Restatements of the Law seek to inform legal audiences on general principles of common law.

First, the jurisdictional question whether cases can be heard in one state where a product has been manufactured in another. *Ford Motor Co v Montana Eighth Judicial District*,[24] a case heard by the Supreme Court relating to product liability lawsuits brought against Ford, provides that even where a product is designed and manufactured in other states or jurisdictions, cases can be brought in the state where the product itself is sold. This means that state-specific laws, such as, for example, Maine's law on strict liability applies to products sold in Maine:

> One who sells any goods or products in a defective condition unreasonably dangerous to the user or consumer or to his property is subject to liability for physical

[21] Consumer Protection Act 1987.

[22] Consumer Rights Act 2015, s 65(1).

[23] Although there is a US Department of Commerce, 'Model Uniform Products Liability Act', which attempts to encourage uniformity.

[24] *Ford Motor Co v Montana*, Eighth Judicial District 592 US.

> harm thereby caused to a person whom the manufacturer, seller or supplier might reasonably have expected to use, consume or be affected by the goods, or his property, if the seller is engaged in the business of selling such a product and it is expected to and does reach the user or consumer without significant change in the condition in which it is sold. This section applies although the seller has exercised all possible care in the preparation and sale of his product and the user or consumer has not bought the product from or entered into any contractual relation with the seller.[25]

Second, product liability claims in the United States 'can be based on negligence, strict liability, or breach of warranty of fitness', depending on the jurisdiction.[26] Product liability 'is generally considered a strict liability issue', whereby a plaintiff is liable simply if the product was defective. There are three types of product defects: design defects, which 'exist before the product is manufactured'; manufacturing defects, which 'occur during the construction or production of the item'; and defects in marketing which 'deal with improper instructions and failures to warn consumers of latent dangers in the product'.[27]

In the case of Bob and the AI chainsaw, the defect is either a design defect and/or a marketing defect. There is nothing to suggest that there was a distinct issue that occurred during the construction of the chainsaw; rather that the issue was inherent to the product's enabling AI. Alternatively, there may be a case made that the AI manufacturer did not provide proper warnings as to the potential dangers of the product.

Cornell's Legal Information Institute notes that '[e]ven when a product is defective due to a design flaw, some courts will use one of two tests to find that the defendant has no liability':

1. Risk-Utility Test
    1. the defendant is not liable for a design defect if evidence shows that the product's utility outweighs its inherent risk of harm.
2. Consumer Expectation Test
    1. a reasonable consumer would find the product defective when using the product in a reasonable manner
    2. if a reasonable consumer would not find the product to be defective even when using it in a reasonable manner, then the defendant is not liable, even if the product's design flaw resulted in injury.[28]

The American Law Institute's Restatement of the Law (Torts), third volume, provides, as noted by the court in *Bifolck v Philip Morris, Inc*,[29] that the risk-utility

[25] 14 Main Revised Statutes Annotated (MRSA) § 221.
[26] 'Products Liability' (Cornell Law School Legal Information Institute): law.cornell.edu/wex/products_liability.
[27] ibid.
[28] ibid.
[29] *Bifolck v Philip Morris USA Inc*, No 17-3927 (2d Cir 2019).

test 'recognizes that the risk-utility analysis is functionally equivalent to the analysis applicable to a negligence claim – each asks whether the manufacturer's design choice was reasonable in light of available alternatives or the risks presented by the product design'.[30]

Perkins notes that the Restatement abandoned the consumer expectation test in favour of the risk-utility analysis, requiring that the plaintiff prove a 'reasonable alternative design', and that 'in jurisdictions that follow the consumer expectations test, a product is defective in design if it fails to meet an ordinary consumer's reasonable expectations of safety'.[31]

Additionally, there is the Federal Trade Commission Act, which empowers the Federal Trade Commission to, in part,

> (a) prevent unfair methods of competition and unfair or deceptive acts or practices in or affecting commerce;
> (b) seek monetary redress and other relief for conduct injurious to consumers;
> (c) prescribe rules defining with specificity acts or practices that are unfair or deceptive, and establishing requirements designed to prevent such acts or practices;
> (d) gather and compile information and conduct investigations relating to the organization, business, practices, and management of entities engaged in commerce; and
> (e) make reports and legislative recommendations to Congress and the public.[32]

In essence, this appears to be primarily directed at consumer protection by ensuring that companies cannot deliberately deceive consumers.

In a nutshell, the US approach starts to sound very similar to the UK approach: asking whether the design choices were reasonable, and if the product matched an ordinary consumer's reasonable expectations of safety. There are potential additional changes by state: while Hawaii does indeed have snow, and a snowblower to boot,[33] there could be an argument that reasonable consumer expectations in Hawaii would not include using equipment in sub-zero temperatures, given that snow typically only occurs on one specific mountain. However, given that every other US state had snow in the 2023–24 winter season, this argument is unlikely to hold much water[34] anywhere else. A reasonable AI producer, working specifically on safety mechanisms that function on human contact, should likely have accounted for the effects of sub-zero temperatures on an activity carried out outside.

[30] ibid, I(2).

[31] C Perkins, 'The Increasing Acceptance of the Restatement (Third) Risk Utility Analysis in Design Defect Claims' (2004) 4 *Nevada Law Journal* 609, 614.

[32] 'Federal Trade Commission Act' (Federal Trade Commission): ftc.gov/legal-library/browse/statutes/federal-trade-commission-act.

[33] Gabe Lehman, 'Stunning photos show snow falling on Hawaii peaks' (*SFGate*, 1 December 2023): sfgate.com/hawaii/article/hawaii-snow-falls-maunakea-mauna-loa-18527778.php.

[34] Crystallised or otherwise.

8.2.3. AI Chainsaw Singapore

Let us assume that the AI chainsaw has not otherwise contravened Singaporean AI law, such as the Model Framework, and that the AI chainsaw passed preliminary verification with AI Verify.

Aligning with the blueprint, Singapore too has its roots in English common law tort, although naturally has its own distinct catalogue of precedent. It also takes into account cases from other common law countries.[35] *Thomson Reuters* notes that 'there is no single comprehensive legislation governing the manufacture, import, or supply of a defective product [; p]roduct liability claims are instead governed under various statutes and the common law', namely contract and tort law. Associate Professor at the National University of Singapore, Tay Swee Kian, notes that the case *Slim 10* 'enunciates' negligence law in Singapore.[36] In the case of *Slim 10*, the court identifies the following as the elements needed for a finding of negligence:

(a) foreseeability of damage
(b) proximity of relationship between the parties; and
(c) that it is fair, just and reasonable to impose such a duty.[37]

As discussed in section 2.1, these are the elements on which the English law of negligence is based.

Relevant statutes for products such as the AI chainsaw include the Sale of Goods Act 1999 and the Unfair Contract Terms Act 1994; and for consumer protection, the Consumer Protection (Fair Trading) Act 2003 and the Consumer Protection (Consumer Goods Safety Requirements) Regulations 2011.

Terms from these statutes will sound very familiar; namely those requiring that 'goods are of satisfactory quality if they meet the standard that a reasonable person would regard as satisfactory, taking into account any description of the goods, the price (if relevant) and all the other relevant circumstances',[38] and that '[a] person cannot by reference to any contract term or to a notice given to persons generally or to particular persons exclude or restrict his liability for death or personal injury resulting from negligence'.[39] The Consumer Protection (Fair Trading) Act 2003 supplies that the consumer may claim against the supplier for unfair practices: those by which a consumer might 'reasonably be deceived or misled'; false claims; or taking 'advantage of a consumer if the supplier knows or

[35] See, eg, the reference to *Leitz v Saskatoon Drug and Stationery Co and TC Distributors* (1970) Ltd (1980), 4 Sask R 35 (QB) in *TV Media Pte Ltd v De Cruz Andrea Heidi and Another Appeal* ('Slim 10') [2004] SGCA 29.

[36] CTS Kian, 'New Developments in Duty of Care: The Singapore Approach to Negligence in Product Liability after the *Slim 10* case' (2005) 26 *Business Law Review* 116.

[37] *TV Media Pte Ltd v De Cruz Andrea Heidi and Another Appeal* ('Slim 10') [2004] SGCA 29, para 44.

[38] Sale of Goods Act 1999, s 14(2)(A).

[39] Unfair Contract Terms Act 1994, s 2(1).

ought reasonably to know that the consumer' cannot protect their own interest or 'is not reasonably able to understand the character, nature, language or effect of the transaction or any matter related to the transaction'.[40] The Consumer Protection (Trade Descriptions and Safety Requirements) Act 1975, unsurprisingly, prohibits false trade descriptions, which:

> (i) means a trade description which by reason of anything contained in or omitted from the trade description is false or likely to mislead in a material respect as regards the goods to which it is applied or in connection with which it is used; and
>
> (ii) includes every alteration of a trade description whether by way of addition, effacement or otherwise which makes the description false or likely to mislead in a material respect.[41]

Lastly, the Consumer Protection (Consumer Goods Safety Requirements) Regulations 2011 requires consumer goods 'for which safety standards have been formulated or adopted and published' by the International Organisation for Standardisation (ISO), International Electrotechnical Commission (IEC), the European Committee for Standardisation, or ASTM International.[42]

In reverse order: let us assume that the details of the AI chainsaw have not yet been tackled by the noted standard bodies. The AI chainsaw company has not engaged in any sort of false trade descriptions, nor did they know or reasonably ought to know that they had taken advantage of the consumer. They have also not deliberately deceived or misled the consumer. The AI chainsaw company cannot contract out of personal injury resulting from negligence. We are then left with whether the goods were 'of satisfactory quality if they meet the standard that a reasonable person would regard as satisfactory, taking into account any description of the goods, the price (if relevant) and all the other relevant circumstances'.[43] Ultimately, the question is whether producers had matched the standard of a reasonable producer under the circumstances.

Stepping back from the legal question at hand, the obvious question is where, exactly, Bob managed to be working in such chilly conditions in Singapore. One guide company states that 'the lowest temperature recorded till date has been 19.4 degrees Celsius on January 31, 1934'.[44] Perhaps Bob is part of an initiative to create a climate-controlled habitat for arctic creatures in the Singapore Zoo. In any case, it becomes very difficult to argue that an AI producer should reasonably have foreseen that the AI chainsaw would encounter the specific factors, caused by severe temperatures, that would cause Bob to suffer. The AI chainsaw producer in Bob's

[40] Consumer Protection (Fair Trading) Act 2003, s 4.

[41] Consumer Protection (Trade Descriptions and Safety Requirements) Act 1975, s 5(a).

[42] Consumer Protection (Consumer Goods Safety Requirements) Regulations 2011, s 2(1).

[43] Sale of Goods Act 1999, s 14(2)(A).

[44] 'Weather and Climate in Singapore' (*GuideMeSingapore*): guidemesingapore.com/business-guides/immigration/get-to-know-singapore/weather-and-climate-in-singapore#:~:text=Based%20on%20climate%20records%20since,1998%20at%2036%20degrees%20Celsius.

case has likely 'matched the standard of a reasonable producer under the circumstances', so long as the problem at hand was not already known to the field.[45]

8.2.4. Product Liability and Consumer Protection in the European Union

The EU of course has the potential inclusion of the EU AI Act, depending on when the case is brought. While unlikely to be included in the initial list of high-risk AI systems, the EU AI Act would in principle define the AI chainsaw to be high risk '[i]n order to ensure a consistent and high level of protection of public interests as regards health, safety and fundamental rights'.[46] 'Additionally, the chainsaw would likely be considered high risk given that the AI system is 'intended to be used as a safety component of a product', and that it would need to 'undergo a third-party conformity assessment'.[47] Datasets for training, validation and testing are required to be 'relevant, sufficiently representative, and to the best extent possible free of errors and complete in view of the intended purpose of the system'.[48] Hindsight provides that this dataset should have contained more data, such as trees in a range of climactic conditions, but while this would certainly be a consideration for future assessments, it might be argued to be the 'state of the art' at the time of training.

The Act requires that each Member State establish a notified body which will perform conformity assessments. Let us assume that the AI chainsaw has successfully passed the conformity assessment stage as a high-risk AI.

The EU AI Act notes in Preamble 9 that 'harmonised rules laid down in this Regulation should apply across sectors and, in line with the New Legislative Framework, should be without prejudice to existing Union law … [including, among others] product safety'. AI is subject to the revised Product Liability Directive (PLD), although the data it employs is not. As discussed in section 5.3.2, in the long term this will likely raise specific questions as to which elements of an AI constitute its data. For the moment, let us assume that the separability of the AI and its data is not at issue.

The PLD provides that a producer is liable where a product is defective, and that '[a] product is defective when it does not provide the safety which a person is entitled to expect, taking all circumstances into account'.[49] The PLD

[45] Such as if the incident occurred first in a snowy jurisdiction.

[46] Regulation (EU) 2024/… of the European Parliament and of the Council of… laying down harmonised rules on artificial intelligence and amending Regulations (EC) No 300/2008, (EU) No 167/2013, (EU) No 168/2013, (EU) 2018/858, (EU) 2018/1139 and (EU) 2019/2144 and Directives 2014/90/EU, (EU) 2016/797 and (EU) 2020/1828 (Artificial Intelligence Act) Preamble (7).

[47] ibid, Art 6(1)(a)–(b).

[48] ibid, Preamble (67).

[49] 'Proposal for a directive of the European Parliament and of the Council on adapting non-contractual civil liability rules to artificial intelligence' (AI Liability Directive) (2022) COM.

also provides defences for development risks and the state of the art: that 'the producer could not reasonably have been expected to discover the defect given the state of scientific and technical knowledge at the time',[50] and that the defect was not discoverable when the product was put into circulation,[51] respectively.

The 'defect' analysis would follow similar lines to that of the United Kingdom; namely that it seems a reasonable expectation that the AI be safe to use in sub-zero temperatures in the EU single market, which has a number of climates that would be in areas falling below freezing. This encompasses a level of the development risks and state of the art defences: that the producer *could* reasonably have been expected to discover the defect as EU temperatures have not suddenly and drastically changed to include cold temperatures. While the defect is certainly obscure, in that it is a specific combination of circumstances, it was in fact discoverable at the time the product was put into circulation: the defect was as discoverable and present at the time of release as it was during Bob's incident. Additionally, the EU AI Act requires that the dataset for the AI 'take into account, to the extent required by their intended purpose, the features, characteristics or elements that are particular to the specific geographical, contextual, behavioural or functional setting which the AI system is intended to be used'.[52] Moreover, the fact that the flesh sensor would always override the density sensor would in most instances be an acceptable outcome, but could indeed have been better handled by instead having the AI chainsaw stop where there was a mismatch between the two – much like the Tempe Arizona vehicle's inability to differentiate between a cyclist and a pedestrian should have resulted in the vehicle stopping, not waiting to decide the nature of the obstacle.

We then come to the AI Liability Directive. Again, this Directive does not and cannot control Member States' liability approaches, although it does attempt to 'prevent the emergence of fragmented AI-specific adaptations of national civil liability rules'.[53]

The Directive itself 'covers national liability claims mainly based on the fault of any person with a view of compensating any type of damage and any type of victim',[54] and focuses on 'the disclosure of evidence on high-risk artificial intelligence (AI) systems to enable a claimant to substantiate a non-contractual fault-based civil law claim for damages; [and] the burden of proof in the case of non-contractual fault-based civil law claims'.[55] It does so by lowering a barrier

[50] Council Directive 85/374/EEC of 25 July 1985 on the approximation of the laws, regulations and administrative provisions of the Member States concerning liability for defective products [1985] OJ L210/29 (Product Liability Directive).

[51] ibid.

[52] EU AI Act (n 46) Preamble (67).

[53] Tambiama Madiega, 'European Parliament Briefing: EU Legislation in Progress – Artificial intelligence liability directive' (2023 European Parliamentary Research Service): www.europarl.europa.eu/RegData/etudes/BRIE/2023/739342/EPRS_BRI(2023)739342_EN.pdf,5 citing AI Liability Directive (n 49).

[54] Draft Liability Directive (n 49).

[55] ibid, Art 1(1).

between proving the causal link between fault and the AI output where certain conditions are met, conditions that require the AI producer to have certain portions of the AI Act. As discussed in section 5.3.2, these requirements essentially mean that the lowered barrier is only present if the AI system can be proved at fault; that it is reasonably likely that the fault has resulted in the questionable AI output; and that the claimant can show that the AI output gave rise to the damage.

For the current case, we must consider the meaning of fault, and whether it has been demonstrated. Given that the AI application at hand is specifically a safety feature, it seems a reasonable argument that a fault has occurred. However, there will certainly be cases where this is a harder element to determine, such as in medical cases, where harm occurring does not inherently mean that there has been a fault or defect. This is why chapter seven and the regulatory blueprint as a whole argue for a reverse burden of proof within the bounds of *res ipsa loquitur* – where there is a clear factual connection between the AI and harm caused, there should be a rebuttable assumption that the harm is caused by the AI. The EU Liability Directive does not go anywhere near as far, and while Bob is likely to be able to successfully argue that the safety feature had failed, other claimants with more complex cases may not be so fortunate, and may need to spend a great deal of time, money and effort to show the fault, assuming they can get sufficient information at all.

The second portion asks whether the fault has influenced the output of the AI. This is likely a reasonable argument in Bob's case, as it is the combination of safety mechanisms that has clearly failed, caused by competing outputs between the flesh and density sensors. Again, however, other cases may not be so straightforward, particularly without the technical knowledge that may be needed to disentangle a complex AI's inner workings.

Third, the Directive asks whether it has been demonstrated that the output produced by the failure of the AI gave rise to damage. As is becoming a refrain: yes, Bob likely can, but this may be needlessly complex in other cases. At this stage, and only at this stage, would the presumption of causality that the Directive proposes arise.

Ultimately, these three questions and the specific approach of the EU Member States brings us to those questions asked of the scenario initially: whether harm was prima facie caused by AI, etc. While Member States may have different specific heads of liability,[56] the fact that the EU Member States have agreed to adopt

[56] The French civil code 'does not contain … a general clause of fault liability', but rather sections of the code 'are treated as if they constituted a general clause of fault-based liability, ie, liability of persons and other actors (enterprises, etc), for intentional and negligent causes of damage'; whereas German civil code, conversely, has three areas of liability: general fault-based liability, culpable breach of statutory duty, and culpability for intentional causation of damage to public good (good morals)'. G Brüggemeier, 'The Civilian Law of Delict: A Comparative and Historical Analysis' (2020) 7 *European Journal of Comparative Law and Governance* 339.

the EU AI Act and may in future adopt the EU Liability Directive means that there will likely be a specific liability heading under which consumers may bring a case. Additionally, as discussed, consumers will not in any way be barred from existing rights, such as those under the PLD. Bob will in all likelihood be compensated for the AI chainsaw failure.

8.2.5. Negligence versus Product and Consumer Protection Law

What the product liability and consumer legislation applications demonstrate, by jurisdiction, is that they ultimately have similar conclusions to negligence liability. While the European Union has taken a more specific look as to how evidence and access to information may be treated, the end result is the same. This makes sense: the evolution of regulation does not happen in a vacuum, and both negligence liability and the blueprint specifically have evolved with complementary legislation in mind. However, we must consider one very important factor about the test case: the AI chainsaw is an embodied AI product. It directly and physically affects the world around it. There is a much, much larger ecosystem of AI that does not impact the world directly. This would make consumer protection and product liability in such cases considerably more nebulous: we have a much better idea of what a chainsaw should achieve than a software program with novel harms. It is much more conceptually difficult to assess the 'safety of a product' or a 'use in a reasonable manner' of something without a direct physical presence. Risk-utility tests become all the more difficult for a non-expert to apply, even in comparison to embodied AI as a baseline. The EU's updates to the Product Liability Directive now state that AI is a product, which should provide some level of clarity at a base level, but not how to answer the questions invoked by stating that even non-embodied AI is a product, particularly where there will be many parties in an AI production chain.

The blueprint, however, has the potential to fill this gap: it leverages an emphasis on due diligence that product and consumer liability do not. This is not to say that consumers are left unprotected, but that it incentivises producers to internally assess design decisions prior to harm occurring. This means that there is not only a mechanism for those harmed to be compensated – in a way that is ultimately not dissimilar to product and consumer liability – but for that harm to be avoided in the first place. Producers must explain what tests were done and why: which metrics were chosen, and why these were the most suitable metrics. They must consciously be aware of the need to defend why other methods were not chosen: not just that those metrics chosen best aligned with the purpose of the product, but also why certain methods were chosen over others – others that might be, for example, more explainable. This is an aspect that absolute liability does not incentivise: absolute liability incentivises avoiding being caught; building to the test, rather than the intent of the test; and ultimately to make cost-benefit decisions over harm decisions. Rewarding producers for designing to the purpose of regulation incentivises innovation, while simultaneously providing pressure on that innovation to be defensibly produced.

In essence, the blueprint poses a bridge between the intended functions of regulation – the prevention of harm – and the functions of liability – to compensate when harm occurs. The better the former, the less the need for the latter. This turns the hurdle of foreseeability for obligations in advance, and potentially without context, into a benefit for the consumer and society as a whole: the producer is forced to confront as wide a range of circumstances as they can produce and think through the design process with these in mind. It showcases what is potentially a detriment of AI – the inability to handle context – against the human ability to provide explanations without grounding in retrospect. AI does not think. An AI is a series of statistics in a trenchcoat. Yet these statistics are not random, and it is crucial that regulation reinforces the ground truth that there are humans deciding which statistics are used, how they are used, and that we leverage that truth to stop harm before it occurs.

9

Conclusion

This book has examined how we should regulate AI causing accidental death. It makes two fundamental assumptions:

1. Regulation must be based on a clear understanding of how AI works – more specifically, how AI makes decisions.
2. Regulation must be capable of responding when harm occurs but must also incentivise the production of as safe AI as possible.

Chapter two, 'Drivers, Doctors, Devices', explains that no matter how liability is expressed in law, it is at heart based on fault. Fault, in turn, is based on the ideas of foreseeability of risks, and what contextually reasonable steps can be taken to mitigate those risks. In order to attribute fault-based liability, three aspects are required: an explanation of how the harm was caused; what harms were foreseeable; and what mitigatory steps were taken to avoid those harms.

This need for explanations is an obstacle because any complex AI is difficult to explain, particularly in advance of an incident which might lead to a liability claim. Fortunately, technology can assist us here. Chapter three, 'Explainable AI (XAI)', details how the technical side of the AI process can begin to provide the explanations needed for fault, although on a statistical rather than certainty level. Explanations are also tools for regulators, in that regulators can require explanations both before and after an AI is placed on the market. While the regulatory understanding of reasonableness comes from the build-up of expectations over time, XAI tools can help bridge the gap between judges and regulators on one side – opening the black box – and technologists on the other – so that each can understand how to develop safe and responsible innovation practices. These approaches allow for societally beneficial AI, where producers can show their work in terms of due diligence with regard to risk identification and mitigation.

Once we can explain why an AI might cause, or has caused, harm, we need to decide what the basis should be for regulating to prevent harm and allocating liability if it occurs. Chapter four, 'Law Using XAI', argues that AI that can cause accidental death or serious harm need to be at least as safe as the human systems they replace and need to avoid creating new risks such as rogue or unpredictable decisions. Assessing these matters requires appropriate standards, and those standards are of a reasonable human (undertaking that task), and of a reasonable producer (creating that AI). The former is assessed in direct comparison – whether the action taken would be considered reasonable if done by the human counterpart; whereas the latter is a question of prediction of risk and appropriate safeguarding – what the producer knew, ought to have known or anticipated and what they ought to have tested for in the AI creation process. The producer must clear both hurdles, but may call on their own logged evidence, including XAI explanations, to show that they have acted with all due diligence.

How far has law and regulation gone in this respect? Chapter five, 'Current Regulatory Approaches', examines several of the jurisdictions taking on the challenge of regulating AI. The most active[1] in this regulatory arena are Singapore, the European Union, the United States and the United Kingdom. Each of these jurisdictions have taken on different goals and treatments of risk and harm in structuring regulation, but where regulation is present, two commonalities are present: they focus on risk identification and mitigation; and they engage in co-regulation – regulation in discussion with the regulated. The difference between jurisdictional approaches can be explained by their different approaches to economic considerations and the need to protect individuals' rights and safety. While the European Union has begun to address liability directly, it is the only jurisdiction to do so, and it does not yet address liability in terms of what negligence might mean.

Chapter six, 'Sectoral Regulation', analyses sectoral regulation, which is where we might expect to find more detail about liability. Sectoral regulation will and already is forming a crucial part of AI regulation, for the key reason that sectoral regulators have specialist knowledge. Existing sectoral regulation already covers issues such as technology approval and insurance, and often validates technical standards. These aim at harm prevention. However, such regulation has a narrow scope based on the known risks in the field. AI will gradually permeate more and more aspects of human life and have the potential to cause harm in ways we cannot yet predict. We cannot specifically regulate every sector of human activity, so there is a need for more general regulation of AI-caused harm.

What, then, is the way forward? Based on the principles set out in chapter four, illuminated by the progress already made in the jurisdictions examined, chapter seven, 'Blueprint for Liability Regulation', sets out a blueprint for how AI causing accidental death should be regulated based on risk foresight and mitigation. It explains how to structure regulation to incentivise safe, explainable AI, and provide a way to deal with incidents when they occur, without formalising standards that fossilise the state of the art too early. This high-level structure should flow down into sectoral legislation, shaping it and setting out its high-level principles but leaving the sector-specific risks to be dealt with by specific provisions (eg, flexible standards) at that level.

[1] And accessible in large part in English – China is active in the AI regulatory sphere, but much less accessible in terms of English sources and commentary.

This blueprint makes several important contributions to guide national lawmakers and regulators. First, it establishes a working definition of what fault in the case of AI should look like, based on the 'reasonable human counterpart' and 'reasonable producer' standards. None of the jurisdictions discussed have yet defined fault, either through active avoidance of the issue as too difficult, or because doing so might upset current policy or political trade-offs. Second, the blueprint integrates XAI as a necessary tool for law and regulation, to be used by both the regulator and the regulated: in investigation, as part of responsible development, and in defence of liability. Third, it navigates the trade-offs between incentivising innovation and prioritising safety by allowing for a high-bar due diligence defence based on the knowledge of the field. Fourth, while multiple jurisdictions have created or proposed a central AI regulator, an inquisitorial body and its proposed functions have hitherto been lacking for AI.[2] I argue that this is a necessary addition, given the specialist knowledge needed to investigate. Fifth, the blueprint proposes a novel harm classification that is based on how the AI actually works, and the foreseeability of the consequences based on the knowability of input and harm – known/unknown, and high/low/unknown, respectively. This allows for more targeted regulation, such as requiring high/unknown harms AI to meet preconditions before market entry such as disclosing the key decisions made in developing the AI,[3] and integration of design considerations such as scope control. This would mean less unnecessary regulation of AI that does not need such intervention. Sixth and finally, the blueprint can be layered onto any jurisdiction.

This integrative potential can be seen in the UK government's July 2022 policy statement on its approach to AI governance in which it engaged in promising new directions of regulatory adaptability.[4] Although several areas of expansion were dialled back to an extent in the 2023 White Paper, the blueprint not only meets but exceeds these guidelines, particularly in focusing on high risk, providing cross-sectoral principles based on the distinct characteristics of AI, and maintaining proportionate adaptability. Where more splintered jurisdictional approaches such as the United States give states the power to determine liability, regulation at the federal system can nonetheless provide model rules, particularly in inter-state commerce – something that producers will find highly desirable. The United States also has a history of federal level investigative bodies, such as the Federal Aviation Administration (FAA) or Federal Aviation Administration's office of Accident Investigation, so might find it appropriate to follow the blueprint in at least that respect.

[2] Although they have been proposed for sectoral uses, including automated driving. See, eg, 'Responsible Innovation in Self-Driving Vehicles' (GOV.UK, 19 August 2022): gov.uk/government/publications/responsible-innovation-in-self-driving-vehicles/responsible-innovation-in-self-driving-vehicles.

[3] See, eg, section 7.2.1.

[4] 'Establishing a Pro-Innovation Approach to Regulating AI' (GOV.UK, 20 July 2022): gov.uk/government/publications/establishing-a-pro-innovation-approach-to-regulating-ai/establishing-a-pro-innovation-approach-to-regulating-ai-policy-statement.

The blueprint does not solve every liability challenge that AI will pose. First and foremost, as discussed throughout, it looks specifically at physical harms rather than more insidious and difficult to discover systemic harms. However, within the realm of high-risk physical harms, it is structured such that currently unanticipated harms are still caught: the blueprint places AI whose harm levels are unknown in a category that requires producers to engage with due diligence responsible production, but without assuming that all harms can be predicted. The blueprint does not suggest that the general regulator engage in standard setting, but that it benefit from expertise both in the field and by sectoral governance bodies, who are much better placed to do so; nor does it state which XAI tools should be used to produce a due diligence defence: it requires producers to use those tools which are most appropriate, and show that they are, in fact, the most appropriate. The standards for producers do not require producers to be perfect, as the AI's human counterparts are also not required to be perfect, but places additional expectations on the producers in order to maintain as high safety standards as possible.

Lastly, chapter eight, 'Test Case Study', details how the blueprint could be applied in practice to the four jurisdictions facing a hypothetical case. While the treatment of the case will differ by jurisdiction, it is remarkable how similar the criteria ultimately are: while common law jurisdictions such as the United Kingdom differ from civil law systems, shared (historical) features such as the Product Liability Directive mean that there is considerable overlap in what remedies are available to victims. Each ultimately asks what is reasonable of society to expect, and the producer to provide.

It is difficult indeed to predict the future, and tricky to presume what may be next. Yet perhaps we can begin to see the outlines. Donald Michie's neural network of matchboxes, or MENACE, 'learned' to play tic tac toe in the 1960s.[5] While one would not have sat down next to the 300 matchbox MENACE and predicted the use of neural networks in everything from medical diagnostics[6] to identifying pastries[7] – sometimes with the same AI – perhaps one might have wondered what challenge might be solved next. While it would not be until 2016 that Deepmind's AlphaGo would beat Go champion Lee Se-dol,[8] the game was

[5] ODSC-Open Data Science, 'How 300 Matchboxes Learned to Play Tic-Tac-Toe Using MENACE' (*Medium*, 23 October 2018):odsc.medium.com/how-300-matchboxes-learned-to-play-tic-tac-toe-using-menace-35e0e4c29fc.

[6] Y Kumar et al, 'Artificial Intelligence in Disease Diagnosis: A Systematic Literature Review, Synthesizing Framework and Future Research Agenda' (2022) *Journal of Ambient Intelligence and Humanized Computing* 1: ncbi.nlm.nih.gov/pmc/articles/PMC8754556/.

[7] 'An AI Built to Tell Apart Pastries Was Great at Spotting Cancers' (*Futurism*): futurism.com/the-byte/ai-pastries-cancers.

[8] James Vincent 'Former Go Champion Beaten by DeepMind Retires after Declaring AI Invincible' (*The Verge*, 27 November 2019): theverge.com/2019/11/27/20985260/ai-go-alphago-lee-se-dol-retired-deepmind-defeat.

already afoot.[9] This must shape our legislation: we can see the outlines of what may be ahead, but not what innovative leaps will be made along the way. We know some of the harms that will occur, but not precisely why – if we knew the why, we could prevent them. Most of all, however, we know what we must protect: the very reason why we allow inevitable harms to occur – to chase, over time, the preservation, protection and progress of humanity. To save progressively more lives as knowledge improves. To never have the same impact twice. To stop, once and for all, the metaphorical trolley.

[9] Or perhaps a metre, depending on one's preferred system of measurement.

BIBLIOGRAPHY

Electronic Material

'2020 Autonomous Vehicles Readiness Index', KPMG International 70: kpmg.com/xx/en/home/insights/2020/06/autonomous-vehicles-readiness-index.html#download.

'4 Reasons For Loss of Taste' (Atlanta ENT Institute/Ear, Nose and Throat Specialists in Georgia, 19 September 2019): entinstitute.com/4-reasons-for-loss-of-taste/.

'A Guide to Job Redesign in the Age of AI': file.go.gov.sg/ai-guide-to-jobredesign.pdf.

'About the AI Safety Summit 2023' (GOV.UK): gov.uk/government/topical-events/ai-safety-summit-2023/about.

'Access to Medical Treatments (Innovation) Act' (MRC Medical Research Council, 11 September 2018): mrc.ukri.org/about/policy/mrc-position-statements/access-to-medical-treatments-innovation-act/.

'Access to Medical Treatments (Innovation) Bill Will Not Serve Healthcare Professionals' (*Pharmaceutical Journal*): pharmaceutical-journal.com/article/opinion/access-to-medical-treatments-innovation-bill-will-not-serve-healthcare-professionals.

'An AI Built to Tell Apart Pastries Was Great at Spotting Cancers' (*Futurism*): futurism.com/the-byte/ai-pastries-cancers.

'An overview of national AI strategies' (2018): medium.com/politics-ai/an-overview-of-national-ai-strategies-2a70ec6edfd.

'Annex A Fact Sheet – Open sourcing of AI Verify and set up of AI Verify Foundation': imda.gov.sg/-/media/imda/files/news-and-events/media-room/media-releases/2023/06/7-jun---ai-annoucements---annex-a.pdf.

anzba.org.au/assets/ANZBA-Factsheet-Aerosol-SC-v2.pdf.

'Artificial Intelligence, Automation, and the Economy' (Executive Office of the President): obamawhitehouse.archives.gov/sites/whitehouse.gov/files/documents/Artificial-Intelligence-Automation-Economy.PDF.

'Artificial Intelligence/Machine Learning (AI/ML)-Based Software as a Medical Device (SaMD) Action Plan' (US Food and Drug Administration, January 2021): fda.gov/media/145022/download.

'Artificial Intelligence Commission Report' (US Chamber of Commerce, 9 March 2023): uschamber.com/technology/artificial-intelligence-commission-report.

'Artificial Intelligence' (*Villains Wiki*): villains.fandom.com/wiki/Category:Artificial_Intelligence.

'Automated Cars – Technical Specifications' (European Commission, 5 May 2022): ec.europa.eu/info/law/better-regulation/have-your-say/initiatives/12152-Automated-cars-technical-specifications_en.

'Automated Deep Learning May Allow Doctors to Develop AI Systems for Healthcare' (Moorfields Eye Hospital NHS Foundation Trust, 2019): moorfields.nhs.uk/news/automated-deep-learning-may-allow-doctors-develop-ai-systems-healthcare.

'Automated Vehicles', Law Commission: lawcom.gov.uk/project/automated-vehicles/.

'Automated Vehicles', Summary of joint report: s3-eu-west-2.amazonaws.com/cloud-platform-e218f50a4812967ba1215eaecede923f/uploads/sites/30/2022/01/AV-Summary-25-01-22-2.pdf.

'Autonomous Vehicle Testing Permit Holders' (California DMV): dmv.ca.gov/portal/vehicle-industry-services/autonomous-vehicles/autonomous-vehicle-testing-permit-holders/.

'Autonomous vehicles – Part 1: Basic behaviour' (Singapore Standards): singaporestandardseshop.sg/Product/SSPdtDetail/df6492de-c92b-435c-a979-d9ad211621c3.

'Autonomous Vehicles/Self-Driving Vehicles Enacted Legislation' (National Conference of State Legislatures, 18 February 2020): ncsl.org/research/transportation/autonomous-vehicles-self-driving-vehicles-enacted-legislation.aspx.

'Autopilot': www.tesla.com/autopilot.

'Benz Patent Motor Car: The First Automobile (1885–1886)' (Daimler): group.mercedes-benz.com/company/tradition/company-history/1885-1886.html.

'Blueprint for an AI Bill of Rights/OSTP', White House: whitehouse.gov/ostp/ai-bill-of-rights/.

'California Axes Self-Driving Car Rule Limiting Liability for Crashes' (*Engadget*): engadget.com/2017-12-02-california-axes-self-driving-car-rule-limiting-liability.html.

'California Regulators Nix Rules Limiting Carmaker Liability' *AP NEWS* (6 May 2021): apnews.com/article/north-america-technology-business-california-mi-state-wire-ce707c88718446c5b9b93b3180c70e6e.

California Senate Floor Analyses, 'Vehicles: autonomous vehicles: safety and performance requirements' (2011–2012) SB-1298: leginfo.legislature.ca.gov/faces/billAnalysisClient.xhtml?bill_id=201120120SB1298.

Center for Devices and Radiological Health, 'Artificial Intelligence and Machine Learning (AI/ML)-Enabled Medical Devices' (US Food and Drug Adminsitration, 2021): fda.gov/medical-devices/software-medical-device-samd/artificial-intelligence-and-machine-learning-aiml-enabled-medical-devices.

—— 'Classify Your Medical Device' (US Food and Drug Administration, 22 October 2020): fda.gov/medical-devices/overview-device-regulation/classify-your-medical-device.

—— 'Overview of Device Regulation' (US Food and Drug Administration, 9 April 2020): www.fda.gov/medical-devices/device-advice-comprehensive-regulatory-assistance/overview-device-regulation.

'Overview of Medical Device Classification and Reclassification' (US Food and Drug Administration, 2018): fda.gov/about-fda/cdrh-transparency/overview-medical-device-classification-and-reclassification.

'Companion to the Model AI Governance Framework – Implementation and Self-Assessment Guide for Organizations': pdpc.gov.sg/-/media/Files/PDPC/PDF-Files/Resource-for-Organisation/AI/SGIsago.pdf.

'Compendium of Use Cases: Practical Illustrations of the Model AI Governance Framework (Volume I)': pdpc.gov.sg/-/media/Files/PDPC/PDF-Files/Resource-for-Organisation/AI/SGAIGovUseCases.pdf.

'Connected Automated Driving/ | Regulations and Policies' (*Connected automated driving.eu*, 12 December 2023): connectedautomateddriving.eu/regulation-and-policies/.

'Consultation on New Guidelines for the Application of ISO 14971 to AI and ML' (*Compliance Navigator*, 21 June 2021): compliancenavigator.bsigroup.com/en/medicaldeviceblog/consultation-on-new-guidelines-for-the-application-of-iso-14971-to-artificial-intelligence-and-machine-learning/.

'Digital Regulation: Driving Growth and Unlocking Innovation' (GOV.UK, 10 October 2023): gov.uk/government/publications/digital-regulation-driving-growth-and-unlocking-innovation.

digital-strategy.ec.europa.eu/en/policies/regulatory-framework-ai#:~:text=The%20European%20AI%20Office%2C%20established,dignity%2C%20rights%2C%20and%20trust.

'Driverless Testing of Autonomous Vehicles': dmv.ca.gov/portal/dmv/detail/vr/autonomous/auto.

'Duty of Care/Advice Guides | Royal College of Nursing' (Royal College of Nursing, 4 December 2015): rcn.org.uk/get-help/rcn-advice/duty-of-care.

'English Law of Obligations module' (University of Dundee): dundee.ac.uk/module/lw31026#:~:text=English%20law%20has%20a%20very,areas%20of%20nuisance%20and%20defamation.

'Establishing a Pro-Innovation Approach to Regulating AI' (GOV.UK, 20 July 2022): gov.uk/government/publications/establishing-a-pro-innovation-approach-to-regulating-ai/establishing-a-pro-innovation-approach-to-regulating-ai-policy-statement.

'EU Legislation and UK Law': legislation.gov.uk/eu-legislation-and-uk-law.

'Europe on the Move: Questions & Answers on the Commission's initiatives' (European Commission, 17 May 2018): ec.europa.eu/commission/presscorner/detail/pt/MEMO_18_3681.

'European Commission Adopts the "Delegated Act" for the Deployment of C-ITS' (*InterCor*, 14 March 2019): intercor-project.eu/european-commission-adopts-the-delegated-act-for-the-deployment-of-c-its/.

European Commission, 'AI Act' (*Shaping Europe's digital future*): digital-strategy.ec.europa.eu/en/policies/regulatory-framework-ai#:~:text=The%20European%20AI%20Office%2C%20established,dignity%2C%20rights%2C%20and%20trust.

—— 'White Paper on Artificial Intelligence: A European Approach to Excellence and Trust': commission.europa.eu/publications/white-paper-artificial-intelligence-european-approach-excellence-and-trust_en.

European Commission. Directorate General for Health and Food Safety, and others, *Patients' Rights in the European Union: Mapping Exercise: Final Report* (Publications Office 2016): data.europa.eu/doi/10.2875/751285.

European Commission Joint Research Centre, *Artificial Intelligence in EU Medical Device Legislation* (Publications Office, 2020): data.europa.eu/doi/10.2760/382730.

European Union, 'European Data Protection Supervisor Glossary': edps.europa.eu/data-protection/data-protection/glossary/d_en.

—— 'Types of Legislation': european-union.europa.eu/institutions-law-budget/law/types-legislation_en.

'Executive Order 12859: Maintaining American Leadership in Artificial Intelligence' (White House, 11 February 2019): web.archive.org/web/20190212000146/https://www.whitehouse.gov/presidential-actions/executive-order-maintaining-american-leadership-artificial-intelligence/.

'Executive Order 13859: Maintaining American Leadership in Artificial Intelligence' (White House, 11 February 2019): trumpwhitehouse.archives.gov/presidential-actions/executive-order-maintaining-american-leadership-artificial-intelligence/.

'Executive Orders', Bureau of Justice Assistance, US Department of Justice: bja.ojp.gov/program/it/privacy-civil-liberties/authorities/executive-orders#:~:text=%E2%80%9CExecutive%20Orders%20(EOs)%20are,and%20statute%20(sometimes%20specified).

'Fact Sheet: AV Policy Section II: Model State Policy', US Department of Transportation: transportation.gov/AV/av-fact-sheet-model-state-policy.

'FACT SHEET: President Biden Issues Executive Order on Safe, Secure, and Trustworthy Artificial Intelligence' (White House, 30 October 2023) whitehouse.gov/briefing-room/statements-releases/2023/10/30/fact-sheet-president-biden-issues-executive-order-on-safe-secure-and-trustworthy-artificial-intelligence/.

'Federal Trade Commission Act' (Federal Trade Commission): ftc.gov/legal-library/browse/statutes/federal-trade-commission-act.

'Financial Conduct Authority' (GOV.UK): gov.uk/government/organisations/financial-conduct-authority.

'Frostbite' (NHS): nhs.uk/conditions/frostbite/.

'FTC Authorizes Compulsory Process for AI-related Products and Services' (Federal Trade Commission, 21 November 2023): ftc.gov/news-events/news/press-releases/2023/11/ftc-authorizes-compulsory-process-ai-related-products-services.

'FTC Chair Khan and Officials from DOJ, CFPB and EEOC Release Joint Statement on AI' (Federal Trade Commission, 25 April 2023): ftc.gov/news-events/news/press-releases/2023/04/ftc-chair-khan-officials-doj-cfpb-eeoc-release-joint-statement-ai.

'Future Risks of Frontier AI' (Government Office for Science, October 2023): assets.publishing.service.gov.uk/media/653bc393d10f3500139a6ac5/future-risks-of-frontier-ai-annex-a.pdf.

'General Purpose AI and the AI Act (Future of Life Institute, May 2022): artificialintelligenceact.eu/wp-content/uploads/2022/05/General-Purpose-AI-and-the-AI-Act.pdf.

'Government Paves the Way for Self-Driving Vehicles on UK Roads' (GOV.UK): gov.uk/government/news/government-paves-the-way-for-self-driving-vehicles-on-uk-roads.

'How Google's Autonomous Car Passed the First U.S. State Self-Driving Test' (*IEEE Spectrum*, 10 September 2014): spectrum.ieee.org/how-googles-autonomous-car-passed-the-first-us-state-selfdriving-test.

imda.gov.sg/resources/press-releases-factsheets-and-speeches/press-releases/2023/singapore-launches-ai-verify-foundation-to-shape-the-future-of-international-ai-standards-through-collaboration.

imda.gov.sg/resources/press-releases-factsheets-and-speeches/press-releases/2024/public-consult-model-ai-governance-framework-genai.

'In Which State Can You Sue and Which Law Applies?' (National Contact Point for cross-border healthcare): eu-patienten.de/en/behandlung_deutschland/behandlungsfehler/klageort_und_anwendbares_recht/klageort_und_anwendbares_recht.jsp.

'It's Here: The Top 10 Greatest Cyborg and AI Villains' (*Horror Made*, 21 August 2015): horrormade.com/2015/08/20/its-here-the-top-10-greatest-cyborg-and-ai-villians/.

'Joint Media Release by the Land Transport Authority, Enterprise Singapore, Standards Development Organisation & Singapore Standards Council – Singapore Develops Provisional National Standards to Guide Development of Fully Autonomous Vehicles', Land Transport Authority: lta.gov.sg/content/ltagov/en/newsroom/2019/1/2/joint-media-release-by-the-land-transport-authority-lta-enterprise-singapore-standards-development-organisation-singapo.html.

'Joint Press Release: New Collaboration Under the U.S.–Singapore Partnership for Growth and Innovation (PGI)', US Department of Commerce: commerce.gov/news/press-releases/2022/03/joint-press-release-new-collaboration-under-us-singapore-partnership.

'Klobuchar, Thune, Commerce Committee Colleagues Introduce Bipartisan AI Bill to Strengthen Accountability and Boost Innovation' (United States Senator Amy Klobuchar, 15 November 2023): klobuchar.senate.gov/public/index.cfm/2023/11/klobuchar-thune-commerce-committee-colleagues-introduce-bipartisan-ai-bill-to-strengthen-accountability-and-boost-innovation#:~:text=The%20bipartisan%20legislation%20establishes%20a,highest%2Dimpact%20applications%20of%20AI.

Land Transport Authority, 'Autonomous Vehicles': lta.gov.sg/content/ltagov/en/industry_innovations/technologies/autonomous_vehicles.html.

Law Commission, *Automated Vehicles: joint report*: www.lawcom.gov.uk/project/automated-vehicles/.

'Legal Obligations of Drivers and Riders' (GOV.UK): gov.uk/legal-obligations-drivers-riders.

'Legislation Related to Artificial Intelligence', National Conference of State Legislatures (31 Janaury 2023): ncsl.org/research/telecommunications-and-information-technology/2020-legislation-related-to-artificial-intelligence.aspx.

'Medical Devices' (European Medicines Agency, 26 November 2018): ema.europa.eu/en/human-regulatory/overview/medical-devices.

'Memorandum for the Heads of Executive Departments and Agencies' (Executive Office of the President, 2018) M-18-22: whitehouse.gov/wp-content/uploads/2018/10/m10-32.pdf.

'Model Artificial Intelligence Governance Framework Second Edition': pdpc.gov.sg/-/media/files/pdpc/pdf-files/resource-for-organisation/ai/sgmodelaigovframework2.pdf.

'Moral Machine' (*Moral Machine*): moralmachine.mit.edu.

'National AI Strategy' (GOV.UK, 18 December 2022): gov.uk/government/publications/national-ai-strategy.

'National Artificial Intelligence Advisory Committee (NAIAC)' (*NIST*, 1 March 2024): nist.gov/itl/national-artificial-intelligence-advisory-committee-naiac.

National Research Council (US) Division of Health Promotion and Disease Prevention, 'Liability for the Production and Sale of Vaccines' in *Vaccine Supply and Innovation* (National Academies Press (US) 1985): www.ncbi.nlm.nih.gov/books/NBK216813/.

'New Liability Rules on Products and AI to Protect Consumers' (European Commission, 22 September 2022): ec.europa.eu/commission/presscorner/detail/en/ip_22_5807.

'New UK Initiative to Shape Global Standards for Artificial Intelligence' (GOV.UK, 12 January 2022): gov.uk/government/news/new-uk-initiative-to-shape-global-standards-for-artificial-intelligence.

ODSC-Open Data Science, 'How 300 Matchboxes Learned to Play Tic-Tac-Toe Using MENACE' (*Medium*, 23 October 2018): odsc.medium.com/how-300-matchboxes-learned-to-play-tic-tac-toe-using-menace-35e0e4c29fc.

'Our Legal System' (Singapore Ministry of Law): mlaw.gov.sg/about-us/our-legal-system/.

'Our Principles' (*Google AI*): ai.google/principles/.

'Oversight of A.I: Rules for Artificial Intelligence' (US Senate Committee on the Judiciary, 16 March 2023): judiciary.senate.gov/committee-activity/hearings/oversight-of-ai-rules-for-artificial-intelligence.

'Oxford Bus Company Crash: Second House Evacuated' *BBC News* (8 October 2021): bbc.com/news/uk-england-oxfordshire-58846457.

Personal Data Protection Commission Singapore (PDPC), 'Discussion Paper on Artificial Intelligence (AI) and Personal Data – Fostering Responsible Development and Adoption of AI' (5 June 2018).

—— 'PDPC/Singapore's Approach to AI Governance': pdpc.gov.sg/Help-and-Resources/2020/01/Model-AI-Governance-Framework.

—— 'Singapore's Approach to AI Governance': pdpc.gov.sg/help-and-resources/2020/01/model-ai-governance-framework.

—— 'PDPC/Who We Are' (*Who we are*): pdpc.gov.sg/Who-We-Are.

'Policy paper: A pro-innovation approach to AI regulation' (GOV.UK, 3 August 2023): www.gov.uk/government/publications/ai-regulation-a-pro-innovation-approach/white-paper.

'Preparing for the future of artificial intelligence' (Executive Office of the President National Science and Technology Council Committee on Technology): obamawhitehouse.archives.gov/sites/default/files/whitehouse_files/microsites/ostp/NSTC/preparing_for_the_future_of_ai.pdf.

'Prevention of Aerosol Col Burns ("Frosty")' (Australia & New Zealand Burn Association): anzba.org.au/assets/ANZBA-Factsheet-Aerosol-SC-v2.pdf.

'Privacy by Design' (*General Data Protection Regulation* (GDPR)): gdpr-info.eu/issues/privacy-by-design/.

'Product Liability and Safety in the UK (England and Wales): Overview' (*Practical Law*): uk.practicallaw.thomsonreuters.com/w-013-0564?transitionType=Default&contextData=(sc.Default).

'Products Liability' (Cornell Law School Legal Information Institute): law.cornell.edu/wex/products_liability.

'Proposed Model AI Governance Framework for Generative AI', AI Verify Foundation and Infocomm Media Development Authority: aiverifyfoundation.sg/downloads/Proposed_MGF_Gen_AI_2024.pdf.

'Regime for Artificial Intelligence (2020/2014(INL))'.

'Regulate to Innovate' (Ada Lovelace Institute, 2021): adalovelaceinstitute.org/report/regulate-innovate/.

'Regulating Medical Devices in the UK' (GOV.UK, 31 December 2020): gov.uk/guidance/regulating-medical-devices-in-the-uk.

'Regulating the AI Ecosystem' (NHS Transformation Directorate): www.nhsx.nhs.uk/ai-lab/ai-lab-programmes/regulating-the-ai-ecosystem/.

'Regulations – NHTSA issues Federal Motor Vehicle Safety Standards' (United States Department of Transportation): nhtsa.gov/laws-regulations/fmvss.

'Report of the Global Forum for Road Traffic Safety on Its Eighty-First Session' (UNECE, 12 January 2021): unece.org/transport/documents/2021/01/reports/report-global-forum-road-traffic-safety-its-eighty-first a.

'Report on Strict Liability' (*Cycle Law Scotland*, 2012): parliament.act.gov.au/__data/assets/pdf_file/0006/534678/05_Research-Report-on-Strict-Liability.pdf.

'Responsible Innovation in Self-Driving Vehicles' (GOV.UK, 19 August 2022): gov.uk/government/publications/responsible-innovation-in-self-driving-vehicles/responsible-innovation-in-self-driving-vehicles.

'Road Traffic (Autonomous Motor Vehicles) Rules 2017 – Singapore Statutes Online': sso.agc.gov.sg/SL/RTA1961-S464-2017?ValidDate=20170824&ProvIds=av-.

'Robotics and Artificial Intelligence in the Homeric Epics' (*Novo Scriptorium*, 22 April 2019): novoscriptorium.com/2019/04/23/robotics-and-artificial-integillence-in-the-homeric-epics/.

'Rules on Safe Use of Automated Vehicles on GB Roads' (GOV.UK): gov.uk/government/consultations/safe-use-rules-for-automated-vehicles-av/rules-on-safe-use-of-automated-vehicles-on-gb-roads.

'SAE Levels of Driving Automation™ Refined for Clarity and International Audience': sae.org/site/blog/sae-j3016-update.

'Safety and Security Risks of Generative Artificial Intelligence to 2025', HM Government: assets.publishing.service.gov.uk/media/653932db80884d0013f71b15/generative-ai-safety-security-risks-2025-annex-b.pdf.

'Self-driving vehicles listed for use in Great Britain': gov.uk/guidance/self-driving-vehicles-listed-for-use-in-great-britain.

'Self-driving vehicles set to be on roads by 2026 as Automated Vehicles Act becomes law' (GOV.UK, 20 May 2024): https://www.gov.uk/government/news/self-driving-vehicles-set-to-be-on-roads-by-2026-as-automated-vehicles-act-becomes-law#:~:text=The%20act%20delivers%20the%20most,for%20how%20the%20vehicle%20drives.

'Self-Regulation: The End of an Era? Lawyer Discipline and the Role of Law Societies' (*Canadian Lawyer*, 14 November 2019): canadianlawyermag.com/resources/professional-regulation/self-regulation-the-end-of-an-era-lawyer-discipline-and-the-role-of-law-societies/321919.

'Signs and Symptoms' (Centre for Disease Control and Prevention, 2017): cdc.gov/leprosy/symptoms/index.html.

'Singapore launches AI Verify Foundation to shape the future of international AI standards through collaboration', Infocomm Media Development Authority (7 June 2023): imda.gov.sg/resources/press-releases-factsheets-and-speeches/press-releases/2023/singapore-launches-ai-verify-foundation-to-shape-the-future-of-international-ai-standards-through-collaboration.

'Singapore proposes framework to foster trusted Generative AI development', Infocomm Media Development Authority (16 January 2024): imda.gov.sg/resources/press-releases-factsheets-and-speeches/press-releases/2024/public-consult-model-ai-governance-framework-genai.

Singapore Health Sciences Authority, 'Digital Health' (HSA): hsa.gov.sg/medical-devices/digital-health.

—— 'Regulatory Overview of Medical Devices' (HSA): hsa.gov.sg/medical-devices/regulatory-overview.

Singapore Ministry of Health, 'Artificial Intelligence in Healthcare Guidelines (AIHGle)': moh.gov.sg/docs/librariesprovider5/eguides/1-0-artificial-in-healthcare-guidelines-(aihgle)_publishedoct21.pdf.

Singapore Workplace Safety and Health (Amendment) Act 2017 (Act 44 of 2017): sso.agc.gov.sg//SL/S766-2017?DocDate=20171227.

'Software and AI as a Medical Device Change Programme – Roadmap' (GOV.UK, 14 June 2023): gov.uk/government/publications/software-and-ai-as-a-medical-device-change-programme/software-and-ai-as-a-medical-device-change-programme-roadmap.

'Software and AI As a Medical Device Change Programme' (GOV.UK, 14 June 2023): gov.uk/government/publications/software-and-ai-as-a-medical-device-change-programme.

'Stare Decisis' (Legal Information Institute, 2021): law.cornell.edu/wex/stare_decisis 4.

'Summary of the 2018 White House summit on artificial intelligence for American Industry' (White House Office of Science and Technology Policy, 2018): trumpwhitehouse.archives.gov/wp-content/uploads/2018/05/Summary-Report-of-White-House-AI-Summit.pdf.

'The Legal Framework for Autonomous Vehicles in the European Union' (*Business Going Digital*, 12 February 2020): www.businessgoing.digital/the-legal-framework-for-autonomous-vehicles-in-the-european-union/.

'The Roadmap to an Effective AI Assurance Ecosystem' (GOV.UK, 8 December 2021): gov.uk/government/publications/the-roadmap-to-an-effective-ai-assurance-ecosystem.

'Tracheotomy: Does TV Get it Right?' (*American Lung Association*, 2016): lung.org/blog/tracheotomy-does-tv-get-right.

'Uber Driver in Fatal Tempe Crash May Have Been Watching The Voice Behind the Wheel' (*Gizmodo*, 22 June 2018): gizmodo.com/uber-driver-in-fatal-tempe-crash-may-have-been-watching-1827039127.

'Uber Self-Driving Car Crash in Tempe, Arizona' (Directed by *VentureBeat*, 2018): youtube.com/watch?v=XtTB8hTgHbM.

University of Georgia, 'People may trust computers more than humans: New research shows that people are more likely to rely on algorithms (*ScienceDaily*): sciencedaily.com/releases/2021/04/210413114040.htm.

'UK Government Issues New Autonomous Testing Code of Practice' (*ITS United Kingdom: Better Transport Through Technology*, 7 February 2019): its-uk.org.uk/uk-government-issues-new-autonomous-testing-code-of-practice/.

US Department of Transportation, 'Automated Driving Systems: A Vision for Safety' 36: www.transportation.gov/policy-initiatives/automated-vehicles/automated-driving-systems-vision-safety; www.nhtsa.gov/sites/nhtsa.gov/files/documents/13069a-ads2.0_090617_v9a_tag.pdf.

'USDOT Automated Vehicles Activities', USDOT Automated Vehicles Activities: transportation.gov/AV.

US Government, 'The National Artificial Intelligence Research and Development Strategic Plan' (National Science and Technology Council; Networking and Information Technology Research and Development Subcommittee): obamawhitehouse.archives.gov/sites/default/files/whitehouse_files/microsites/ostp/NSTC/national_ai_rd_strategic_plan.pdf.

'US Leadership in AI: A Plan for Federal Engagement in Developing Technical Standards and Related Tools' (US Department of Commerce 2019): nist.gov/system/files/documents/2019/08/10/ai_standards_fedengagement_plan_9aug2019.pdf.

'U.S. Senate: The Interstate Commerce Act Is Passed': www.senate.gov/artandhistory/history/minute/Interstate_Commerce_Act_Is_Passed.htm.

'US State-by-state AI legislation snapshot', BCLP: bclplaw.com/en-US/events-insights-news/2023-state-by-state-artificial-intelligence-legislation-snapshot.html.

'Vehicle Insurance' (GOV.UK): gov.uk/vehicle-insurance.

'Weather and Climate in Singapore' (*GuideMeSingapore*): guidemesingapore.com/business-guides/immigration/get-to-know-singapore/weather-and-climate-in-singapore#:~:text=Based%20on%20climate%20records%20since,1998%20at%2036%20degrees%20Celsius.

'What Is It Like Driving in Texas Compared to California? – AIS Insurance' (*AIS Insurance Specialists Blog*, 28 August 2020): blog.aisinsurance.com/2020/08/27/driving-in-texas-compared-to-california/.

'What we do' (Accidental Compensation Corporation, 2018): www.acc.co.nz/about-us/who-we-are/what-we- do/ 8.

'Who Regulates Health Care' (Health and Safety Executive): hse.gov.uk/healthservices/arrangements.htm.

'WHO Target Product Profiles for COVID-19 Vaccines' (World Health Organization, 9 April 2020): www.who.int/publications/m/item/who-target-product-profiles-for-covid-19-vaccines.

'Working with chainsaws' (Health and Safety Executive): hse.gov.uk/treework/safety-topics/chainsaw-operator.htm.

'U.S. General Aviation Safety Data' (Bureau of Transportation Statistics, United States Department of Transportation): bts.gov/content/us-general-aviationa-safety-data.

Ajana, B, 'Augmented Borders: Big Data and the Ethics of Immigration Control' (2015) 13 Journal of Information, Communication and Ethics in Society 58: doi.org/10.1108/JICES-01-2014-0005.

Alexander, K and Clarkson, PJ, 'Good design practice for medical devices and equipment, Part I: A review of current literature' (2009) 24 *Journal of Medical Engineering & Technology* 1: tandfonline.com/doi/abs/10.1080/03091900029398.

Alter, R, 'Bill Skarsgård's Eyes Really Did Spook Sweet Angel Bill Hader on the Set of *It*' (*Vulture*, 9 September 2019): vulture.com/2019/09/bill-hader-bill-skarsgard-eyes-memes.html.

Amirthalingam, K, 'Medical Negligence and Patient Autonomy – Bolam Rules in Singapore and Malaysia – Revisited' (2015) 27 *Singapore Academy of Law Journal* 666: journalsonline.academypublishing.org.sg/Journals/Singapore-Academy-of-Law-Journal-Special-Issue/e-Archive/ctl/eFirstSALPDFJournalView/mid/513/ArticleId/1067/Citation/JournalsOnlinePDF.

Anderson, DQ, 'Medical Negligence Proceedings in Singapore: Instilling a Gentler Touch' [2021] *Global Studies in Comparative Law* 53: doi.org/10.1007/978-3-030-67000-9_14.

Arrieta, AB et al, 'Explainable Artificial Intelligence (XAI): Concepts, Taxonomies, Opportunities and Challenges toward Responsible AI' (2019): arxiv.org/abs/1910.10045.

Arya, V et al, 'One Explanation Does Not Fit All: A Toolkit and Taxonomy of AI Explainability Techniques' (2019): arxiv.org/abs/1909.03012.

Bal, BS, 'An Introduction to Medical Malpractice in the United States' (2009) 467(2) *Clinical Orthopaedics and Related Research* 339: www.ncbi.nlm.nih.gov/pmc/articles/PMC2628513/.

Baldwin, R and J Black, J, 'Really Responsive Regulation' (2008) 71 Modern Law Review 59: onlinelibrary.wiley.com/doi/abs/10.1111/j.1468-2230.2008.00681.x.

Ball, P, 'The Lightning-Fast Quest for COVID Vaccines – and What It Means for Other Diseases' (2020) 589 *Nature* 16: nature.com/articles/d41586-020-03626-1.

Barker, G, 'The Airbnb Effect On Housing And Rent' (*Forbes*, 21 February 2020) forbes.com/sites/garybarker/2020/02/21/the-airbnb-effect-on-housing-and-rent/.

Barre, E and Jin, YE, 'In Brief: Regulation of Healthcare M&A in Singapore' (*Lexology*, 30 June 2021): lexology.com/library/detail.aspx?g=84157a29-02a2-4755-a472-3cc0705aeb49.

Bellan, R, 'Musk Admits Full Self-Driving System "Not Great", Blames a Single Stack for Highway and City Streets' (*TechCrunch*): social.techcrunch.com/2021/08/24/musk-admits-full-self-driving-system-not-great-blames-a-single-stack-for-highway-and-city-streets/.

Bellon, T, 'U.S. Will See "meaningful" Autonomous Vehicle Policy in 2020s – U.S. Transportation Secretary' *Reuters* (17 March 2022): reuters.com/world/us/us-will-see-meaningful-autonomous-vehicle-policy-2020s-us-transportation-2022-03-16/.

Ben-Shahar, O, 'Should Carmakers Be Liable When a Self-Driving Car Crashes?' (*Forbes*, 22 September 2016): perma.cc/U22K-B4H4.

Black, J, 'Forms and Paradoxes of Principles Based Regulation' (2008) LSE Studies Working Paper No 13: ssrn.com/abstract=1267722.

Blumenthal, R and Hawley, J, 'Bipartisan Framework for U.S. AI Act': blumenthal.senate.gov/imo/media/doc/09072023bipartisanaiframework.pdf.

Bonner, A, 'The Complete Beginners Guide to Deep Learning' (*Medium*, 13 January 2019): towardsdatascience.com/intro-to-deep-learning-c025efd92535.

Bowal, P and Iss, L, 'Whatever Happened to R. v. Sault Ste. Marie: The Due Diligence Defence' (2013) 37(3) *Lawnow* 63: hdl.handle.net/1880/49667.

Braithwaite, V, 'Closing the Gap between Regulation and the Community' in P Drahos (ed), *Regulatory Theory* (ANU Press 2017): jstor.org/stable/j.ctt1q1crtm.9.

Brdiczka, O, 'Contextual AI: The Next Frontier of Artificial Intelligence' (*Digital Transformation*, 8 April 2019): blog.adobe.com/en/publish/2019/04/09/contextual-ai-the-next-frontier-of-artificial-intelligence.html.

Brown, C, 'Autonomous Vehicle Technology in Mining' (2012) 213 *Engineering and Mining Journal* 30: proquest.com/openview/ae4f7afb678c263bfe38727071f82d30/1?pq-origsite=gscholar&cbl=39.

Butcher, J and Beridze, I, 'What Is the State of Artificial Intelligence Governance Globally?' (2019) 164 *RUSI Journal* 88: tandfonline.com/doi/full/10.1080/03071847.2019.1694260.

Bygrave, LA, 'Data Protection by Design and by Default : Deciphering the EU's Legislative Requirements' (*Oslo Law Review*, 25 August 2017): idunn.no/doi/10.18261/issn.2387-3299-2017-02-03.

Cain, DM and Detsky, AS, 'Everyone's a Little Bit Biased (Even Physicians)' (25 June 2008) 299(24) *Journal of the American Medical Association* 2893: doi: 10.1001/jama.299.24.2893.

Cameron, S and W Seinen, W, 'AI Liability Addressed in Fresh EU Proposals', Pinsent Masons: pinsentmasons.com/out-law/news/ai-liability-addressed-eu-proposals.

Cellan-Jones, R, 'Uber's Self-Driving Operator Charged over Fatal Crash' *BBC News* (16 September 2020): bbc.com/news/technology-54175359.

Chen, S, Lim, JHS and Lim, BKL, 'Attribution of Civil Liability for Accidents Involving Automated Cars' (2020) Research Collection School Of Law 1: ink.library.smu.edu.sg/sol_research/3369.

Cushman, F, 'Rationalization Is Rational' (2020) 43 *Behavioral and Brain Sciences* 28 cambridge.org/core/journals/behavioral-and-brain-sciences/article/abs/rationalization-is-rational/2A13B99ED0 9BD802C0924D3681FEC55B.

Dahlawi, S et al, 'Medical Negligence in Healthcare Organizations and Its Impact on Patient Safety and Public Health: A Bibliometric Study' (2021) 10 F1000 Research 174: ncbi.nlm.nih.gov/pmc/articles/PMC8156516/.

Daly, A et al, 'Artificial Intelligence, Governance and Ethics: Global Perspectives' (2019) SSRN Electronic Journal: ssrn.com/abstract=3414805.

Dastin, J, 'Amazon Scraps Secret AI Recruiting Tool That Showed Bias against Women' *Reuters* (10 October 2018): www.reuters.com/article/us-amazon-com-jobs-automation-insight-idUSKCN-1MK08G.

Davies, A, 'Oh Look, More Evidence Humans Shouldn't Be Driving' (*Wired*, 21 May 2015): wired.com/2015/05/oh-look-evidence-humans-shouldnt-driving/.

Dietterich, TG, 'Exchange between Thomas G Dietterich and Cynthia Rudin on Explainable Machine Learning and Interpretability': twitter.com/tdietterich/status/1053487106193002496.

Doshi-Velez, F et al, 'Accountability of AI Under the Law: The Role of Explanation' (2019): arxiv.org/abs/1711.01134.

Drahos, P and Krygier, M, 'Regulation, Institutions and Networks' in P Drahos (ed), *Regulatory Theory* (ANU Press 2017): jstor.org/stable/j.ctt1q1crtm.7.

Dutton, T, 'An overview of national AI strategies' (2018): medium.com/politics-ai/an-overview-of-national-ai-strategies-2a70ec6edfd.

Elli, MS and Weast, J, 'Analysis of Draft EU ADS Performance Requirements' (2021): arxiv.org/abs/2106.02148.

Evas, T, 'A common EU approach to liability rules and insurance for connected and automated vehicles', European Parliamentary Research Service, 2018: europarl.europa.eu/RegData/etudes/STUD/2018/615635/EPRS_STU(2018)615635_EN.pdf.

Feldstein, S, 'The Global Expansion of AI Surveillance' (Carnegie Endowment for International Peace, 2019) jstor.org/stable/resrep20995.1.

Fenn, P, Gray, A and Rickman, N, 'The Economics of Clinical Negligence Reform in England' (2004) 114 *Economic Journal* F272: academic.oup.com/ej/article/114/496/F272-F292/5089438.

Fisher, J, 'Autonomous Truck Testing Heats up under the Texas Sun' (*FleetOwner*, 27 May 2021): fleetowner.com/perspectives/trucks-at-work/blog/21165424/autonomous-truck-testing-heats-up-under-the-texas-sun.

Fjelland, R, 'Why General Artificial Intelligence Will Not Be Realized' (2020) 7(1) *Humanities and Social Sciences Communications*: nature.com/articles/s41599-020-0494-4.

Ford, C, 'Prospects for Scalability: Relationships and Uncertainty in Responsive Regulation: Prospects for Scalability' (2013) 7 *Regulation & Governance* 14: doi.wiley.com/10.1111/j.1748-5991.2012.01166.x.

Franklin-Wallis, O, 'Inside X, Google's Top-Secret Moonshot Factory' (*Wired UK*, 2020): wired.co.uk/article/ten-years-of-google-x.

Garcia, M, 'What Air Canada Lost in "Remarkable" Lying AI Chatbot Case' (*Forbes*, 19 February 2024): www.forbes.com/sites/marisagarcia/2024/02/19/what-air-canada-lost-in-remarkable-lying-ai-chatbot-case/.

Gbade, AO, 'Reflection on Development Risk Defence Under Product Liability Law' (2017) 10:9 *OIDA International Journal of Sustainable Development* 29–38: ssrn.com/link/OIDA-Intl-Journal-Sustainable-Dev.html.

Gerke, S, Minssen, T and Cohen, G, 'Ethical and Legal Challenges of Artificial-Intelligence-Driven Healthcare' (2020) *Artificial Intelligence in Healthcare* 295: ncbi.nlm.nih.gov/pmc/articles/PMC7332220/.

Gheraibia, Y et al, 'Review of Legal Frameworks, Standards and Best Practices in Verification and Assurance for Infrastructure Inspection Robotics' (2020) SSRN Electronic Journal: papers.ssrn.com/sol3/papers.cfm?abstract_id=3645997.

Gill, SS, 'Legal Systems in Singapore: Overview' *Thomson Reuters Practical Law*: uk.practicallaw.thomsonreuters.com/w-008-9647?transitionType=Default&contextData=(sc.Default)&firstPage=true.

Gilligan, G, 'The Origins of UK Financial Services Regulation' (26 March 1997): papers.ssrn.com/abstract=2213218.

Goldberg, R, 'Medical Malpractice and Compensation in the UK' (2012) 87 *Chicago-Kent Law Review*: heinonline.org/HOL/LandingPage?handle=hein.journals/chknt87&div=9&id=&page=.

Grady, D, 'A.I. Took a Test to Detect Lung Cancer. It Got an A' *New York Times* 920 May 2019): nytimes.com/2019/05/20/health/cancer-artificial-intelligence-ct-scans.html.

Green, E, 'The Reasonable Man: Legal Fiction or Psychosocial Reality?' (1968) 2 *Law & Society Review* 241: jstor.org/stable/3052783.

Grieman, K, 'Hard Drive Crash' (2019) 9 *Journal of Intellectual Property, Information Technology and Electronic Commerce Law* 294: jipitec.eu/issues/jipitec-9-3-2018/at_download/CompleteIssue.

Grønsund, T and Aanestad, M 'Augmenting the Algorithm: Emerging Human-in-the-Loop Work Configurations' (2020) 29 *Journal of Strategic Information Systems* 101614 sciencedirect.com/science/article/pii/S0963868720300226.

Hall, W and Presenti, J, 'Growing the artificial intelligence industry in the UK' (2017): assets.publishing.service.gov.uk/media/5a824465e5274a2e87dc2079/Growing_the_artificial_intelligence_industry_in_the_UK.pdf.

Hancox-Li, L, 'Robustness in Machine Learning Explanations' (Proceedings of the 2020 Conference on Fairness, Accountability, and Transparency, 27 January 2020) 640: doi.org/10.1145/3351095.3372836.

Hao, K, 'We Read the Paper That Forced Timnit Gebru out of Google. Here's What It Says' (*MIT Technology Review*): technologyreview.com/2020/12/04/1013294/google-ai-ethics-research-paper-forced-out-timnit-gebru/.

Harrison, C, 'Holy Cow! Cops Step in as Herd of Cattle Blocks Road in Warwickshire' (*CoventryLive*, 28 July 2021): coventrytelegraph.net/news/local-news/holy-cow-police-step-herd-21166875.

Hawkins, AJ, 'These Nine States Will Serve as Testing Grounds for Self-Driving Cars' (*The Verge*, 23 January 2017): theverge.com/2017/1/23/14357564/dot-self-driving-car-testing-sites-nine-states.

Hawkins, AJ, 'Waymo Sues California DMV to Keep Driverless Crash Data under Wraps' (*The Verge*, 28 January 2022): theverge.com/2022/1/28/22906513/waymo-lawsuit-california-dmv-crash-data-foia.

Helms, MM and Hutchins, BA, 'Poor Quality Products: Is Their Production Unethical?' (1992) 30 *Management Decision* 5: doi.org/10.1108/00251749210015661.

Hong, J-W and Williams, D, 'Racism, Responsibility and Autonomy in HCI: Testing Perceptions of an AI Agent' (2019) 100 *Computers in Human Behavior* 79: www.sciencedirect.com/science/article/abs/pii/S0747563219302389.

Hotten, R, 'Volkswagen: The Scandal Explained' *BBC News* (10 December 2015) bbc.co.uk/news/business-34324772.

Huberman, P, 'Tort Law, Corrective Justice and the Problem of Autonomous-Machine-Caused Harm' (2021) 34 *Canadian Journal of Law & Jurisprudence* 105: cambridge.org/core/journals/canadian-journal-of-law-and-jurisprudence/article/abs/tort-law-corrective-justice-and-the-problem-of-autonomousmachinecaused-harm/723467C9EF5CF11C29E1AB2E1BCA2D73.

Jones, R, 'Archaic Man Meets a Marvellous Automaton: Posthumanism, Social Robots, Archetypes' (2017) 62 *Journal of Analytical Psychology* 338: onlinelibrary.wiley.com/doi/abs/10.1111/1468-5922.12316.

Katsivela, M, 'The notion of injury in the tort of negligence (common law) and the personal extra-contractual liability (civil law) in Canada: A comparative study' (2018) *translation* 96 Canadian Bar Review 3: ssrn.com/abstract=3373986.

Khaleghi, B, 'The How of Explainable AI: Post-Modelling Explainability' (*Medium*, 3 August 2019): towardsdatascience.com/the-how-of-explainable-ai-post-modelling-explainability-8b4cbc7adf5f.

Kingston, J, 'Artificial Intelligence and Legal Liability' (2018): arxiv.org/abs/1802.07782.

Kowert, W, 'The Foreseeability of Human–Artificial Intelligence Interactions' (2017) 96 *Texas Law Review* 181: semanticscholar.org/paper/The-Foreseeability-of-Human%E2%80%93Artificial-Intelligence-Kowert/f512cdf9a190b32af0e730a404944c677f8278d0.

Kudina, O and Verbeek, P-P, 'Ethics from Within: Google Glass, the Collingridge Dilemma, and the Mediated Value of Privacy' (2019) 44 *Science, Technology, & Human Values* 291: doi.org/10.1177/0162243918793711.

Kumar, Y et al, 'Artificial Intelligence in Disease Diagnosis: A Systematic Literature Review, Synthesizing Framework and Future Research Agenda' (2022) *Journal of Ambient Intelligence and Humanized Computing* 1: ncbi.nlm.nih.gov/pmc/articles/PMC8754556/.

Lambert, F, 'Tesla Starts Releasing Big Full Self-Driving Beta Update' (*Electrek*, 14 March 2022): electrek.co/2022/03/14/tesla-full-self-driving-fsd-beta-update-10-11/.

Land, MK and Aronson, JD, 'Human Rights and Technology: New Challenges for Justice and Accountability' (2020) 16 *Annual Review of Law and Social Science* 223 doi.org/10.1146/annurev-lawsocsci-060220-081955.

Lee, TB, 'Tesla Autopilot Director Contradicts Musk's Self-Driving Timeline' (*Ars Technica*, 5 July 2021): arstechnica.com/cars/2021/05/tesla-autopilot-director-contradicts-musks-self-driving-timeline/.

Lehman, G, 'Stunning photos show snow falling on Hawaii peaks' (*SFGate*, 1 December 2023): sfgate.com/hawaii/article/hawaii-snow-falls-maunakea-mauna-loa-18527778.php.

Levin, S and Wong, JC, 'Self-Driving Uber Kills Arizona Woman in First Fatal Crash Involving Pedestrian' *Guardian* (19 March 2018): theguardian.com/technology/2018/mar/19/uber-self-driving-car-kills-woman-arizona-tempe.

Liang, F et al, 'Constructing a Data-Driven Society: China's Social Credit System as a State Surveillance Infrastructure' (2018) 10 *Policy & Internet* 415: onlinelibrary.wiley.com/doi/abs/10.1002/poi3.183.

Lin, P, Abney, K and Jenkins, R, *Robot Ethics 2.0: New Challenges in Philosophy, Law, and Society* (Oxford University Press 2017): philarchive.org/rec/LINRE-3.

Liza, FF, 'Challenges of Enforcing Regulations in Artificial Intelligence Act --- Analyzing Quantity Requirement in Data and Data Governance' (2022) 1st International Workshop on Imagining the AI Landscape After the AI Act (In conjunction with the First International Conference on Hybrid Human-Artificial Intelligence): 10 ueaeprints.uea.ac.uk/id/eprint/85717/1/IAIL2022.pdf.

Losoncz, I, 'Methodological Approaches and Considerations in Regulatory Research' in P Drahos (ed), *Regulatory Theory* (ANU Press 2017): jstor.org/stable/j.ctt1q1crtm.12.

Madiega, T, 'European Parliament Briefing: EU Legislation in Progress – Artificial intelligence liability directive' (2023 European Parliamentary Research Service): www.europarl.europa.eu/RegData/etudes/BRIE/2023/739342/EPRS_BRI(2023)739342_EN.pdf.

Marshall, A, 'Uber's Self-Driving Car Saw the Woman It Killed, Report Says' (*Wired*, 24 May 2018): wired.com/story/uber-self-driving-crash-arizona-ntsb-report/.

Maruf, R, 'Super Bowl ad slams Tesla's 'Full Self-Driving' tech' (*CNN Business*, 12 February 2023) edition.cnn.com/2023/02/12/business/super-bowl-ad-tesla-full-self-driving/index.html.

Marr, B, '28 Best Quotes About Artificial Intelligence' (*Forbes*, 25 July 2017): www.forbes.com/sites/bernardmarr/2017/07/25/28-best-quotes-about-artificial-intelligence/.

McFarlane, A, 'How the UK's First Fatal Car Accident Unfolded' (*BBC News*, 17 August 2010): bbc.com/news/magazine-10987606.

Miller, KP, 'America's political future is a California-Texas duel' (2023) USA Today eu.usatoday.com/story/opinion/2020/11/01/how-california-and-texas-u-s-s-great-rivals-policy-column/6060779002/.

Molnar, C, *Interpretable Machine Learning*: christophm.github.io/interpretable-ml-book/index.html.

Mullen, D, 'Mercedes to Accept Legal Responsibility for Accidents Involving Self-Driving Cars' (*Driving.co.uk from The Sunday Times*, 28 March 2022): driving.co.uk/news/technology/mercedes-to-accept-legal-responsibility-for-accidents-involving-self-driving-cars/.

Nestoras, A (ed), *EU Policy Review Volume 1* (*European Policy Review* 2021) 1: liberalforum.eu/wp-content/uploads/2022/01/ELF-POLICY-REVIEW-Vol-1-2021.pdf.
Newdick, C, 'The Development Risk Defence of the Consumer Protection Act 1987' 47 *Cambridge Law Journal* 455: cambridge.org/core/product/identifier/S0008197300120458/type/journal_article.
Nurfikri, F, 'Artificial Intelligence, Machine Learning, and Deep Learning – What the Difference?' (*Medium*, 14 June 2020): towardsdatascience.com/artificial-intelligence-machine-learning-and-deep-learning-what-the-difference-8b6367dad790.
Othman, K 'Public Acceptance and Perception of Autonomous Vehicles: A Comprehensive Review' [2021] 1 *AI and Ethics* 355: doi.org/10.1007/s43681-021-00041-8.
Pandey, P, 'Interpretable Machine Learning' (*Medium*, 10 April 2019): towardsdatascience.com/interpretable-machine-learning-1dec0f2f3e6b.
Piccolo, R, 'AI in Criminal Sentencing: A Risk to Our Human Rights?' (Law Society of South Australia, 2018): Bulletin search.informit.org/doi/abs/10.3316/agispt.20190121005803.
Pradeep Kumar, R, 'Are ML, DL, DS the Unique Relations of AI?' (*Medium*, 29 March 2020): medium.com/@4deep.prk/are-ml-dl-ds-the-unique-relations-of-ai-a52d7735c88.
Purnama, A and Drago, D, 'FDA Regulatory Pathways for Medical Devices' (Organisation for Professionals in Regulatory Affairs): topra.org/topra/topra_member/pdfs/CPD-May-2019-Medical-Devices-and-FDA.pdf.
Pyper, J, 'Self-Driving Cars Could Cut Greenhouse Gas Pollution' (*Scientific American*, 15 September 2014): scientificamerican.com/article/self-driving-cars-could-cut-greenhouse-gas-pollution/.
Rachum-Twaig, O, 'Whose Robot is it Anyway? Liability for Artificial-Intelligence-Based Robots' (Social Science Research Network 2019) papers.ssrn.com/abstract=3339230.
Radu, R, 'Steering the Governance of Artificial Intelligence: National Strategies in Perspective' (2021) 40 Policy and Society 178: doi.org/10.1080/14494035.2021.1929728.
Reed, C, 'How to Make Bad Law: Lessons from Cyberspace' (2010) 73 *Modern Law Review* 903: jstor.org/stable/40926555.
Richmond, K, '15 Unbelievable Self-Driving Car Statistics & Facts' (*Future Insights*, 2019): futureinsights.com/15-unbelievable-self-driving-car-statistics-facts-2019/.
Roberts, R, 'Laws of Maths Don't Apply Here, Says Australian Prime Minister' *Independent* (15 July 2017): independent.co.uk/news/malcolm-turnbull-prime-minister-laws-mathematics-do-not-apply-australia-encryption-l-a7842946.html.
Roff, HM and Moyes, R, 'Meaningful Human Control, Artificial Intelligence and Autonomous Weapons', Informal Meeting of Experts on Lethal Autonomous Weapons Systems: article36.org/wp-content/uploads/2016/04/MHC-AI-and-AWS-FINAL.pdf.
Rubinstein, I, 'The Future of Self-Regulation Is Co-Regulation' (2016) Social Science Research Network SSRN Scholarly Paper ID 2848513: papers.ssrn.com/abstract=2848513.
Rudin, C, 'Stop explaining black box machine learning models for high stakes decisions and use interpretable models instead' (2019) 1 *Natural Machine Intelligence* 206: doi.org/10.1038/s42256-019-0048-x.
Samp, T et al, 'Landmark Artificial Intelligence Legislation Advances toward Becoming Law/ Insights/ DLA Piper Global Law Firm', DLA Piper: dlapiper.com/en/us/insights/publications/2020/12/landmark-artificial-intelligence-legislation-advances-toward-becoming-law/.
Santuosuosso, A, Boscarato, C, Caroleo, F, Labruto, R and Leroux, C, 'Robots, Market and Civil Liability: A European Perspective' (21st IEEE International Symposium on Robot and Human Interactive Communication 2012) 1051 as cited in Y Gheraibia et al, 'Review of Legal Frameworks, Standards and Best Practices in Verification and Assurance for Infrastructure Inspection Robotics' (2020) SSRN Electronic Journal: papers.ssrn.com/sol3/papers.cfm?abstract_id=3645997.
Saria, S, Butte, A and Sheikh, A, 'Better Medicine through Machine Learning: What's Real, and What's Artificial?' (2018) 15 *Public Library of Science Medicine* 12: dx.plos.org/10.1371/journal.pmed.1002721.
Schaffer, J, 'Contrastive Causation in the Law' (2010) 16(1) *Legal Theory* 259: cambridge.org/core/journals/legal-theory/article/contrastive-causation-in-the-law/C649A3D07D99D8FB05F-D1EF0042338A3.

Schütte, B, Majewski, L and Havu, K 'Damages Liability for Harm Caused by Artificial Intelligence – EU Law in Flux' (Social Science Research Network 2021): papers.ssrn.com/abstract=3897839.

Sendak, MP et al, 'Presenting machine learning model information to clinical end users with model facts labels' (23 March 2020) *NPJ Digital Medicine*: semanticscholar.org/paper/Presenting-machine-learning-model-information-to-Sendak-Gao/15bab838342b7fc6897e8729e92697d705d8e2e1.

Sgueo, G, 'Using technology to 'co-create' EU policies' (2020) European Parliamentary Research Service: europarl.europa.eu/RegData/etudes/BRIE/2020/646127/EPRS_BRI(2020)646127_EN.pdf.

Shacklett, M, 'Algorithmic Accountability Act: What Tech Leaders Need to Know and Do Now' (*TechRepublic*, 28 July 2022): techrepublic.com/article/know-algorithmic-accountability-act/.

Shepardson, D, 'Tesla Driver in Fatal "Autopilot" Crash Got Numerous Warnings: US Government' *Reuters* (20 June 2017): reuters.com/article/us-tesla-crash-idUSKBN19A2XC.

—— 'U.S. Eliminates Human Controls Requirement for Fully Automated Vehicles' *Reuters* (11 March 2022): reuters.com/business/autos-transportation/us-eliminates-human-controls-requirement-fully-automated-vehicles-2022-03-11/.

Shevlane, T and Dafoe, A, 'The Offense–Defense Balance of Scientific Knowledge: Does Publishing AI Research Reduce Misuse?' (Proceedings of the AAAI/ACM Conference on AI, Ethics, and Society, 2020): dl.acm.org/doi/10.1145/3375627.3375815.

Shulayeva, O, Siddharthan, A and Wyner, A, 'Recognizing Cited Facts and Principles in Legal Judgements' (2017) 25 *Artificial Intelligence and Law* 107: doi.org/10.1007/s10506-017-9197-6.

Simmler, M and Markwalder, N, 'Guilty Robots? – Rethinking the Nature of Culpability and Legal Personhood in an Age of Artificial Intelligence' (2019) 30 *Criminal Law Forum* 1: doi.org/10.1007/s10609-018-9360-0.

Simmons, R, 'Big Data, Machine Judges, and the Legitimacy of the Criminal Justice System' (2018) 52 *University of California Davis Law Review* 1067: lawreview.law.ucdavis.edu/issues/52/2/articles/52-2_Simmons.pdf.

Simon, M, 'Despite Proven Technology, Attempts to Make Table Saws Safer Drag On' (NPR, 10 August 2017): npr.org/2017/08/10/542474093/despite-proven-technology-attempts-to-make-table-saws-safer-drag-on.

Sinha, N, 'Self-Supervised Learning' (*Medium*, 3 October 2019) towardsdatascience.com/self-supervised-learning-78bdd989c88b.

Sprenger, F, 'Microdecisions and Autonomy in Self-Driving Cars: Virtual Probabilities' (2020) *AI & SOCIETY*: doi.org/10.1007/s00146-020-01115-7.

Stephanow, C, 'Sask. Alpaca Becomes Internet Sensation after Road Trip through Regina' *CTV News Regina* (15 May 2020): regina.ctvnews.ca/sask-alpaca-becomes-internet-sensation-after-road-trip-through-regina-1.4942137.

Storey, T, *Unlocking Criminal Law*, 7th edn (Routledge, 2019), citing RE Nisbett and TD Wilson, 'Telling More than We Can Know: Verbal Reports on Mental Processes' (1977) 84 *Psychological Review* 231; CM Funk and MS Gazzaniga, 'The Functional Brain Architecture of Human Morality' (2009) 19 *Current Opinion in Neurobiology* 678.

Strantz, NJ, 'Beyond R v Sault Ste Marie: The Creation and Expansion of Strict Liability and the Due Diligence Defence' (1992) 30 *Alberta Law Review* 1233: canlii.org/en/commentary/doc/1992CanLIIDocs182#!fragment//BQCwhgziBcwMYgK4DsDWszIQewE4BUBTADwBdoByCgSgBpltTCIB-FRQ3AT0otokLC4EbDtyp8BQkAGU8pAELcASgFEAMioBqAQQByAYRW1SYAEbRS2ONWpA.

Sullivan, HR and Schweikart, SJ, 'Are Current Tort Liability Doctrines Adequate for Addressing Injury Caused by AI?' (2019) 21 *AMA Journal of Ethics* 160: journalofethics.ama-assn.org/article/are-current-tort-liability-doctrines-adequate-addressing-injury-caused-ai/2019-02.

Tan, SY and Taeihagh, A, 'Adaptive Governance of Autonomous Vehicles: Accelerating the Adoption of Disruptive Technologies in Singapore' (2021) 38 *Government Information Quarterly* 101546: sciencedirect.com/science/article/pii/S0740624X20303257.

Taylor, S, 'Introduction' (2019) 2 *Journal Du Droit de la Santé et de l'Assurance* – Maladie 9: cairn.info/revue-journal-du-droit-de-la-sante-et-de-l-assurance-maladie-2019-2-page-9.htm;www.cairn.info/revue-journal-du-droit-de-la-sante-et-de-l-assurance-maladie-2019-2-page-9.htm.

Thorley, C and Kumar, D, 'Eyewitness Susceptibility to Co-Witness Misinformation Is Influenced by Co-Witness Confidence and Own Self-Confidence' (2017) 23 *Psychology, Crime & Law* 342: doi.org/10.1080/1068316X.2016.1258471.

Trump, BD, 'Synthetic Biology Regulation and Governance: Lessons from TAPIC for the United States, European Union, and Singapore' (2017) 121 *Health Policy* 1139: sciencedirect.com/science/article/pii/S0168851017301999.

van de Poel, I, 'Why New Technologies Should Be Conceived as Social Experiments' (2013) 16 *Ethics, Policy & Environment* 352: doi.org/10.1080/21550085.2013.844575.

Vellinga, NE, 'From the Testing to the Deployment of Self-Driving Cars: Legal Challenges to Policy-makers on the Road Ahead' (2017) 33 *Computer Law & Security Review* 847: sciencedirect.com/science/article/pii/S0267364917301334.

Vincent, J, 'Former Go Champion Beaten by DeepMind Retires after Declaring AI Invincible' (*The Verge*, 27 November 2019): theverge.com/2019/11/27/20985260/ai-go-alphago-lee-se-dol-retired-deepmind-defeat.

Vought, RT, 'Memorandum for the Heads of Executive Departments and Agencies' whitehouse.gov/wp-content/uploads/2020/01/Draft-OMB-Memo-on-Regulation-of-AI-1-7-19.pdf.

Vranaki, A and Reed, C, 'The Rise of Investigations by European Data Protection Authorities in the Context of Cloud Computing' (2014) SSRN Electronic Journal: researchgate.net/publication/315336890_The_Rise_of_Investigations_by_European_Data_Protection_Authorities_in_the_Context_of_Cloud_Computing.

Walch, K, 'Is AI Overhyped?' (*Forbes*, 4 June 2020): forbes.com/sites/cognitiveworld/2020/06/04/is-ai-overhyped/.

Wedro, B, 'Frostbite vs. Hypothermia Differences in Symptoms and Stages' (emedicinehealth): emedicinehealth.com/frostbite_and_hypothermia_symptoms_and_stages/article_em.htm.

Whitney, L, 'Google's Self-Driving Cars Hit the Roads in Austin, Texas' (*Roadshow*) cnet.com/roadshow/news/googles-self-driving-cars-hit-the-roads-in-austin-texas/.

Widen, WH and Koopman, P, 'Autonomous Vehicle Regulation, Does Tesla's Full Self-Driving Beta Release Comply with Law? (2021) SSRN Scholarly Paper ID 3931341: papers.ssrn.com/abstract=3931341.

Yadron, D and Tynan, D, 'Tesla Driver Dies in First Fatal Crash While Using Autopilot Mode' *Guardian* (30 June 2016): theguardian.com/technology/2016/jun/30/tesla-autopilot-death-self-driving-car-elon-musk.

Zinkevich, M, 'Rules of Machine Learning' (*Google Developers*): developers.google.com/machine-learning/guides/rules-of-ml.

Other

Abbott, R, *The Reasonable Robot* (Cambridge University Press 2020).

Abbott, R and Sarch, A 'Punishing Artificial Intelligence: Legal Fiction or Science Fiction' (2019) 53 *University of California Davis Law Review* 323.

Angwin, J, Larson, J, Kirchner, L and Mattu, S, 'Machine bias' (2016) ProPublica in J-W Hong and D Williams, 'Racism, Responsibility and Autonomy in HCI: Testing Perceptions of an AI Agent' (2019) 100 *Computers in Human Behavior* 79.

Asimov, I, *I, Robot* (Gnome Press 1950).

'Bill Analysis' ((*Texas) Senate Research Center*, 2017) SB 2205.

Bhuta, N et al (eds), *Autonomous Weapons Systems: Law, Ethics, Policy* (Cambridge University Press 2016).

Black, J, 'Talking about Regulation' [1988] *Practical Law* 77.

—— 'Decentring Regulation: Understanding the Role of Regulation and Self-Regulation in a "Post-Regulatory" World' (2001) 54 *Current Legal Problems* 103.

—— 'Critical Reflections on Regulation' (2002) 27 *Australasian Journal of Legal Philosophy* 1.
Brüggemeier, G, 'The Civilian Law of Delict: A Comparative and Historical Analysis' (2020) 7 *European Journal of Comparative Law and Governance* 339.
Ciatto, G et al, 'Agent-Based Explanations in AI: Towards an Abstract Framework' in D Calvaresi et al (eds), *Explainable, Transparent Autonomous Agents and Multi-Agent Systems* (Springer International Publishing 2020).
Clarke, YD, 'Text – H.R.6580 – 117th Congress (2021–2022): Algorithmic Accountability Act of 2022' (2 April 2022).
Dick, PK, *Do Androids Dream of Electric Sheep?* (Doubleday 1968).
Drexler, DA and T Haidegger, T 'Handover Process of Autonomous Vehicles – Technology and Application Challenges' (2019) 16 *Acta Polytechnica Hungarica* 235.
European Parliament, 'Report with Recommendations to the Commission on a Civil Liability Regime for Artificial Intelligence (2020/2014(INL))'.
Farrell, A-M and Dove, ES, 'Clinical Negligence' in Mason and McCall Smith (eds), *Law and Medical Ethics*, 12th edn (Oxford University Press 2023).
Franks, N, *Sharks among Minnows: Germany's First Fighter Pilots and the Fokker Eindecker Period, July 1915 to September 1916* (London, Grub Street, 2001).
Giuffrida, I, 'Liability for AI Decision-Making: Some Legal and Ethical Considerations' (2019) 88 *Fordham Law Review* 439.
Hanne, M and Weisberg, R, *Narrative and Metaphor in the Law* (Cambridge University Press 2018).
Hazard, GC, 'Discovery and the Role of the Judge in Civil Law Jurisdictions' (1998) 73 *Notre Dame Law Review* 1017.
Johann-Liang, R et al, 'Analysis of anaphylaxis cases after vaccination: 10-year review from the National Vaccine Injury Compensation Program' (2011) 106(5) *Ann Allergy Asthma Immunology* 440.
Josephson, JR and SG Josephson, SG, *Abductive Inference: Computation, Philosophy, Technology* (Cambridge University Press 1996).
Kasap, A, *Tracing the Locus of Regulation and Liability* (Edward Elgar Publishing 2022).
Kian, CTS, 'New Developments in Duty of Care: The Singapore Approach to Negligence in Product Liability after the *Slim 10* case' (2005) 26 *Business Law Review* 116.
Miller, T, 'Explanation in Artificial Intelligence: Insights from the Social Sciences' (2019) 267 *Artificial Intelligence* 1.
Monett, D, Lewis, CWP and Thórisson, KR, Introduction to the JAGI Special Issue 'On Defining Artificial Intelligence' Commentaries and Author's Response (2020) 11 *Journal of Artificial General Intelligence* 1.
Morgan, N and Yeo, S, 'Defining the Fault Elements of Driving Offences' (2007) 19 *Singapore Academy of Law Journal* 205.
Mota, SA, 'Federal Preemption after Medtronic, Altia Group, and Wyeth' (2010) *Oklahoma City University Law Review* 23.
National Highway Traffic Safety Administration, 'Occupant Protection for Vehicles with Automated Driving Systems' (2022).
Needham, J, Science and Civilisation in China: Physics and Physical Technology – Mechanical Engineering, vol 4, 2nd edn (Cambridge University Press 1965).
'On the road to automated mobility: An EU strategy for mobility of the future 2018' (Communication from the Commission to the European Parliament, The Council, The European Economic and Social Committee, The Committee of the Regions, 2018).
'Overview of Standards: Specifying Formats of Advanced Electronic Signatures and Seals' (European Union Agency for Cybersecurity, 2019).
'Reported Road Casualties in Great Britain, Final Estimates Involving Illegal Alcohol Levels: 2018' (Department for Transport, 2020).
Pejovic, C, 'Civil Law and Common Law: Two Different Paths Leading to the Same Goal' (2001) 155 *Poredbeno Pomorsko Pravo* 7.

Perkins, C, 'The Increasing Acceptance of the Restatement (Third) Risk Utility Analysis in Design Defect Claims' (2004) 4 *Nevada Law Journal* 609.
Pinto, C, 'How Autonomous Vehicle Policy in California and Nevada Addresses Technological and Non-Technological Liabilities' (2012) 5 *Intersect* 1.
Pratchett, T, *Hogfather* (Corgi Books 1997).
Richardson, A and Rosefeld, A, 'A Survey of Interpretability and Explainability in Human-Agent Systems' (Proceedings of the 2nd Workshop on Explainable Artificial Intelligence, 2018).
Selbst, AD, 'Negligence and AI's Human Users' (2020) 100 *Boston University Law Review* 62 1315.
Select Committee on Artificial Intelligence, *AI in the UK: Ready, Willing and Able* (HL 2017–19) 183.
Silver, DL, 'Machine Lifelong Learning: Challenges and Benefits for Artificial General Intelligence' in J Schmidhuber, KR Thórisson and M Looks (eds), *Artificial General Intelligence* (Springer 2011).
Solum, LB, 'Legal Personhood for Artificial Intelligences' in W Wendell and P Asaro (eds), *Machine Ethics and Robot Ethics* (Routledge 2017).
Steiner, E, *French Law*, 2nd edn (Oxford University Press 2018).
Toglia, MP et al, *The Handbook of Eyewitness Psychology: Volume I: Memory for Events* (Psychology Press 2017).
Turing, A, 'Computing Machinery and Intelligence' (1950) 59 *Mind*, New Series 433.
US Congress, 116th Congress (2019–2020): National Defense Authorization Act for Fiscal Year 2021.
Wang, P, What Do You Mean by "AI"?' in P Wang, B Goertzel and S Franklin (eds), *Artificial General Intelligence: Proceedings of the First AGI Conference, Frontiers in Artificial Intelligence and Applications* vol 17 (IOS Press 2008).
Wells, M, *Murderbot* (Tor.com 2017).
Westbrook, H, 'Look Ma, No Hands: Providing Automated Vehicle Regulations and Precedents Inclusive of Disabled Individuals' (2018) 19 *Texas Tech Administrative Law Journal* 385.
Zhu, X and Goldberg, A, 'Introduction to Semi-Supervised Learning' (2009) 3 *Synthesis Lectures on Artificial Intelligence and Machine Learning* 1.

INDEX

NB – page locators given in *italics* refer to information in figures

www.ingramcontent.com/pod-product-compliance
Ingram Content Group UK Ltd.
Pitfield, Milton Keynes, MK11 3LW, UK
UKHW020135290926
15471UKWH00003B/498

9 781509 977406